Jus Internationale et Europaeum

herausgegeben von
Thilo Marauhn und Christian Walter

202

Nils-Hendrik Grohmann

Strengthening the UN Human Rights Treaty Bodies

An Analysis of the Committees' Legal Powers and Possibilities for Reform

Mohr Siebeck

Nils-Hendrik Grohmann, born 1992; Law studies at the University of Münster and Oslo; 2018 Research assistant at the Chair of European and International Law at the University of Potsdam; 2022 Legal clerk at the Kammergericht Berlin.
orcid.org/0000-0001-8328-2944

At the same time doctoral thesis, University of Potsdam, 2023

ISBN 978-3-16-162825-2 / eISBN 978-3-16-162826-9
DOI 10.1628/978-3-16-162826-9

ISSN 1861-1893 / eISSN 2568-8464 (Jus Internationale et Europaeum)

The Deutsche Nationalbibliothek lists this publication in the Deutsche Nationalbibliographie; detailed bibliographic data are available at *https://dnb.dnb.de*.

© 2024 Mohr Siebeck Tübingen, Germany. www.mohrsiebeck.com

This work is licensed under the license "Attribution-NonCommercial-NoDerivatives 4.0 International" (CC BY-NC-ND 4.0). A complete version of the license text can be found at: https://creativecommons.org/licenses/by-nc-nd/4.0/.

Any use not covered by the above license is prohibited and illegal without the permission of the publisher.

The book was printed on non-aging paper and bound by Gulde Druck in Tübingen.

Printed in Germany.

Preface

This thesis was accepted at the Faculty of Law of the University of Potsdam in the winter semester 2022/2023. Due to the ongoing reform process of the UN Human Rights Treaty Bodies, new developments are constantly emerging and unfolding. Available sources and documents were taken into account as far as possible until summer 2023.

Special thanks go first and foremost to my supervisor and Doktorvater, Professor Dr. Andreas Zimmermann LL.M. (Harvard). This thesis was written during my time as a research assistant at his Chair of European and International Public Law. The success of the work is largely due to his constant support and encouragement. I always enjoyed working at the Chair, it opened up new areas of international law for me and was decisive for the success of my PhD. I would also like to thank Professor Dr. Wojciech Burek for the speedy preparation of his review of my thesis.

Representing the entire team at the Chair, I would like to mention Ullrike Schiller in particular, who, along with Mr. Zimmermann, always has an open ear for all members of staff and, like everyone else, made me feel very welcome from the very first day in September 2018.

Among those in my private life, I would like to thank Dr. Lena Gumnior first, who wrote her PhD at the same time as me and who was always open for discussions and encouraging conversations; and who also accompanied me many times at the Staatsbibliothek Berlin. I would also like to mention Johannes Becker, Charlotte Föcking, Marcin Korbanek, Lydia Kühn, Kamil Pawłowski and Dr. Frauke Rödel. They have learned almost as much as I have about the UN treaty bodies over the past few years and have therefore always been able and willing to make critical comments on my writing.

The same holds true for my husband, Marco Štorman, who was probably more closely and constantly involved in the writing process than any other person. Thank you for your encouragement and support, for bearing with me during some stressful times and for patiently listening when I shared my thoughts out loud.

Finally, the greatest thanks go to my parents, Martina and Dr. Olaf Grohmann, who have supported me in every conceivable way throughout my entire life and without whom I would probably never have started and completed a PhD. This thesis is dedicated to them.

Berlin, December 2023

Overview

Preface	V
Table of Contents	IX
Introduction	1
A. *United Nations human rights treaty bodies*	1
B. *Problems faced by human rights treaty bodies*	4
C. *Fragmentation of human rights law within the treaty body system*	9
D. *Aim and scope of the thesis at hand*	12
Part I: Growth of the treaty body system	15
A. *Discussions on the suitable enforcement mechanisms under the two Covenants*	16
B. *CERD Committee*	19
C. *CEDAW Committee*	20
D. *Committee against Torture*	21
E. *CRC Committee*	22
F. *CMW Committee*	23
G. *CED Committee*	24
H. *CRPD Committee*	27
I. *Interim conclusion and outlook*	29
Part II: Past attempts at reform	31
A. *"Alston proposals" between 1989 and 1997*	31
B. *Consolidated single State report proposal*	35
C. *Unified standing treaty body proposal*	38

D.	*Origins of the current treaty body strengthening process*	41
E.	*Human rights treaty bodies as the main drivers for attempts at reform*	51

Part III: Delineating the mandate of treaty bodies 55

A.	*Interpretation of human rights treaties*	55
B.	*Broadening of competencies with the involvement of State parties*	115

Part IV: Reform proposals under the reporting procedure and their implementation 133

A.	*Object and purpose of human rights reporting*	134
B.	*Simplified Reporting Procedure*	139
C.	*Comprehensive reporting calendar*	183
D.	*Reviews in the absence of a report*	212
E.	*Concluding observations and follow-up activities*	231
F.	*Conclusion on attempts at reform under the reporting procedure*	254

Part V: Institutionalized Cooperation among human rights treaty bodies 257

A.	*Establishment and evolution of the "linkage Committees"*	258
B.	*Decision-making powers of "linkage Committees"*	268
C.	*Conclusion and outlook*	284

Conclusions 287

Bibliography 293

Index 313

Table of Contents

Preface V

Overview VII

Introduction 1
- A. United Nations human rights treaty bodies 1
- B. Problems faced by human rights treaty bodies 4
- C. Fragmentation of human rights law within the treaty body system ... 9
- D. Aim and scope of the thesis at hand 12

Part I: Growth of the treaty body system 15
- A. Discussions on the suitable enforcement mechanisms under the two Covenants 16
  - I. ICCPR 16
  - II. ICESCR 17
    1. Monitoring of the ICESCR by ECOSOC 17
    2. Establishment of the CESCR Committee 18
- B. CERD Committee 19
- C. CEDAW Committee 20
- D. Committee against Torture 21
- E. CRC Committee 22
- F. CMW Committee 23
- G. CED Committee 24
- H. CRPD Committee 27
- I. Interim conclusion and outlook 29

Part II:	Past attempts at reform	31
A.	*"Alston proposals" between 1989 and 1997*	31
I.	1989 initial report	31
II.	1993 interim report	32
III.	1997 final report	33
B.	*Consolidated single State report proposal*	35
C.	*Unified standing treaty body proposal*	38
D.	*Origins of the current treaty body strengthening process*	41
I.	*Pillay's* multistakeholder approach	41
	1. 2012 strengthening report	41
	2. Interference by the intergovernmental process	44
	3. Resolution 68/268	46
II.	Review process set in motion via Resolution 68/268	48
III.	Co-facilitators' review process 2020	49
E.	*Human rights treaty bodies as the main drivers for attempts at reform*	51

Part III:	Delineating the mandate of treaty bodies	55
A.	*Interpretation of human rights treaties*	55
I.	Specialized rules of interpretation	56
II.	Interpretative methods under regional and UN human rights treaties	59
	1. "Living-instrument" doctrine	59
	2. Effectiveness-orientated and teleological approaches	61
	3. Legal effects of the interpretative approaches	62
III.	Interpretative task at hand	65
	1. Legal nature of human rights treaty bodies	67
	2. Application of specialized methods of interpretation to procedural provisions	69
	3. Implied Powers	73
	a) Origin and legal effects of the doctrine	74
	b) Implications for the determination of treaty bodies' powers	77
IV.	Confirmation of the hypothesis established	79
	1. Adoption of concluding observations	79
	a) Discussions within the Human Rights Committee	80
	b) Discussions within the early CEDAW Committee	82
	c) Other treaty bodies	83
	2. Adoption of General Comments	84
	a) Committees with an explicit normative basis	86
	b) CESCR Committee	87
	c) Committee against Torture, the CMW and the CED Committee	87

		3. Follow-up under the reporting procedure	89
		a) Normative basis for follow-up activities	90
		b) The CESCR Committee as the exception	92
		4. Follow-up under the individual complaints procedure	93
		5. Adoption of interim measures	96
		a) Competence to adopt interim measures	96
		b) Binding force of interim measures	98
		aa) Evolving practice by treaty bodies	99
		bb) Criticism by State parties	100
		cc) Arguments in favour of interim measures' binding force	102
		6. Reservations to human rights treaties	103
		a) Developing positions by treaty bodies	103
		b) Criticism of General Comment No. 24	105
		c) Question of competence	106
		aa) Competence to formulate recommendations as regards reservations	107
		bb) Competence to determine the legal consequences of invalid reservations	110
		cc) Interim conclusion on the topic of reservations	112
		7. Conclusion on past extensions of powers	113
B.		*Broadening of competencies with the involvement of State parties*	115
I.		Subsequent practice	115
		1. Relevant authors of subsequent practice	116
		2. Constituent elements of subsequent practice under article 31(3)(b) VCLT	120
II.		Authority of the United Nations General Assembly	123
		1. Involvement in treaty amendments	123
		2. Endorsement/authorization of Committee activities	127
		3. General Assembly as a Conference of State parties	128

Part IV: Reform proposals under the reporting procedure and their implementation 133

A.	*Object and purpose of human rights reporting*	134
I.	Initially perceived functions of reporting by treaty bodies	136
II.	Changing perception of the functions attributed to reporting	137
B.	*Simplified Reporting Procedure*	139
I.	Simplified and standard reporting procedure compared	140
II.	Origins and dissemination of the simplified reporting procedure . . .	140
	1. Committee against Torture	140
	2. Human Rights Committee	142
	3. CMW Committee	143

	4. CRPD Committee		143
	5. CERD Committee		144
	6. CEDAW Committee		144
	7. CESCR Committee		145
	8. CRC Committee		146
	9. CED Committee as the exception		146
	10. Developments at the 2019 Meeting of Chairpersons		149
	11. Interim conclusion		150
III.	Further alignment of the simplified reporting procedure		152
	1. Application to initial reports		152
	2. Format of Lists of Issues Prior to Reporting		153
	a)	Format of LOIPRs under CAT	154
	b)	Format of LOIPRs under the ICCPR	155
	c)	Format of LOIPRs under CMW	157
	d)	Format of LOIPRs under CRPD	158
	e)	Format of LOIPRs under CERD	158
	f)	Format of LOIPRs under CEDAW	159
	g)	Format of LOIPRs under the ICESCR	160
	h)	Format of LOIPRs under CRC	161
	i)	Comparison and detection of best practices	161
	3. Solutions to the problem of substantive overlap		164
	a)	Cross-references to external documents	165
		aa) Rationales for including cross-references in LOIPRs	166
		bb) Practice of the Committee against Torture	168
	b)	Internal coordination	170
	c)	Interim conclusion on the avoidance of substantial overlap	171
IV.	Treaty bodies' mandates to implement the simplified reporting procedure		172
	1. Sequence of actions under the standard reporting procedure		173
	2. Content to include in reports according to treaty provisions		174
	a)	Entity to define a report's content	175
		aa) Article 17 ICESCR	175
		bb) Articles 73(3) CMW and 35(3) CRPD	176
	b)	Rules governing the follow-up procedure	177
	3. Final evaluation		178
	4. Introduction of LOIPRs via subsequent practice		180
V.	Conclusion on the simplified reporting procedure and outlook		182
C.	*Comprehensive reporting calendar*		183
I.	Necessity of a comprehensive reporting calendar		184
II.	Possible calendar schemes		186
	1. Pairing of treaty bodies with annual reviews		186
	2. Clustered reviews		187

	3. Single consolidated review	188
	4. Evaluation	189
III.	Discussions and practice among treaty bodies	191
	1. Steps taken by the CMW Committee	192
	2. Steps taken by the Human Rights Committee	192
	3. Steps taken by the CESCR Committee	193
	4. Steps taken by the CED Committee	193
	5. Treaty body position paper and 2022 Meeting of Chairpersons	194
IV.	Legal questions concerning a reporting calendar	196
	1. Increase of reporting frequencies	196
	2. Decrease of reporting frequencies	197
	a) Practice by treaty bodies	197
	aa) CERD Committee	198
	bb) CEDAW Committee	199
	cc) Committee against Torture	200
	dd) CRC Committee	201
	ee) CRPD Committee	202
	ff) CMW Committee	202
	gg) General tendencies among the treaty bodies	203
	b) Legal arguments	204
	c) Extending reporting intervals via subsequent practice	207
IV.	Possible synergies with the UPR	208
V.	Conclusion on the comprehensive reporting calendar	211
D.	*Reviews in the absence of a report*	212
I.	Practice by treaty bodies	213
	1. CERD Committee	213
	2. CESCR Committee	214
	3. CRC Committee	215
	4. Committee against Torture	215
	5. Human Rights Committee	216
	6. CEDAW Committee	217
	7. CMW Committee	218
	8. CED Committee	218
	9. CRPD Committee	219
	10. Evaluation	219
II.	Developments at the Meeting of Chairpersons	220
III.	Legal mandate of treaty bodies with regard to reviews in the absence of a report	221
	1. Text-based interpretation	222
	a) Sources of information according to treaty provisions	223
	b) Committees with a wider mandate	224
	2. Effectiveness-orientated interpretation	225

	3. Alternative reading of article 36(2) CRPD	227
	4. Remaining aspects of concern	227
	a) Actual need to review State parties in the absence of a report	227
	b) Sources of information for reviews in the absence of a report	228
IV.	Conclusion on reviews in the absence of a report	230
E.	*Concluding observations and follow-up activities*	231
I.	Alignment of concluding observations	231
	1. Common format for concluding observations	231
	2. References to other treaty bodies' concluding observations	233
II.	Prioritization	234
	1. Follow-up to concluding observations	235
	a) Time frame for the follow-up report	236
	b) Criteria for the selection of concluding observations	236
	aa) Committee practice	237
	bb) Evaluation	238
	c) Criteria for assessing State compliance	239
	aa) Committees with a single grading scheme	240
	bb) Committees with two grading schemes	241
	cc) Evaluation	243
	2. Prioritization by means of an integrated follow-up procedure ...	243
	a) Practice by the CRPD Committee	244
	b) Possible content of concluding observations	245
	c) Legal arguments for an integrated follow-up procedure	247
	d) Practical arguments for an integrated follow-up procedure	248
	e) Identification of suitable topics for an integrated follow-up procedure	249
	aa) Equality clauses	250
	bb) Congruent treaty provisions	251
	cc) Example of the right to water	252
	III. Conclusion on the follow-up procedure	253
F.	*Conclusion on attempts at reform under the reporting procedure*	254

Part V: Institutionalized Cooperation among human rights treaty bodies 257

A.	*Establishment and evolution of the "linkage Committees"*	258
I.	Initial phase	258
II.	Phase of increased and improved organization	260
III.	Phase of parallel existence	262
	1. Inter-Committee Meeting	262

	2. Meeting of Chairpersons	263
IV.	Phase of "constitutionalization" of the Meeting of Chairpersons	265
V.	Evaluation of the two "linkage committees"	266
B.	*Decision-making powers of "linkage Committees"*	268
I.	Vesting Chairs with decision-making powers	268
II.	Hesitant implementation of the "Poznan formula"	269
III.	Recent discussion on decision-making powers	271
IV.	Legal mandate of treaty bodies in implementing the "Poznan formula"	271
	1. Legal problems in the application of the "Poznan formula"	273
	2. Internal rules governing the Chairpersons' mandates	273
	a) Ordinary powers during treaty body sessions	273
	b) Rules governing a Committee's control over its Chairperson	274
	c) Exceptional intersessional powers	275
	d) Methods of voting	275
	3. Relevant treaty provisions	276
	a) Requirement of acting as "the Committee"	277
	b) External influence via the Meeting of Chairpersons	279
	aa) Article 28 CED	279
	bb) Article 38(b) CRPD	281
	4. Reconciliation between autonomy and external influence	282
C.	*Conclusion and outlook*	284

Conclusions 287

Bibliography 293

Index 313

Introduction

A. United Nations human rights treaty bodies

At the global level, the main responsibility for the protection and advancement of human rights standards resides with the United Nations human rights treaty bodies.[1] These are the Human Rights Committee, established by the International Covenant on Civil and Political Rights (ICCPR),[2] the Committee on Economic, Social and Cultural Rights (CESCR Committee), which monitors the implementation of the International Covenant on Economic, Social and Cultural Rights (ICESCR),[3] the Committee on the Elimination of Racial Discrimination (CERD Committee), established by the International Convention on the Elimination of All Forms of Racial Discrimination (CERD),[4] the Committee on the Elimination of Discrimination against Women (CEDAW Committee), established by the Convention on the Elimination of All Forms of Discrimination against Women (CEDAW),[5] the Committee against Torture, established by the Convention against Torture and Other Cruel, Inhuman or Degrading Treatment or Punishment (CAT),[6] the Committee on the Rights of the Child (CRC Committee), established by the Convention on the Rights of the Child (CRC),[7] the Committee on the Protection of the Rights of All Migrant Workers and Members of their Families (CMW Committee), established by the International Convention on the Protection of the Rights of All Migrant Workers and Members of their Families (CMW),[8] the Committee on Enforced Disappearances (CED Committee), established by the International Convention for the Protection of All Persons from Enforced Disappearance (CED),[9] and finally the Committee on the Rights of Persons with Disabilities (CRPD Committee), which has been established by the Convention on the Rights of Persons with Disabilities.[10]

---

[1] *Keller/Ulfstein*, Introduction, in: Keller/Ulfstein (eds.), UN Human Rights Treaty Bodies: Law and Legitimacy, 2012, p. 2.
[2] Adopted 16 December 1966, entered into force 23 March 1977, 999 UNTS 171.
[3] Adopted 16 December 1966, entered into force 03 January 1976, 993 UNTS 3.
[4] Adopted 21 December 1965, entered into force 04 January 1969, 660 UNTS 195.
[5] Adopted 18 December 1979, entered into force 03 September 1981, 1249 UNTS 13.
[6] Adopted 10 December 1984, entered into force 26 June 1987, 1465 UNTS 85.
[7] Adopted 20 November 1989, entered into force 02 September 1990, 1577 UNTS 3.
[8] Adopted 18 December 1990, entered into force 01 July 2003, 2220 UNTS 3.
[9] Adopted 20 December 2006, entered into force 23 December 2010, 2716 UNTS 3.
[10] Adopted 13 December 2006, entered into force 03 May 2008, 2515 UNTS 3.

The Subcommittee on Prevention of Torture and other Cruel, Inhuman or Degrading Treatment or Punishment, established by the Optional Protocol to the Convention against Torture and Other Cruel, Inhuman or Degrading Treatment or Punishment,[11] is yet another treaty body operating at the UN level.[12] However, it differs from the other nine treaty bodies in that its mandate is limited to preventive action against torture by establishing a system of regular visits and providing advice and assistance to State parties and national preventive mechanisms.[13] It will thus not be considered in the work at hand.

These monitoring bodies are composed of independent experts who serve in their personal capacity and who normally meet not more than three months a year in total. By ratifying one of the UN human rights core treaties, a State party automatically submits itself to the mandatory State reporting procedure, existent under each of the UN human rights core treaties. Among various possible enforcement mechanisms, State reporting presents the arguably weakest and the most sovereign-friendly solution,[14] and is hence the procedure that is most likely accepted by contracting parties.

Under the reporting procedure, each State party is obliged to periodically submit reports on measures taken to implement treaty guarantees. These reports are subsequently reviewed by the respective treaty body.[15] After the examination, the Committees adopt concluding observations, which reflect the Committee's dialogue with the State party under review and comprise both positive developments and areas of concern with regard to the State party's human rights record. A reporting cycle is terminated with a written follow-up procedure, under which the State party concerned is expected to submit information on the implementation of specific recommendations identified by the Committees.

In addition, treaty bodies may receive and consider individual communications, but subject to the acceptance of State parties, as they must either ratify the respective Optional Protocol foreseeing such a procedure,[16] or make a decla-

---

[11] Adopted 18 December 2002, entered into force 22 June 2006, 2375 UNTS 237.

[12] Adopted 18 December 2002, entered into force 22 June 2006, 2375 UNTS 237.

[13] For an overview of the mandate of the Subcommittee on the Prevention of Torture, see *Buchinger*, Article 11, Mandate of the Subcommittee, in: Nowak/Birk/Monina (eds.), The United Nations Convention Against Torture and its Optional Protocol: A Commentary, Second Edition, 2019; see also *Byrnes*, The Committee against Torture and the Subcommittee for the Prevention of Torture, in: Mégret/Alston (eds.), The United Nations and Human Rights: A Critical Appraisal, Second Edition, 2020, pp. 513–517; *Kessing*, New Optional Protocol to the UN Torture Convention, Nordic Journal of International Law 72 (2003), 571.

[14] *Kälin*, Examination of state reports, in: Keller/Ulfstein (eds.), UN Human Rights Treaty Bodies: Law and Legitimacy, 2012, p. 17; *O'Flaherty*, The United Nations Human Rights Treaty Bodies as Diplomatic Actors, in: O'Flaherty et al. (eds.), Human Rights Diplomacy: Contemporary Perspectives, 2011, p. 157.

[15] The review by independent experts sets the review process decisively apart from the Universal Periodic Review, which serves as the second "main" forum at the global level to evaluate State parties as regards their compliance with human rights standards.

[16] The individual complaints procedure before the Human Rights Committee is provided

ration to accept said complaints procedure pursuant to relevant treaty provisions.[17] Especially in countries that are not members of one of the three regional human rights systems, the UN human rights treaty bodies constitute the only supervisory system as far as human rights are concerned and thus provide individual redress and relief for victims at the international level.

Next to these two kinds of supervisory mechanisms, most of the UN human rights treaty bodies adopt so-called General Comments, by which they clarify their own understanding of substantive treaty provisions or provide guidance to State parties as to how to meet the requirements of periodic reports, for instance.[18] Further functions discharged by treaty bodies and that complete the picture include the inter-State complaints mechanism,[19] the early warnings and urgent actions procedure,[20] and the inquiry procedure.[21] Specifically, the last of these constitutes a complementary function to both the reporting and complaints

---

for by the First Optional Protocol to the International Covenant on Civil and Political Rights (adopted 16 December 1966, entered into force 23 March 1976), 999 UNTS 171; before the CESCR Committee by the Optional Protocol to the International Covenant on Economic, Social and Cultural Rights (adopted 10 December 2008, entered into force 05 May 2013), UN General Assembly, Resolution 63/117, UN Doc. A/RES/63/117; before the CEDAW Committee by the Optional Protocol to the Convention on the Elimination of All Forms of Discrimination against Women (adopted 06 October 1999, entered into force 22 December 2000), 2131 UNTS 83; before the CRPD Committee by the Optional Protocol to the Convention on the Rights of Persons with Disabilities (adopted 13 December 2006, entered into force 03 May 2008), 2518 UNTS 283; before the CRC Committee by the Optional Protocol to the Convention on the Rights of the Child on a communications procedure (adopted 19 December 2011, entered into force 14 April 2014), UN General Assembly, Resolution 66/138, UN Doc. A/RES/66/138.

[17] Article 14(1) CERD; article 22(1) CAT; article 31(1) CED; and article 77(1) CMW, however, so far, the required number of ten submitted declarations pursuant to article 77(8) CMW has not yet been reached.

[18] See generally *Keller/Grover*, General Comments of the Human Rights Committee and their legitimacy, in: Keller/Ulfstein (eds.), UN Human Rights Treaty Bodies: Law and Legitimacy, 2012, pp. 116–198.

[19] Until recently, the inter-state complaints mechanism has been lying dormant, but three procedures are currently pending before the CERD Committee, see for their documentation: https://www.ohchr.org/EN/HRBodies/CERD/Pages/InterstateCommunications.aspx (last access: 21.08.2023).

[20] The CERD Committee developed said procedure under article 9(1)(b) CERD, Report of the Committee on the Elimination of Racial Discrimination (42nd and 43rd session), UN Doc. A/48/18 (1993), Annex III; *Thornberry*, The International Convention on the Elimination of All Forms of Racial Discrimination: A Commentary, 2016, The Convention and the Committee, pp. 49–51; under the CED, it is article 30 that provides for the urgent action procedure.

[21] The inquiry procedure is provided for by article 20 CAT, article 33 CED, article 8 OP CEDAW, article 6 OP CRPD, article 11 OP ICESCR and article 3 Third OP CRC.

procedure, as it allows the treaty bodies to react to "allegations of systematic, grave, or serious violations".[22]

Provided that a State party has ratified all of the nine UN human rights core treaties, it will be subject to international scrutiny regarding a wide range of human rights, covering both civil and political rights and socio-economic rights, as well as more group- and issue-specific treaties. Next to their manifold functions and mandates, treaty bodies are also said to have contributed to the development of both international law in general, and human rights law in particular,[23] for instance the approach to invalid reservations or the broadening of substantive standards.

Against this backdrop, the UN human rights treaty bodies might appear to be an unprecedented success story in terms of implementing human rights and developing international standards further. But what may sound promising on paper is anything but entirely positive in reality. Instead, the human rights treaty bodies are confronted with a considerable number of challenges when exercising their mandates.

B. Problems faced by human rights treaty bodies

First, there are inherent weaknesses, such as the non-binding status of treaty body recommendations or views adopted under the individual complaints procedure,[24] which sets treaty bodies apart from regional human rights courts, for instance. At the same time, this kind of finding does not necessarily signify that treaty body pronouncements are void of any effect.[25] They are accorded "great

---

[22] *Oette*, The UN Human Rights Treaty Bodies: Impact and Future, in: Oberleitner (ed.), International Human Rights Institutions, Tribunals, and Courts, 2018, p. 107.

[23] *Oette*, The UN Human Rights Treaty Bodies: Impact and Future, in: Oberleitner (ed.), International Human Rights Institutions, Tribunals, and Courts, 2018, p. 104, with specific reference to the CESCR Committee and socio-economic rights; *van Alebeek/Nollkaemper*, The legal status of decisions by human rights treaty bodies in national law, in: Keller/Ulfstein (eds.), UN Human Rights Treaty Bodies: Law and Legitimacy, 2012, p. 357; *Klein*, Impact of Treaty Bodies on the International Legal Order, in: Wolfrum/Röben (eds.), Developments of International Law in Treaty Making, 2005, p. 575, who detects a "norm creating function" in relation to General Comments.

[24] *Tomuschat*, Human Rights: Between Idealism and Realism, Third Edition, 2014, p. 233; *Ulfstein*, Individual Complaints, in: Keller/Ulfstein (eds.), UN Human Rights Treaty Bodies: Law and Legitimacy, 2012, p. 94; *O'Flaherty*, The Concluding Observations of United Nations Human Rights Treaty Bodies, Human Rights Law Review 6 (2006), 27, 32, who accords "advisory" character to concluding observations; see *Helfer/Slaughter*, Toward a Theory of Effective Supranational Adjudication, Yale Law Journal 107 (1997), 273, 280, who nonetheless argue that the Human Rights Committee began to act more and more like a court.

[25] See for instance *Neuman*, Giving Meaning and Effect to Human Rights, The Contribution of Human Rights Committee Members, in: Moeckli/Keller/Heri (eds.) The Human Rights Covenants at 50: Their Past, Present, and Future, 2018, p. 34, who observes that treaty

weight"[26] or an "authoritative status",[27] and State parties that have ratified the human rights core treaties are at least expected to comply in good faith with their treaty obligations, which also entails giving due respect to the output generated by the Committees.[28] Second, looking at the implementation of recommendations, treaty bodies exhibit a weak mandate with regard to the enforcement of recommendations and views.[29] Most of the treaties do not provide for any express power to follow-up the implementation of recommendations or views. The missing "legal and actual capacity to enforce the obligations"[30] signifies that treaty bodies may well articulate useful and valuable recommendations in the course of examining a State party's human rights record, but once the constructive dialogue in Geneva is over, there is hardly any possibility for treaty bodies to influence the situation on the ground.

Among the various functions and tasks exercised by treaty bodies, it is especially the State reporting procedure that has given rise to serious concerns. State parties do not comply with their reporting obligations, both in terms of non-submission as well as reports of low quality.[31] State reports often do not even provide a minimum of sufficient information for treaty bodies to examine the respective State party's human rights record in a reasonable manner. In these cases, treaty bodies need to rely on other sources of information, but these may present themselves equally "highly selective" or just focus on a particular prob-

---

body findings may persuade State parties or may "reinforce internal political forces and social movements arguing for reform."

[26] *Ahmadou Sadio Diallo (Republic of Guinea v Democratic Republic of the Congo)*, Merits, Judgment, I.C.J. Reports 2010, p. 639, at para. 66.

[27] *Reiners*, Transnational Lawmaking Coalitions for Human Rights, 2021, pp. 33–35; *Kälin/Künzli*, The Law of International Human Rights Protection, Second Edition, 2019, p. 218; *Payandeh*, Fragmentation within international human rights law, in: Andenas/Bjorge (eds.), A Farewell to Fragmentation: Reassertion and Convergence in International Law, 2015, p. 305, who states that treaty body pronouncements are "highly authoritative and significantly influence legal discourse and human rights practice"; *O'Flaherty*, The Concluding Observations of United Nations Human Rights Treaty Bodies, Human Rights Law Review 6 (2006), 27, 36, speaking of "notable authority", but under the restriction that the recommendation must be linked to the respective treaty body's instrument and must not refer to extraneous and unrelated matters.

[28] Human Rights Committee, General Comment No. 33, Obligations of States parties under the Optional Protocol to the International Covenant on Civil and Political Rights, UN Doc. CCPR/C/GC/33, 25.06.2009, para. 15, which states that a "duty to cooperate with the Committee arises from an application of the principle of good faith to the observance of all treaty obligations."

[29] *Ramcharan*, Modernizing the UN Human Rights System, 2019, p. 176.

[30] *Gaer*, Implementing Treaty Body Recommendations: Establishing Better Follow-Up Procedures, in: Bassiouni/Schabas (eds.), New Challenges for the UN Human Rights Machinery: What Future for the UN Treaty Body System and the Human Rights Council Procedures?, 2011, p. 107.

[31] *Giegling*, Challenges and Chances of a Written State Report: Analysis and Improvement of a Monitoring Instrument on the Implementation of Human Rights, 2021, p. 66.

lem and thus do not provide a comprehensive overview of the situation in the State party concerned.[32] In line with the weaker institutional design of treaty bodies, possible reactions on the part of treaty bodies to put an end to non-compliance are likewise scarce. And even when State parties have submitted their reports in a timely manner, appeared before the treaty bodies and have participated in the constructive dialogue, this does not automatically signify that the State party under review will eventually respect and implement the recommendations made by the respective Committee. At the same time, however, it must not be overlooked that non-compliance does not always represent a deliberate breach of reporting obligations, but can also result from a State party simply being unable to meet all of its numerous reporting obligations.[33] Provided that a State party has ratified all of the UN human rights core treaties, it theoretically must submit an average of two reports per year,[34] not to mention the preparation and submission of other reports under regional human rights treaties.[35]

Moreover, quite paradoxically, the treaty body system is also taken to be a victim of its own success.[36] Both the uncoordinated growth of the system and the increasing number of ratifications have pushed it to its limits.[37] Due to prevailing resource constraints, treaty bodies would not be able to handle the workload that would exist if all State parties were fully compliant with their reporting obligations under each treaty, let alone the increasing number of filed and pending individual communications that await consideration.[38]

---

[32] *Bayefsky*, Introduction, in: Bayefsky (ed.), The UN Human Rights Treaty System in the 21st Century, 2000, p. xviii.

[33] *Kälin*, Examination of state reports, in: Keller/Ulfstein (eds.), UN Human Rights Treaty Bodies: Law and Legitimacy, 2012, p. 18.

[34] *Morijn*, Reforming United Nations Human Rights Treaty Monitoring Reform, Netherlands International Law Review 58 (2011), 295, 302.

[35] In the European context, a comparable reporting system, which is to entail periodic reports submitted to an independent expert organ, is established by articles 21 to 29 of the European Social Charter, for an overview of the system, see *de Schutter/Sant'Ana*, The European Committee of Social Rights (the ECSR), in: de Beco (ed.), Human Rights Monitoring Mechanisms of the Council of Europe, 2012, pp. 71–99; in the African context, article 62 of the African Charter on Human and Peoples' Rights requires State parties to submit every two years a report on the legislative or other measures taken to give effect to rights and freedoms enshrined in the Charter. For an overview of the procedure, see *Murray*, The African Charter on Human and Peoples' Rights: A Commentary, 2019, Article 62, State Reporting.

[36] *Crawford*, The UN human rights treaty system: A system in crisis?, in: Alston/Crawford (eds.), The Future of UN Human Rights Treaty Monitoring, 2000, p. 3.

[37] *Abashidze/Koneva*, The Process of Strengthening the Human Rights Treaty Body System: The Road towards Effectiveness or Inefficiency?, Netherlands International Law Review 66 (2019), 357, 362; between 2004 and 2012, the treaty body system has doubled in size with the addition of four new treaties and three additional individual complaints procedures, *Pillay*, Strengthening the United Nations human rights treaty body system, p. 17; see also the Concept Paper on the High Commissioner's Proposal for a Unified Standing Treaty Body, UN Doc. HRI/MC/2006/2, 22.03.2006, para. 18.

[38] *Kälin*, Examination of state reports, in: Keller/Ulfstein (eds.), UN Human Rights Treaty

B. Problems faced by human rights treaty bodies

Further problems which add up to the system's shortcomings are the quality and independence of treaty body members,[39] the lack of visibility of and knowledge about the system,[40] and the growing volume of documentation, which is a logical consequence of more and more State parties ratifying and reporting under UN human rights treaties.[41] The latter specifically requires additional costs of translation, which again has negative repercussions on the system's already scarce resources.

Probably the most disillusioning aspect of the whole treaty body system is the fact that the above-described findings have been threatening the system almost since its inception and despite repeated attempts at reform, no significant improvements have been achieved yet.[42] The fact that the Committees are chronically lacking the necessary resources is not a novelty, but recent calls made indicate that the situation has only deteriorated.[43] Unexpected budgetary constraints would have almost led to the cancellation of treaty body sessions in autumn 2019, which posed a serious threat to undermine the system and would have had a considerable impact on all of the functions performed by the various Commit-

---

Bodies: Law and Legitimacy, 2012, pp. 71–72; *Rodley*, Duplication and Divergence in the Work of the United Nations Human Rights Treaty Bodies: A Perspective from a Treaty Body Member, American Society of International Law Proceedings 105 (2011), 512; *Bayefsky*, Introduction, in: Bayefsky (ed.), The UN Human Rights Treaty System in the 21st Century, 2000, p. xviii.

[39] *Carraro*, Electing the experts: Expertise and independence in the UN human rights treaty bodies, European Journal of International Relations 25 (2019), 826, 828, who describes the election of treaty body members as "highly politicized" and marked by "negotiations and exchanges of votes between countries". The author also detects variances with a view to the level of expertise and independence of Committee members; *Ulfstein*, Individual Complaints, in: Keller/Ulfstein (eds.), UN Human Rights Treaty Bodies: Law and Legitimacy, 2012, pp. 85–86, suggesting to elect treaty body members openly, contrary to the current *modus operandi* with elections by secret ballot; cf. Concept Paper on the High Commissioner's Proposal for a Unified Standing Treaty Body, UN Doc. HRI/MC/2006/2, 22.03.2006, para. 22.

[40] *Pillay*, Strengthening the United Nations human rights treaty body system, p. 88; *Morijn*, Reforming United Nations Human Rights Treaty Monitoring Reform, Netherlands International Law Review 58 (2011), 295, 302.

[41] *Pillay*, Strengthening the United Nations human rights treaty body system, p. 24.

[42] See *Egan*, Transforming the UN Human Rights Treaty System: A Realistic Appraisal, Human Rights Quarterly 42 (2020), 762, 765, speaking of a "perpetual crisis"; UN General Assembly, Status of the human rights treaty body system, Report of the Secretary-General, UN Doc. A/77/279, 10.01.2020, paras. 14–18, with an overview of the reporting compliance by State parties. 86 per cent of all State parties have at least one report outstanding. Under current working methods, the Committees would need approximately 3.2 years to clear the backlog of reports, see in the same document para. 18. With a view to individual communications pending before the Committees, the situation seems equally dramatic with 1.800 communications currently pending paras. 19–21.

[43] See exemplary the call made by the Human Rights Committee in one of its more recent annual reports, Report of the Human Rights Committee (126th, 127th and 128th session), UN Doc. A/75/40 (2020), paras. 39–40.

tees. As one can imagine, the COVID-19 pandemic also played its part in exacerbating the situation and has brought the system to a halt.[44]

Last but not least, it is one thing for a State party to formally participate in the State reporting procedure, but quite another for it to accept and eventually implement the recommendations adopted by the treaty bodies. Whereas the lack of political will at the national level might be one explanation for implementation deficits, the phenomenon of low compliance might also be the result of imprecise and superficial concluding observations, leaving it unclear to the State party how to comply with their substantive treaty obligations.[45] Yet, given that concluding observations reflect the dialogue with the State party concerned, which in turn is (partially) based on the State report submitted, reports of low quality will also lead to the adoption of concluding observations with limited informative value.[46] It is in these cases that information submitted by NGOs and civil society representatives can close this lacuna.[47] However, this does not guarantee that the treaty's implementation is comprehensively covered by this information and such approach presupposes the existence of active and participating NGOs in the country under review.[48] Ultimately, notwithstanding the fact that the quality of concluding observations is said to have improved, it hinges on the will of State parties to implement treaty body findings, and the exact influence of treaty bodies is generally considered hard to measure.[49]

---

[44] "Work of human rights treaty bodies at risk, warn UN Committee Chairs", https://www.ohchr.org/EN/NewsEvents/Pages/DisplayNews.aspx?NewsID=26147&LangID=E (last access: 21.08.2023); see also Discussion paper of the Informal Working Group on COVID-19, https://www.ohchr.org/EN/HRBodies/AnnualMeeting/Pages/Session32.aspx (last access: 21.08.2023).

[45] See generally for the quality of concluding observations *O'Flaherty*, The Concluding Observations of United Nations Human Rights Treaty Bodies, Human Rights Law Review 6 (2006), 27.

[46] *Kälin*, Examination of state reports, in: Keller/Ulfstein (eds.), UN Human Rights Treaty Bodies: Law and Legitimacy, 2012, p. 60.

[47] See exemplarily for the importance of NGOs under the reporting procedure, *Mutzenberg*, NGOs, Essential Actors for Embedding Covenants in the National Context, in: Moeckli/Keller/Heri (eds.), The Human Rights Covenants at 50: Their Past, Present, and Future, 2018, pp. 77–84.

[48] *Kälin*, Examination of state reports, in: Keller/Ulfstein (eds.), UN Human Rights Treaty Bodies: Law and Legitimacy, 2012, pp. 62–63.

[49] For studies on the effect of treaty bodies at the domestic level, see *Creamer/Simmons*, The Proof Is in the Process: Self-Reporting Under International Human Rights Treaties, American Journal of International Law 114 (2020), 1; *Krommendijk*, The Domestic Impact and Effectiveness of the Process of State Reporting under UN Human Rights Treaties in the Netherlands, New Zealand and Finland: Paper-pushing or policy prompting?, Intersentia, 2014; *Heyns/Viljoen* (eds.), The Impact of the United Nations Human Rights Treaties on the Domestic Level, 2002.

C. Fragmentation of human rights law within the treaty body system

The underlying theoretical reason for the system's shortfalls may well be the fragmented status of human rights law, and the arguably equally fragmented state of the UN human rights treaty system. Under general international law, the debate about the fragmented state of the law, its negative and positive implications and how to overcome or deal with fragmentation might have had their "heydays" in the 2000s and the proliferation of sub-regimes, and its consequences might have been largely accepted by now.[50] It now primarily focuses on ways and means of dealing with the fragmented state of international law.[51]

As a matter of fact, all characteristics of the fragmentation of the general international legal order can be found in the specialized field of human rights law.[52] Due to increased norm-setting activities at the universal and regional level, several "human rights sub-treaty regimes" have been developed. Group- and issue-specific treaties have been added, driven by the belief or necessity to focus on the respective vulnerable and marginalized group of individuals or the specific form of violation of rights. The establishment of yet another treaty often entails the establishment of another monitoring body, which applies and interprets its own constituent instrument. Ensuing from said multiplication of entities entrusted with applying and monitoring their own treaties, which overlap to a great extent as far as substantive rights and guarantees are concerned,[53] "decisional fragmentation" might occur. This term signifies that "two courts seized of the

---

[50] *Peters*, The refinement of international law: From fragmentation to regime interaction and politicization, International Journal of Constitutional Law 15 (2017), 671, 674; see also *Broude*, Keep Calm and Carry on: Martti Koskenniemi and the Fragmentation of International Law, Temple International & Comparative Law Journal 27 (2013), 279, 280.

[51] See for example *Andenas/Bjorge* (eds.), A Farewell to Fragmentation: Reassertion and Convergence in International Law, 2015; with specific focus on human rights law, *Heyns/Killander*, Universality and the Growth of Regional Systems, in: Shelton (ed.), The Handbook of International Human Rights Law, 2013, p. 695, who state that "the dangers of the fragmentation of international human rights law by breakaway movements have not come to pass."

[52] *Payandeh*, Fragmentation within international human rights law, in: Andenas/Bjorge (eds.), A Farewell to Fragmentation: Reassertion and Convergence in International Law, 2015, pp. 298–299, who argues that similar problems related to fragmentation can be found between the UN human rights treaties and treaty bodies themselves; see also *Ajevski*, Fragmentation in International Human Rights Law – Beyond Conflict of Laws, Nordic Journal of Human Rights 32 (2014), 87.

[53] *Morijn*, Reforming United Nations Human Rights Treaty Monitoring Reform, Netherlands International Law Review 58 (2011), 295, 317; the research on diverging or congruent interpretations in international human rights law often compares the approaches taken by the regional bodies or compares regional bodies with selected human rights treaty bodies, see for instance the contributions in Buckley/Donald/Leach (eds.), Towards Convergence in International Human Rights Law: Approaches of Regional and International Systems, 2016.

same issue render contradictory decisions."[54] While diverging interpretations as such might lead to a broader and "denser"[55] body of case law in the first place and could secondly prompt international courts and tribunals to develop the most sophisticated and well-reasoned solution to a legal problem,[56] State parties could as well shield themselves behind contradicting judgments, views or recommendations.[57] They could just accept the less far-reaching solution as to the restriction of governmental powers, or could simply refuse to comply with *any* of the recommendations made if they contradict each other.[58] On the other hand, diverging opinions offer at the same time the possibility of filing petitions with the one institution that is deemed to render the most applicant-friendly decision. In this case, forum shopping proves to be a positive means that offers advantages and thus strategic opportunities to individuals seeking legal protection at the international level.[59]

Applied to UN human rights treaty bodies, it is hence very likely that the outcome of similar communications might be different, or even diametrically opposed to each other, as different treaty bodies might prioritize different interests or rights.[60] Such a result seems all the more imaginable given the fact that the establishment of group- or issue-specific treaty was driven by a "specialization logic",[61] and that the respective treaty body will consider itself an advocate of the

---

[54] *Webb*, International Judicial Integration and Fragmentation, 2013, p. 6.

[55] *Peters*, The refinement of international law: From fragmentation to regime interaction and politicization, International Journal of Constitutional Law 15 (2017), 671, 681.

[56] *Ulfstein*, The international Judiciary, in: Klabbers/Peters/Ulfstein (eds.), The Constitutionalization of International Law, 2009, p. 138.

[57] Cf. *Walker*, International Human Rights Law: Towards Pluralism or Harmony? The Opportunities and Challenges of Coexistence: The View from the UN Treaty Bodies, in: Buckley/Donald/Leach (eds.), Towards Convergence in International Human Rights Law: Approaches of Regional and International Systems, 2016, p. 493, who observes that contradictions might lead to confusion and could also challenge the credibility of human rights courts and tribunals.

[58] By way of example, reference shall be made to an order rendered by the German Constitutional Court in which it relied, inter alia, on contradicting treaty body recommendations to reinforce its position that domestic courts neither had to abide by the jurisprudence of treaty bodies nor that the position of the CRPD Committee was legally convincing, BVerfG, Order of the Second Senate of 29 January 2019 – 2 BvC 62/14, para. 77.

[59] On the possibility of forum shopping for individuals in the context of human rights law generally, see *Helfer*, Forum Shopping for Human Rights, University of Pennsylvania Law Review 148 (1999), 285.

[60] *Payandeh*, Fragmentation within international human rights law, in: Andenas/Bjorge (eds.), A Farewell to Fragmentation: Reassertion and Convergence in International Law, 2015, p. 308; *Ulfstein*, The international Judiciary, in: Klabbers/Peters/Ulfstein (eds.), The Constitutionalization of International Law, 2009, p. 139.

[61] *Brems*, Smart human rights integration, in: Brems/Ouald-Chaib (eds.), Fragmentation and Integration in Human Rights Law: Users' Perspectives, 2018, pp. 170–178.

C. Fragmentation of human rights law within the treaty body system

group of vulnerable individuals the treaty was intended to provide protection for.[62]

While contradictory decisions and recommendations may both pose opportunities and challenges, it must be reiterated that the work at hand will mostly focus on the State reporting procedure, at the end of which concluding observations tailored to the State party under review will be adopted. Openly divergent and contradictory recommendations adopted by two or more treaty bodies initially seem less likely. Contrary to the communications procedure, recommendations under the reporting procedure serve as guiding devices in overcoming structural deficits. As all treaty bodies strive for full implementation of treaty guarantees by State parties, recommendations under the reporting procedure will generally seek to improve a State party's human rights record. Differences between concluding observations will rather reside in their protective scopes, thus they will differ in the extent to which State parties shall take appropriate measures.

Nevertheless, the overlap between substantive treaty provisions has been identified as one of the major causes exacerbating the so-called "reporting fatigue".[63] Due to the uncoordinated approaches among the various Committees and the sometimes considerable substantive overlap between the treaties,[64] it is very likely that a State party is called before several treaty bodies with only short intervals in between and is asked to report on the same issue again and again.[65] Besides, despite the less imminent risk of contradictory statements under the reporting procedure, the proliferation of treaty bodies has led, at least in the past, to different working methods among treaty bodies and different requirements State reports have to fulfil. The adherence to treaty body-specific requirements thus only further aggravates the reporting burden imposed on State parties.[66] The cause for

---

[62] *Payandeh*, Fragmentation within international human rights law, in: Andenas/Bjorge (eds.), A Farewell to Fragmentation: Reassertion and Convergence in International Law, 2015, p. 311, speaking of a "structural bias" of treaty bodies with a view to their own constituent instrument.

[63] *Morijn*, Reforming United Nations Human Rights Treaty Monitoring Reform, Netherlands International Law Review 58 (2011), 295, 297; *Tyagi*, The UN Human Rights Committee, Practice and Procedure, 2011, p. 748, speaking of "competing reporting procedures"; see also *Johnstone*, Streamlining the Constructive Dialogue: Efficiency from States' Perspectives, in: Bassiouni/Schabas (eds.), New Challenges for the UN Human Rights Machinery, 2011, p. 64, who observes that "providing multiple accounts of overlapping information is not an efficient use of resources."

[64] For possible substantive overlap among the UN human rights treaties, see Guidelines on an expanded core document and treaty-specific targeted reports and harmonized guidelines on reporting under the international human rights treaties, Report of the secretariat, UN Doc. HRI/MC/2004/3, 09.04.2004, para. 20 with the so-called "chart of congruence".

[65] *Krommendijk*, Less is more: Proposals for how UN human rights treaty bodies can be more selective, Netherlands Quarterly of Human Rights 38 (2020), 5, 8; *Johnstone*, Cynical Savings or Reasonable Reform? Reflections on a Single Unified UN Human Rights Treaty Body, Human Rights Law Review 7 (2007), 173, 183–184, pointing to the burden of small and developing State parties in this context.

[66] Concept Paper on the High Commissioner's Proposal for a Unified Standing Treaty

the system's shortfalls is thus to be located at the intersection of the various manifestations of fragmentation: substantive overlap between the treaties, the proliferation of oversight bodies that work in isolation from each other, rather than cooperating, and procedural fragmentation, which denotes the development of diverging working methods among the treaty bodies, and which renders it very burdensome for State parties to respect all the treaty-specific particularities.[67] Coupled with enormous resource constraints and a high number of delinquent State parties, all this has led to a vicious circle, from which withdrawal seems almost impossible.[68]

D. Aim and scope of the thesis at hand

As the treaty body system is, and has probably always been, in crisis, a significant number of academic writings has been produced, either focusing on previously proposed attempts at reform or suggesting new recommendations.[69] The work at

---

Body, UN Doc. HRI/MC/2006/2, 22.03.2006, para. 17, stating that different working methods among the Committees might compromise "the system's coherence" and can create "a lack of clarity for States parties".

[67] See *O'Flaherty*, Reform of the UN Human Rights Treaty Body System: Locating the Dublin Statement, Human Rights Law Review 10 (2010), 319, 326, who notes that the development of working methods does not appear to always happen in cooperation.

[68] *Morijn*, Reforming United Nations Human Rights Treaty Monitoring Reform, Netherlands International Law Review 58 (2011), 295, 304; cf. *Shany*, The Effectiveness of the Human Rights Committee, in: Breuer et al. (eds.), Der Staat im Recht, Festschrift für Eckart Klein zum 70. Geburtstag, 2013, p. 1323, who identifies "serious capacity problems" and "limited legal powers" as the fundamental problems of the treaty bodies.

[69] *Giegling*, Challenges and Chances of a Written State Report: Analysis and Improvement of a Monitoring Instrument on the Implementation of Human Rights, 2021; *Egan*, Reform of the UN Human Rights Treaty Body System, in: Mégret/Alston (eds.), The United Nations and Human Rights: A Critical Appraisal, Second Edition, 2020, p. 645; *Abashidze/Koneva*, The Process of Strengthening the Human Rights Treaty Body System: The Road towards Effectiveness or Inefficiency?, Netherlands International Law Review 66 (2019), 357; *Gaer*, The Institutional Future of the Covenants, A World Court for Human Rights?, in: Moeckli/Keller/Heri (eds.) The Human Rights Covenants at 50: Their Past, Present, and Future, 2018, p. 334; *O'Flaherty*, The Strengthening Process of the Human Rights Treaty Bodies, American Society of International Law, Proceedings of the Annual Meeting 108 (2014), 285; *Oberleitner*, Agenda for Strengthening Human Rights Institutions, in: Oberleitner (ed.), International Human Rights Institutions, Tribunals, and Courts, 2018, 551; *Egan*, Strengthening the United Nations Human Rights Treaty Body System, Human Rights Law Review 13 (2013), 209; *O'Flaherty*, Reform of the UN Human Rights Treaty Body System: Locating the Dublin Statement, Human Rights Law Review 10 (2010), 319; *Schöpp-Schilling*, Treaty Body Reform: The Case of the Committee on the Elimination of Discrimination Against Women, Human Rights Law Review 7 (2007), 201; *O'Flaherty/O'Brien*, Reform of UN Human Rights Treaty Monitoring Bodies: A Critique of the Concept Paper on the High Commissioner's Proposal for a Unified Standing Treaty Body, Human Rights Law Review 7 (2007), 141; *Hampson*, An Overview of the Reform of the UN Human Rights Machinery, Human Rights

hand is intended to complement this series, but the treaty bodies, their current *modus operandi* and their obvious need for reform shall be approached from a perspective which has not been pursued before.

The thesis' main argument is that the Committees themselves can and should be primarily responsible for reforming the system. Both the uncoordinated growth and past attempts at reform prove that State parties, thus "the masters of the treaties", are lacking the decisive will or capacity to ultimately provide the system with the impetus required for sufficient and sustainable reform. At the same time, to fully understand current reform efforts, previous reform initiatives must be taken into consideration. Present attempts at reform are often the result of preceding actions. The first main section will therefore shed light on the growth of the treaty body system with a specific view on the rationales for establishing each time yet another treaty body and on past attempts at reform.

Since treaty bodies enjoy a certain autonomy, albeit not easy to conceptualize, which allows them to implement certain measures on their own without the consent of State parties, they have to navigate a small strait between acting *ultra vires* and remaining within their boundaries.[70] It is also one thing to consider their actions from the perspective of State parties, sometimes accusing treaty bodies of exceeding their legitimate powers, but another to establish in purely legal terms whether treaty bodies ultimately enjoy certain powers or not.

Therefore, the second main section will provide answers to the question of how to interpret the treaty bodies' constituent instruments, from which they derive their mandate, and where to set the boundaries for their autonomous actions. For that purpose, possible interpretative methods in the realm of human rights treaties will be put under closer scrutiny, which also raises the question of whether there are different interpretative approaches regarding substantive or procedural provisions.

To clarify the question, the extension of powers that had previously been undertaken by treaty bodies in the past will be analysed. These examples will provide determinants for a possible general framework in the delineation of a human rights treaty body's mandate. The section is also intended to explore possible extensions of powers via subsequent practice in accordance with article 31(3)(b) VCLT, and which authority to ascribe to the United Nations General Assembly in relation to the human rights treaty bodies. On that note, one of the underlying assumptions of the thesis at hand is that all UN human rights treaty bodies are considered equal in their mandates and functions. By implication,

---

Law Review 7 (2007), 7; *Bayefsky* (ed.), The UN Human Rights Treaty System in the 21st Century, 2000; Alston/Crawford (eds.), The Future of UN Human Rights Treaty Monitoring, 2000.

[70] See *Shelton*, The Legal Status of Normative Pronouncements of Human Rights Treaty Bodies, in: Hestermeyer et al. (eds.), Coexistence, Cooperation and Solidarity, Liber Amicorum Rüdiger Wolfrum Volume I, 2012, pp. 559–560, illustrating said problem with the requirement of having to walk the "Goldilocks line".

findings in legal literature and Committee statements that solely focus on an individual treaty body will be considered transferable to all other Committees, unless indicated otherwise.

The third main section will then focus on current reform efforts, all of which are deemed realizable by the Committees themselves, and thus without State consent. These are, in particular, proposals which are currently discussed among treaty bodies, as well as other stakeholders, and which might bear the potential to oppose and resolve the reporting fatigue and the system's major shortcomings.

The underlying assumption in the third main section is that the implementation of all proposals analysed there are interdependent. The proposals will be portrayed in "chronological order" along the steps under the reporting procedure. This approach also allows each subsequent step to be based on what has been previously discussed, which ultimately leads to a comprehensive and holistic overview of the system and possible actions for refinement. The section will focus on the simplified reporting procedure, the establishment of a comprehensive reporting calendar, possible reviews in the absence of a report, and on ways and means to mitigate possible reporting gaps which could ensue in the event of introducing a comprehensive reporting calendar. Despite the thesis' major focus on attempts of reform concerning working methods and procedural aspects under the reporting procedure, the substantive overlap will be addressed as well, where deemed appropriate.

In the last section, the possibility of enhanced cooperation between the various treaty bodies will be analysed. Currently, the Chairs of each treaty body meet annually in the so-called Meeting of Chairpersons, which could be described as a body of *sui generis* status and which serves as a linking element. The Meeting of Chairpersons itself has undergone a considerable evolution and it might provide the necessary impetus for accelerating and improving the harmonization of working methods and procedures among the various Committees. In this sense, it might also serve to reduce incoherencies and can thereby contribute to alleviating the reporting burden resting on State parties.

Part I

Growth of the treaty body system

One of the main causes for the inefficiency of the United Nations human rights treaty body system is its fragmented institutional structure, stemming from its uncoordinated growth in the past.[1] The drafters of the Universal Declaration of Human Rights originally intended to develop an international bill of human rights comprising a declaration, a binding convention, containing both civil and socio-economic rights, and measures for implementation and supervision of compliance.[2] If said international bill of human rights had come into existence, arguably many, if not most, of the problems the treaty body system is facing today could have been avoided. An international court of human rights would likely be tasked with monitoring the implementation of all the UN human rights core treaties.[3]

After the adoption of the Universal Declaration of Human Rights, December 10 1948 by Resolution A/RES/217/A (III), the General Assembly adopted the same day Resolution A/RES/217/E (III) by which it requested ECOSOC to ask the UN Commission on Human Rights to continue its work and elaborate both a covenant on human rights and adequate measures of implementation. But as political tensions grew bigger amidst the Cold War, and due to the fact that civil and political rights and socio-economic rights were considered two opposing and thus mutually exclusive categories of rights,[4] it was decided in 1952 to split the

---

[1] See *Rodley*, The Role and Impact of Treaty Bodies, in: Shelton (ed.), The Oxford Handbook of International Human Rights Law, 2013, p. 643, who identifies the multiplication of treaty bodies as the main cause for their various problems.

[2] *Hertig Randall*, The History of the Covenants: Looking Back Half a Century and Beyond, in: Moeckli/Keller/Heri (eds.), The Human Rights Covenants at 50: Their Past, Present, and Future, 2018, p. 7; *Tomuschat*, International Covenant on Civil and Political Rights (1966), in: Peters (ed.), Max Planck Encyclopedia of Public International Law, April 2019, para. 3; see also *Tolley*, The U.N. Commission on Human Rights, Boulder 1987, p. 21 with a summary of the proposals suggested in relation to the bill of rights and its three main features.

[3] *Nowak*, A World Court of Human Rights, in: Oberleitner (ed.), International Human Rights Institutions, Tribunals, and Courts, 2018, p. 272; see for the Australian proposal dating from 1947, UN Commision on Human Rights, Draft resolution for an International Court on Human Rights, UN Doc. E/CN.4/15, 05.02.1947.

[4] *Hertig Randall*, The History of the Covenants: Looking Back Half a Century and Beyond, in: Moeckli/Keller/Heri (eds.), The Human Rights Covenants at 50: Their Past, Present, and Future, 2018, p. 18; *Tomuschat*, International Covenant on Civil and Political Rights (1966), in: Peters (ed.), Max Planck Encyclopedia of Public International Law, Online

drafting in two separate Covenants.⁵ With the abandonment of the project to draft a single and binding treaty, efforts for the establishment of any monitoring body for such a treaty simultaneously receded into the background.

A. Discussions on the suitable enforcement mechanisms under the two Covenants

While the following discussions on the suitable enforcement mechanisms for both the ICESCR and ICCPR were vigorously conducted, they did not so much focus on the proliferation of treaty bodies, a question which was obviously less pressing at that time, but more on the question to which extent and by which means an international body of any kind could interfere with State sovereignty.⁶

I. ICCPR

As far as the ICCPR was concerned, particularly the measures on implementation proved to be one of the most controversial topics during the drafting.⁷ State parties from the Eastern Bloc not only opposed the inclusion of a mandatory reporting procedure, as they did during early stages of the drafting process,⁸ but also opposed the adoption of an inter-State complaints mechanism or the inclusion of an individual complaints procedure.⁹ Others questioned the reporting procedure's appropriateness, which ultimately became the only mandatory implementation mechanism, owing to the direct applicability of civil and political

---

version, April 2019, para. 4; *Odello/Seatzu*, The UN Committee on Economic, Social and Cultural Rights: The Law, Process and Practice, 2013, p. 6.

⁵ *Nowak*, CCPR Commentary, Second revised Edition, 2005, Introduction, para. 8; *Boerefijn*, The Reporting Procedure under the Covenant on Civil and Political Rights: Practice and Procedures of the Human Rights Committee, 1999, p. 17; *Tolley*, The U.N. Commission on Human Rights, Boulder 1987, p. 25.

⁶ *Boerefijn*, The Reporting Procedure under the Covenant on Civil and Political Rights: Practice and Procedures of the Human Rights Committee, 1999, pp. 20–23; *McGoldrick*, The Human Rights Committee: Its Role in the Development of the International Covenant on Civil and Political Rights, 1991, pp. 13–14; *Tolley*, The U.N. Commission on Human Rights, Boulder 1987, p. 26; *Alston*, Out of the Abyss: The Challenges Confronting the New U. N. Committee on Economic, Social and Cultural Rights, Human Rights Quarterly 9 (1987), 332, 336–337.

⁷ *Nowak*, CCPR Commentary, Second revised Edition, 2005, Article 40, State Reports, para. 2; see generally for the drafting of the ICCPR *Bossuyt*, Guide to the "travaux préparatoires" of the International Covenant on Civil and Political Rights, 1987.

⁸ *Nowak*, CCPR Commentary, Second revised Edition, 2005, Article 40, State Reports, para. 2.

⁹ *Schwelb*, Civil and Political Rights: The International Measures of Implementation, American Journal of International Law 62 (1968), 827, 833.

rights as opposed to socio-economic rights, the latter only to be realized progressively.[10]

II. ICESCR

1. Monitoring of the ICESCR by ECOSOC

The first "formal" proposal in relation to any kind of supervisory organ under the ICESCR was presented by the Lebanese representative in April 1951 and provided for an independent committee composed of 15 members. Nevertheless, the proposed committee, which was "remarkably similar" to the CESRC Committee's current design, did not find much support.[11] The early debates on the Convention's implementation mechanism triggered the introduction of other suggestions, though none of them included the establishment of an expert body.[12] Interestingly, when discussions on the topic were briefly resumed in 1954, the French representative pointed out the possibility of assigning the soon to be established Human Rights Committee with the task of monitoring the implementation of the ICESCR. Several other representatives, however, clearly rejected the proposal and it was not even put to a vote.[13]

During the final stage of the drafting process within the Third Committee of the UN General Assembly in 1966, calls for the establishment of either an ad hoc committee or an independent committee modelled after the provisions installing the CERD Committee were made again.[14] Both proposals met with much opposition for various reasons. Especially African states remarked that an "undue proliferation of new bodies should be avoided" and pointed out unnecessary bureaucratic overhead.[15] Ultimately, ECOSOC was assigned with oversight of the Covenant, which was influenced by the widespread attitude among State

---

[10] *Hertig Randall*, The History of the Covenants: Looking Back Half a Century and Beyond, in: Moeckli/Keller/Heri (eds.), The Human Rights Covenants at 50: Their Past, Present, and Future, 2018, p. 24; *Nowak*, CCPR Commentary, Second revised Edition, 2005, Article 40, State Reports, para. 17; for the discussions during the drafting process concerning the "immediacy" of civil and political under the ICCPR, see *Schwelb*, Civil and Political Rights: The International Measures of Implementation, American Journal of International Law 62 (1968), 827, 838–842.

[11] *Alston*, The Committee on Economic, Social and Cultural Rights, in: Alston (ed.), The United Nations and Human Rights: A Critical Appraisal, First Edition, 1992, pp. 476–477.

[12] *Alston*, The Committee on Economic, Social and Cultural Rights, in: Alston (ed.), The United Nations and Human Rights: A Critical Appraisal, First Edition, 1992, p. 477.

[13] *Alston*, The Committee on Economic, Social and Cultural Rights, in: Alston (ed.), The United Nations and Human Rights: A Critical Appraisal, First Edition, 1992, p. 477.

[14] *Craven*, The International Covenant on Economic, Social, and Cultural Rights, 1995, p. 21; *Alston*, Out of the Abyss: The Challenges Confronting the New U. N. Committee on Economic, Social and Cultural Rights, Human Rights Quarterly 9 (1987), 332, 338.

[15] *Alston*, The Committee on Economic, Social and Cultural Rights, in: Alston (ed.), The United Nations and Human Rights: A Critical Appraisal, First Edition, 1992, pp. 478–479.

parties that monitoring should serve the providence of technical assistance rather than the critical examination of a State party's human rights record.[16]

2. Establishment of the CESCR Committee

In order to fulfil its monitoring obligation, ECOSOC established a "Sessional Working Group", tasked with the assistance of the Council in the review of reports submitted. The Sessional Working Group's members were appointed by the Council's president after consultations with regional groups.[17] As the necessary expertise of members in the field of socio-economic rights was seemingly missing, the Sessional Working Group became the Working Group of Governmental Experts in 1982, whose members were nominated by State parties and elected by the Council.[18]

Nevertheless, due to heavy criticism of the Economic and Social Council's overall performance in monitoring the Covenant's implementation,[19] it was already decided in 1980 to reopen deliberations on the entity charged with monitoring. For that purpose, the Economic and Social Council called upon the Secretary-General to engage in consultations with all State parties to the ICESCR and with members of the Council.[20]

The participating State parties were almost equally divided on the issue. One half preferred another independent committee, comparable to the Human Rights Committee, whereas the other half did not wish to tamper with the way things were.[21] Finally, also because of the Working Group's own proposal to transform itself into a committee composed of independent experts,[22] ECOSOC created the Committee on Economic, Social, and Cultural Rights by Resolution 1985/17.[23]

---

[16] *Craven*, The International Covenant on Economic, Social, and Cultural Rights, 1995, p. 49.

[17] *Craven*, The International Covenant on Economic, Social, and Cultural Rights, 1995, p. 39.

[18] *Harvey*, Monitoring Mechanisms for International Agreements Respecting Economic and Social Human Rights, Yale Journal of International Law 12 (1987), 396, 405.

[19] For a summary of the points of criticism, see *Craven*, The International Covenant on Economic, Social, and Cultural Rights, 1995, pp. 40–41; see also *Coomans*, The UN Committee on Economic, Social, and Cultural Rights, in: Oberleitner (ed.), International Human Rights Institutions, Tribunals, and Courts, 2018, p. 145, who notes that the discussions on State parties' human rights records were of a "politicized nature".

[20] *Alston*, The Committee on Economic, Social and Cultural Rights, in: Alston (ed.), The United Nations and Human Rights: A Critical Appraisal, First Edition, 1992, p. 484.

[21] *Alston*, The Committee on Economic, Social and Cultural Rights, in: Alston (ed.), The United Nations and Human Rights: A Critical Appraisal, First Edition, 1992, p. 484.

[22] *Alston*, Out of the Abyss: The Challenges Confronting the New U. N. Committee on Economic, Social and Cultural Rights, Human Rights Quarterly 9 (1987), 332, 345.

[23] See *Craven*, The International Covenant on Economic, Social, and Cultural Rights, 1995, p. 42, who critically remarks that there had been no "substantial re-evaluation" of the reporting system under the ICESCR prior to the establishment of the CESCR Committee.

The only State party voting against were the United States of America. It explained its voting behaviour with the expenses incurred by the Committee's establishment.[24] According to the US representative, it was not justified to install another treaty body "at a time of extreme budgetary austerity".[25]

The CESCR Committee thereby holds a unique position among the other human rights treaty bodies. It receives its mandate from ECOSOC and has only been indirectly established by the treaty it is supposed to monitor.[26] While the Committee's origin may play a role in the delineation of its mandate, it will be considered functionally equal to the other human rights treaty bodies in this thesis, as it performs the same functions and has developed similar working methods.[27] Although it has been stated that the Committee may more easily extend its powers due to the fact that it derives its existence from Resolution 1985/17,[28] it cannot interpret its mandate in such a manner that would contravene provisions in the ICESCR, or that would contradict its mandate as stipulated in its establishing resolution.

B. CERD Committee

Originally, the first draft of the CERD, as submitted by the Sub-Commission on the Prevention of Discrimination and Protection of Minorities, did not include the establishment of an independent monitoring body, but opted for the submission of reports to the Economic and Social Council.[29] Over the course of drafting, another article was introduced which provided for a "Good Offices and Conciliation Committee", which first became a "Committee" and then slowly took on

---

[24] *Alston*, The Committee on Economic, Social and Cultural Rights, in: Alston (ed.), The United Nations and Human Rights: A Critical Appraisal, First Edition, 1992, p. 487.

[25] US statement cited at *Alston*, The Committee on Economic, Social and Cultural Rights, in: Alston (ed.), The United Nations and Human Rights: A Critical Appraisal, First Edition, 1992, p. 487.

[26] *Riedel*, Committee on Economic, Social and Cultural Rights (CESCR), in: Peters (ed.), Max Planck Encyclopedia of Public International Law, Online version, November 2010, para. 2.

[27] *Odello/Seatzu*, The UN Committee on Economic, Social and Cultural Rights: The Law, Process and Practice, 2013, p. 110 and 112, noting that the CESCR Committee is decisively similar to all the other human rights treaty bodies; *Riedel*, International Covenant on Economic, Social and Cultural Rights (1966), in: Peters (ed.), Max Planck Encyclopedia of Public International Law, Online version, April 2011, para. 20, who observes that the CESCR Committee functions like all other treaty bodies; *Coomans*, The Role of the UN Committee on Economic, Social and Cultural Rights in Strengthening Implementation and Supervision of the International Covenant on Economic, Social and Cultural Rights, Verfassung und Recht in Übersee 35 (2002), 182, 184.

[28] *Beiter*, The Protection of the Right to Education by International Law, 2006, p. 348.

[29] *Thornberry*, The International Convention on the Elimination of All Forms of Racial Discrimination: A Commentary, 2016, The Convention and the Committee, p. 37.

the shape of what it is now the CERD Committee.[30] Although the CERD Committee was one of the first UN human rights treaty bodies to come into existence and the problem of overlapping mandates was hence less imminent than today, one delegate raised the issue of proliferation of monitoring bodies during the discussions.[31] His statement can be considered all the more astonishing, given that it precisely foreshadowed what was to become one of the system's major shortfalls.

According to the Dutch delegate, it was questionable "whether it was really desirable to establish several similar institutions each designed to ensure the implementation of a separate international instrument."[32] He further wondered if there was "not a danger, in view of the growing number of international instruments, that that might lead to organizational complications, and would not it be preferable to consider the possibility of creating only one single machinery for the implementation of all the international instruments in the field of human rights, which raised the same problems of application?"[33]

C. CEDAW Committee

In case of the CEDAW, the debates on the suitable supervisory organ mainly centred around the question whether to establish another committee by a provision modelled after article 28 ICCPR, or to assign the Commission on the Status of Women (CSW) with monitoring.[34] At a later stage of the drafting process, it was also proposed to establish an ad hoc group composed of fifteen members serving in their personal capacity and elected by the CSW from among State parties to the Convention. Alternatively, according to another suggestion, the ad hoc group could have been composed of twenty-three State parties and members of the Economic and Social Council.[35] The Third Committee eventually

---

[30] *Thornberry*, The International Convention on the Elimination of All Forms of Racial Discrimination: A Commentary, 2016, The Convention and the Committee, pp. 37–38.

[31] *Egan*, The United Nations Human Rights Treaty System: Law and Procedure, 2011, p. 459, footnote 40.

[32] UN General Assembly, Official Records, Third Committee, 1344th Meeting, UN Doc. A/C.3/SR.1344, 16.11.1965, para. 62.

[33] UN General Assembly, Official Records, Third Committee, 1344th Meeting, UN Doc. A/C.3/SR.1344, 16.11.1965, para. 62.

[34] See *Rehof*, Guide to the *Travaux Préparatoires* of the United Nations Convention on the Elimination of All Forms of Discrimination Against Women, 1993, pp. 191–193 with a summary of State parties' opinions on "the need for a supervisory committee".

[35] *Boerefijn*, Article 17, in: Freeman/Chinkin/Rudolf (eds.), The UN Convention on the Elimination of All Forms of Discrimination Against Women: A Commentary, 2012, p. 477; *Rehof*, Guide to the *Travaux Préparatoires* of the United Nations Convention on the Elimination of All Forms of Discrimination Against Women, 1993, pp. 193–196 with a summary of State opinions on this issue.

opted for the establishment of another independent expert body. Surprising about the debates, according to commentators, is the absence of any arguments relating to the overlapping substantive mandates of the CSW and the additional monitoring body that was established.[36]

D. Committee against Torture

Said duplication of mandates with a view to substantive treaty provisions became more relevant in the drafting of the Convention against Torture. In the event of having accepted the original "Swedish proposal", the monitoring would have been delegated to the Human Rights Committee and no additional supervisory body would have been established by virtue of the Convention.[37]

The main rationales for possibly assigning the Human Rights Committee with supervision were to "ensure consistency in the interpretation of the overlapping guarantees"[38] between article 7 ICCPR and the Convention against Torture as such, "to avoid unnecessary procedural duplication and complexity"[39] and to minimize the extra expenses inevitably accompanying the establishment of another supervisory body.[40]

However, partially due to arguments contained in a requested advice from the Legal Counsel of the UN, the idea of assigning the Human Rights Committee with the Convention's implementation was rejected. Concerns were raised over delegating oversight of the treaty to the Human Rights Committee, as this would entail "serious legal obstacles".[41] Not only was the "general concordance" between article 7 ICCPR and the Convention considered insufficient, but charging the Human Rights Committee with supervision also constituted a modification of the ICCPR. Consequently, the argument went, such a modification could only be realized via a formal treaty amendment in accordance with article 51 ICCPR.[42]

---

[36] *Burrows*, The 1979 Convention on the Elimination of All Forms of Discrimination Against Women, Netherlands International Law Review 32 (1985), 419, 454.

[37] See for the original Swedish proposal and other possibilities advanced by participating delegations *Monina*, Article 17, Committee against Torture, in: Nowak/Birk/Monina (eds.), The United Nations Convention Against Torture and its Optional Protocol: A Commentary, Second Edition, 2019, pp. 477–480.

[38] *Byrnes*, The Committee against Torture, in: Alston (ed.), The United Nations and Human Rights: A Critical Appraisal, First Edition, 1992, p. 510.

[39] *Byrnes*, The Committee against Torture, in: Alston (ed.), The United Nations and Human Rights: A Critical Appraisal, First Edition, 1992, p. 511.

[40] *Ingelse*, The UN Committee against Torture: An Assessment, 2001, p. 76; *Byrnes*, The Committee against Torture, in: Alston (ed.), The United Nations and Human Rights: A Critical Appraisal, First Edition, 1992, p. 511.

[41] *Burgers/Danelius*, The United Nations Convention against Torture, 1988, p. 76.

[42] *Burgers/Danelius*, The United Nations Convention against Torture, 1988, p. 76.

After lengthy discussions, the drafters adopted the final version of article 17 CAT, which foresaw the Committee in its current design.[43]

E. CRC Committee

Unsurprisingly, the drafting process of the Convention on the Rights of the Child also gave rise to the meanwhile well-known question of what kind of implementation organ to choose. Several proposals had been tabled, such as the submission of periodic reports to the Economic and Social Council,[44] or the creation of an independent "Committee of Experts".[45] Interestingly, the drafters were well aware of "the enormous strain affecting the reporting system of international human rights instruments",[46] but many voices still preferred the establishment of another independent expert body over assigning already existing bodies with the implementation of the Convention.[47] Others warned about the "proliferation of committees" and proposed to empower either the Human Rights Committee or the CESCR Committee with monitoring.[48] Eventually, the CRC brought about the creation of another treaty body, which might have been decisively motivated by the lack of a "legal entity which had the overall view of the rights of the child".[49]

---

[43] *Monina*, Article 17, Committee against Torture, in: Nowak/Birk/Monina (eds.), The United Nations Convention Against Torture and its Optional Protocol: A Commentary, Second Edition, 2019, pp. 482–484.

[44] Economic and Social Council, Report of the Working Group on a Draft Convention on the Rights of the Child, UN Doc. E/CN.4/1987/25, 09.03.1987, para. 139.

[45] Economic and Social Council, Report of the Working Group on a Draft Convention on the Rights of the Child, UN Doc. E/CN.4/1987/25, 09.03.1987, para. 140.

[46] Economic and Social Council, Report of the Working Group on a Draft Convention on the Rights of the Child, UN Doc. E/CN.4/1987/25, 09.03.1987, para. 144.

[47] See for instance Economic and Social Council, Report of the Working Group on a Draft Convention on the Rights of the Child, UN Doc. E/CN.4/1987/25, 09.03.1987, paras. 145, 148, 149, 151 and 153.

[48] Economic and Social Council, Report of the Working Group on a Draft Convention on the Rights of the Child, UN Doc. E/CN.4/1987/25, 09.03.1987, para. 146.

[49] Economic and Social Council, Report of the Working Group on a Draft Convention on the Rights of the Child, UN Doc. E/CN.4/1988/28, 06.04.1988, para. 82; *Verheyde/Goedertier*, A Commentary on the United Nations Convention on the Rights of the Child, Articles 43–45: The UN Committee on the Rights of the Child, 2006, para. 7.

F. CMW Committee

During the drafting of the CMW, the controversy on which monitoring body to choose arose between mostly Western States, which argued for the International Labour Organization as the appropriate monitoring organ, and States from the Global South, who preferred the establishment of a monitoring body comparable to those already existing under other human rights core treaties.[50] These differing opinions ultimately constituted the manifestation of a deeper cleavage which permeated whole drafting process on whether to proceed with standard-setting of the rights of migrant workers within the ILO framework, or to adopt an additional and separate human rights treaty under the auspices of the United Nations.[51]

To assign the ILO with whatsoever role in monitoring the Convention's implementation was justified by its wide experience and recognized competence.[52] At minimum, the ILO should be entitled to appoint a certain number of experts in the Committee.[53] Furthermore, vesting the ILO with oversight of implementation activities undertaken by State parties would have solved the problems of consistency in substantive terms.[54] Proponents of the establishment of another treaty body, however, argued that the substantive scope of the Convention would exceed the mandate of the ILO since the Convention would not exclusively address

---

[50] *Chetail*, The Committee on the Protection of the Rights of All Migrant Workers and Members of Their Families, in: Mégret/Alston (eds.), The United Nations and Human Rights: A Critical Appraisal, Second Edition, 2020, p. 604.

[51] On the historical background to the Convention, see *Bohning*, The ILO and the New UN Convention on Migrant Workers: The Past and Future, International Migration Review 25 (1991), 698, 699–702.

[52] UN General Assembly, Report of the Open-ended Working Group on the Elaboration of an International Convention on the Protection of the Rights of All Migrant Workers and Their Families, UN Doc. A/C.3/39/1, 14.06.1984, para. 47; *Chetail*, Committee on the Protection of the Rights of All Migrant Workers and Members of their Families (CMW), in: Ruiz Fabri (ed.), Max Planck Encyclopedia of International Procedural Law, Online version, August 2018, para. 2; the ILO and its periodic reporting system under article 22 are considered to be effective and enjoy "high reputation", see *Wagner*, Internationaler Schutz sozialer Rechte, Die Kontrolltätigkeit des Sachverständigenausschusses der IAO, 2002, p. 67, 280, 299; *Cabrera-Ormaza*, International Labour Organization, in: Oberleitner (ed.), International Human Rights Institutions, Tribunals, and Courts, 2018, p. 246, who reaches the conclusion that the monitoring machinery of the ILO is "robust"; *Leary*, The International Labour Organisation, in: Alston (ed.), The United Nations and Human Rights: A Critical Appraisal, First Edition, 1992, p. 618, who considers the supervision machinery as "highly developed" and "relatively effective".

[53] *Chetail*, The Committee on the Protection of the Rights of All Migrant Workers and Members of Their Families, in: Mégret/Alston (eds.), The United Nations and Human Rights: A Critical Appraisal, Second Edition, 2020, p. 604.

[54] *Chetail*, The Committee on the Protection of the Rights of All Migrant Workers and Members of Their Families, in: Mégret/Alston (eds.), The United Nations and Human Rights: A Critical Appraisal, Second Edition, 2020, p. 604.

labour-related issues, but would extend to a wider range of human rights and other than those contained in previously adopted ILO Conventions.[55]

Ultimately, a compromise between the competing positions could be reached in that the Convention provides for the establishment of another independent expert body, but with the International Labour Office being invited by the Committee to nominate representatives to attend the meetings of the Committee in a consultative capacity, according to article 74(5) CMW.[56]

G. CED Committee

An interesting aspect of the CED's drafting is that it coincided with the second treaty body reform initiative. It is therefore of particular interest to examine why the drafters ultimately opted for the creation of yet another treaty body, notwithstanding increasing evidence for the system's constant overloading, its precarious financial situation, and its by then well-known shortfalls.

In 2004, debates among drafters focused for the first time more thoroughly on the selection of the appropriate monitoring body to the Convention.[57] Many participants voiced concerns over the proliferation of treaty bodies and stressed the need to find "the least costly solution in financial and human terms."[58] Due to the topic's potential threat to the negotiation process as such, however, the Working Group's Chair proposed to discuss the Convention's substantive scope first, and then, secondly, to resume deliberations on suitable enforcement mechanisms.[59]

Essentially, three proposals were tabled as to the future design of the monitoring body, whose establishment was considered necessary in any event by al-

---

[55] UN General Assembly, Report of the Open-ended Working Group on the Elaboration of an International Convention on the Protection of the Rights of All Migrant Workers and Their Families, UN Doc. A/C.3/39/1, 14.06.1984, para. 50; *Chetail*, The Committee on the Protection of the Rights of All Migrant Workers and Members of Their Families, in: Mégret/Alston (eds.), The United Nations and Human Rights: A Critical Appraisal, Second Edition, 2020, p. 604.

[56] *Chetail*, The Committee on the Protection of the Rights of All Migrant Workers and Members of Their Families, in: Mégret/Alston (eds.), The United Nations and Human Rights: A Critical Appraisal, Second Edition, 2020, p. 604; *Bohning*, The ILO and the New UN Convention on Migrant Workers: The Past and Future, International Migration Review 25 (1991), 698, 704.

[57] Economic and Social Council, Report of the intersessional open-ended working group to elaborate a draft legally binding normative instrument for the protection of all persons from enforced disappearance, UN Doc. E/CN.4/2004/59, 23.02.2004, paras. 143–148.

[58] Economic and Social Council, Report of the intersessional open-ended working group to elaborate a draft legally binding normative instrument for the protection of all persons from enforced disappearance, UN Doc. E/CN.4/2004/59, 23.02.2004, para. 144.

[59] *de Frouville*, The Committee on Enforced Disappearances, in: Mégret/Alston (eds.), The United Nations and Human Rights: A Critical Appraisal, Second Edition, 2020, p. 584.

G. CED Committee

most all delegations.[60] The first idea was the drafting of an optional protocol to the ICCPR, and to assign the Human Rights Committee with monitoring.[61] Since enforced disappearances constituted violations of several provisions under the ICCPR, in particular articles 6, 7 and 9,[62] vesting the Human Rights Committee with oversight of the Convention could arguably serve to ensure coherence and "continuity in the practice of the Human Rights Committee in that area".[63] Others opted for the drafting of an optional protocol as well, but with the difference of establishing a subcommittee of the Human Rights Committee specifically tasked with monitoring.[64] Lastly, the creation of another independent monitoring body was proposed,[65] an idea which gained increasing support throughout the discussions for various reasons.[66]

First, it was observed that the Human Rights Committee itself was already overburdened and monitoring another human rights instrument would incur additional costs anyways.[67] Second, the parties to the ICCPR and the CED would not necessarily have to be congruent, which could potentially entail legal difficulties, such as impairments on possible ratifications, as the ratification of the two existing Optional Protocols to the ICCPR requires States to be a party to the

---

[60] Economic and Social Council, Report of the Intersessional Open-ended Working Group to elaborate a draft legally binding normative instrument for the protection of all persons from enforced disappearance, UN Doc. E/CN.4/2005/66, 10.03.2005, para. 147; "quite isolated" the Chinese delegation suggested to leave monitoring to the assembly of State parties, *de Frouville*, The Committee on Enforced Disappearances, in: Mégret/Alston (eds.), The United Nations and Human Rights: A Critical Appraisal, Second Edition, 2020, p. 584.

[61] Economic and Social Council, Report of the Intersessional Open-ended Working Group to elaborate a draft legally binding normative instrument for the protection of all persons from enforced disappearance, UN Doc. E/CN.4/2005/66, 10.03.2005, para. 151.

[62] Economic and Social Council, Report of the Intersessional Open-ended Working Group to elaborate a draft legally binding normative instrument for the protection of all persons from enforced disappearance, UN Doc. E/CN.4/2005/66, 10.03.2005, para. 151.

[63] Economic and Social Council, Report of the Intersessional Open-ended Working Group to elaborate a draft legally binding normative instrument for the protection of all persons from enforced disappearance, UN Doc. E/CN.4/2005/66, 10.03.2005, para. 152.

[64] Economic and Social Council, Report of the Intersessional Open-ended Working Group to elaborate a draft legally binding normative instrument for the protection of all persons from enforced disappearance, UN Doc. E/CN.4/2005/66, 10.03.2005, para. 155.

[65] Economic and Social Council, Report of the Intersessional Open-ended Working Group to elaborate a draft legally binding normative instrument for the protection of all persons from enforced disappearance, UN Doc. E/CN.4/2005/66, 10.03.2005, para. 157.

[66] *de Frouville*, The Committee on Enforced Disappearances, in: Mégret/Alston (eds.), The United Nations and Human Rights: A Critical Appraisal, Second Edition, 2020, p. 584.

[67] Economic and Social Council, Report of the Intersessional Open-ended Working Group to elaborate a draft legally binding normative instrument for the protection of all persons from enforced disappearance, UN Doc. E/CN.4/2005/66, 10.03.2005, para. 158 and para. 162 with a preliminary cost estimate.

Covenant itself.[68] Third, concerns over incoherent jurisprudence were rebutted by pointing out existing areas of overlapping scopes of protection, with particular reference to the prohibition of torture.[69]

Yet, the Working Group did not reach a conclusion until its last session, and only because of the introduction of "some compromise provisions" by the Chairperson of the Working Group.[70] He proposed to establish another independent treaty body, but which would be subject to reassessment six years after the entry into force of the Convention, in order to be able to react to the processing of the treaty body reform.[71] Eventually, and despite some delegations still opting to assign the Human Rights Committee with oversight for the very same reasons as advanced during previous sessions, the Working Group agreed on a draft that provided for the establishment of another independent Committee, with the inclusion of the compromise clause subjecting the newly established Committee to possible revision after six years.[72]

Pursuant to article 27 CED, said conference of State parties was convened on 19 December 2016 and reached by consensus the conclusion "that the Committee on Enforced Disappearances continue to monitor the International Convention for the Protection of All Persons from Enforced Disappearance in accordance with the functions defined in articles 28 to 36."[73] The outcome of the assessment comes as no big surprise, as reopening the discussions on the Convention's implementation and its supervisory body would inevitably have caused renegotiations and lengthy debates on possible treaty amendments.

---

[68] Economic and Social Council, Report of the Intersessional Open-ended Working Group to elaborate a draft legally binding normative instrument for the protection of all persons from enforced disappearance, UN Doc. E/CN.4/2005/66, 10.03.2005, para. 158.

[69] Economic and Social Council, Report of the Intersessional Open-ended Working Group to elaborate a draft legally binding normative instrument for the protection of all persons from enforced disappearance, UN Doc. E/CN.4/2005/66, 10.03.2005, para. 159.

[70] *de Frouville*, The Committee on Enforced Disappearances, in: Mégret/Alston (eds.), The United Nations and Human Rights: A Critical Appraisal, Second Edition, 2020, p. 585.

[71] Economic and Social Council, Report of the Intersessional Open-ended Working Group to elaborate a draft legally binding normative instrument for the protection of all persons from enforced disappearance, UN Doc. E/CN.4/2006/57, 02.02.2006, para. 70.

[72] Economic and Social Council, Report of the Intersessional Open-ended Working Group to elaborate a draft legally binding normative instrument for the protection of all persons from enforced disappearance, UN Doc. E/CN.4/2006/57, 02.02.2006, para. 83; *Citroni*, Committee on Enforced Disappearances (CED), in: Ruiz Fabri/Wolfrum (eds.), Max Planck Encyclopedia of International Procedural Law, Online version, December 2018, para. 9, who refers to article 27 CED as a "safety clause".

[73] Conference of the States parties, Report of the Conference of the States Parties to the International Convention for the Protection of All Persons from Enforced Disappearance on its first session, held on 19 December 2016, UN Doc. CED/CSP/2016/4, 18.01.2017, para. 11, decision 1.

H. CRPD Committee

The drafters of the Convention on the Rights of Persons with Disabilities were well aware of the ongoing treaty body strengthening process. They held that due account should be taken of lessons learned from previous drafting processes regarding the establishment of an additional treaty body.[74] Even though specific provisions on the Convention's implementation and the possible accompanying monitoring organ were not included in the draft up until the Ad Hoc Committee's report on its eighth session, this should not obscure the fact that the question on the establishment of another treaty body was prevalent throughout the whole drafting process from the very beginning.[75]

In keeping with the lines of argumentation and logics developed in the context of previous drafting processes, it is possible to array the proposals which emerged during the CRPD's negotiations accordingly. While some delegations proposed the establishment of an independent body in whatsoever ultimate and concrete design, other delegations pointed out that monitoring mechanisms already in existence under other international human rights treaties were sufficient.[76] It was also proposed to create the mandate of a United Nations Disability Ombudsperson assigned with the task of promoting implementation and receiving communications, accompanied by the obligation of State parties to report to other existing treaty bodies.[77] Acknowledging that the treaty body system and its monitoring machinery were facing several challenges, such as substantive overlap, onerous reporting obligations, growing backlogs of reports awaiting consideration, not to mention the chronic lack of resources, the drafters eventually considered it necessary to establish an effective supervisory organ which should be in no way inferior to already existing bodies.[78] It is interesting to note that they still

---

[74] *Guernsey*, Article 34, Committee on the Rights of Persons with Disabilities, in: Bantekas/Stein/Anastasiou (eds.), The UN Convention on the Rights of Persons with Disabilities: A Commentary, 2018, p. 1019.

[75] *Guernsey*, Article 34, Committee on the Rights of Persons with Disabilities, in: Bantekas/Stein/Anastasiou (eds.), The UN Convention on the Rights of Persons with Disabilities: A Commentary, 2018, p. 1016; see also *Stein/Lord*, Monitoring the Convention on the Rights of Persons with Disabilities: Innovations, Lost Opportunities, and Future Potential, Human Rights Quarterly 32 (2010), 689, 691–694 with references to further documents that contain "the relatively wide range of viewpoints by states".

[76] *Guernsey*, Article 34, Committee on the Rights of Persons with Disabilities, in: Bantekas/Stein/Anastasiou (eds.), The UN Convention on the Rights of Persons with Disabilities: A Commentary, 2018, p. 1018.

[77] *Guernsey*, Article 34, Committee on the Rights of Persons with Disabilities, in: Bantekas/Stein/Anastasiou (eds.), The UN Convention on the Rights of Persons with Disabilities: A Commentary, 2018, p. 1018.

[78] *Stein/Lord*, Monitoring the Convention on the Rights of Persons with Disabilities: Innovations, Lost Opportunities, and Future Potential, Human Rights Quarterly 32 (2010), 689, 692–693.

considered the adding of yet another supervisory organ to be appropriate. Pointing out the treaty body system's shortcomings would rather argue against the establishment of another treaty body, as one might have guessed.

During the Ad Hoc Committee's sixth session, it was stated that "that the Committee should not be held hostage by timeframes imposed by the reforms",[79] with this statement being reiterated during the Ad Hoc Committee's seventh session. Overall, delegates expressed that "the international community should not wait for the completion of the treaty body reform effort to establish an international monitoring mechanism"[80] and it was remarked, for instance, that the drafting of the Convention "should not get too caught up in the process of reform",[81] or that there was no alternative to the establishment of another treaty body.[82] Similar to the drafting of CED, it was also raised that "adjustments" could always be made to the Committee.[83] Also in keeping with the positions developed during previous drafting processes, some voices considered it more suitable to make use of already existing treaty bodies, as these possessed "immediate expertise on nondiscrimination" and would already cover many of the topics to be included in the new Convention.[84] As no consensus could be reached at the seventh session, it was decided to conduct "inter-sessional informal discussions" on the topic of enforcement and monitoring. The eighth session then

---

[79] General Assembly, Report of the Ad Hoc Committee on a Comprehensive and Integral International Convention on the Protection and Promotion of the Rights and Dignity of Persons with Disabilities on its sixth session, UN Doc. A/60/266, 17.08.2005, Annex II, para. 158; *Guernsey*, Article 34, Committee on the Rights of Persons with Disabilities, in: Bantekas/Stein/Anastasiou (eds.), The UN Convention on the Rights of Persons with Disabilities: A Commentary, 2018, p. 1020.

[80] *Guernsey*, Article 34, Committee on the Rights of Persons with Disabilities, in: Bantekas/Stein/Anastasiou (eds.), The UN Convention on the Rights of Persons with Disabilities: A Commentary, 2018, p. 1021.

[81] Mexican intervention, Daily summary of discussion at the seventh session 23 January 2006, https://www.un.org/esa/socdev/enable/rights/ahc7sum23jan.htm (last access: 21.08.2023).

[82] Intervention of Liechtenstein, Daily summary of discussion at the seventh session 23 January 2006, https://www.un.org/esa/socdev/enable/rights/ahc7sum23jan.htm (last access: 21.08.2023).

[83] Brazilian remark, Daily summary of discussion at the seventh session 03 February 2006, https://www.un.org/esa/socdev/enable/rights/ahc7sum03feb.htm (last access: 21.08.2023).

[84] Position advanced by the US, Daily summary of discussion at the seventh session 03 February 2006, https://www.un.org/esa/socdev/enable/rights/ahc7sum03feb.htm (last access: 21.08.2023); the US received partial support from China, the Russian Federation and Australia, *Guernsey*, Article 34, Committee on the Rights of Persons with Disabilities, in: Bantekas/Stein/Anastasiou (eds.), The UN Convention on the Rights of Persons with Disabilities: A Commentary, 2018, p. 1022.

first discussed the provisions on monitoring and implementation.[85] Ultimately, the consensus was reached that a Convention on the rights of persons with disabilities should only come into existence with another separate body monitoring its implementation.[86]

I. Interim conclusion and outlook

As has become apparent, the proliferation of human rights treaty bodies and the accompanying repercussions on the efficiency and effectivity of existing Committees were taken into consideration by many drafters, particularly by those who were tasked with the elaboration of the CED and CRPD. However, all of them ultimately opted for the establishment of yet another independent treaty body, various concerns over financial implications or the substantive overlap and duplication of mandates notwithstanding. As the formation of multilateral treaties, especially human rights treaties, is often dependent on a certain political climate and may also be the result of contingencies, it might be understandable that the growth of the treaty body system did not follow a consistent and stringent pattern.

Regarding developments as regards three further possible international human rights treaties, one on business and human rights, one on the rights of elderly people and one on the rights of peasants,[87] caution is warranted, at minimum.[88] At some point, the treaty body system will certainly reach a critical point. Particularly the drafting of the possible future treaty on business and human rights is revealing, and it is questionable whether "compromise solutions", such as in the case of CED, will present themselves as suitable means.

The current third revised draft for a possible treaty on business and human rights provides for an independent expert body, which is charged, inter alia, with

---

[85] See *Guernsey*, Article 34, Committee on the Rights of Persons with Disabilities, in: Bantekas/Stein/Anastasiou (eds.), The UN Convention on the Rights of Persons with Disabilities: A Commentary, 2018, p. 1022, who notes that no daily summaries of the eighth session are available.

[86] *Guernsey*, Article 34, Committee on the Rights of Persons with Disabilities, in: Bantekas/Stein/Anastasiou (eds.), The UN Convention on the Rights of Persons with Disabilities: A Commentary, 2018, p. 1022.

[87] With a view to the rights of peasants, the Human Rights Council adopted a respective declaration, Human Rights Council, Resolution 39/12, United Nations Declaration on the Rights of Peasants and Other People Working in Rural Areas, UN Doc. A/HRC/RES/39/12, 28.09.2018.

[88] *Gaer*, The Institutional Future of the Covenants, A World Court for Human Rights?, in: Moeckli/Keller/Heri (eds.) The Human Rights Covenants at 50: Their Past, Present, and Future, 2018, p. 345; literature has also proposed to consider the drafting of a UN treaty on violence against women, *McQuigg*, Is it time for a UN treaty on violence against women?, The International Journal of Human Rights 22 (2018), 305.

the examination of reports submitted by State parties.[89] As is apparent from the available documentation, it seems that history is repeating itself. For instance, delegates have been questioning whether it was necessary to establish another independent expert body, due to both the possible duplication of mandates with already existing treaty bodies, and financial repercussions on the overall system.[90] Comparable to the drafting of the CRPD, delegations proposed to adjourn deliberations on the enforcement machinery until the 2020 treaty body review process finds its end.[91] It was also suggested to make use of already existing mechanisms to monitor the implementation of the treaty, keeping in mind financial implications when establishing another treaty body.[92] Taking into consideration the very similar discussions and arguments of the drafting processes analysed above, it seems likely that the drafters of this treaty will eventually opt for the introduction of another treaty body, even though the CESCR Committee appears to be a competent and experienced treaty body in the subject matter.[93]

---

[89] Third revised draft 17.08.2021, article 15(1), available at: https://www.ohchr.org/Doc uments/HRBodies/HRCouncil/WGTransCorp/Session6/LBI3rdDRAFT.pdf (last access: 21.08.2023); for the discussion in legal literature on possible remedies and enforcement mechanisms under a new treaty on business and human rights, see *McConnell*, Assessing the Feasibility of a Business and Human Rights Treaty, International and Comparative Law Quarterly 66 (2017), 143, 173–179; pointing to the budgetary implications another reporting procedure would entail, *de Schutter*, Towards a New Treaty on Business and Human Rights, Business and Human Rights Journal 1 (2015), 41, 57–58; arguing for the establishment of another treaty body *Bernaz*, Conceptualizing Corporate Accountability in International Law: Models for a Business and Human Rights Treaty, Human Rights Review 22 (2021), 45, 61.

[90] UN General Assembly, Report on the sixth session of the open-ended intergovernmental working group on transnational corporations and other business enterprises with respect to human rights, UN Doc. A/HRC/46/73, 14.01.2021, para. 40.

[91] UN General Assembly, Report on the fifth session of the open-ended intergovernmental working group on transnational corporations and other business enterprises with respect to human rights, UN Doc. A/HRC/43/55, 09.01.2020, para. 92.

[92] UN General Assembly, Report on the fourth session of the open-ended intergovernmental working group on transnational corporations and other business enterprises with respect to human rights, UN Doc. A/HRC/40/48, 02.01.2019, para. 86.

[93] CESCR Committee, General comment No. 24 (2017) on State obligations under the International Covenant on Economic, Social and Cultural Rights in the context of business activities, UN Doc. E/C.12/GC/24, 10.08.2017.

Part II

Past attempts at reform

Not only the drafters of new UN human rights treaties were aware of the challenges and problems that accompanied the growth of the treaty body system. From the late 1980s onward, treaty bodies themselves and entities within the United Nations also contributed to the shaping of the system by proposing and initiating attempts at reform. In order to understand the current strengthening process, previous reform initiatives must be taken into consideration, as the most recent efforts are influenced by and based on past experiences.

A. "Alston proposals" between 1989 and 1997

Between 1989 and 1997, the independent expert *Philipp Alston*, who served as a member of the CESCR Committee between 1986 and 1998, at the request of the General Assembly which was made in reaction to the already prevalent shortcomings of the UN human rights treaty body system at that time,[1] delivered three reports on the treaty body system,[2] focusing both on its then *status quo* and on ways and means to enhance its efficacy and efficiency.

I. 1989 initial report

In his initial report, *Alston* first identified the treaty body system's shortfalls, such as non-submitted reports or reports of low quality, duplication of mandates concerning substantive provisions, a lack of financial and human resources and a corresponding lack of sufficient meeting time; many of which still threat to

---

[1] See UN General Assembly, Resolution 43/115, Reporting obligations of State parties to international instruments on human rights and effective functioning of bodies established pursuant to such instruments, UN Doc. A/RES/43/115, 08.12.1988.
[2] The initial report is contained in UN General Assembly, Effective Implementation of International Instruments on Human Rights, Including Reporting Obligations under International Instruments on Human Rights, UN Doc. A/44/668, 08.11.1989; the interim report can be found in UN General Assembly, Interim Report on Updated Study by Mr. Philipp Alston, UN Doc. A/CONF.157/PC/62/Add.11/Rev. 1, 22.04.1993; and the final report is contained in Economic and Social Council, Final report on enhancing the long-term effectiveness of the United Nations human rights treaty system, UN Doc. E/CN.4/1997/74, 27.03.1997.

undermine the system today.³ In order to overcome these pitfalls, *Alston* included various proposals in his initial report. He suggested, inter alia, to extend the reporting periodicities under the treaties, to consolidate reporting guidelines or to allow State parties to include cross-references in their reports. The latter could indicate that State parties had provided relevant information to another treaty body before, thereby avoiding the submission of reports with almost identical content over and over again.⁴

Next to these rather short-term orientated suggestions, another part of the initial report briefly took sight of long-term orientated solutions.⁵ According to *Alston*, long-term solutions were necessary to mitigate the negative effects stemming from the uncoordinated growth of the system and the constant adding of new treaty bodies. He concluded that they should therefore be considered "a natural and eventually unavoidable response".⁶ Due to the finding that the then existing treaty body system was "untidy in virtually every respect",⁷ he tabled his most far-reaching avenue for reform, which entailed to consolidate all single treaty bodies into one or two remaining bodies.⁸

II. 1993 interim report

In 1993, *Alston* delivered his interim report, which focused in an even more thorough and extensive manner on possible reform proposals related to the re-

---

³ *Egan*, The United Nations Human Rights Treaty System: Law and Procedure, 2011, pp. 453–454.

⁴ For all these suggestions, see UN General Assembly, Effective Implementation of International Instruments on Human Rights, Including Reporting Obligations under International Instruments on Human Rights, UN Doc. A/44/668, 08.11.1989, paras. 39–48; *Giegling*, Challenges and Chances of a Written State Report: Analysis and Improvement of a Monitoring Instrument on the Implementation of Human Rights, 2021, p. 76.

⁵ UN General Assembly, Effective Implementation of International Instruments on Human Rights, Including Reporting Obligations under International Instruments on Human Rights, UN Doc. A/44/668, 08.11.1989, paras. 175–197; *Gaer*, The Institutional Future of the Covenants, A World Court for Human Rights?, in: Moeckli/Keller/Heri (eds.) The Human Rights Covenants at 50: Their Past, Present, and Future, 2018, p. 339.

⁶ UN General Assembly, Effective Implementation of International Instruments on Human Rights, Including Reporting Obligations under International Instruments on Human Rights, UN Doc. A/44/668, 08.11.1989, para. 175.

⁷ UN General Assembly, Effective Implementation of International Instruments on Human Rights, Including Reporting Obligations under International Instruments on Human Rights, UN Doc. A/44/668, 08.11.1989, para. 179.

⁸ UN General Assembly, Effective Implementation of International Instruments on Human Rights, Including Reporting Obligations under International Instruments on Human Rights, UN Doc. A/44/668, 08.11.1989, para. 179; arguably less radical and drawing upon ideas that emerged in the drafting of the Convention against Torture, he further explored the possibility of assigning new functions to already existing treaty bodies by means of new treaties or by means of additional protocols, see in the same document paras. 184–192.

porting procedure.[9] Noteworthy about the interim report and of interest for the project at hand are above all those suggestions which bear a strong resemblance to current reform initiatives pursued by treaty bodies themselves. Worth mentioning are possible reviews in the absence of a report, though only as a measure of last resort according to *Alston*,[10] extending periodicities of reporting intervals,[11] and the introduction of a modified reporting procedure. The latter consisted of replacing comprehensive reports, covering all treaty guarantees, with "a limited range of specific issues identified in advance by the responsible committee."[12]

Obviously, all three proposals strongly correspond to current efforts initiated by treaty bodies, such as reviews in the absence of reports of non-compliant State parties on a regular basis, the possible introduction of a comprehensive reporting calendar and the application of the simplified reporting procedure, all of which are dealt with in detail further below.[13] In keeping with the initial report, the interim report additionally suggested long-term solutions, such as allowing State parties to prepare and submit a single consolidated report to all treaty bodies for consideration.[14]

III. 1997 final report

The final report was presented in 1997 and focused on the progress achieved since the submission of the initial report and contained the independent expert's final recommendations. The implementation of some recommendations and certain progress achieved by that time notwithstanding,[15] *Alston* reached the conclusion that the treaty body system in its condition at the time was "unsuitable" and required "significant reforms".[16] He concluded his final report with "medium-

---

[9] *Giegling*, Challenges and Chances of a Written State Report: Analysis and Improvement of a Monitoring Instrument on the Implementation of Human Rights, 2021, pp. 77–78 with a detailed account of the interim's report content.

[10] UN General Assembly, Interim Report on Updated Study by Mr. Philipp Alston, UN Doc. A/CONF.157/PC/62/Add.11/Rev. 1, 22.04.1993, para. 120.

[11] UN General Assembly, Interim Report on Updated Study by Mr. Philipp Alston, UN Doc. A/CONF.157/PC/62/Add.11/Rev. 1, 22.04.1993, paras. 136–138.

[12] UN General Assembly, Interim Report on Updated Study by Mr. Philipp Alston, UN Doc. A/CONF.157/PC/62/Add.11/Rev. 1, 22.04.1993, para. 174.

[13] See *infra* Part IV B., C., and D.

[14] UN General Assembly, Interim Report on Updated Study by Mr. Philipp Alston, UN Doc. A/CONF.157/PC/62/Add.11/Rev. 1, 22.04.1993, paras. 164–173.

[15] *Giegling*, Challenges and Chances of a Written State Report: Analysis and Improvement of a Monitoring Instrument on the Implementation of Human Rights, 2021, p. 78; *Egan*, The United Nations Human Rights Treaty System: Law and Procedure, 2011, p. 454.

[16] Economic and Social Council, Final report on enhancing the long-term effectiveness of the United Nations human rights treaty system, UN Doc. E/CN.4/1997/74, 27.03.1997, para. 10; *Egan*, The United Nations Human Rights Treaty System: Law and Procedure, 2011, p. 454.

term and long-term reform issues", encompassing four options for possible subsequent actions to ensure the functioning of the treaty body system.[17]

The first and second proposals, either to simply ignore the current challenges[18] or, alternatively, to introduce reforms within the limited financial possibilities at the time (which would have involved, inter alia, reducing the length of constructive dialogues or translating fewer documents into other official United Nations working languages),[19] were put aside fast. The third possibility, "the provision of greatly enhanced budgetary resources to support all aspects of the procedures with a view to more or less maintaining the status quo",[20] was considered unrealistic and hence discarded as well.[21]

The fourth option proposed, being "a more complex one",[22] consisted of various elements. These could have been implemented comprehensively as a package or only partially. *Alton's* "far-reaching" reforms included the idea of drafting a consolidated report, the elimination of comprehensive reports which would be replaced by State- and situation-specific reporting guidelines. Even more far-reaching, he suggested the consolidation and merger of all treaty bodies. Even though these proposals found their way into the final report, it has been observed that *Alston's* suggestions "ultimately tended toward the practical".[23]

---

[17] The proposals took equally into consideration the expected increase of ratifications and the accompanying increase of reports submitted, the addition of a seventh treaty body with the CMW Committee soon to come into existence and the additional expenses and costs coming along with the expected developments, Economic and Social Council, Final report on enhancing the long-term effectiveness of the United Nations human rights treaty system, UN Doc. E/CN.4/1997/74, 27.03.1997, paras. 80–101; *Egan*, The United Nations Human Rights Treaty System: Law and Procedure, 2011, p. 454.

[18] Economic and Social Council, Final report on enhancing the long-term effectiveness of the United Nations human rights treaty system, UN Doc. E/CN.4/1997/74, 27.03.1997, para. 85.

[19] Economic and Social Council, Final report on enhancing the long-term effectiveness of the United Nations human rights treaty system, UN Doc. E/CN.4/1997/74, 27.03.1997, paras. 86–87.

[20] Economic and Social Council, Final report on enhancing the long-term effectiveness of the United Nations human rights treaty system, UN Doc. E/CN.4/1997/74, 27.03.1997, para. 88.

[21] *Egan*, The United Nations Human Rights Treaty System: Law and Procedure, 2011, pp. 454–455.

[22] Economic and Social Council, Final report on enhancing the long-term effectiveness of the United Nations human rights treaty system, UN Doc. E/CN.4/1997/74, 27.03.1997, para. 89.

[23] *Gaer*, The Institutional Future of the Covenants, A World Court for Human Rights?, in: Moeckli/Keller/Heri (eds.) The Human Rights Covenants at 50: Their Past, Present, and Future, 2018, p. 340; see also *Egan*, The United Nations Human Rights Treaty System: Law and Procedure, 2011, p. 455, who rightly points out that many of the proposals formed the basis for "concrete improvements" to the reporting procedure; reaching a similar conclusion, *Devereux/Anderson*, Reporting under International Human Rights Treaties: Perspectives from Timor Leste's Experience of the Reformed Process, Human Rights Law Review 8 (2008), 69, 76.

In academic circles, however, the idea of establishing a single treaty body, or at least some kind of unification or consolidation seemed to have gained the most support at the time of *Alston's* reports.[24] They were joined by UN Secretary General *Kofi Annan*, who set the incentives for the second reform initiative.[25]

B. Consolidated single State report proposal

The second reform initiative began with the Secretary-General's report "Strengthening of the United Nations: an agenda for further change"[26], which also gave "new momentum" to the treaty body strengthening process.[27] Within this comprehensive report on possible reform initiatives concerning the United Nations, one section was specifically devoted to the "growing complexity of the human rights machinery and the corresponding burden of reporting obligations".[28]

Two proposals were brought forward by *Annan* to overcome said obstacles. Treaty bodies should first aim for "a more coordinated approach to their activities and standardize their varied reporting requirements", and second, State parties should be allowed to draft a single consolidated report which would comprehensively cover all of their reporting obligations under each of the human rights core treaties.[29] The report by the Secretary-General simultaneously requested the High Commissioner for Human Rights to consult with treaty bodies on new streamlined reporting procedures, which led to a meeting in 2003 (Malbun I) between treaty bodies and other stakeholders.[30]

A wide array of stakeholders attended the Malbun I meeting, most of which, however, "clearly rejected" the idea of allowing State parties to submit a single

---

[24] See *Gaer*, The Institutional Future of the Covenants, A World Court for Human Rights?, in: Moeckli/Keller/Heri (eds.) The Human Rights Covenants at 50: Their Past, Present, and Future, 2018, p. 340 with further references; *Egan*, The United Nations Human Rights Treaty System: Law and Procedure, 2011, p. 456.

[25] *Gaer*, The Institutional Future of the Covenants, A World Court for Human Rights?, in: Moeckli/Keller/Heri (eds.) The Human Rights Covenants at 50: Their Past, Present, and Future, 2018, p. 341.

[26] UN General Assembly, Strengthening of the United Nations: an agenda for further change, Report of the Secretary-General, UN Doc. A/57/387 09.09.2002.

[27] *Schöpp-Schilling*, Treaty Body Reform: The Case of the Committee on the Elimination of Discrimination Against Women, Human Rights Law Review 7 (2007), 201, 205.

[28] UN General Assembly, Strengthening of the United Nations: an agenda for further change, Report of the Secretary-General, UN Doc. A/57/387 09.09.2002, para. 52.

[29] UN General Assembly, Strengthening of the United Nations: an agenda for further change, Report of the Secretary-General, UN Doc. A/57/387 09.09.2002, para. 54.

[30] See for the outcome of the Malbun I meeting, Report of a Brainstorming Meeting on Reform of the Human Rights Treaty Body System (Malbun, Liechtenstein, 4–7 May 2003), UN Doc. HRI/ICM/2003/4-HRI/MC/2003/4, 10.06.2003; see for a list of the participants Annex II of the same document.

consolidated report.[31] The human rights treaty bodies, in particular, proved to be one of the most vigorous critics.[32] Arguments against a single consolidated report were, for instance, the marginalization of specific issues or vulnerable groups of persons, which would then run the risk of receiving even less attention in the event of allowing a single consolidated report, the unmanageable length of such a report and the fact that its introduction would not solve the problem of non-reporting.[33]

Instead of the submission of a single report, participants preferred the development of more harmonized reporting guidelines. In 1991, the human rights treaty bodies had already taken the decision to harmonize their reporting requirements to a certain extent with the adoption of consolidated guidelines on a core document. According to these, State parties should ideally submit a basic set of relevant data to the work of all treaty bodies.[34] The approach was now to be refined with the introduction of an expanded core document, jointly submitted with a treaty-specific document. The latter would be shorter and more focused. Relevant information to all treaty bodies, encompassing information and data related to the implementation of congruent or overlapping substantive treaty provisions, could have already been included in said expanded core document.[35]

In the aftermath of the Malbun meeting, both the fifteenth Meeting of Chairpersons and the second Inter-Committee Meeting[36] discussed the consultation's outcome and requested the Secretariat to prepare a draft for harmonized reporting guidelines, including an expanded core document.[37] In light of the discussions and recommendations adopted within both meetings, the decisions taken "certainly foreshadowed" the position of the treaty bodies in the future reform process. "Radical" approaches did not seem to appear at all during the discussions among treaty body members, and the emphasis clearly was on streamlining procedures and harmonization in procedural matters.[38]

---

[31] *Schöpp-Schilling*, Treaty Body Reform: The Case of the Committee on the Elimination of Discrimination Against Women, Human Rights Law Review 7 (2007), 201, 206.

[32] *Johnstone*, Cynical Savings or Reasonable Reform? Reflections on a Single Unified UN Human Rights Treaty Body, Human Rights Law Review 7 (2007), 173, 182, who refers to treaty bodies' responses as "frosty".

[33] Report of a Brainstorming Meeting on Reform of the Human Rights Treaty Body System (Malbun, Liechtenstein, 4–7 May 2003), UN Doc. HRI/ICM/2003/4–HRI/MC/2003/4, 10.06.2003, para. 25.

[34] *Schöpp-Schilling*, Treaty Body Reform: The Case of the Committee on the Elimination of Discrimination Against Women, Human Rights Law Review 7 (2007), 201, 206.

[35] *Schöpp-Schilling*, Treaty Body Reform: The Case of the Committee on the Elimination of Discrimination Against Women, Human Rights Law Review 7 (2007), 201, 207.

[36] For the Inter-Committee Meeting see *infra* Part V A.I.3.

[37] Report of the Chairpersons of the human rights treaty bodies on their fifteenth meeting, UN Doc. A/58/350, 05.09.2003, Annex I, Report of the second inter-committee meeting of human rights treaty bodies, para. 40.

[38] *Egan*, The United Nations Human Rights Treaty System: Law and Procedure, 2011, p. 458; reaching a similar conclusion with regard to the position of treaty bodies, *O'Flaher-*

Following the request made by the treaty bodies, the Secretariat presented its first draft on possible harmonized reporting guidelines in 2004[39] and delivered a second amended version in 2006.[40] Particularly the discussion on an expanded core document and its chart of congruent substantive treaty provisions was to emerge as one of the most problematic aspects.[41] While the chart of congruence seemed to have received support from many State parties, treaty bodies were less open to the introduction of an extended core document that would cover a wide range of substantive provisions.[42] Considerable criticism was levelled by the CEDAW Committee, which argued, inter alia, that the chart was "grounded in a rather schematic interpretation of the norms and provisions of the seven human rights treaties" and that the "specific nature of women's discrimination on the basis of sex and gender as compared to discrimination of men and women on other grounds seems to be neglected."[43] In the end, the Common Core Document only addressed the principle of non-discrimination and equality and effective remedies as congruent treaty guarantees common among the various UN human rights treaties. This leaves the question whether anything was gained thereby.[44] The only mention of these two congruent guarantees is explained by "real disagreement" over which provisions to include in a possible Common Core Document.[45]

A renewed call for treaty body reform stemmed from the Secretary General's report to the General Assembly in 2005,[46] in which he not only recommended to

---

ty/O'Brien, Reform of UN Human Rights Treaty Monitoring Bodies: A Critique of the Concept Paper on the High Commissioner's Proposal for a Unified Standing Treaty Body, Human Rights Law Review 7 (2007), 141, 156–157.

[39] Guidelines on an expanded core document and treaty-specific targeted reports and harmonized guidelines on reporting under the international human rights treaties, Report of the secretariat, UN Doc. HRI/MC/2004/3, 09.06.2004.

[40] Harmonized guidelines on reporting under the international human rights treaties, including guidelines on a common core document and treaty-specific targeted documents, Report of the secretariat, UN Doc. HRI/MC/2005/3, 01.06.2005.

[41] *Schöpp-Schilling*, Treaty Body Reform: The Case of the Committee on the Elimination of Discrimination Against Women, Human Rights Law Review 7 (2007), 201, 207.

[42] *Johnstone*, Streamlining the Constructive Dialogue: Efficiency from States' Perspectives, in: Bassiouni/Schabas (eds.), New Challenges for the UN Human Rights Machinery, 2011, p. 70.

[43] Comments and suggestions concerning the draft harmonized guidelines on reporting under the international human rights treaties, Preliminary views of the Committee on the Elimination of Discrimination against Women, UN Doc. HRI/MC/2005/6/Add.1, 14.06.2005, para. 26; see for the Committee's other arguments/concerns *Schöpp-Schilling*, Treaty Body Reform: The Case of the Committee on the Elimination of Discrimination Against Women, Human Rights Law Review 7 (2007), 201, 212–213.

[44] *Kälin*, Examination of state reports, in: Keller/Ulfstein (eds.), UN Human Rights Treaty Bodies: Law and Legitimacy, 2012, p. 47.

[45] *Devereux/Anderson*, Reporting under International Human Rights Treaties: Perspectives from Timor Leste's Experience of the Reformed Process, Human Rights Law Review 8 (2008), 69, 80.

[46] UN General Assembly, In larger freedom: towards development, security and human rights for all, Report of the Secretary-General, UN Doc. A/59/2005, 21.03.2005.

treaty bodies to finalize the drafting of the Harmonized Reporting Guidelines,[47] but also called upon the High Commissioner for Human Rights to deliver a subsequent plan of action.[48] In reaction to the Secretary-General's call, the then High Commissioner for Human Rights first delivered her plan of action,[49] in which she stressed both the need to finalise the drafting of the Harmonized Guidelines, and the possible creation of a unified standing treaty body in the long-term.[50] The latter was further elaborated in her "concept paper",[51] which also marks the starting point of the third treaty body reform initiative.

C. Unified standing treaty body proposal

In 2006, the then High Commissioner for Human Rights, *Louise Arbour*, submitted her concept paper on the creation of a unified standing treaty body which, if created, would obviously have had greater unification effects than previous attempts at reform. After having summarized the "by now familiar shortcomings"[52] and challenges to the treaty body system,[53] *Arbour* introduced in more detail her proposal to create a unified standing treaty body.

The underlying premises were that "the lack of visibility, authority and access which affects the current system will persist", unless the treaty body system would work and was perceived as a unified and single entity. She also stated that the system in its then *modus operandi* would soon reach its limits.[54] Therefore, *Arbour*

---

[47] UN General Assembly, In larger freedom: towards development, security and human rights for all, Report of the Secretary-General, UN Doc. A/59/2005, 21.03.2005, para. 147; *Egan*, The United Nations Human Rights Treaty System: Law and Procedure, 2011, p. 458, who considers the call for a unified system to be to some extent ambiguous, as it could imply either the harmonization of working methods or the establishment of a unified treaty body.

[48] *Giegling*, Challenges and Chances of a Written State Report: Analysis and Improvement of a Monitoring Instrument on the Implementation of Human Rights, 2021, p. 82.

[49] UN General Assembly, In larger freedom: towards development, security and human rights for all, Report of the Secretary-General, UN Doc. A/59/2005/Add.3, 26.05.2005, Annex, Plan of action submitted by the United Nations High Commissioner for Human Rights.

[50] *Egan*, The United Nations Human Rights Treaty System: Law and Procedure, 2011, p. 459.

[51] Concept Paper on the High Commissioner's Proposal for a Unified Standing Treaty Body, UN Doc. HRI/MC/2006/2, 22.03.2006.

[52] *Gaer*, The Institutional Future of the Covenants, A World Court for Human Rights?, in: Moeckli/Keller/Heri (eds.) The Human Rights Covenants at 50: Their Past, Present, and Future, 2018, p. 343; see also *Egan*, The United Nations Human Rights Treaty System: Law and Procedure, 2011, p. 460, who writes of "the myriad of challenges".

[53] Concept Paper on the High Commissioner's Proposal for a Unified Standing Treaty Body, UN Doc. HRI/MC/2006/2, 22.03.2006, paras. 15–26.

[54] Concept Paper on the High Commissioner's Proposal for a Unified Standing Treaty Body, UN Doc. HRI/MC/2006/2, 22.03.2006, para. 27, the High Commissioner therefore required more "fundamental structural change" in the long-term perspective.

suggested the creation of a single treaty body, composed of permanent and full-time professionals. According to her, the establishment of a permanent treaty body would lead to consistent and authoritative jurisprudence,[55] together with numerous other advantages.[56]

With respect to the unified treaty body's specific design, several ideas were presented. The standing treaty body could either work as a single organ in plenary or could alternatively be divided into chambers. These could be mandated with oversight of all treaties, or they could be established along treaty lines. In this case, each single chamber would be tasked with monitoring one specific treaty.[57] Other ideas entailed establishing chambers with thematic focus, chambers along regional lines or along functional lines, thus creating chambers for single tasks, such as individual complaints or inquiry procedures.[58]

In general, it appears that the High Commissioner's concept paper placed a stronger focus on coherence and mainstreaming human rights standards throughout the system than previous initiatives. Examples of this are the unified treaty body issuing General Comments and thereby following "a holistic approach to overlapping obligations in the treaties",[59] and the aforementioned "consistent approach to the interpretation of provisions in the treaties which are similar or overlap substantively."[60] At the same time, *Arbour* clarified that any reform must not come at the cost of the treaties' particularities and that focus on issue- or group-specific topics had to be kept.[61]

---

[55] Concept Paper on the High Commissioner's Proposal for a Unified Standing Treaty Body, UN Doc. HRI/MC/2006/2, 22.03.2006, para. 27.

[56] Concept Paper on the High Commissioner's Proposal for a Unified Standing Treaty Body, UN Doc. HRI/MC/2006/2, 22.03.2006, paras. 28–36, most notable are the standing body's permanent availability and thus increased visibility and more flexibility with regard to the timing and venue of its sessions; see for a short but detailed account *Egan*, The United Nations Human Rights Treaty System: Law and Procedure, 2011, pp. 460–461; see also *O'Flaherty/O'Brien*, Reform of UN Human Rights Treaty Monitoring Bodies: A Critique of the Concept Paper on the High Commissioner's Proposal for a Unified Standing Treaty Body, Human Rights Law Review 7 (2007), 141, 159–160, with another summary of the arguments by *Arbour* to justify the creation of a single standing treaty body.

[57] *Johnstone*, Cynical Savings or Reasonable Reform? Reflections on a Single Unified UN Human Rights Treaty Body, Human Rights Law Review 7 (2007), 173, 193, arguing that such a division could possibly respect the interests of vulnerable groups.

[58] Concept Paper on the High Commissioner's Proposal for a Unified Standing Treaty Body, UN Doc. HRI/MC/2006/2, 22.03.2006, paras. 40–45; *Egan*, The United Nations Human Rights Treaty System: Law and Procedure, 2011, pp. 461–462.

[59] Concept Paper on the High Commissioner's Proposal for a Unified Standing Treaty Body, UN Doc. HRI/MC/2006/2, 22.03.2006, para. 51.

[60] Concept Paper on the High Commissioner's Proposal for a Unified Standing Treaty Body, UN Doc. HRI/MC/2006/2, 22.03.2006, para. 30.

[61] Concept Paper on the High Commissioner's Proposal for a Unified Standing Treaty Body, UN Doc. HRI/MC/2006/2, 22.03.2006, para. 59.

In legal literature, however, the missing perspective on how to keep the various treaties' specificities had been criticized as one of several major weaknesses,[62] in addition to the omission of concrete steps on how to address the "complex legal challenges"[63] posed by the unification process, let alone the voices which considered the proposed unification to be "fundamentally flawless and irresponsible".[64]

To discuss her proposal in more depth with a range of various stakeholders, a second brainstorming meeting (Malbun II)[65] was convened, but nearly every aspect of her plan of action was criticized by at least one group of stakeholders.[66] Especially the treaty bodies considered the establishment of a unified standing treaty body an ill-fitting means in reaction to the challenges faced. Analogous to criticism levelled against the single consolidated report, the CEDAW Committee raised concerns about the "serious risk to undermine the differentiation and specificity of human rights as enshrined in the seven major international human rights treaties" in the event of unification.[67] Other Committees fell in line and pointed to the legal and political problems, neither easily solvable in the short or

---

[62] *O'Flaherty/O'Brien*, Reform of UN Human Rights Treaty Monitoring Bodies: A Critique of the Concept Paper on the High Commissioner's Proposal for a Unified Standing Treaty Body, Human Rights Law Review 7 (2007), 141, 166; *Kjærum*, The UN Reform Process in an Implementation Perspective, in: Lagoutte/Sano/Scharff Smith (eds.), Human Rights in Turmoil: Facing Threats, Consolidating Achievements, 2007, p. 17, who points out to the possible loss of expertise of treaty body members, which "is a tremendous resource".

[63] *Nowak*, Comments on the UN High Commissioner's Proposals Aimed at Strengthening the UN Human Rights Treaty Body System, Netherlands Quarterly of Human Rights 31 (2013), 3, 5; *O'Flaherty/O'Brien*, Reform of UN Human Rights Treaty Monitoring Bodies: A Critique of the Concept Paper on the High Commissioner's Proposal for a Unified Standing Treaty Body, Human Rights Law Review 7 (2007), 141, 172; *Johnstone*, Cynical Savings or Reasonable Reform? Reflections on a Single Unified UN Human Rights Treaty Body, Human Rights Law Review 7 (2007), 173, 198–199, pointing out to the need for amending the existing treaties, to arguably slow-paced ratification patterns in case of the adoption of either new treaties or additional protocols, both of which could eventually hamper the coming into existence of the unified treaty body.

[64] *Hampson*, An Overview of the Reform of the UN Human Rights Machinery, Human Rights Law Review 7 (2007), 7, 12.

[65] UN General Assembly, Annex to the letter dated 14 September 2006 from the Permanent Representative of Liechtenstein to the United Nations addressed to the Secretary-General Chairperson's summary of a brainstorming meeting on reform of the human rights treaty body system ("Malbun II"), UN Doc. A/61/351, 18.09.2006.

[66] *Gaer*, The Institutional Future of the Covenants, A World Court for Human Rights?, in: Moeckli/Keller/Heri (eds.) The Human Rights Covenants at 50: Their Past, Present, and Future, 2018, p. 344.

[67] Statement by the CEDAW Committee cited at *Schöpp-Schilling*, Treaty Body Reform: The Case of the Committee on the Elimination of Discrimination Against Women, Human Rights Law Review 7 (2007), 201, 210.

medium term,[68] or stressed the need for closer cooperation among treaty bodies instead of aiming for unification in the broader sense.[69]

D. Origins of the current treaty body strengthening process

I. Pillay's *multistakeholder approach*

The last of four reform initiatives began in 2009, when the then High Commissioner for Human Rights *Navanethem Pillay* initiated a further process of reflection on how to streamline and strengthen the treaty body system. Contrary to the three previous attempts at reform, *Pillay* made it clear from the beginning that it would be crucial to invite all stakeholders to take part in the discussions. Sustainable and lasting change could only be reached by respecting the voices of all actors involved.[70] In between November 2009 and November 2011, around twenty meetings with all stakeholders were convened and formed the background to *Pillay's* report submitted in June 2012.[71] Context-wise, these consultations and the resulting report may well be considered the very beginning of the current debate on the treaty body system.

1. 2012 strengthening report

As the outcome of the comprehensive consultation process, six major proposals and recommendations were included in the report, each entailing a range of additional minor proposals to facilitate the realization of the respective overar-

---

[68] Position of the Human Rights Committee contained in Report of the Working Group on the Harmonization of Working Methods of Treaty Bodies, UN Doc. HRI/MC/2007/2, 09.01.2007, para. 7.

[69] Report of the Working Group on the Harmonization of Working Methods of Treaty Bodies, UN Doc. HRI/MC/2007/2, 09.01.2007, para. 6, and reflecting the general position among treaty bodies para. 11; see also *Egan*, Reform of the UN Human Rights Treaty Body System, in: Mégret/Alston (eds.), The United Nations and Human Rights: A Critical Appraisal, Second Edition, 2020, p. 651, who summarizes the positions taken by the treaty bodies as inclined towards "a more incremental approach"; *Connors*, The Human Rights Treaty Body System, in: Chesterman/Malone/Villalpando (eds.), The Handbook of United Nations Treaties, 2019, p. 393.

[70] *Pillay*, Strengthening the United Nations human rights treaty body system, p. 9; *Egan*, Strengthening the United Nations Human Rights Treaty Body System, Human Rights Law Review 13 (2013), 209, 213–214.

[71] For a detailed account of the consultations with the various stakeholders involved, see *Giegling*, Challenges and Chances of a Written State Report: Analysis and Improvement of a Monitoring Instrument on the Implementation of Human Rights, 2021, pp. 87–93; for a detailed description and analysis of three important meetings within the consultation process, see *Egan*, The United Nations Human Rights Treaty System: Law and Procedure, 2011, pp. 466–473, including the Dublin, Marrakesh and Poznan meeting.

ching suggestion.[72] The first idea presented by *Pillay* was the introduction of a comprehensive reporting calendar with fixed deadlines for the submission of reports, covering each human rights core treaty and the implementation of which would lead to "predictability and stability in reporting".[73]

Second, the strengthening report discussed the advantages of adopting a simplified reporting procedure as the default reporting procedure among all treaty bodies.[74] At the time of publication, three treaty bodies had gained first experiences in implementing the newly developed procedure, which differs from the standard reporting procedure in that the Committees send a questionnaire to the contracting parties and the responses to this already count as a State report. Under the simplified reporting procedure, State parties hence do not submit a comprehensive report anymore. *Pillay* considered its application an opportunity to "significantly streamline and enhance the reporting procedure".[75]

Third, the report explicitly addressed strengthening activities with respect to the individual communications procedures, inquiries and country visits.[76] The section's probably most far-reaching suggestion, presumably also in the overall context of the report as such, was the possible establishment of a joint treaty body working group on communications.[77] The proposal had been submitted by the CERD Committee during the preceding consultation process, which had also raised the very same idea when discussing the former High Commissioner's plan of action.[78] Nevertheless, similar to criticism against *Arbour's* proposal of unification "virtually no attempt to elucidate the substantive merits of this proposal"[79] can be detected in her strengthening report.[80]

---

[72] For a detailed consideration and evaluation of the potential of *Pillay's* report, see *Egan*, Strengthening the United Nations Human Rights Treaty Body System, Human Rights Law Review 13 (2013), 209.

[73] *Pillay*, Strengthening the United Nations human rights treaty body system, pp. 37–46.

[74] *Pillay*, Strengthening the United Nations human rights treaty body system, pp. 47–50; for the simplified reporting procedure, see *infra* Part IV B.

[75] *Pillay*, Strengthening the United Nations human rights treaty body system, p. 48, in conjunction with the proposal to adopt the simplified reporting, various other suggestions were introduced, such as the submission of a common core document and regular updates thereof, strict adherence to page limitations, an aligned methodology for the constructive dialogues, reducing the translation of summary records, focused concluding observations, further institutionalization of engagement with other United Nations entities and aligned models of interaction among treaty bodies, national human rights institutions and civil society organizations and addressing reprisals.

[76] *Pillay*, Strengthening the United Nations human rights treaty body system, pp. 68–73.

[77] *Pillay*, Strengthening the United Nations human rights treaty body system, p. 68.

[78] Report of the Working Group on the Harmonization of Working Methods of Treaty Bodies, UN Doc. HRI/MC/2007/2, 09.01.2007, para. 5.

[79] *Egan*, Strengthening the United Nations Human Rights Treaty Body System, Human Rights Law Review 13 (2013), 209, 230.

[80] See in this matter also *Riedel*, Global Human Rights Protection at the Crossroads: Strengthening or Reforming the System, in: Breuer et al. (eds.), Der Staat im Recht, Fest-

D. Origins of the current treaty body strengthening process

Fourth, the independence and expertise of treaty body members were considered in more detail.[81] In fact, these required characteristics of treaty body members have at times not been met, and the quality of Committee members also forms part of current debates within the treaty body strengthening process.[82] Moreover, *Pillay* added several minor proposals revolving around the modalities of the nomination and election process of treaty body members.[83]

Fifth, headed "strengthening capacity of States to implement the treaties", the follow-up procedures undertaken by treaty bodies were addressed. *Pillay* suggested developing a set of common guidelines in this domain and additionally called upon treaty bodies to simplify and improve their follow-up procedures by simultaneously striving for greater coherence and harmonization in that matter.[84] Further proposals relating to the capacity of State parties in implementing the treaties included the introduction of standing national reporting and coordination mechanisms.[85] With regard to more coherence in treaty interpretation, *Pillay* called for an aligned consultation process for the elaboration of General Comments.[86]

The last section of the proposals dealt with the visibility and accessibility of treaty bodies. Observing that treaty bodies "[remained] relatively unknown at the national level", *Pillay* suggested various practical ideas for enhancing the system's visibility, such as webcasting and videoconferencing, improving the web-appearance of treaty bodies or making targeted use of social media to better disseminate treaty body output.[87]

In summary, *Pillay's* report contained many feasible ideas and was the outcome of intensive and profound discussions, meetings, and deliberation between all stakeholders relevant to the treaty body system.[88] Further noteworthy is the

---

schrift für Eckart Klein zum 70. Geburtstag, 2013, p. 1303, who proposes that the existing communication procedures could be reformed by introducing a "communication committee". He equally admits that its creation and functioning would require more resources.

[81] *Pillay*, Strengthening the United Nations human rights treaty body system, pp. 74–79.

[82] In literature, cf. *Carraro*, Electing the experts: Expertise and independence in the UN human rights treaty bodies, European Journal of International Relations 25 (2019), 826.

[83] *Pillay*, Strengthening the United Nations human rights treaty body system, pp. 75–79.

[84] *Pillay*, Strengthening the United Nations human rights treaty body system, pp. 80–82.

[85] *Pillay*, Strengthening the United Nations human rights treaty body system, pp. 85–87.

[86] *Pillay*, Strengthening the United Nations human rights treaty body system, p. 82.

[87] *Pillay*, Strengthening the United Nations human rights treaty body system, p. 88.

[88] *Egan*, Strengthening the United Nations Human Rights Treaty Body System, Human Rights Law Review 13 (2013), 209, 242–243; *Broecker/O'Flaherty*, The Outcome of the General Assembly's Treaty Body Strengthening Process, p. 27, considering the report suitable in terms of "enabling each treaty body to fulfil its valuable and unique role in contributing to the promotion and protection of human rights"; see, however, *Nowak*, Comments on the UN High Commissioner's Proposals Aimed at Strengthening the UN Human Rights Treaty Body System, Netherlands Quarterly of Human Rights 31 (2013), 3, 6–7, who questions whether the proposals might have a significant effect on the system, as they are "fairly modest", and he further argues that the report does not include meaningful proposals with a view to procedures other than State reporting.

fact that most of the proposals were realizable without treaty amendments, which was also one of the underlying key criteria.[89]

2. Interference by the intergovernmental process

However, while the consultation process and the drafting of the report were still underway, a group of a considerable number of State parties (often referred to as the "cross-regional group" or "like-minded group") intervened in *Pillay's* initiative. Led by Russia, the like-minded group asserted that "the process of strengthening or reforming the treaty bodies should primarily be subject to an interstate discussion", thereby challenging *Pillay's* multi-stakeholder approach and claiming a leading role for State parties.[90]

Furthermore, State parties used this occasion to level further criticism against treaty bodies, accused them of operating beyond their mandates and acting *ultra vires*. Russia asserted for instance that the backlog of reports awaiting consideration was a consequence of "additional responsibilities not envisaged"[91] under the various treaties. China criticized treaty bodies for the introduction of follow-up activities, which were allegedly "burden[ing] the States parties with extraneous obligations"[92] and which were hence considered beyond the legal mandate of treaty bodies. The intergovernmental process must therefore be primarily understood as efforts to undermine the independence of treaty bodies[93] and to "[rein] in"[94] their activities.[95]

In February 2012, Russia then submitted a draft resolution to the General Assembly which called for the establishment of an intergovernmental process and justified the submission by arguing that it was "unacceptable to ignore the views of Member States".[96] In the course of the emerging discussion within the General Assembly, the United States eventually called for a vote and the pro-

---

[89] *Egan*, Strengthening the United Nations Human Rights Treaty Body System, Human Rights Law Review 13 (2013), 209, 214.

[90] *Broecker/O'Flaherty*, The Outcome of the General Assembly's Treaty Body Strengthening Process, p. 14.

[91] Russian statement cited by *Broecker/O'Flaherty*, The Outcome of the General Assembly's Treaty Body Strengthening Process, p. 14.

[92] Chinese submission cited by *Broecker/O'Flaherty*, The Outcome of the General Assembly's Treaty Body Strengthening Process, p. 14.

[93] *Gaer*, The Institutional Future of the Covenants, A World Court for Human Rights?, in: Moeckli/Keller/Heri (eds.) The Human Rights Covenants at 50: Their Past, Present, and Future, 2018, p. 345.

[94] *Egan*, Reform of the UN Human Rights Treaty Body System, in: Mégret/Alston (eds.), The United Nations and Human Rights: A Critical Appraisal, Second Edition, 2020, p. 657.

[95] *O'Flaherty*, The High Commissioner and the Treaty Bodies, in: Gaer/Broecker (eds.), The United Nations High Commissioner for Human Rights: Conscience for the World, 2014, p. 115, who notes that the "ploy was entirely political".

[96] *Broecker/O'Flaherty*, The Outcome of the General Assembly's Treaty Body Strengthening Process, p. 14.

D. Origins of the current treaty body strengthening process   45

posed resolution was adopted by 85 votes in favour, 66 members abstaining and no State party was voting against. The voting result, particularly with regard to the 66 members abstaining, mirrors concern as to the timing and the objective of the proposal.[97] The Swiss delegate, for example, articulated strong criticism of the intervention by the like-minded group. He argued that the parties to the human rights treaties could not "support an initiative that would compromise the independence of its bodies and their experts."[98] In the same vein, other abstaining State parties stressed the importance of respecting the treaty bodies' legal competencies and that the intergovernmental process should not result in undermining the work and autonomy of the Committees in any event.[99]

The draft was adopted by Resolution 66/254 and set in motion a second and hence parallel reform process, which only allowed very limited participation of stakeholders other than State parties.[100] *Pillay's* report, originally intended to serve as the basis for what should become a final and concluding General Assembly Resolution, was thus reduced to a mere political interim report.[101]

The following intergovernmental process and its accompanying negotiations are best characterized by the struggle between the two main competing positions on the treaty body system's future. On one side, the smaller like-minded group insisted on exerting more formal control over treaty bodies, held that treaty interpretation by the adoption of General Comments and the establishment of follow-up activities were beyond the Committees' legal mandates, and wished to adopt a code of conduct for treaty body members.[102] On the other side, the

---

[97] *Egan*, Reform of the UN Human Rights Treaty Body System, in: Mégret/Alston (eds.), The United Nations and Human Rights: A Critical Appraisal, Second Edition, 2020, p. 657; *Broecker/O'Flaherty*, The Outcome of the General Assembly's Treaty Body Strengthening Process, p. 14.

[98] UN General Assembly, Official Records, Sixty-sixth session, 98th plenary meeting, 23.02.2012, 10 a.m. New York, UN Doc. A/66/PV. 98, p. 4.

[99] UN General Assembly, Official Records, Sixty-sixth session, 98th plenary meeting, 23.02.2012, 10 a.m. New York, UN Doc. A/66/PV. 98, p. 6 and 10.

[100] *Volger*, Die Stärkung der Vertragsorgane im UN-Menschenrechtssystem, MenschenRechtsMagazin 20 (2015), 107, 112; *Egan*, Strengthening the United Nations Human Rights Treaty Body System, Human Rights Law Review 13 (2013), 209, 241; *Broecker/O'Flaherty*, The Outcome of the General Assembly's Treaty Body Strengthening Process, p. 14; see, however, *O'Flaherty*, The Strengthening Process of the Human Rights Treaty Bodies, American Society of International Law, Proceedings of the Annual Meeting 108 (2014), 285, 286, who writes that "the widening of the space for the voices of non-state actors constitutes a notable precedent in terms of how human rights are discussed at the level of the General Assembly"; Report of the Chairs of the human rights treaty bodies on their twenty-fourth meeting, UN Doc. A/67/222, 02.08.2012, para. 6, with the Chairs noting that they "had a central role to play regarding the future of the treaty body system and as such, their presence during the deliberations of the open-ended intergovernmental process, […], was essential."

[101] *Volger*, Die Stärkung der Vertragsorgane im UN-Menschenrechtssystem, MenschenRechtsMagazin 20 (2015), 107, 112.

[102] *Reiners*, Transnational Lawmaking Coalitions for Human Rights, 2021, p. 127, who observes that State parties tried to put "additional pressure" on the Committees by means of

WEOG Group (consisting of Western European and other State parties) sought to preserve the independence and autonomy of treaty bodies and wished to protect "their essential function, the independent assessment of state compliance with treaty obligations."[103]

3. Resolution 68/268

The intergovernmental process ultimately culminated in the adoption of General Assembly Resolution 68/268,[104] which was considered a compromise between the conflicting positions.[105] In comparison to the High Commissioner's report, the adopted resolution contained fewer reform proposals and was less far-reaching in terms of potential for actual change. The most significant reform proposals stemming from the intergovernmental process related to budgetary issues, financing and the allocation of additional resources to treaty bodies.[106] One promising proposal advanced by *Pillay*, the establishment of a comprehensive reporting calendar,[107] positively appraised in legal literature and by NGOs,[108] did not find its way into Resolution 68/268. Its omission is most likely attributable to several arguments forwarded by State parties during the discussions.[109] Inter alia, the

---

"year-long reform pro- cesses with possibly limited effect"; *Egan*, Reform of the UN Human Rights Treaty Body System, in: Mégret/Alston (eds.), The United Nations and Human Rights: A Critical Appraisal, Second Edition, 2020, p. 658; *Volger*, Die Stärkung der Vertragsorgane im UN-Menschenrechtssystem, MenschenRechtsMagazin 20 (2015), 107, 114; *Broecker/O'Flaherty*, The Outcome of the General Assembly's Treaty Body Strengthening Process, p. 16.

[103] *Broecker/O'Flaherty*, The Outcome of the General Assembly's Treaty Body Strengthening Process, p. 15.

[104] UN General Assembly, Resolution 68/268, Strengthening and enhancing the effective functioning of the human rights treaty body system, UN Doc. A/RES/68/268, 09.04.2014.

[105] *Egan*, Reform of the UN Human Rights Treaty Body System, in: Mégret/Alston (eds.), The United Nations and Human Rights: A Critical Appraisal, Second Edition, 2020, p. 658.

[106] *Broecker/O'Flaherty*, The Outcome of the General Assembly's Treaty Body Strengthening Process, p. 27; inter alia, Resolution 68/268 contained an allocation formula for further meeting time, UN General Assembly, Resolution 68/268, Strengthening and enhancing the effective functioning of the human rights treaty body system, UN Doc. A/RES/68/268, 09.04.2014, paras. 26–27.

[107] See *Pillay*, Strengthening the United Nations human rights treaty body system, pp. 37–46.

[108] *Egan*, Strengthening the United Nations Human Rights Treaty Body System, Human Rights Law Review 13 (2013), 209, 215–217, who nevertheless identifies two factors mitigating potential support. First of all, the fixed and inflexible nature of such a calendar and second, the capacity of treaty bodies and the extra workload accompanied by the establishment of a comprehensive reporting calendar; interestingly, the proposal was broadly endorsed by NGOs, see footnote 37 at page 215.

[109] *Shany/Cleveland*, Treaty Body Reform 2020: Has the time come for adopting a Global Review Calendar?, p. 3, https://www.geneva-academy.ch/joomlatools-files/docman-files/Draft%20List%20of%20Submissions%20–%20Academic%20Platform%202020%20Review%20without%20Propositions%20.pdf (last access: 21.08.2023).

D. Origins of the current treaty body strengthening process   47

feasibility of such an endeavour was contested and legal concerns with respect to the varying reporting periodicities under the different treaties were raised.[110] However, paragraph 34 of Resolution 68/268 still alludes to the concept of a comprehensive reporting calendar. According to said paragraph, the human rights treaty bodies and the OHCHR are invited "to continue to work to increase coordination and predictability in the reporting process, […], with the aim of achieving a clear and regularized schedule for reporting by State parties."[111]

Other topics addressed in the High Commissioner's strengthening report, but unfortunately omitted in Resolution 68/268, are questions related to follow-up and implementation, and features concerning the individual complaints procedure, with the latter not even remotely addressed.[112] Similarly striking is the absence of any mention of cross-cutting issues or the duplication of mandates and the corresponding substantive overlap among treaty bodies. Whereas previous reform initiatives at least highlighted the importance of coherent jurisprudence, Resolution 68/268 remains completely silent in this regard. However, notwithstanding the resolution's evaluation as "modest"[113] and in spite of one commentator's judgement of it being "mundane, technical, timid and cosmetic",[114] the several shortcomings portrayed above must not obscure the positive features contained in Resolution 68/268.

Contrary to initial fears, the intergovernmental process did not result in undermining the autonomy of the treaty bodies, as it "ended up technically respecting the competencies of treaty bodies".[115] The reaffirmation of treaty bodies being independent actors,[116] not subject to direct control by State parties, must be

---

[110] *Broecker/O'Flaherty*, The Outcome of the General Assembly's Treaty Body Strengthening Process, p. 21.

[111] UN General Assembly, Resolution 68/268, Strengthening and enhancing the effective functioning of the human rights treaty body system, UN Doc. A/RES/68/268, 09.04.2014, para. 34; *Broecker/O'Flaherty*, The Outcome of the General Assembly's Treaty Body Strengthening Process, p. 21, who detect "potential for future reform" with regard to the topic at hand.

[112] See also *Egan*, Reform of the UN Human Rights Treaty Body System, in: Mégret/Alston (eds.), The United Nations and Human Rights: A Critical Appraisal, Second Edition, 2020, p. 659, who remarks that it is "conspicuous" that the quality and independence of treaty body members have been curtailed by the intergovernmental process and that the proposal to establish and strengthen national reporting and coordination mechanisms has regrettably been minimized to a voluntary option for State parties.

[113] *Egan*, Reform of the UN Human Rights Treaty Body System, in: Mégret/Alston (eds.), The United Nations and Human Rights: A Critical Appraisal, Second Edition, 2020, p. 659; *Broecker/O'Flaherty*, The Outcome of the General Assembly's Treaty Body Strengthening Process, p. 27.

[114] *Subedi*, The Effectiveness of the UN Human Rights System: Reform and the Judicalisation of Human Rights, 2017, p. 97.

[115] *Gaer*, The Institutional Future of the Covenants, A World Court for Human Rights?, in: Moeckli/Keller/Heri (eds.) The Human Rights Covenants at 50: Their Past, Present, and Future, 2018, p. 345.

[116] UN General Assembly, Resolution 68/268, Strengthening and enhancing the effective

evaluated even more positively given that their autonomy had been under attack several times during the intergovernmental process.[117]

What is more, the code of conduct, as proposed by the cross-regional group, was not introduced.[118] While all these aspects could equally be considered damage limitation, other purely positive features are the explicit acknowledgement of treaty bodies being entitled to issue General Comments,[119] the envisioned enhanced mandate of the Meeting of Chairpersons,[120] and the fact that the treaty bodies were referred to as a system for the first time in an international document.[121]

II. Review process set in motion via Resolution 68/268

Besides the recommendations addressed to both State parties and treaty bodies, paragraphs 40 and 41 of Resolution 68/268 set in motion a review process for further treaty body reform. According to its paragraph 40, the Secretary-General was requested to submit biennial comprehensive reports on the status of the human rights treaty body system and the progress achieved by the human rights treaty bodies in realizing greater efficiency and effectiveness in their work.[122]

---

functioning of the human rights treaty body system, UN Doc. A/RES/68/268, 09.04.2014, para. 35.

[117] *O'Flaherty*, The Strengthening Process of the Human Rights Treaty Bodies, American Society of International Law, Proceedings of the Annual Meeting 108 (2014), 285, 287.

[118] *Egan*, Reform of the UN Human Rights Treaty Body System, in: Mégret/Alston (eds.), The United Nations and Human Rights: A Critical Appraisal, Second Edition, 2020, p. 658.

[119] UN General Assembly, Resolution 68/268, Strengthening and enhancing the effective functioning of the human rights treaty body system, UN Doc. A/RES/68/268, 09.04.2014, para. 14.

[120] UN General Assembly, Resolution 68/268, Strengthening and enhancing the effective functioning of the human rights treaty body system, UN Doc. A/RES/68/268, 09.04.2014, para. 38; *Egan*, Reform of the UN Human Rights Treaty Body System, in: Mégret/Alston (eds.), The United Nations and Human Rights: A Critical Appraisal, Second Edition, 2020, pp. 658–659; *Broecker/O'Flaherty*, The Outcome of the General Assembly's Treaty Body Strengthening Process, p. 17.

[121] Cf. *Flinterman*, The United Nations Human Rights Committee, Some Reflections of a Former Member, Netherlands Quarterly of Human Rights 33 (2015), 4, 5, who argues that the overall impact of Resolution 68/268 "can certainly be regarded as very positive"; *O'Flaherty*, The Strengthening Process of the Human Rights Treaty Bodies, American Society of International Law, Proceedings of the Annual Meeting 108 (2014), 285, 287.

[122] UN General Assembly, Resolution 68/268, Strengthening and enhancing the effective functioning of the human rights treaty body system, UN Doc. A/RES/68/268, 09.04.2014, paras. 40 and 41; *Giegling*, Challenges and Chances of a Written State Report: Analysis and Improvement of a Monitoring Instrument on the Implementation of Human Rights, 2021, p. 97; the first biennial report covered the period between the adoption of Resolution 68/268 and June 2016, UN General Assembly, Status of the human rights treaty body system, Report of the Secretary-General, UN Doc. A/71/118, 18.07.2016; the second biennial report covered the period between January 2016 and December 2017, UN General Assembly, Status of the human rights treaty body system, Report of the Secretary-General, UN Doc. A/73/309,

D. Origins of the current treaty body strengthening process

A perusal of all reports submitted, however, paints a rather negative picture, as no real improvement concerning the State reporting procedure and compliance with reporting obligations seems to have been achieved since the adoption of General Assembly Resolution 68/268.[123] Besides, although input by stakeholders was sought, it mostly consisted of replies to questionnaires sent to State parties in the preparation of the second and third biennial report.[124]

In 2020, pursuant to paragraph 41 of Resolution 68/268, the therein envisaged treaty body review process was initiated with the appointment of two co-facilitators.[125] Their mandate was "to undertake informal consultations with Member States, in both New York and Geneva, with contributions, as appropriate, from the Office of the United Nations High Commissioner for Human Rights (OHCHR), from the treaty bodies, and from other relevant stakeholders."[126]

III. Co-facilitators' review process 2020

The phrasing of the co-facilitators' mandate clearly indicates that the treaty body strengthening process was still considered mainly State party-centred. Yet, during the three-month consultations, a considerably wide array of stakeholders provided input, encompassing State parties, treaty bodies, national human rights institutions, NGOs and others.[127] Against the backdrop of the three preceding biennial reports submitted by the Secretary-General and the debate's previous major focus, the report's focus on issues which had been prevalent in Resolution 68/268 does not come as a big surprise.[128]

06.08.2018; the third and final report considered activities up until October 2019, UN General Assembly, Status of the human rights treaty body system, Report of the Secretary-General, UN Doc. A/74/643, 10.01.2020.

[123] *Giegling*, Challenges and Chances of a Written State Report: Analysis and Improvement of a Monitoring Instrument on the Implementation of Human Rights, 2021, p. 102; reaching the same conclusion in 2018, *Egan*, Reform of the UN Human Rights Treaty Body System, in: Mégret/Alston (eds.), The United Nations and Human Rights: A Critical Appraisal, Second Edition, 2020, p. 661.

[124] For an arguably non-comprehensive overview of the responses submitted, see *Giegling*, Challenges and Chances of a Written State Report: Analysis and Improvement of a Monitoring Instrument on the Implementation of Human Rights, 2021, pp. 99–102.

[125] https://www.ohchr.org/Documents/HRBodies/TB/Letter_PGA_8April20_co_facilitatorsmeeting.pdf, (last access: 21.08.2023).

[126] UN General Assembly, Report on the process of the consideration of the state of the United Nations human rights treaty body system, UN Doc. A/75/601, 17.11.2020, para. 3.

[127] For a complete list, see https://www.ohchr.org/en/calls-for-input/co-facilitation-process-treaty-body-review-2020, (last access: 21.08.2023).

[128] The report addresses the use of information and communication technologies, alignment of working methods and rules of procedure, the accessibility of the system by different stakeholders, capacity-building and technical assistance and, how could it be otherwise, budgetary issues.

Noteworthy, however, is the re-emergence of the introduction of a fixed master calendar comprising the reporting obligations under each UN human rights core treaty.[129] Although there seems to have been differing opinions during the consultations, first on its establishment,[130] and second on its specific design,[131] the co-facilitators eventually recommended to the OHCHR and the treaty bodies to prepare a draft comprehensive calendar with an accompanying estimate of concomitant expenses required for its realization.[132] Resuming discussions on a possible master calendar might have been owed to the input provided for by treaty bodies themselves. Their joint position paper submitted to the co-facilitators entails the establishment of an eight-year review cycle among Covenant Committees and predictable reviews with fixed schedules among Conventions Committees,[133] and might have served as a blueprint.

Also notable is the report's express reference to streamlined and enhanced follow-up activities to concluding observations,[134] as well as the mention of recommendations concerning the individual complaints procedure, although confined to the establishment of a digital case management system for individual communications and urgent actions.[135] Reform proposals of such kind had been almost completely absent during both, the intergovernmental process and the biennial review process.

Terminating the report with recommendations for the way forward, the co-facilitators considered a follow-up process as the "most appropriate way to achieve the goal of strengthening and enhancing the effective functioning of the human rights treaty body system."[136] As the most recent step, the General As-

---

[129] UN General Assembly, Report on the process of the consideration of the state of the United Nations human rights treaty body system, UN Doc. A/75/601, 17.11.2020, paras. 50–56.

[130] UN General Assembly, Report on the process of the consideration of the state of the United Nations human rights treaty body system, UN Doc. A/75/601, 17.11.2020, para. 55.

[131] UN General Assembly, Report on the process of the consideration of the state of the United Nations human rights treaty body system, UN Doc. A/75/601, 17.11.2020, paras. 53–54.

[132] UN General Assembly, Report on the process of the consideration of the state of the United Nations human rights treaty body system, UN Doc. A/75/601, 17.11.2020, para. 56.

[133] For the treaty bodies' position conveyed to the co-facilitators, see Report of the Chairs of the human rights treaty bodies on their thirty-second annual meeting, UN Doc. A/75/346, 14.09.2020, para. 46.

[134] UN General Assembly, Report on the process of the consideration of the state of the United Nations human rights treaty body system, UN Doc. A/75/601, 17.11.2020, paras. 45–47.

[135] UN General Assembly, Report on the process of the consideration of the state of the United Nations human rights treaty body system, UN Doc. A/75/601, 17.11.2020, para. 22.

[136] UN General Assembly, Report on the process of the consideration of the state of the United Nations human rights treaty body system, UN Doc. A/75/601, 17.11.2020, para. 83.

sembly adopted Resolution 75/174 in reaction to the co-facilitators' report, by which it only continued the review process provided for in Resolution 68/268.[137]

Next to the invitation to the Chairs of the treaty bodies to participate in the General Assembly's discussions on the topic of treaty body strengthening at its two upcoming general sessions,[138] Resolution 75/174 merely reiterates the request addressed to the Secretary-General under paragraph 40 of Resolution 68/268 to submit another report on the status of the human rights treaty body system at the General Assembly's seventy-seventh session.[139] With the resolution being the anticipated culmination of a six-year long review process, including input by various stakeholders, and the quite intensive three months consultation process in 2020, the result is disappointing and underwhelming, both in terms of specific recommendations and the lack of tangible future steps.

E. Human rights treaty bodies as the main drivers for attempts at reform

Not as many different proposals as one might have guessed emerged during the above portrayed treaty body reform initiatives. Oscillating between the two extremes of the merger of all Committees on one side, and providing only minimum additional resources to keep the status quo of the system on the other side, numerous, though equally manageable, proposals were presented. These proposals either focused on the system's institutional design or, on a smaller scale, on treaty bodies' working methods and the assistance provided to State parties.

As has become apparent, initiatives with the aim of transforming the system more radically, e.g., merging various treaty bodies, have progressively vanished from the agenda. The last proposal of this kind was the establishment of a joint working group on communications.[140] In the same vein, other less radical proposals calling for unification were rejected and eventually discarded, such as the proposed submission of a single consolidated State report. Specifically, treaty bodies were little or not at all inclined to accept a consolidated reporting system and became one of the idea's most vocal critics. Prevalent objections were based on the fear of the marginalization of already vulnerable groups of people, or the unmanageable length of consolidated State reports, imposing burdens on both State parties and treaty bodies rather than to alleviate them.

---

[137] UN General Assembly, Resolution 75/174, Human rights treaty body system, UN Doc. A/RES/75/174, 16.12.2020.

[138] UN General Assembly, Resolution 75/174, Human rights treaty body system, UN Doc. A/RES/75/174, 16.12.2020, para. 3.

[139] UN General Assembly, Resolution 75/174, Human rights treaty body system, UN Doc. A/RES/75/174, 16.12.2020, para. 9.

[140] *Pillay*, Strengthening the United Nations human rights treaty body system, p. 68.

There is thus a clear trend within the strengthening efforts towards a focus on working methods and procedural harmonization. Noteworthy is the fact that many suggestions of the current debate find their origin in the independent expert's reports dating from the late 1980s and early 1990s respectively. What is more, together with shifting the focus towards procedural harmonization, the avoidance of treaty amendments has emerged as one of the essential criteria for any reform proposal.

While this excludes more prompt and immediate changes, it grants at the same time some leeway to the treaty bodies in the context of the strengthening process. Many activities below the formal level of treaty amendments arguably rest in their hands, at least as long as these are governed by their legal mandates. Provided that the lack of political will for further reaching reform initiatives has been, and probably will continue to prevail, and given that the political climate towards treaty bodies has even been hostile sometimes,[141] it is all the more essential for treaty bodies to take actions on their own and to take a firm stand against any attempts at undermining their independence.

The obvious need to focus on the Committees becomes even more evident when one considers that not only have previous reform initiatives ultimately failed due to a lack of political will, but also that the establishment of further treaty bodies has often only proved to be a compromise solution during the respective drafting process. Therefore, it will be explored in the following which potential and, most importantly, which legal possibilities are intrinsic to treaty bodies in the context of the ongoing strengthening process. Treaty bodies themselves might prove to be one of the most promising stakeholders in bringing sustainable and lasting change to the system.[142]

On that note, it is also submitted here that there are certainly limits for what the treaty bodies can achieve on their own. Due to the facts that the Committees are composed of independent experts, serving in their personal capacity, that they do not meet on a permanent basis and that they are clearly dependent on the allocation of very scarce financial resources, one might wonder whether it is not

---

[141] Cf. *Ramcharan*, Modernizing the UN Human Rights System, 2019, p. 171, who notes that the "politicization of the human rights treaty bodies should not be permitted to continue".

[142] *Egan*, Strengthening the United Nations Human Rights Treaty Body System, Human Rights Law Review 13 (2013), 209, 243, who sees the main responsibility for changing the system lying with the State parties and treaty bodies; *Broecker/O'Flaherty*, The Outcome of the General Assembly's Treaty Body Strengthening Process, p. 27, who also emphasize the role of the treaty bodies in the reform process with special attention to the aligning and coordination process of working methods; see also *O'Flaherty*, The Strengthening Process of the Human Rights Treaty Bodies, American Society of International Law, Proceedings of the Annual Meeting 108 (2014), 285, 288, who states that the treaty bodies "hold in their own hands so much of the work of strengthening and improving the system"; *Morijn*, Reforming United Nations Human Rights Treaty Monitoring Reform, Netherlands International Law Review 58 (2011), 295, 333.

E. Human rights treaty bodies as the main drivers for attempts at reform

indeed a viable and alternative idea to establish a permanent World Court of Human Rights.[143] Alternatively, one could endeavour the possibility of merging treaty bodies without treaty amendments, such as the proposed merger of the Human Rights Committee and the CESCR Committee.[144] However, despite the (sometimes justified) critique of the performance of the UN human rights treaty bodies, it must not be overlooked that they remain the main bodies responsible for monitoring compliance with human rights standards at the global level. As long as no serious initiative pushes the idea of a permanent international human rights body further, which would then also have to be clearly supported by the will of the contracting parties, it is all the more sensible and important to deal with the existing structures and render them as resilient as possible.

---

[143] The probably most vehement proponent of a World Court of Human Rights is *Manfred Nowak*, see, by way of example, one of his various contributions to this topic, *Nowak*, A World Court of Human Rights, in: Oberleitner (ed.), International Human Rights Institutions, Tribunals, and Courts, 2018, 271; also supportive of the idea to establish a Court, *Kirkpatrick*, A Modest Proposal: A Global Court of Human Rights, Journal of Human Rights 13 (2014), 230, 239–244; see, however, *Alston*, Against a World Court for Human Rights, Ethics & International Affairs 28 (2014), 197, who emerges as one of the most vocal critics of the idea to establish a World Court; see further *Tyagi*, The UN Human Rights Committee, Practice and Procedure, 2011, p. 760, arguing for a "step-by-step approach" as regards possible institutional reforms.

[144] Such a merger has been proposed by *Scheinin*, who argued that the review of State reports under the ICESCR could be allocated to the Human Rights Committee by means of an ECOSOC-Resolution, thus without any treaty amendment, *Scheinin*, The Proposed Optional Protocol to the Covenant on Economic, Social and Cultural Rights: A Blueprint for UN Human Rights Treaty Body Reform Without Amending the Existing Treaties, Human Rights Law Review 6 (2006), 131.

Part III

Delineating the mandate of treaty bodies

After having demonstrated above that the Committees themselves are the most promising stakeholder in bringing about real and lasting change to the treaty body system, the next step is to determine the scope of their powers and possible sources of legitimacy for their actions. Since all Committees derive their mandates from their respective constituent instrument, by virtue of which they are already endowed with certain powers, these are obviously the first sources of legitimacy to analyse and turn to. In performing their mandates, treaty bodies enjoy a certain degree of autonomy, which is possibly best reflected by the fact that they are entitled to adopt their own Rules of Procedure.[1] The crucial question is to define how far treaty bodies can reach when filling the gaps, which result from the treaties' vague language.[2] The determination of their powers is ultimately situated between the autonomy accorded to them and the point at which the alteration of procedures is so significant that State consent is required.[3] In the latter case, attempts at reform are beyond the mandate of treaty bodies. To conclusively answer the question of whether the Committees are legally capable of implementing reform proposals on their own, it is therefore necessary to interpret the United Nations human rights core treaties accordingly.

A. Interpretation of human rights treaties

As regards the interpretation of international treaties, the general applicable rules are provided for in articles 31 to 33 Vienna Convention on the Law of Treaties.[4] These provisions, as is now generally accepted, reflect international

---

[1] Article 39(2) ICCPR, article 10(1) CERD, article 19(1) CEDAW, article 18(2) CAT, article 43(8) CRC, article 75(1) CMW, article 26(6) CED, article 34(10) CRPD; for the CESCR Committee, thus under ICESCR, there exists no comparable provision.

[2] Highlighting the need to fil the "gaps", *Pappa*, Das Individualbeschwerdeverfahren des Fakultativprotokolls zum Internationalen Pakt über bürgerliche und politische Rechte, 1996, p. 35.

[3] See in this regard *Seibert-Fohr*, The UN Human Rights Committee, in: Oberleitner (ed.), International Human Rights Institutions, Tribunals, and Courts, 2018, p. 134, who notes that the competence to adopt Rules of Procedure provides "some leeway" to the Committee "within the outer boundaries of the Covenant".

[4] Vienna Convention on the Law of Treaties (adopted 23 May 1969, entered into force 27 January 1980) UNTS 1155, 331.

customary law.⁵ They are therefore applicable to all treaties, despite falling under the non-retroactivity clause of article 4 VCLT,⁶ or to treaties concluded between States which are not parties to the Vienna Convention,⁷ for instance. However, while there is general consensus on the customary status of the rules of treaty interpretation, the question of their actual application is much more opaque, and allegedly divergent methods of interpretation have emerged in the context of human rights treaties.⁸

I. Specialized rules of interpretation

Whether human rights treaties require a special set of interpretative rules at variance with those provided for in articles 31 to 33 VCLT has caused much scholarly discussion and research, either focusing on regional human rights regimes,⁹ the work of the United Nations human rights treaty bodies,¹⁰ or posing the more general question of whether interpretative rules applied to human rights

---

⁵ *Dörr*, Article 31, General rule of interpretation, in: Dörr/Schmalenbach (eds.), Vienna Convention on the Law of Treaties: A Commentary, Second Edition, 2018, para. 6; *Gardiner*, The Vienna Convention Rules on Treaty Interpretation, in: Hollis (ed.), The Oxford Guide to Treaties, Second Edition, 2020, p. 460; see also *Aust*, Modern Treaty Law and Practice, Third Edition, 2013, p. 207, who observes that the ICJ and other international courts and tribunals recognize the principles enshrined in articles 31 and 32 VCLT reflecting international customary law; for more recent case law by the ICJ, see for example *Jadhav Case (India v. Pakistan)*, Judgment, I.C.J. Reports 2019, p. 418, para. 71; *Certain Questions of Mutual Assistance in Criminal Matters (Djibouti v. France)*, Judgment, I.C.J. Reports 2008, p. 232, para. 153; *Avena and Other Mexican Nationals (Mexico v. United States of America)*, Judgment, I.C.J. Reports 2004 (I), p. 48, para. 83.

⁶ Which would exclude the ICCPR and the ICESCR from the scope of application, for instance.

⁷ *Dörr*, Article 31, General rule of interpretation, in: Dörr/Schmalenbach (eds.), Vienna Convention on the Law of Treaties: A Commentary, Second Edition, 2018, para. 7, who refers to the USA and France as examples, both of which are not party to the VCLT but still acknowledge the rules of interpretation enshrined in articles 31 to 33 VCLT.

⁸ *Schlütter*, Aspects of human rights interpretation by the UN treaty bodies, in: Keller/Ulfstein (eds.), UN Human Rights Treaty Bodies: Law and Legitimacy, 2012, p. 263.

⁹ For the ECtHR and the ECHR, see *Letsas*, Strasbourg's Interpretive Ethic: Lessons for the International Lawyer, European Journal of International Law 21 (2010), 509; *Orakhelashvili*, Restrictive Interpretation of the Human Rights Treaties in the Recent Jurisprudence of the European Court of Human Rights, European Journal of International Law 14 (2003), 529; for the Inter-American System, see *Lixinski*, Treaty Interpretation by the Inter-American Court of Human Rights: Expansionism at the Service of the Unity of International Law, European Journal of International Law 21 (2010), 585.

¹⁰ *Schlütter*, Aspects of human rights interpretation by the UN treaty bodies, in: Keller/Ulfstein (eds.), UN Human Rights Treaty Bodies: Law and Legitimacy, 2012, p. 261; *Mechlem*, Treaty Bodies and the Interpretation of Human Rights, Vanderbilt Journal of Transnational Law 42 (2009), 905.

treaties might require adjustments, regardless of the treaty's regional or universal character.[11]

The search for or the question of specialized rules in the interpretation of human rights treaties is motivated by the observation that human rights treaties, as opposed to other international multilateral treaties, supposedly exhibit some "special features",[12] rendering them unique to a certain extent. The first feature invoked to justify the special character of human rights treaties is their non-reciprocal nature.[13] Despite being negotiated and concluded between State parties, the real addressees and beneficiaries are individuals, directly entitled with rights opposable to governmental powers. The rights and guarantees enable them, at least in theory, to eventually limit a State party's exercise of powers.[14] A second feature of human rights treaties that is invoked to explain their special character is their "general wording".[15] In this vein, human rights treaties are also referred to as rules with a "high degree of abstraction and vagueness",[16] that also "tend to be vague, broad, and nebulous in scope."[17] Third, human rights treaties are considered treaties that enshrine moral values and are thereby said to constitute a distinct category of treaties due to their "quasi-constitutional" nature.[18]

---

[11] *Çalı*, Specialized Rules of Treaty Interpretation: Human Rights, in: Hollis (ed.), The Oxford Guide to Treaties, Second Edition, 2020, p. 504; *Tobin*, Seeking to Persuade: A Constructive Approach to Human Rights Treaty Interpretation, Harvard Human Rights Journal 23 (2010), 1; *Craven*, Legal differentiation and the concept of the human rights treaty in international law, European Journal of International Law 11 (2000), 489.

[12] *Gardiner*, Treaty Interpretation, Second Edition, 2015, p. 474.

[13] *Fitzmaurice*, Interpretation of Human Rights Treaties, in: Shelton (ed.), The Oxford Handbook of International Human Rights Law, 2013, p. 742, arguing that this may lead to more importance being attached to the object and purpose of the treaty than to the text itself; *Orakhelashvili*, Restrictive Interpretation of the Human Rights Treaties in the Recent Jurisprudence of the European Court of Human Rights, European Journal of International Law 14 (2003), 529, 532; see also *Reservations to the Genocide Convention*, Advisory Opinion, I.C.J. Reports 1951, p. 15, 23.

[14] *Dörr*, Article 31, General rule of interpretation, in: Dörr/Schmalenbach (eds.), Vienna Convention on the Law of Treaties: A Commentary, Second Edition, 2018, para. 28; *McGrogan*, On the Interpretation of Human Rights Treaties and Subsequent Practice, Netherlands Quarterly of Human Rights 32 (2014), 347; *Schlütter*, Aspects of human rights interpretation by the UN treaty bodies, in: Keller/Ulfstein (eds.), UN Human Rights Treaty Bodies: Law and Legitimacy, 2012, p. 264 and p. 309.

[15] *Çalı*, Specialized Rules of Treaty Interpretation: Human Rights, in: Hollis (ed.), The Oxford Guide to Treaties, Second Edition, 2020, p. 508.

[16] *Schlütter*, Aspects of human rights interpretation by the UN treaty bodies, in: Keller/Ulfstein (eds.), UN Human Rights Treaty Bodies: Law and Legitimacy, 2012, p. 265.

[17] *McGrogan*, On the Interpretation of Human Rights Treaties and Subsequent Practice, Netherlands Quarterly of Human Rights 32 (2014), 347.

[18] *de Schutter*, The Formation of a Common Law of Human Rights, in: Bribosia/Rorive (eds.), Human Rights Tectonics: Global Dynamics of Integration and Fragmentation, 2018, p. 9; cf. *Letsas*, The ECHR as a living instrument: its meaning and legitimacy, in: Føllesdal/Peters/Ulfstein (eds.), Constituting Europe: The European Court of Human Rights in a National, European and Global Context, 2013, p. 107, who detects resemblances between international human rights treaties and constitutional bills of rights.

While all these assertions might be challenged, since other multilateral treaties are equally broad and vague in their wording; human rights treaties do also contain reciprocal treaty obligations,[19] and despite a treaty's constitutional character, third parties remain third parties,[20] the alleged specificities have led to certain methods of interpretation within the various regional and universal human rights treaty regimes that may indeed be said to be at variance with the canonical approach to interpretation. The decisive factor in the development of these supposedly special methods of interpretation is who mainly interprets the treaties.

Whereas interpretation is normally a privilege of State parties to a treaty, the situation is different in the realm of human rights treaties, mostly because individuals are the main holders of rights. In order to secure independent and impartial monitoring of State parties' compliance, human rights bodies exercise to a great extent the interpretative role "in lieu" of State parties.[21] This justifies taking a closer look at the interpretative methods developed.

---

[19] *Gardiner*, Treaty Interpretation, Second Edition, 2015, p. 475; *Fitzmaurice*, Interpretation of Human Rights Treaties, in: Shelton (ed.), The Oxford Handbook of International Human Rights Law, 2013, p. 743, who argues that treaties are by no means void of "traditional reciprocal obligations"; *Jardón*, The Interpretation of Jurisdictional Clauses in Human Rights Treaties, Anuario Mexicano de Derecho Internacional 8 (2013), 99, 121; see also *Craven*, Legal differentiation and the concept of the human rights treaty in international law, European Journal of International Law 11 (2000), 489, 498 with the observation that other types of international treaties may equally confer enforceable rights on individuals; Human Rights Committee, General Comment No. 31 [80], The Nature of the General Legal Obligation Imposed on States Parties to the Covenant, UN Doc. CCPR/C/21/Rev. 1/Add. 13, 26.05.2004, para. 2, stating that drawing the attention to a State party's breach of Convention rights should be "considered as a reflection of legitimate community interest."

[20] *Craven*, Legal differentiation and the concept of the human rights treaty in international law, European Journal of International Law 11 (2000), 489, 493.

[21] *Mechlem*, Treaty Bodies and the Interpretation of Human Rights, Vanderbilt Journal of Transnational Law 42 (2009), 905, 919; see also *McGrogan*, On the Interpretation of Human Rights Treaties and Subsequent Practice, Netherlands Quarterly of Human Rights 32 (2014), 347, 352; *Giegerich*, Vorbehalte zu Menschenrechtsabkommen: Zulässigkeit, Gültigkeit und Prüfungskompetenzen von Vertragsgremien: Ein konstitutioneller Ansatz, ZaöRV 55 (1995), 713, 759.

II. Interpretative methods under regional and UN human rights treaties

1. "Living-instrument" doctrine

Similar to the European Court of Human Rights[22] or the Inter-American Court of Human Rights,[23] the UN human rights treaty bodies interpret their respective treaties in light of societal or environmental changes and thus also apply the "living instrument approach", which was initially mainly coined by Strasbourg jurisprudence.[24] It seems that the "principle of dynamic interpretation has been accepted by all UN treaty bodies."[25] In 2002, the Human Rights Committee was the first UN human rights treaty body to expressly refer to its constituent treaty as a living instrument. While the Committee had previously held that the deportation of individuals to a country where they would face capital punishment did not amount to a violation of the right to life under article 6 ICCPR as such, it revised its position on this matter in *Judge v. Canada*.[26] To substantiate its finding, it first noticed a growing acceptance among the international community regarding the abolition of the death penalty and then concluded secondly that the "Convention should be interpreted as a living instrument and the rights protected under it should be applied in context and in the light of present-day conditions."[27]

---

[22] For literature on the living-instrument doctrine applied by the ECtHR, see among various others *Dörr*, The Strasbourg Approach to Evolutionary Interpretation, in: Abi-Saab et al. (eds.), Evolutionary Interpretation and International Law, 2019, p. 115; *Letsas*, The ECHR as a living instrument: its meaning and legitimacy, in: Føllesdal/Peters/Ulfstein (eds.), Constituting Europe: The European Court of Human Rights in a National, European and Global Context, 2013, p. 106.

[23] *Gaggioli*, The Strength of Evolutionary Interpretation in International Human Rights Law, in: Abi-Saab et al. (eds.), Evolutionary Interpretation and International Law, 2019, pp. 106–107; *Fitzmaurice*, Interpretation of Human Rights Treaties, in: Shelton (ed.), The Oxford Handbook of International Human Rights Law, 2013, p. 766.

[24] Early landmark cases are, for instance, *Tyrer v. United Kingdom (Merits)*, Application No. 5856/72, judgment of 25 April 1978, Series A No. 26; or *Marckx v. Belgium (Merits)*, Application No. 6833/74, judgment of 13 June 1979, Series A No. 31; see also *Moeckli/White*, Treaties as 'Living Instruments', in: Bowman/Kritsiotis (eds.), Conceptual and Contextual Perspectives on the Modern Law of Treaties, 2018, p. 146, with a short but detailed account of occurrences of the notion "living instrument" in the ECtHR's jurisprudence.

[25] *Schlütter*, Aspects of human rights interpretation by the UN treaty bodies, in: Keller/Ulfstein (eds.), UN Human Rights Treaty Bodies: Law and Legitimacy, 2012, p. 296; see also *Moeckli/White*, Treaties as 'Living Instruments', in: Bowman/Kritsiotis (eds.), Conceptual and Contextual Perspectives on the Modern Law of Treaties, 2018, p. 143 who argue that the concept of a living instrument can be "attached to the category of human rights treaties as a whole."; see, however, *Keane*, Mapping the International Convention on the Elimination of All Forms of Racial Discrimination as a Living Instrument, Human Rights Law Review 20 (2020), 236, 249, who only detects six communications before treaty bodies which directly refer to the living instrument approach.

[26] Human Rights Committee, *Judge v. Canada*, Communication No. 829/1998, UN Doc. CCPR/C/78/D/829/1998, 05.08.2002.

[27] Human Rights Committee, *Judge v. Canada*, Communication No. 829/1998, UN Doc.

Comparable to the ECtHR's search for domestic consensus,[28] the Human Rights Committee observed "a broadening international consensus in favor of abolition of the death penalty" and thereby relied on national legislative developments as well.[29]

Further examples of treaty bodies invoking the notion of human rights treaties as being a living instrument are communications before the Committee against Torture and the CERD Committee. In both *Hagan v. Australia*[30] and *V.X.N. and H.N. v. Sweden*[31] respectively the Committees reasoned that the interpretation of the respective Convention must take account of contemporary developments.[32] The same applies to the CEDAW Committee, which frames its own approach as the "dynamic instrument doctrine",[33] or to the CRC Committee. The latter noted in its General Comment No. 8 that the "the Convention, like all human rights instruments, must be regarded as a living instrument, whose interpretation develops over time."[34]

CCPR/C/78/D/829/1998, 05.08.2002, para. 10.3; *Moeckli/White*, Treaties as 'Living Instruments', in: Bowman/Kritsiotis (eds.), Conceptual and Contextual Perspectives on the Modern Law of Treaties, 2018, pp. 152–153; see however *Schlütter*, Aspects of human rights interpretation by the UN treaty bodies, in: Keller/Ulfstein (eds.), UN Human Rights Treaty Bodies: Law and Legitimacy, 2012, pp. 275–276, who discusses the same communication, but considers a combination of literal and contextual approaches of interpretation as decisive for the Committee's departure from its previous position; for further relevant case law, see Human Rights Committee, *Yoon and Choi v. Republic of Korea*, Communications Nos. 1321/2004 and 1322/2004, UN Doc. CCPR/C/88/D/1321–1322/2004, 03.11.2006, para. 8.4, in which the Human Rights Committee broadened the scope of protection under article 18 ICCPR by means of the "living-instrument" approach.

[28] For a discussion and analysis of the "European Consensus" among various others, see *Łącki*, Consensus as a Basis for Dynamic Interpretation of the ECHR—A Critical Assessment, Human Rights Law Review 21 (2021), 186; *Dzehtsiarou*, European Consensus and the Evolutive Interpretation of the European Convention on Human Rights, German Law Journal 12 (2010), 1730.

[29] Human Rights Committee, *Judge v. Canada*, Communication No. 829/1998, UN Doc. CCPR/C/78/D/829/1998, adopted 05.08.2002, para. 10.3.

[30] CERD Committee, *Hagan v. Australia*, Communication No. 26/2002, UN Doc. CERD/C/62/D/26/2002, 20.03.2003.

[31] Committee against Torture, *V.X.N. and H.N. v. Sweden*, Communications Nos. 130/1999 and 131/1999, UN Doc. CAT/C/24/D/130 and 131/1999, 15.05.2000.

[32] CERD Committee, *Hagan v. Australia*, Communication No. 26/2002, UN Doc. CERD/C/62/D/26/2002, 20.03.2003, para. 7.3; Committee against Torture, *V.X.N. and H.N. v. Sweden*, Communications Nos. 130/1999 and 131/1999, CAT/C/24/D/130 and 131/1999, 15.05.2000; *Schlütter*, Aspects of human rights interpretation by the UN treaty bodies, in: Keller/Ulfstein (eds.), UN Human Rights Treaty Bodies: Law and Legitimacy, 2012, pp. 296–297.

[33] CEDAW Committee, General recommendation No. 28 on the core obligations of States parties under article 2 of the Convention on the Elimination of All Forms of Discrimination against Women, UN Doc. CEDAW/C/GC/28, 16.12.2010, para. 2; *Çalı*, Specialized Rules of Treaty Interpretation: Human Rights, in: Hollis (ed.), The Oxford Guide to Treaties, Second Edition, 2020, p. 512.

[34] CRC Committee, General Comment No. 8, The right of the child to protection from

2. Effectiveness-orientated and teleological approaches

Another interpretative method that is widely applied in the context of the interpretation of human rights treaties,[35] but which is also discernable within general international law, is the principle of effectiveness.[36] Embraced by both regional courts[37] and UN human rights treaty bodies, the principle of effectiveness in its specific human rights dimension means interpreting human rights treaties in such a way that they "have an impact on the ground."[38]

Although UN human rights treaty bodies do not seem to directly invoke the principle of effectiveness, it has been observed that they too rely on corresponding considerations to render rights and guarantees effective and thus beneficial to individuals.[39] Especially the interpretation of socio-economic rights undertaken

---

corporal punishment and other cruel or degrading forms of punishment, UN Doc. CRC/C/GC/8, 02.03.2007, para. 20; *Moeckli/White*, Treaties as 'Living Instruments', in: Bowman/Kritsiotis (eds.), Conceptual and Contextual Perspectives on the Modern Law of Treaties, 2018, p. 154.

[35] See *Çalı*, Specialized Rules of Treaty Interpretation: Human Rights, in: Hollis (ed.), The Oxford Guide to Treaties, Second Edition, 2020, p. 522, who argues that all the different approaches in the interpretation of human rights treaties can be summarized under the "overarching umbrella of effectiveness"; but see also *Crawford/Keene*, Interpretation of the human rights treaties by the International Court of Justice, The International Journal of Human Rights 24 (2020), 935, 945, who rightly state that "effectivity originates from the interplay of criteria within the VCLT, rather than representing a new and somehow distinctive interpretive technique"; *Dörr*, Article 31, General rule of interpretation, in: Dörr/Schmalenbach (eds.), Vienna Convention on the Law of Treaties: A Commentary, Second Edition, 2018, para. 34, who observes that effectiveness "is not an isolated goal or concept", but represents "a specific application of the object and purpose test and the good faith rule and, therefore an integral part of the general rule of interpretation laid down in Art 31."

[36] *Ulfstein*, Interpretation of the ECHR in light of the Vienna Convention on the Law of Treaties, The International Journal of Human Rights 24 (2020), 917, 919; *Çalı*, Specialized Rules of Treaty Interpretation: Human Rights, in: Hollis (ed.), The Oxford Guide to Treaties, Second Edition, 2020, p. 513; *Schlütter*, Aspects of human rights interpretation by the UN treaty bodies, in: Keller/Ulfstein (eds.), UN Human Rights Treaty Bodies: Law and Legitimacy, 2012, p. 286; *Christoffersen*, Impact on General Principles of Treaty Interpretation, in: Kamminga/Scheinin (eds.), The Impact of Human Rights Law on General International Law, 2009, p. 42 with an enumeration of cases in which the ECtHR took recourse to the principle of effectiveness; *Orakhelashvili*, The Interpretation of Acts and Rules in Public International Law, 2008, p. 401.

[37] In the Inter-American system, the effectiveness-orientated interpretation prevails in form of the so-called "pro homine" approach, as the Court will seek to find the one interpretation which is most favourable to the individual, see *Killander*, Interpreting Regional Human Rights Treaties, Sur-International Journal on Human Rights 13 (2010), 145, 147; *Lixinski*, Treaty Interpretation by the Inter-American Court of Human Rights: Expansionism at the Service of the Unity of International Law, European Journal of International Law 21 (2010), 585, 588.

[38] *Orakhelashvili*, The Interpretation of Acts and Rules in Public International Law, 2008, p. 404.

[39] *Schlütter*, Aspects of human rights interpretation by the UN treaty bodies, in: Keller/

by the CESCR Committee is said to be driven by a maximum of effectiveness-related considerations,[40] but also treaty bodies entrusted with monitoring civil and political rights argue for the effective protection of human rights within the framework of their interpretations.[41]

Closely related to the principle of effectiveness is strong reliance on the very object and purpose of human rights treaties, hence granting the individual the best possible protection against the exercise of (unjustified) governmental authority.[42] UN human rights treaty bodies "strategically" lend weight to the object and purpose of their treaties to underpin their lines of argumentation,[43] which may, nonetheless, be subject to criticism by contracting parties.[44] In line with the observation that the treaty bodies seldom specifically label their methods of interpretation as such, teleological interpretation nevertheless occurs quite frequently, at least as far as the Human Rights Committee is concerned.[45]

3. Legal effects of the interpretative approaches

By interpreting the respective provision in the light of changing social circumstances, taking recourse to a treaty's object and purpose or deploying considerations of effectiveness, sometimes to their maximum or even beyond, regional human rights courts and treaty bodies constantly redefined their constituent instruments.[46] The application of the portrayed interpretative methods, e.g. in

---

Ulfstein (eds.), UN Human Rights Treaty Bodies: Law and Legitimacy, 2012, pp. 286–287, with a brief but detailed account of relevant case law of the Human Rights Committee, Committee against Torture and the CERD Committee.

[40] *Fitzmaurice*, Interpretation of Human Rights Treaties, in: Shelton (ed.), The Oxford Handbook of International Human Rights Law, 2013, p. 763; *Orakhelashvili*, The Interpretation of Acts and Rules in Public International Law, 2008, p. 406.

[41] *Pazartzis/Merkouris*, Final Report on The UN Human Rights Committee and other Human Rights Treaty Bodies, TRICI-Law Paper No. 007/2020, pp. 7–8.

[42] For instance, see *Chinkin*, Human Rights, in: Bowman/Kritsiotis (eds.), Conceptual and Contextual Perspectives on the Modern Law of Treaties, 2018, p. 519, who argues that the interpretation of human rights treaties generally "accords greater significance to the object and purpose" than to the wording.

[43] *Schlütter*, Aspects of human rights interpretation by the UN treaty bodies, in: Keller/Ulfstein (eds.), UN Human Rights Treaty Bodies: Law and Legitimacy, 2012, p. 284; cf. *Pazartzis/Merkouris*, Final Report on The UN Human Rights Committee and other Human Rights Treaty Bodies, TRICI-Law Paper No. 007/2020, p. 9, who note that the object and purpose of the ICCPR is "critical for the interpretative process".

[44] *Moeckli*, Interpretation of the ICESCR: Between Morality and State Consent, in: Moeckli/Keller/Heri (eds.), The Human Rights Covenants at 50: Their Past, Present, and Future, 2018, p. 59, who observes in relation to the CESCR Committee the "central role that it accords to the object and purpose element."

[45] *Pazartzis/Merkouris*, Final Report on The UN Human Rights Committee and other Human Rights Treaty Bodies, TRICI-Law Paper No. 007/2020, p. 9.

[46] *Letsas*, The ECHR as a living instrument: its meaning and legitimacy, in: Føllesdal/Peters/Ulfstein (eds.), Constituting Europe: The European Court of Human Rights in a National, European and Global Context, 2013, p. 122.

response to technological progress or changing social relationships,[47] has thus led to an extension of the scopes of protection granted by the treaties.[48] To the extent that this is beneficial to individuals, said methods of interpretation simultaneously result in the treaties "[retaining] their relevance in changing political, social and economic circumstances".[49] But at the same time, the approaches are subject to criticism.

Progressive interpretations might reach far beyond the drafters' original intentions and do not necessarily meet the consent of State parties.[50] State parties seem to "favour a positivist or dogmatic view that gives priority to the ordinary meaning of the words",[51] and also tend to rely on the intention of the drafters when carrying out any interpretative act.[52] And although there seems to be general consensus in legal literature that the methods of interpretation presented above are all ultimately reconcilable with the general rules of interpretation pro-

---

[47] See for instance *Mowbray*, Between the will of the Contracting Parties and the needs of today, in: Brems/Gerards (eds.), Shaping Rights in the ECHR: The Role of the European Court of Human Rights in Determining the Scope of Human Rights, 2013, pp. 20–25, with an overview of external circumstances requiring the Court's response and related case law analyses.

[48] See for example *Medina*, The Role of International Tribunals: Law-Making or Creative Interpretation?, in: Shelton (ed.), The Handbook of International Human Rights Law, 2013, pp. 649–669 with particular focus on the practice of the Human Rights Committee and the Inter-American Court; or *Schlütter*, Aspects of human rights interpretation by the UN treaty bodies, in: Keller/Ulfstein (eds.), UN Human Rights Treaty Bodies: Law and Legitimacy, 2012, pp. 311–317, with a detailed assessment of the Human Rights Committee's changing jurisprudence on the right to conscientious objection under article 18 ICCPR; *Lixinski*, Treaty Interpretation by the Inter-American Court of Human Rights: Expansionism at the Service of the Unity of International Law, European Journal of International Law 21 (2010), 585, 604, who concludes that "[new] dimensions are added to pre-existing rights";

[49] *Chinkin*, Human Rights, in: Bowman/Kritsiotis (eds.), Conceptual and Contextual Perspectives on the Modern Law of Treaties, 2018, p. 518; see also *Buga*, Modification of Treaties by Subsequent Practice, 2018, p. 93, referring to a treaty's "survival".

[50] *Gaggioli*, The Strength of Evolutionary Interpretation in International Human Rights Law, in: Abi-Saab et al. (eds.), Evolutionary Interpretation and International Law, 2019, p. 111; *Schlütter*, Aspects of human rights interpretation by the UN treaty bodies, in: Keller/Ulfstein (eds.), UN Human Rights Treaty Bodies: Law and Legitimacy, 2012, p. 266; *Letsas*, Strasbourg's Interpretive Ethic: Lessons for the International Lawyer, European Journal of International Law 21 (2010), 509, 515; see also *Çalı*, Specialized Rules of Treaty Interpretation: Human Rights, in: Hollis (ed.), The Oxford Guide to Treaties, Second Edition, 2020, p. 522, who observes that it is an "important consequence" of the specific interpretative methods in the realm of human rights treaties to "disregard original intent".

[51] *Chinkin*, Human Rights, in: Bowman/Kritsiotis (eds.), Conceptual and Contextual Perspectives on the Modern Law of Treaties, 2018, p. 522.

[52] *de Schutter*, The Formation of a Common Law of Human Rights, in: Bribosia/Rorive (eds.), Human Rights Tectonics: Global Dynamics of Integration and Fragmentation, 2018, p. 5; *Letsas*, Strasbourg's Interpretive Ethic: Lessons for the International Lawyer, European Journal of International Law 21 (2010), 509, 513–514.

vided for by the VCLT,[53] State parties might also vocally object to interpretations undertaken by international human rights bodies and might accuse courts and treaty bodies of rewriting "clear provisions of the treaty under the guise of interpretation".[54] In that regard, they might even challenge progressive interpretations as "illegitimate",[55] "activism" or "judicial imperialism".[56] These conflicting views are therefore ultimately a manifestation of the question of who holds the prerogative of interpretation over the treaties.[57] Any interpretative result could arguably be placed on a scale that ranges between the two extremes of strict adherence to the wording and maximum considerations of effectiveness.

---

[53] *Jardón*, The Interpretation of Jurisdictional Clauses in Human Rights Treaties, Anuario Mexicano de Derecho Internacional 8 (2013), 99, 121; *Fitzmaurice*, Interpretation of Human Rights Treaties, in: Shelton (ed.), The Oxford Handbook of International Human Rights Law, 2013, p. 769; *Schlütter*, Aspects of human rights interpretation by the UN treaty bodies, in: Keller/Ulfstein (eds.), UN Human Rights Treaty Bodies: Law and Legitimacy, 2012, p. 317; *Rietiker*, The Principle of "Effectiveness" in the Recent Jurisprudence of the European Court of Human Rights: Its Different Dimensions and Its Consistency with Public International Law – No Need for the Concept of Treaty Sui Generis, Nordic Journal of International Law 79 (2010), 245, 255; *Christoffersen*, Impact on General Principles of Treaty Interpretation, in: Kamminga/Scheinin (eds.), The Impact of Human Rights Law on General International Law, 2009, p. 61; *Mechlem*, Treaty Bodies and the Interpretation of Human Rights, Vanderbilt Journal of Transnational Law 42 (2009), 905, 913; *Orakhelashvili*, Restrictive Interpretation of the Human Rights Treaties in the Recent Jurisprudence of the European Court of Human Rights, European Journal of International Law 14 (2003), 529, 533–534, who observes that "[general] guidance is still provided by the [VCLT]".

[54] This was the position of the USA towards the Committee against Torture's General Comment No. 2, in which the Committee clarified that articles 3 to 15 CAT are applicable to both torture and ill-treatment, cited at *Chinkin*, Human Rights, in: Bowman/Kritsiotis (eds.), Conceptual and Contextual Perspectives on the Modern Law of Treaties, 2018, p. 521; an instructive example, among various other instances of open criticism concerning allegedly too progressive interpretations, are reactions by State parties with regard to draft General Comment No. 36 by the Human Rights Committee. The Russian Federation labelled one of the Committee's assertions as an "arbitrary interpretation", Canada held that the Committee's approach in draft General Comment No. 36 was "too extensive" and the US referred to a number of topics included in draft General Comment No. 36 as "overly expansive", the comments by State parties are available under: https://www.ohchr.org/en/calls-for-input/general-comment-no-36-article-6-right-life (last access: 21.08.2023).

[55] *Schlütter*, Aspects of human rights interpretation by the UN treaty bodies, in: Keller/Ulfstein (eds.), UN Human Rights Treaty Bodies: Law and Legitimacy, 2012, p. 319.

[56] *Gaggioli*, The Strength of Evolutionary Interpretation in International Human Rights Law, in: Abi-Saab et al. (eds.), Evolutionary Interpretation and International Law, 2019, p. 111.

[57] With regard to the ECtHR, see *Mowbray*, Between the will of the Contracting Parties and the needs of today, in: Brems/Gerards (eds.), Shaping Rights in the ECHR: The Role of the European Court of Human Rights in Determining the Scope of Human Rights, 2013, p. 37.

III. Interpretative task at hand

The section above has shown that the interpretation of human rights treaties is based on effectiveness-oriented considerations, often giving priority to the object and purpose of the treaty in question. Nevertheless, as has also become apparent, these interpretative approaches were mainly used to broaden the scope of substantive provisions, whereas the question at stake is how to determine the powers of treaty bodies. The task of delineating powers also "poses a well-known challenge of interpretation",[58] but with the decisive difference that the provisions subject to interpretation are of procedural character.

Procedural provisions, which endow treaty bodies with powers, are comparably vague and broad as their substantive counterparts. An example of that is article 28(1) CED.[59] The provision principally imposes the duty on the CED Committee to cooperate with all stakeholders enumerated in article 28(1) CED. At the same time, the duty to cooperate finds its limits "in the framework of the competencies granted by this Convention". This is circular in that the Convention does not reveal anything about possible forms of cooperation or how far the scope of such cooperation might reach, and only spells out the usual powers conferred on human rights treaty bodies.

Similar observations were made about article 40 ICCPR, for instance, which does not give much guidance to the Human Rights Committee on how to conduct the examination of State reports.[60] This finding can easily be applied to other provisions that govern the State reporting procedure under the various UN human rights core treaties. Moreover, some treaties, as will be demonstrated further

---

[58] *Oette*, The UN Human Rights Treaty Bodies: Impact and Future, in: Oberleitner (ed.), International Human Rights Institutions, Tribunals, and Courts, 2018, p. 99; cf. *Møse/ Opsahl*, The Optional Protocol to the International Covenant on Civil and Political Rights, Santa Clara Law Review 21 (1981), 271, 278, who observe a difficulty in distinguishing between extensions of powers that contradict the First Optional Protocol and would consequently be prohibited, and extensions of powers that would supplement treaty provisions, and would consequently be permitted.

[59] Article 28(1) CED reads as follows: "In the framework of the competencies granted by this Convention, the Committee shall cooperate with all relevant organs, offices and specialized agencies and funds of the United Nations, with the treaty bodies instituted by international instruments, with the special procedures of the United Nations and with the relevant regional intergovernmental organizations or bodies, as well as with all relevant State institutions, agencies or offices working towards the protection of all persons against enforced disappearances."

[60] See for example *Kretzmer*, The UN Human Rights Committee and International Human Rights Monitoring, Straus Institute Working Paper No. 12, 2010, p. 20, who describes the provisions relating to the reporting procedure under the ICCPR as "laconic"; *Oette*, The UN Human Rights Treaty Bodies: Impact and Future, in: Oberleitner (ed.), International Human Rights Institutions, Tribunals, and Courts, 2018, p. 101, noting that the provisions governing the reporting procedure provide "limited guidance on the format or reports and the process of review."

below, are even silent on certain issues, and do not reveal anything about a treaty body's competence in a certain domain.[61] Hence, the above portrayed methods of interpretation qualify as promising means when seeking to enhance the effectiveness and efficiency of treaty bodies, at least initially. Whenever the treaties remain silent and do not provide for a certain power, or the possibility of implementation remains uncertain because of the treaty's vague wording, treaty bodies could extend their competences by means of teleological interpretation; possibly with reference to the positive effects for more effective human rights protection ensuing from such an interpretation.

Nonetheless, two decisive features must be considered first in the delineation of treaty bodies' powers. It is their arguably special legal status which may require a different approach to the definition of competencies than is the case with regional human rights courts. In this context, a second question arises as to whether the above portrayed methods of interpretation are also applicable to procedural provisions. They do bear the potential to significantly widen the scope of the provision under interpretation, but any such alteration might have an impact on the relationship between the treaty body and the State parties, and may also significantly alter the institutional set-up under the treaties.[62]

As a first step, it is thus necessary to define the treaty bodies' legal nature. They exercise "multidimensional"[63] functions and are therefore not easy to categorize.[64] In comparison to the classical branches of power in domestic systems, it has been argued that the examinations of State reports and inquiries conducted resemble administrative or investigative activities; the adoption of views is said to be similar to the functioning of domestic courts; and the issuance of General Comments "has elements that resemble legislation."[65]

These distinct functions might require treaty bodies to proceed differently when defining their own powers, depending on which of their various functions is concerned.[66] The adherence to any kind of differentiation might possibly require

---

[61] Some treaties do not vest their respective treaty body with the power to issue interim measures, or the power to monitor the implementation of views and concluding observations adopted is not expressly provided for by UN human rights treaties.

[62] *Oette*, The UN Human Rights Treaty Bodies: Impact and Future, in: Oberleitner (ed.), International Human Rights Institutions, Tribunals, and Courts, 2018, p. 99; cf. *Opsahl*, The Human Rights Committee, in: Alston (ed.), The United Nations and Human Rights: A Critical Appraisal, First Edition, 1992, p. 369, who notes that the Committee's function can "evolve significantly".

[63] *Hennebel*, The Human Rights Committee, in: Mégret/Alston (eds.), The United Nations and Human Rights: A Critical Appraisal, Second Edition, 2020, p. 346.

[64] *Wolf*, Aktivlegitimation im UN-Individualbeschwerdeverfahren, 2018, p. 76; *McGoldrick*, The Human Rights Committee: Its Role in the Development of the International Covenant on Civil and Political Rights, 1991, p. 55, who refers to the nature of the Human Rights Committee as "amorphous".

[65] *Keller/Ulfstein*, Introduction, in: Keller/Ulfstein (eds.), UN Human Rights Treaty Bodies: Law and Legitimacy, 2012, p. 3.

[66] *Hennebel*, The Human Rights Committee, in: Mégret/Alston (eds.), The United Nations

different methods of interpretation, since a "one size fits all-approach" could easily neglect particularities that exclusively pertain to one of a treaty body's features. On the other hand, a differentiating approach could lead to treaty bodies being accused of cherry-picking when they strive to extend their powers and could thus provide a disservice to them.

1. Legal nature of human rights treaty bodies

UN human rights treaty bodies are neither international organizations nor are they international courts.[67] While human rights treaty bodies might meet some of the criteria of an international organization – such as having been established by an international treaty, exercising functions conferred on them by their constituent treaty and possibly articulating a "will" that is distinct from the one of the parties to the treaty – they are ultimately lacking the decisive criterion of having an own legal personality.[68] With regard to a possible classification as international courts, all human rights treaty bodies can potentially examine individual complaints,[69] which is considered "the most court-like function of the treaty bodies",[70] but it is still only a *court-like* function. Said function leads some commentators to assert that treaty bodies are quasi-judicial organs,[71] which consequently sets them apart from international organizations in this domain, but also does not fully qualify them as international courts.

Those who consider treaty bodies to be quasi-judicial bodies invoke the "adversarial decision-making process, and its procedural safeguards" under the in-

---

and Human Rights: A Critical Appraisal, Second Edition, 2020, p. 346; see also *McGoldrick*, The Human Rights Committee: Its Role in the Development of the International Covenant on Civil and Political Rights, 1991, p. 55, who proposes that the nature of the Human Rights Committee "may alter in accordance with its exercise of the various functions and roles it performs or could perform."

[67] *Ulfstein*, Law-making by human rights treaty bodies, in: Liivoja/Petman (eds.), International Law-making, 2014, p. 249.

[68] *Engström*, Understanding Powers of International Organizations: A Study of the Doctrines of Attributed Powers, Implied Powers and Constitutionalism – with a Special Focus on the Human Rights Committee, Åbo 2009, pp. 8–9.

[69] The complaints procedure under CMW has not yet entered into force as the required number of 10 declarations under article 77 CMW has not yet been reached.

[70] *Rodley*, The Role and Impact of Treaty Bodies, in: Shelton (ed.), The Oxford Handbook of International Human Rights Law, 2013, p. 634.

[71] Characterizing the Committee against Torture as a "quasi-judicial treaty-based organ", *Monina*, Article 17, Committee against Torture, in: Nowak/Birk/Monina (eds.), The United Nations Convention Against Torture and its Optional Protocol: A Commentary, Second Edition, 2019, p. 476; *Nowak*, CCPR Commentary, Second revised Edition, 2005, Article 28, Human Rights Committee, para. 1; *Scheinin*, How to Untie a Tie in the Human Rights Committee, in: *Alfredsson et al.* (eds.), International Human Rights Monitoring Mechanism, First Edition, 2001, p. 129.

dividual complaints procedure to justify their characterization.[72] Others, in turn, only consider the individual complaints procedure as being of "quasi-judicial" nature,[73] but do not deduce any general character ascribed to human rights treaty bodies from this finding. Similarly, the Human Rights Committee asserted itself a quasi-judicial character in the exercise of its mandate under the First Optional Protocol. It held that its views adopted "exhibit some important characteristics of a judicial decisions" and that "[they] are arrived at in a judicial spirit".[74] Nevertheless, contrary to judgments handed down by the ECtHR for instance, views adopted by treaty bodies are not legally binding as such, and the very terminology used in the context of the individual complaints procedure indicates that treaty bodies are somewhat different from international courts.[75] Moreover, the quasi-judicial function, although with regard to the Human Rights Committee possibly the closest to what could be described as "universal human rights jurisprudence",[76] only makes up one third of the Committee's main features. In addition, when compared to other human rights treaty bodies, particularly in terms of quantity, almost three quarters of all individual complaints filed with human rights treaty bodies are examined by the Human Rights Committee. It is followed by the Committee against Torture, which considers approximately 20 per cent of the communications submitted to the treaty bodies.[77] As follows, all other seven treaty bodies have not yet developed a similar (quasi-)judicial profile and devote most of their meeting time to the examination of State reports or the adoption of General Comments, for instance. Both of these activities are functions that apparently do not exhibit a judicial character in the traditional sense.[78]

---

[72] *Seibert-Fohr*, The UN Human Rights Committee, in: Oberleitner (ed.), International Human Rights Institutions, Tribunals, and Courts, 2018, p. 118.

[73] *Kälin/Künzli*, The Law of International Human Rights Protection, Second Edition, 2019, p. 205; *Oette*, The UN Human Rights Treaty Bodies: Impact and Future, in: Oberleitner (ed.), International Human Rights Institutions, Tribunals, and Courts, 2018, p. 105; *Subedi*, The Effectiveness of the UN Human Rights System: Reform and the Judicalisation of Human Rights, 2017, p. 77; *Hartman*, Derogation from Human Rights Treaties in Public Emergencies – A Critique of Implementation by the European Commission and Court of Human Rights and the Human Rights Committee of the United Nations, Harvard International Law Journal 22 (1981), 1, 42.

[74] Human Rights Committee, General Comment No. 33, The Obligations of States Parties under the Optional Protocol to the International Covenant on Civil and Political Rights, UN Doc. CCPR/C/GC/33, 05.11.2008, para. 11.

[75] See *Wolf*, Aktivlegitimation im UN-Individualbeschwerdeverfahren, 2018, p. 75, who refers to the terms "communications" and "opinions" used instead of "judgment".

[76] *Engström*, Understanding Powers of International Organizations: A Study of the Doctrines of Attributed Powers, Implied Powers and Constitutionalism – with a Special Focus on the Human Rights Committee, Åbo 2009, p. 11.

[77] *Gaer*, The Institutional Future of the Covenants, A World Court for Human Rights?, in: Moeckli/Keller/Heri (eds.) The Human Rights Covenants at 50: Their Past, Present, and Future, 2018, p. 352.

[78] For the functions of General Comments, see *infra* Part III C.II.; *O'Flaherty*, The United

To conclusively identify the nature of UN human rights treaty bodies, it is thus argued here to consider all their functions comprehensively. This signifies that treaty bodies in their entirety are not only of a "quasi-judicial" character, but that they do encompass more characteristics. In line with this, it has been suggested to include treaty bodies among those interpreters who operate at least partially in an institutional law context, as long as their activities are "not limited to (semi-) judicial review of cases".[79]

Therefore, in the final analysis, those who consider treaty bodies to have a *sui generis* status must be agreed with.[80] It is only the classification as bodies *sui generis* which is able to capture all of their different functions at once without relying too narrowly on one particular feature. Furthermore, the classification of bodies *sui generis* entails the benefit of applying a consistent and uniform approach to the delineation of their competencies, irrespective of the precise field of application, be it the individual complaints procedure or the State reporting procedure.

2. Application of specialized methods of interpretation to procedural provisions

Recalling that evolutionary interpretation is mainly understood as "evolution intended",[81] it is questionable if progressive interpretation can be applied to procedural provisions. The same might hold true for other interpretative techniques portrayed above, which have the potential to widen the scope of procedural provisions significantly. It was a deliberate choice of the drafters to establish a treaty body,[82] which is endowed with a weaker institutional design than a regional human rights court. The presumption against having intended procedural pro-

---

Nations Human Rights Treaty Bodies as Diplomatic Actors, in: O'Flaherty et al. (eds.), Human Rights Diplomacy: Contemporary Perspectives, 2011, p. 171, who accords a diplomatic character to the State reporting procedure.

[79] *Brölmann*, Specialized Rules of Treaty Interpretation: International Organizations, in: Hollis (ed.), The Oxford Guide to Treaties, Second Edition, 2020, p. 537.

[80] *Wolf*, Aktivlegitimation im UN-Individualbeschwerdeverfahren, 2018, p. 79; *O'Flaherty*, The High Commissioner and the Treaty Bodies, in: Gaer/Broecker (eds.), The United Nations High Commissioner for Human Rights: Conscience for the World, 2014, p. 101; *Tyagi*, The UN Human Rights Committee, Practice and Procedure, 2011, p. 44 with reference to monitoring bodies as "*sui generis* organs" and pp. 110–111, where the Human Rights Committee is referred to as a "unique body" with a "special status"; *Boerefijn*, The Reporting Procedure under the Covenant on Civil and Political Rights: Practice and Procedures of the Human Rights Committee, 1999, p. 169.

[81] *Bjorge*, The Evolutionary Interpretation of Treaties, 2014, p. 188; *Arato*, Subsequent Practice and Evolutive Interpretation: Techniques of Treaty Interpretation over Time and Their Diverse Consequences, The Law and Practice of International Courts and Tribunals 9 (2010), 443, who observes that the intention of the parties is the basis for any interpretation of a treaty over time.

[82] *Ulfstein*, Treaty Bodies and Regimes, in: Hollis (ed.), The Oxford Guide to Treaties, Second Edition, 2020, pp. 415 and 424, who argues that treaty bodies are established when State parties seek to "minimize" interference with the sovereignty of contracting parties.

visions, and related powers being capable of evolving as much as substantive treaty guarantees, is further amplified by the fact that the drafters of the most recent treaties, CED and CRPD, opted for another treaty body with only a few more powers as compared to the already existing seven UN human rights treaty bodies. Furthermore, against the background of the strengthening process so far and the observations made in relation to the broadening of substantive treaty provisions, State parties are very likely to criticize extensive interpretations of procedural provisions.[83] They might argue that treaty bodies are acting *ultra vires* when relying too prominently on considerations of effectiveness when it comes to the extension of their powers.[84]

On the other hand, it has been proposed that the principle of effectiveness is applicable to procedural provisions too, which are thus to be "interpreted in a pro-active rather than a passive fashion".[85] Also the case law of regional human rights courts demonstrates to a certain extent that it is not only substantive provisions which are reinterpreted by means of an effectiveness-orientated interpretation, or by recourse to the "living-instrument" approach. In both, *Loizidou v. Turkey (Preliminary Objections)*[86] and in *Mamatkulov and Askarov v. Turkey*,[87]

---

[83] Strongly advocating a limited mandate of treaty bodies in legal literature *Pedone/Kloster*, New Proposals for Human Rights Treaty Body Reform, Journal of Transnational Law & Policy 22 (2012–2013), 29, 36.

[84] *Ulfstein*, The Human Rights Treaty Bodies and Legitimacy Challenges, in: Grossmann et al. (eds.), Legitimacy and International Courts, 2018, p. 298, with reference to the criticism articulated by China and Russia in the context of the multi-stakeholder strengthening process; cf. *Helfer*, Pushback Against Supervisory Systems: Lessons for the ILO from International Human Rights Institutions, in: Politakis et al. (eds.), ILO100 – LAW FOR SOCIAL JUSTICE, Geneva 2019, p. 262, who argues that some expansions of powers have been "audacious"; see also *Helfer/Slaughter*, Toward a Theory of Effective Supranational Adjudication, Yale Law Journal 107 (1997), 273, 344. As an example can serve the Russian submission to the co-facilitators of the 2020 review process. It was argued that "the efficiency of treaty bodies depends on the strict adherence by Committees to the mandates granted by States". China stressed in its submission that it "would like to reiterate that the treaty bodies are established by the respective treaties and should operate strictly within the terms of their mandates provided for under the respective treaties. The mandate, mode of work, rules of procedure and future development of the treaty bodies should be determined in accordance with the treaties. The States parties' views in this regard should be fully respected and considered", https://www.ohchr.org/en/calls-for-input/co-facilitation-process-treaty-body-review-2020 (last access: 21.08.2023).

[85] *Çalı*, Enforcement, in: Langford et al. (eds.), The Optional Protocol to the International Covenant on Economic, Social and Cultural Rights: A Commentary, 2016, p. 367, who advances her argument in the context of provisions governing the follow-up procedure to views adopted under the OP-ICESCR; see also *Wolf*, Aktivlegitimation im UN-Individualbeschwerdeverfahren, 2018, p. 96, arguing that the application of dynamic interpretation to procedural provisions can be considered possible.

[86] *Loizidou v. Turkey (Preliminary Objections)*, Application No. 15318/89, judgment of 23 March 1995, Series A No. 310.

[87] *Mamatkulov and Askarov v. Turkey (Merits and Just Satisfaction)* [GC], Application Nos. 46827/99 and 46951/99, judgment of 04 February 2005, ECHR 2005-I.

the ECtHR referred to the living instrument approach in the context of interpreting procedural provisions.[88] In the former, the Court held that the living instrument approach "is not confined to the substantive provisions of the Convention, but also applies to those provisions, such as [former] Articles 25 and 46 (art. 25, art. 46), which govern the operation of the Convention's enforcement machinery."[89] In *Mamatkulov and Askarov v. Turkey*, the question at hand was whether the ECtHR could render binding interim measures by which contracting State parties had to abide. In the judgment, the Court confirmed the binding status of interim measures and relied, inter alia, on the fact that the Convention "is a living instrument which must be interpreted in the light of present-day conditions".[90]

Similar to the European Court of Human Rights, the Inter-American Commission on Human Rights indicated that it was possible to apply the living instrument approach to procedural provisions.[91] The Inter-American Court of Human Rights is also said to have altered its advisory function by "heavily relying on evolutionary interpretation" to the effect that the Court asserted that it had the right not only to interpret the treaties explicitly mentioned in the Inter-American Convention on Human Rights, but also non-binding legal documents which are not referred to in its founding instrument.[92]

With a view to the CERD Committee, according to legal literature, one of its findings in relation to the requirement of the exhaustion of domestic remedies under the inter-State mechanism "could be considered an evolutive interpretation".[93] Furthermore, in one of its admissibility decisions concerning the inter-

---

[88] *Moeckli/White*, Treaties as 'Living Instruments', in: Bowman/Kritsiotis (eds.), Conceptual and Contextual Perspectives on the Modern Law of Treaties, 2018, p. 147.

[89] *Loizidou v. Turkey* (Preliminary Objections), No. 15318/89, Judgment of 23 March 1995, para. 71, Series A No. 310.

[90] *Mamatkulov and Askarov v. Turkey (Merits and Just Satisfaction)* [GC], Application Nos. 46827/99 and 46951/99, judgment of 04 February 2005, para. 121, ECHR 2005-I; however, it has been critically noted that reliance on the "living-instrument" approach was not to achieve a certain interpretative result, but to leave behind contradicting precedents, which the Court did not want to uphold any longer, *Wyatt*, Intertemporal Linguistics in International Law: Beyond Contemporaneous and Evolutionary Treaty Interpretation, 2020, pp. 78–79. But even if one assumes that the judgment only uses the narrative of the "living-instrument" approach without actually applying the doctrine, it cannot be denied that there are at least considerations of effectiveness that led the Court to leave behind its previous jurisprudence; in that regard, see also *Mowbray*, A New Strasbourg Approach to the Legal Consequences of Interim Measures, Human Rights Law Review 5 (2005), 377, 386, who reaches the critical conclusion that "a very desirable procedural reform has been achieved by judicial creativity that extends beyond the permissible limits of Convention interpretation."

[91] *Moeckli/White*, Treaties as 'Living Instruments', in: Bowman/Kritsiotis (eds.), Conceptual and Contextual Perspectives on the Modern Law of Treaties, 2018, p. 152.

[92] *Gaggioli*, The Strength of Evolutionary Interpretation in International Human Rights Law, in: Abi-Saab et al. (eds.), Evolutionary Interpretation and International Law, 2019, pp. 104–105.

[93] *Keane*, Mapping the International Convention on the Elimination of All Forms of Racial Discrimination as a Living Instrument, Human Rights Law Review 20 (2020), 236,

State complaint *Palestine v. Israel*, the Committee reasoned that the mechanism under articles 11 to 13 CERD must be approached in an effective manner to the end that the procedure "should be practical, constructive and effective."[94] The Committee held further that it "considers that a formalistic approach cannot be adopted in this regard."[95] While this might demonstrate that the CERD Committee considers an effectiveness-orientated interpretation in particular suited to its own instrument, it must be equally taken into account that the Committee specifically referred to the inter-State mechanism's "special nature". Therefore, it could just as well be that it only interprets the provisions governing the inter-State complaints procedure in a dynamic manner, with the result that no general statements can be inferred from this with respect to other procedures before the Committee.[96]

To distinguish between the various provisions or procedures in question would allow for more flexibility, but could likewise lead to even more insecurities inherent in the interpretative process. There could be exceptions to the classifications made, for instance.[97] Additionally, any classification undertaken beforehand might prove to be extremely complex.[98] That is why the idea to allow possible exceptions within an individual human rights treaty, or the exclusion of a complete treaty, e.g. a UN human rights treaty, from the application of certain methods of interpretation should be rejected.[99] Nevertheless, if the extension of

---

265, he thereby refers to the CERD Committee's finding, relating to article 11(3) CERD, that "exhaustion of domestic remedies is not a requirement where a 'generalised policy and practice' has been authorised."

[94] CERD Committee, *State of Palestine v. Israel*, Decision on the jurisdiction of the Committee under article 11(2) CERD, UN Doc. CERD/C/100/5, 30.04.2021, para. 3.41.

[95] CERD Committee, *State of Palestine v. Israel*, Decision on the jurisdiction of the Committee under article 11(2) CERD, UN Doc. CERD/C/100/5, 30.04.2021, para. 3.41.

[96] For a detailed analysis of the approaches taken by the UN human rights treaty bodies with regard to the extension of powers, see *infra* Part III A.IV. 1.–6.

[97] *Djeffal*, Static and Evolutive Treaty Interpretation: A Functional Reconstruction, 2016, p. 176.

[98] *Djeffal*, Static and Evolutive Treaty Interpretation: A Functional Reconstruction, 2016, p. 176, who mentions a possible differentiation between procedural and substantive human rights treaty provisions, but questions at the same time whether exceptions should be made, e.g., in relation to territorial jurisdiction clauses.

[99] See for instance *Banković and others v. Belgium and others (Admissibility)* [GC], Application no. 52207/99, Decision of 12 December 2001, para. 65, ECHR 2001-XII, where the ECtHR held that article 1 ECHR was not approachable by the "living-instrument" doctrine; critical in legal literature, however, *Bjorge*, The Convention as a Living Instrument: Rooted in the Past, Looking to the Future, Human Rights Law Journal 36 (2016), 243, 252–253, who notes, first, that even jurisdictional clauses do not require "special doctrines of interpretation" and who concludes, second, that the very concept of jurisdiction under article 1 ECHR has not evolved as much as other Convention provisions; see also *Bjorge*, The Evolutionary Interpretation of Treaties, 2014, pp. 136–137, with further arguments against the ECtHR's reasoning concerning article 1 ECHR and its non-evolutionary interpretation; see also *Jardón*, The Interpretation of Jurisdictional Clauses in Human Rights Treaties, Anuario Mexi-

substantive treaty provisions requires the definition of limits,[100] the same holds true for expansion of powers, particularly in the case of human rights treaty bodies, as they exhibit by their very nature a weaker mandate when compared to international organizations or judicial bodies in the traditional sense.

3. Implied Powers

To shed light on possible limitations of an effectiveness-orientated interpretation, one might also approach the question via the doctrine of implied powers. It has been suggested that the doctrine of implied powers, originally developed in the context of international organizations, might be equally applicable to treaty bodies.[101] Specifically related to the Committee against Torture, it has been proposed that the Committee may derive "an infinite number of powers" from the objectives of the Convention, as long as the powers in question are considered necessary in the effective fulfilment of its tasks, and as long as these do not contradict the Convention or international law in general.[102] As will be demonstrated further below, many other commentators do mention the doctrine of implied powers for the justification of further powers to be exercised by treaty bodies. Yet, it is only rarely explained why human rights treaty bodies are deemed to possess implied powers, let alone is the legal process itself addressed, by which the powers in question are constructed.

In terms of interpretative techniques, implied powers are the result of an effectiveness-orientated interpretation,[103] with a particular emphasis on the ob-

---

cano de Derecho Internacional 8 (2013), 99, 142–143, who argues with a view to jurisdictional clauses that the same methods of interpretation apply as in the case of substantive provisions.

[100] See for instance *Gaggioli*, The Strength of Evolutionary Interpretation in International Human Rights Law, in: Abi-Saab et al. (eds.), Evolutionary Interpretation and International Law, 2019, pp. 111–114.

[101] *Ulfstein* in particular has repeatedly argued for the application of implied powers to treaty bodies, *Ulfstein*, Treaty Bodies and Regimes, in: Hollis (ed.), The Oxford Guide to Treaties, Second Edition, 2020, p. 425; *Ulfstein*, Law-making by human rights treaty bodies, in: Liivoja/Petman (eds.), International Law-making, Klabbers, 2014, pp. 252, 254, 256; *Ulfstein*, The Human Rights Treaty Bodies and Legitimacy Challenges, in: Grossman et al. (eds.), Legitimacy and International Courts, 2018, p. 298; see also *Engström*, Understanding Powers of International Organizations: A Study of the Doctrines of Attributed Powers, Implied Powers and Constitutionalism – with a Special Focus on the Human Rights Committee, Åbo 2009, p. 214, who notes that even though the doctrine was developed in the realm of international organization, "there is no a priori obstacle to relying on the doctrine" in relation to other institutions; alluding to the implied powers doctrine in connection with the CESCR Committee, *Odello/Seatzu*, The UN Committee on Economic, Social and Cultural Rights: The Law, Process and Practice, 2013, p. 131.

[102] *Ingelse*, The UN Committee against Torture: An Assessment, 2001, p. 92; it is submitted here that such an approach may equally be applicable to all other human rights treaty bodies.

[103] *Dörr*, Article 31, General rule of interpretation, in: Dörr/Schmalenbach (eds.), Vienna Convention on the Law of Treaties: A Commentary, Second Edition, 2018, para. 56; *Bröl-

74 Part III: Delineating the mandate of treaty bodies

ject and purpose of the treaty concerned; hence an interpretation which seeks to guarantee the provisions being interpreted to their "fullest effect".[104] With regard to their legal consequences, both the approaches portrayed above and the implied powers doctrine thereby allow for the broadening of provisions, whereby the latter is more likely to be associated with the powers of an organization or a court.[105]

a) Origin and legal effects of the doctrine

Three advisory opinions of the ICJ are said to "constitute the core of the evolution of implied powers doctrine in international law",[106] of which the *Reparation for Injuries Advisory Opinion* is commonly referred to as the very origin of the

---

mann, Specialized Rules of Treaty Interpretation: International Organizations, in: Hollis (ed.), The Oxford Guide to Treaties, Second Edition, 2020, pp. 529–531; *Engström*, Constructing the Powers of International Institutions, 2012, p. 41, referring to a "dynamic approach to interpretation"; *Orakhelashvili*, The Interpretation of Acts and Rules in Public International Law, 2008, p. 431; *Alvarez*, Constitutional Interpretation, in: Coicaud/Heiskanen (eds.), The legitimacy of international organizations, 2001, p. 121; see also *Moeckli/ White*, Treaties as 'Living Instruments', in: Bowman/Kritsiotis (eds.), Conceptual and Contextual Perspectives on the Modern Law of Treaties, 2018, pp. 138–143, who consider the United Nations Charter as the "paradigmatic" example of an living instrument.

[104] *Klabbers*, An Introduction to International Institutional Law, Second Edition, 2009, p. 59.

[105] Sometimes legal commentators also invoke the notion of "inherent powers" when describing the mandate of treaty bodies, see for instance *Pappa*, Das Individualbeschwerdeverfahren des Fakultativprotokolls zum Internationalen Pakt über bürgerliche und politische Rechte, 1996, pp. 33–35; the concept of inherent powers is normally invoked to explain those powers of international tribunals and courts which are not expressly provided for in their treaties and constituent instruments, see *Orakhelashvili*, The Interpretation of Acts and Rules in Public International Law, 2008, p. 435. Even though inherent powers and implied powers serve "alternative explanations" for the establishment and deduction of powers, their respective legal effects come close to each other. Some commentators consider inherent and implied powers even jointly, *Wolf*, Aktivlegitimation im UN-Individualbeschwerdeverfahren, 2018, p. 87. The doctrine of implied powers is furthermore considered as one of the various possible sources for inherent powers. For possible sources of inherent powers, see *Brown*, Inherent Powers in International Adjudication, in: Romano et al. (eds.), The Oxford Handbook of International Adjudication, 2013, pp. 838–842; due to the special *sui generis* character of human rights treaty bodies and the fact that inherent powers normally pertain to international courts, which treaty bodies obviously are not, the doctrine will be treated as equivalent to the implied powers doctrine.

[106] *Engström*, Understanding Powers of International Organizations: A Study of the Doctrines of Attributed Powers, Implied Powers and Constitutionalism – with a Special Focus on the Human Rights Committee, Åbo 2009, p. 55, the three advisory opinions are: *Reparation for Injuries Suffered in the Service of the United Nations*, Advisory Opinion of 11 April 1949, I.C.J. Reports 1949, p. 174; *Effect of Awards of Compensation Made by the United Nations Administrative Tribunal*, Advisory Opinion of 13 July 1954, I.C.J. Reports 1954, p. 47; *Certain Expenses of the United Nations (Article 17, paragraph 2, of the Charter)*, Advisory Opinion of 20 July 1962, I.C.J. Reports 1962, p. 151.

doctrine in modern international law.[107] The Court famously held: "Under international law, the Organisation must be deemed to have those powers which, though not expressly provided in the Charter, are conferred upon it by necessary implication as being essential to the performance of its duties."[108] Nevertheless, any application of the implied powers doctrine to treaty bodies requires caution. The doctrine finds its origins in the law of international organizations and might therefore prove itself incompatible with treaty bodies, being a different international actor and deliberately set up with fewer competencies.[109]

The first reason to invoke the doctrine of implied powers in the context of international institutional law is that it is impossible to spell out in full detail each "specific power an international organization will need to perform its functions."[110] The second reason for international organizations to possess implied powers is that it is equally impossible to "foresee in sufficient detail what specific powers are necessary to perform their functions effectively in an uncertain future."[111] Without possible recourse to implied powers, international organizations would lack the "necessary flexibility" in discharging their given mandate in ever changing circumstances.[112] Implied powers hence provide an "adaptation mechanism" to ensure that the treaty in question retains its effectiveness.[113] In light of the manifold functions and purposes conferred upon international or-

---

[107] *Schermers/Blokker*, International Institutional Law: Unity within Diversity, Sixth Revised Edition, 2018, p. 196, para 233; *Alvarez*, Constitutional Interpretation, in: Coicaud/Heiskanen (eds.), The legitimacy of international organizations, 2001, p. 122; *Gautier*, The Reparation for Injuries Case Revisited: The Personality of the European Union, Max Planck Yearbook of United Nations Law 4 (2000), 331, 332 and 340; *Campbell*, The Limits of the Powers of International Organisations, International Comparative Law Quarterly 32 (1983), 523.

[108] *Reparation for Injuries Suffered in the Service of the United Nations*, Advisory Opinion of 11 April 1949, I.C.J. Reports 1949, p. 174, 182.

[109] *Ulfstein*, Treaty Bodies and Regimes, in: Hollis (ed.), The Oxford Guide to Treaties, Second Edition, 2020, p. 430; *Leckie*, The Committee on Economic, Social and Cultural Rights: Catalyst for change in a system needing reform, in: Alston/Crawford (eds.), The Future of UN Human Rights Treaty Monitoring, 2000, p. 129, speaking of "restricted powers" with regard to the CESCR Committee; *Evatt*, The Future of the Human Rights Treaty System: Forging Recommendations, in: Bayefsky (ed.), The UN Human Rights Treaty System in the 21st Century, 2000, p. 296, who refers to the "limited mandates" of human rights treaty bodies, which results in less possibilities for change without the consent of State parties.

[110] *Blokker*, International Organizations or Institutions, Implied Powers, in: Peters (ed.), Max Planck Encyclopedia of Public International Law, Online version, April 2009, para. 5.

[111] *Blokker*, International Organizations or Institutions, Implied Powers, in: Peters (ed.), Max Planck Encyclopedia of Public International Law, Online version, April 2009, para. 6.

[112] *Blokker*, International Organizations or Institutions, Implied Powers, in: Peters (ed.), Max Planck Encyclopedia of Public International Law, Online version, April 2009 para. 6; *Crawford*, Brownlie's Principles of Public International Law, Ninth Edition, 2019, p. 177.

[113] *Buga*, Modification of Treaties by Subsequent Practice, 2018, p. 105.

ganizations, it then seems at least problematic to transfer the doctrine to treaty bodies without any hesitation.[114]

It is further crucial to highlight that the doctrine in its own rights does not come uncontested with a view to its traditional subject of application. Principally, a distinction is drawn between a broad and a narrow construction of implied powers.[115] A broad approach, as formulated by the ICJ in its famous passage handed down in the *Reparation for Injuries Advisory Opinion*, relies upon the test of whether the power in question is necessary for the organization to perform its duties.[116] In contrast, a narrow approach, as formulated by the then dissenting Judge Hackworth, presupposes that "[powers] not expressed cannot freely be implied. Implied powers flow from a grant of express powers, and are limited to those that are 'necessary' to the exercise of powers expressly granted."[117] Put differently, a narrow approach requires at least a textual basis in the respective constituent instrument, which serves as the basis for the interpretative act ultimately arriving at implying the power in question.[118] A broader approach may instead rely on the very duties or functions conferred upon the organization, which consequently opens up wide-ranging possibilities for the extension of powers.[119]

Reliance on a broad approach thus bears the risk, or to put it the other way, brings with it the potential of enlarging an organization's powers almost infinitely, the only requirement being here that the powers "can be hooked up to the purpose of the organization".[120] At the same time, the question of what is "nec-

---

[114] *Ulfstein*, Treaty Bodies and Regimes, in: Hollis (ed.), The Oxford Guide to Treaties, Second Edition, 2020, p. 419, who holds that the limited functions of treaty bodies argue against a wide set of implied powers.

[115] *White*, The law of international organisations, Third Edition, 2017, p. 125; *Blokker*, International Organizations or Institutions, Implied Powers, in: Peters (ed.), Max Planck Encyclopedia of Public International Law, Online version, April 2009, para. 10; cf. *Klabbers*, An Introduction to International Institutional Law, Second Edition, 2009, pp. 59–64.

[116] *Klabbers*, An Introduction to International Institutional Law, Second Edition, 2009, pp. 61–62.

[117] *Reparation for Injuries Suffered in the Service of the United Nations*, Advisory Opinion of 11 April 1949, I.C.J. Reports 1949, p. 174, dissenting opinion by Judge Hackworth, p. 198, cited by *Klabbers*, An Introduction to International Institutional Law, Second Edition, 2009, p. 60.

[118] *Dörr*, Article 31, General rule of interpretation, in: Dörr/Schmalenbach (eds.), Vienna Convention on the Law of Treaties: A Commentary, Second Edition, 2018, para. 57, who notes that "[the] consideration of object and purpose finds its limits in the ordinary meaning of the text of the treaty."

[119] For instance, in *Certain Expenses of the United Nations (Article 17, paragraph 2, of the Charter)*, Advisory Opinion of 20 July 1962, I.C.J. Reports 1962, p. 151, the ICJ held that "when the Organization takes action which warrants the assertion that it was appropriate for the fulfilment of one of the stated purposes of the United Nations, the presumption is that such action is not ultra vires the Organization."; see also *Klabbers*, An Introduction to International Institutional Law, Second Edition, 2009, p. 62.

[120] *Klabbers*, An Introduction to International Institutional Law, Second Edition, 2009,

essary" or "essential" for an international actor in performing its tasks and duties embodies uncertainties with a view to the precise meaning of this "highly flexible" formulation and concept.[121] Unless there is a judicial body entrusted with determining what powers are necessary or essential, positions between the organization (or treaty body) and those of members States are likely to differ.[122]

b) Implications for the determination of treaty bodies' powers

Despite the fact that the human rights treaty bodies ultimately serve the promotion and advancement of human rights standard, a broad concept of implied powers should not be easily transferred to them. Such an approach would inevitably result in a carte blanche when adding new powers.[123] Any creation of new powers and competencies whatsoever might be justified by highlighting their positive impact on the promotion and advancement of human rights standards, ultimately beneficial to individuals. If applicable at all, implied powers enjoyed by treaty bodies should thus only be construed in the narrow sense, which denotes that any additional power should find its roots in the wording of a treaty body's constituent instrument. What is more, the necessity of the contentious power has to be understood in a restrictive manner.[124] This signifies that new

---

p. 62; see also *Klabbers*, Formal Intergovernmental Organizations, in: Katz Cogan/Hurd/Johnstone (eds.), The Oxford Handbook of International Organizations, 2016, p. 148, who provides the absurd as well as apt example that the United Nations can host the Miss Universe contest, as this could possibly contribute to the maintenance of international peace and security as well as to the development of friendly relations between states; *Blokker*, International Organizations or Institutions, Implied Powers, in: Peters (ed.), Max Planck Encyclopedia of Public International Law, Online version, April 2009, para. 9.

[121] *Schermers/Blokker*, International Institutional Law: Unity within Diversity, Sixth Revised Edition, 2018, p. 195, para. 233; see also *Engström*, Understanding Powers of International Organizations: A Study of the Doctrines of Attributed Powers, Implied Powers and Constitutionalism – with a Special Focus on the Human Rights Committee, Åbo 2009, p. 232; *Klabbers*, An Introduction to International Institutional Law, Second Edition, 2009, p. 61, who also observes that different actors or stakeholders are likely to achieve different results in the determination of what is considered "necessary", which consequently adds another layer of uncertainty to the application of the doctrine; *Skubiszewski*, Implied Powers of International Organizations, in: Dinstein (ed.), International Law at a Time of Perplexity: Essays in Honour of Shabtai Rosenne, 1989, p. 861.

[122] *Schermers/Blokker*, International Institutional Law, Unity within Diversity, Sixth Revised Edition, 2018, p. 195, para. 233.

[123] Cf. *Alvarez*, Constitutional Interpretation, in: Coicaud/Heiskanen (eds.), The legitimacy of international organizations, 2001, p. 122, who notes that when implied powers are construed broadly, "constitutional limitations" become an "important safeguard".

[124] For such a restrictive approach to the topic of implied powers, see *Legality of the Use by a State of Nuclear Weapons in Armed Conflict*, Advisory Opinion, I.C.J. Reports 1996, p. 66, 79; *Dörr*, Article 31, General rule of interpretation, in: Dörr/Schmalenbach (eds.), Vienna Convention on the Law of Treaties: A Commentary, Second Edition, 2018, para. 56, reaching the conclusion that the doctrine might have "lost quite a bit of its appeal".

powers can only be "added" when these are considered indispensable for the proper performance of functions and duties already assigned to treaty bodies by virtue of their constituent instrument. This implies in addition that the focus should not rest on the general purpose of the treaty in question, but rather on the object and purpose of the respective procedure, such as the object and purpose of the articles governing the State reporting procedure.

Said specific determinant in the delineation of powers can simultaneously accommodate the requirement of treaty bodies not to extensively and unduly impose new obligations on contracting parties and may help to avoid a "competence creep".[125] Lastly, as outlined by *Ulfstein*, a distinction should be drawn between the use of implied powers with regard to internal affairs, and the use of implied powers that affects the relationship with State parties.[126] Given that numerous voices during the strengthening process have criticized and attacked treaty bodies for allegedly reaching beyond their mandates by imposing new obligations on contracting parties, a rather cautious approach seems appropriate and should therefore serve the treaty bodies' own interest.

Ultimately, as it has been written concerning the interpretation of treaties establishing an international organization, "the law of treaties *is* the primary legal tool for interpretation."[127] This holds even more true for the interpretation of procedural provisions that establish human rights treaty bodies. Their *sui generis* status does not allow for total reliance on doctrines developed in the realm of international organizations or international courts and tribunals. Additionally, the "borderline"[128] nature of treaty bodies and the respective possible doctrinal approaches to determine their competencies must not lead to cherry-picking in terms of what approach fits best when scopes of powers are ambiguous. This could easily undermine their legitimacy and would provide an eclectic rather than precise framework in the determination of powers.

The easier any interpretation can be reconciled with the very wording of the treaty, the more acceptable extensions of competencies are, which is henceforth in conformity with the observation that even effectiveness-orientated interpretations find their outer limit in the wording of the treaty.[129] At the same time, sole

---

[125] Cf. *Engström*, Constructing the Powers of International Institutions, 2012, pp. 56–59: see also *Schermers/Blokker*, International Institutional Law, Unity within Diversity, Sixth Revised Edition, 2018, p. 199, para. 233A, who state that implied powers "may not change the distribution of functions within an organization."

[126] Drawing a similar distinction with a view to International Organizations, *Skubiszewski*, Implied Powers of International Organizations, in: Dinstein (ed.), International Law at a Time of Perplexity: Essays in Honour of Shabtai Rosenne, 1989, p. 859.

[127] *Brölmann*, Specialized Rules of Treaty Interpretation: International Organizations, in: Hollis (ed.), The Oxford Guide to Treaties, Second Edition, 2020, p. 541.

[128] *Engström*, Understanding Powers of International Organizations: A Study of the Doctrines of Attributed Powers, Implied Powers and Constitutionalism – with a Special Focus on the Human Rights Committee, Åbo 2009, p. 8.

[129] *Buga*, Modification of Treaties by Subsequent Practice, 2018, p. 106.

reliance on effectiveness should be avoided. Provided that a textual basis is weak or even non-existent, new powers should be only added if they are considered necessary in the sense that the treaty body could only insufficiently or no longer perform one of its main tasks without their introduction. Last, what also hinges on the former, another determinant is whether the external relationship between the treaty body and the State parties is affected,[130] which allows treaty bodies more latitude regarding internal affairs.

IV. Confirmation of the hypothesis established

In the following section, expansions of powers and competencies undertaken by human rights treaty bodies themselves will be subjected to closer scrutiny. With a view to the validation of the criteria established above, it will be analysed whether, to what extent, and how, the treaty bodies have extended their powers. The section is intended to shed light on discussions among Committees and arguments advanced, if available and relevant, and also seeks to take into account legal writings on the question as to whether the respective extensions of powers were covered by the mandates of treaty bodies.

1. Adoption of concluding observations

The current State reporting procedure, with the adoption of concluding observations and the subsequent demand for follow-up reports, now common practice among almost all treaty bodies,[131] is the result of lengthy discussions and the outcome of an "evolutionary process" in its own.[132] During the 1980s, the State reporting procedure was confined to the mere consideration of reports submitted in the form of the constructive dialogue, and no comments on State parties' activities in implementing treaty guarantees were made. Yet, in light of the grave breaches of human rights committed by several State parties, such as Chile for instance, it soon became questionable whether a completely non-confrontational approach was appropriate under the reporting procedure.[133]

---

[130] Cf. with regard to international organizations, *White*, The law of international organisations, Third Edition, 2017, p. 125, who points out that discussions on the extent of powers relate to the question of dependence on and independence from contracting parties.

[131] Currently, the CRC Committee is the only treaty body that has not yet adopted a formalized follow-up procedure, for the follow-up procedure in more detail, see *infra* Part IV F.II.1.

[132] *Kälin*, Examination of state reports, in: Keller/Ulfstein (eds.), UN Human Rights Treaty Bodies: Law and Legitimacy, 2012, p. 20.

[133] *Kretzmer*, The UN Human Rights Committee and International Human Rights Monitoring, Straus Institute Working Paper No. 12, 2010, pp. 25–27 with a general overview, and who also notes that the Chilean case "was somewhat of a watershed in the development of the Committee's working methods under article 40."

a) Discussions within the Human Rights Committee

Particularly within the Human Rights Committee, disagreement on how to discharge the mandate under article 40(4) ICCPR prevailed among Committee members. The question arose as to whether the Committee could adopt individually tailored concluding observations vis-à-vis the State party under review.[134] The discussion essentially revolved around the issue of how to interpret the terms "its reports" and "general comments"[135] under article 40(4) ICCPR. Two main positions developed alongside ideological borders between members from socialist and western State parties.[136]

Committee members from the Eastern Bloc held that the Committee did not possess the competence to formulate precise observations on a single State party's human rights record. They argued that the term "its reports" could only refer to the Committees' annual reports to the General Assembly under article 45 ICCPR, since any other meaning of reports under article 40(4) ICCPR would have been clarified by the Covenant.[137] Furthermore, article 40(4) ICCPR only mentioned "State parties" and not "State parties concerned", which would consequently restrict the Committee's power to direct comments only to the State parties in their entirety.[138] Another argument was drawn from the comparison between the reporting procedure under article 40 ICCPR and the inter-State procedure under article 41 ICCPR. It was stressed that the reporting procedure was neither "a control procedure" nor would it allow monitoring of the implementation of Covenant rights in a specific country. Any such activity would hence amount to impermissible interference with the internal affairs of the State party concerned.[139] Ultimately, opposing Committee members held that any evaluation or assessment of State parties "would go far beyond the wording of

---

[134] For a general overview, see *Nowak*, CCPR Commentary, Second revised Edition, 2005, Article 40, State Reports, paras. 48–60.

[135] *Tomuschat*, Human Rights: Between Idealism and Realism, Third Edition, 2014, p. 225; *McGoldrick*, The Human Rights Committee: Its Role in the Development of the International Covenant on Civil and Political Rights, 1991, p. 89; *Fischer*, Reporting under the Covenant on Civil and Political Rights: The First Five Years of the Human Rights Committee, American Journal of International Law 76 (1982), 142, 147.

[136] *McGoldrick*, The Human Rights Committee: Its Role in the Development of the International Covenant on Civil and Political Rights, 1991, pp. 89–91, who refers to the opposing positions as two "schools of thought".

[137] Report of the Human Rights Committee (8th, 9th and 10th session), UN Doc. A/35/40 (1980), para. 380.

[138] *Nowak*, CCPR Commentary, Second revised Edition, 2005, Article 40, State Reports, para. 49.

[139] Report of the Human Rights Committee (8th, 9th and 10th session), UN Doc. A/35/40 (1980), para. 381.

the Covenant".[140] They thereby mainly relied on a text-based interpretation of the Covenant and considered the mandate of the Committee to be limited.[141]

On the other side, proponents of a broader understanding of article 40(4) ICCPR argued that the reporting procedure was not completed until an individual assessment, in the form of a separate report addressing the Covenant's specific implementation, was conducted.[142] Decisive in their line of argumentation was the reading of article 40 ICCPR "in the context of the very objects of the Covenant as a whole instead of in the context of the terminological differences within particular provisions of the Covenant."[143] Given that the objectives of the Covenant were to "promote and ensure the observance" of its rights and guarantees, the Committee had to be able to come to some sort of conclusions after having studied the respective report.[144] Country-specific reports would remain of an advisory nature and would not transform the character of the reporting procedure into adversary or "inquisitory proceedings".[145] It was further stated that reports under article 45 ICCPR encompassed all of the Committee's activities and could include, as appendixes, the separate reports adopted vis-à-vis individual State parties.[146]

Even though proponents undertook a more effectiveness-orientated interpretation of the Covenant, they still solidly built their argumentation upon the wording of article 40(4) ICCPR. That the Human Rights Committee is able to adopt reports in relation to individual State parties was also widely shared in legal literature.[147] Ultimately, "grammatical, systematic and historical-teleological interpretations" lead to the Committee's competence to adopt specific conclusions on individual State parties.[148] Since the Committee tried to reach deci-

---

[140] Report of the Human Rights Committee (8th, 9th and 10th session), UN Doc. A/35/40 (1980), para. 380.
[141] *Boerefijn*, The Reporting Procedure under the Covenant on Civil and Political Rights: Practice and Procedures of the Human Rights Committee, 1999, pp. 197–198.
[142] *Nowak*, CCPR Commentary, Second revised Edition, 2005, Article 40, State Reports, para. 50.
[143] Report of the Human Rights Committee (8th, 9th and 10th session), UN Doc. A/35/40 (1980), para. 375.
[144] Report of the Human Rights Committee (8th, 9th and 10th session), UN Doc. A/35/40 (1980), para. 375.
[145] Report of the Human Rights Committee (8th, 9th and 10th session), UN Doc. A/35/40 (1980), para. 378.
[146] Report of the Human Rights Committee (8th, 9th and 10th session), UN Doc. A/35/40 (1980), para. 378.
[147] *Nowak*, CCPR Commentary, Second revised Edition, 2005, Article 40, State Reports, para. 50; *Dimitrijevic*, State Reports, in: Alfredsson et al. (eds.), International Human Rights Monitoring Mechanism, First Edition, 2001, p. 198; *Opsahl*, The General Comments of the Human Rights Committee, in: Jekewitz et al. (eds.), Des Menschen Rechts zwischen Freiheit und Verantwortung: Festschrift für Karl Joseph Partsch zum 75. Geburtstag, 1989, p. 286; *Jhabvala*, The Practice of the Covenant's Human Rights Committee, 1976–82: Review of State Party Reports, Human Rights Quarterly 6 (1984), 81, 93–94.
[148] *Nowak*, CCPR Commentary, Second revised Edition, 2005, Article 40, State Reports,

sions only by consensus, and taking into consideration the described controversy, it is not surprising that not much of a real improvement was achieved until the end of the Cold War.[149]

b) Discussions within the early CEDAW Committee

Comparable to the controversy among Human Rights Committee members, CEDAW Committee members were also divided on the Committee's mandate under the reporting procedure.

To clarify the powers under article 21 CEDAW, two working groups were established.[150] In reaction to a proposal made by the first working group, Committee members discussed whether it was possible to adopt a "paragraph of general appraisal" at the end of the reporting procedure.[151] The difference between a "general paragraph of appraisal" and concluding observations notwithstanding, Committee members were even divided on this issue.[152] Some members held that the adoption of such a general paragraph violated the Committee's mandate, arguing that the respective provisions only allowed for suggestions and general recommendations after the examination of State reports. Accordingly, they relied on a rigid text-based interpretation.[153] Despite their critique, the Committee eventually took the decision to adopt a "general comment" on each State party, though only when deemed appropriate.[154]

---

paras. 51–55 with a detailed analysis of the travaux préparatoires. He even goes so far to conclude that in the absence of any single report adopted under article 40(4) ICCPR, the Human Rights Committee never completed a reporting procedure satisfactorily up until the 1990s and thus violated its duties imposed by virtue of the Covenant, para. 56; see also *Monina*, Article 19, State Reporting Procedure, in: Nowak/Birk/Monina (eds.), The United Nations Convention Against Torture and its Optional Protocol: A Commentary, Second Edition, 2019, para. 61, who identifies systematic interpretation the decisive factor for the Committee's competence to adopt concluding observations vis-à-vis individual State parties.

[149] As a first step in 1984, "quasi-concluding personal statements" were adopted, and it was not until 1990 that the Human Rights Committee decided to adopt country-specific concluding observations, which have been explicitly referred to as concluding observations since 1997, *Nowak*, CCPR Commentary, Second revised Edition, 2005, Article 40, State Reports, paras. 56–58.

[150] Report of the Committee on the Elimination of Discrimination Against Women (6th session), UN Doc. A/42/38 (1987), paras. 26–30, one working group on ways and means of expediting the work of the Committee and the other working group on ways and means of implementing article 21 CEDAW

[151] *Boerefijn*, Article 21, in: Freeman/Chinkin/Rudolf (eds.) The UN Convention on the Elimination of All Forms of Discrimination Against Women: A Commentary, 2012, p. 522.

[152] *Boerefijn*, Article 21, in: Freeman/Chinkin/Rudolf (eds.) The UN Convention on the Elimination of All Forms of Discrimination Against Women: A Commentary, 2012, p. 522.

[153] Report of the Committee on the Elimination of Discrimination Against Women (6th session), UN Doc. A/42/38 (1987), para. 45.

[154] If no decision could be reached, the only comment included would be that the report had been submitted and considered by the Committee, Report of the Committee on the

The second working group considered the possibility of making suggestions and recommendations addressed to an individual State party, but did not find any definite solution in that regard. In line with arguments brought forward by proponents of a broad understanding of article 40(4) ICCPR, several Committee members approved the possibility of addressing targeted recommendations to State parties, but under the condition that the State party concerned was given the possibility to respond to them.[155]

What is more, proponents highlighted that "article 21 was a very efficient tool for monitoring the implementation of the Convention".[156] Said line of argumentation presumably alludes to an effectiveness-orientated interpretation of article 21 CEDAW. In the final analysis, the Committee took the decision to address recommendations to individual State parties in cases where deemed appropriate, which, however, was not reached by consensus.[157] Taken up again at the 10th session, where once again no ultimate decision could be reached, the Committee eventually decided in 1994 to follow other treaty bodies in the practice of adopting concise "concluding comments", which should reflect the most important aspects raised during the constructive dialogue.[158]

c) Other treaty bodies

Unlike other treaty bodies which commenced their activities before the end of the Cold War, the Committee against Torture is already vested, by virtue of its constituent instrument, with a more explicit basis for adopting concluding observations vis-à-vis individual State parties. Article 19(3) CAT stipulates that the Committee can make general comments on the report received, and can forward these to the State party concerned. In comparison to article 40(4) ICCPR, article 19(3) CAT only mentions a single report, which is subsequently directed to the State party concerned and not to all treaty members in their entirety.[159] Despite its more

---

Elimination of Discrimination Against Women (6th session), UN Doc. A/42/38 (1987), para. 44; *Boerefijn*, Article 21, in: Freeman/Chinkin/Rudolf (eds.) The UN Convention on the Elimination of All Forms of Discrimination Against Women: A Commentary, 2012, p. 522.

[155] Report of the Committee on the Elimination of Discrimination Against Women (6th session), UN Doc. A/42/38 (1987), para. 57.

[156] Report of the Committee on the Elimination of Discrimination Against Women (6th session), UN Doc. A/42/38 (1987), para. 58.

[157] Report of the Committee on the Elimination of Discrimination Against Women (6th session), UN Doc. A/42/38 (1987), para. 59; *Boerefijn*, Article 21, in: Freeman/Chinkin/Rudolf (eds.) The UN Convention on the Elimination of All Forms of Discrimination Against Women: A Commentary, 2012, p. 523.

[158] Report of the Committee on the Elimination of Discrimination Against Women (13th Session), UN Doc. A/49/38 (1994), paras. 812–817; *Boerefijn*, Article 21, in: Freeman/Chinkin/Rudolf (eds.) The UN Convention on the Elimination of All Forms of Discrimination Against Women: A Commentary, 2012, p. 523.

[159] *Monina*, Article 19, State Reporting Procedure, in: Nowak/Birk/Monina (eds.), The United Nations Convention Against Torture and its Optional Protocol: A Commentary,

express normative basis, the Committee discussed repeatedly how to exercise its mandate under article 19(3) CAT and which content to include in such comments.[160] The Committee against Torture hence proceeded as carefully as the Human Rights Committee, initially only publishing conclusions adopted by individual Committee members and adopting its first concluding observations in 1992.[161]

In case of the CESCR and the CERD Committee, it has been noted that both treaty bodies seized the opportunity of the changing political climate in the early 1990s and introduced concluding observations under their reporting procedures.[162] Comparable to the other treaty bodies, the CERD Committee published individual opinions of Committee members in its summary records prior to the introduction of concluding observations.[163] All other treaty bodies, which began to operate after the end of the Cold War, introduced the practice of adopting concluding observations directly from the beginning of their existence. Particularly the CRC Committee, which commenced its activities in 1991, seems to have been inspired by the developments within the Human Rights Committee.[164]

2. Adoption of General Comments

Mirroring the competence to adopt country-specific concluding observations, treaty bodies also developed the practice to issue General Comments. Their adoption is now considered the third main function of human rights treaty bodies.[165] As with concluding observations and adopted views, General Comments are not

---

Second Edition, 2019, para. 63; *Vandenhole*, The Procedures before the UN Human Rights Treaty Bodies: Divergence or Convergence?, 2004, p. 120.

[160] See *Ingelse*, The UN Committee against Torture: An Assessment, 2001, p. 147, with references to relevant summary records in footnote 95.

[161] *Vandenhole*, The Procedures before the UN Human Rights Treaty Bodies: Divergence or Convergence?, 2004, p. 120.

[162] *O'Flaherty*, The Concluding Observations of United Nations Human Rights Treaty Bodies, Human Rights Law Review 6 (2006), 27, 30.

[163] *Thornberry*, The International Convention on the Elimination of All Forms of Racial Discrimination: A Commentary, 2016, The Convention and the Committee, p. 47.

[164] CRC Committee, Report on the second session, UN Doc. CRC/C/10, 19.10.1992, paras. 41 and 42; Report of the Committee on the Protection of the Rights of All Migrant Workers and Members of Their Families, UN Doc. A/59/48 (2004), para. 7 and Annex IV with the Committee's provisional Rules of Procedure; Report of the Committee on the Rights of Persons with Disabilities on its third session, UN Doc. CRPD/C/3/2, 07.03.2011, para. 10; Report of the Committee on Enforced Disappearances (1st and 2nd session), UN Doc. A/67/56 (2012), para. 28.

[165] *Keller/Ulfstein*, Introduction, in: Keller/Ulfstein (eds.), UN Human Rights Treaty Bodies: Law and Legitimacy, 2012, p. 3.

legally binding as such,[166] but are accorded the status of "authoritative statements" or "authoritative interpretations" of the respective treaties.[167]

General Comments serve different objectives, but can above all be characterized as "detailed and comprehensive commentaries on specific treaty provisions or on the relationship between treaty provisions and specific themes"[168] and are directed to all State parties.[169] In a more nuanced fashion, General Comments first serve a "legal analytical function".[170] In this respect, they constitute a means for interpreting and clarifying treaty provisions.[171] The respective treaty body draws upon the experience made under the reporting or individual complaints procedure,[172] and thereby ultimately condenses its understanding of substantive treaty provisions.[173] However, not only substantive treaty provisions are dealt with by General Comments. On the contrary, General Comments were initially devoted to providing guidance to State parties in the fulfilment of their reporting obligations by, for instance, identifying questions to be answered.[174] What is

---

[166] *Keller/Grover*, General Comments of the Human Rights Committee and their legitimacy, in: Keller/Ulfstein (eds.), UN Human Rights Treaty Bodies: Law and Legitimacy, 2012, p. 129.

[167] *Reiners*, Transnational Lawmaking Coalitions for Human Rights, 2021, p. 33; *Keller/Grover*, General Comments of the Human Rights Committee and their legitimacy, in: Keller/Ulfstein (eds.), UN Human Rights Treaty Bodies: Law and Legitimacy, 2012, p. 132.

[168] *Oette*, The UN Human Rights Treaty Bodies: Impact and Future, in: Oberleitner (ed.), International Human Rights Institutions, Tribunals, and Courts, 2018, p. 103.

[169] *Seibert-Fohr*, The UN Human Rights Committee, in: Oberleitner (ed.), International Human Rights Institutions, Tribunals, and Courts, 2018, p. 127.

[170] *Seibert-Fohr*, The UN Human Rights Committee, in: Oberleitner (ed.), International Human Rights Institutions, Tribunals, and Courts, 2018, p. 127; *Keller/Grover*, General Comments of the Human Rights Committee and their legitimacy, in: Keller/Ulfstein (eds.), UN Human Rights Treaty Bodies: Law and Legitimacy, 2012, p. 124.

[171] *Rodley*, The Role and Impact of Treaty Bodies, in: Shelton (ed.), The Oxford Handbook of International Human Rights Law, 2013, p. 631, who considers General Comments as "close to a codification of evolving practice."; *Keller/Grover*, General Comments of the Human Rights Committee and their legitimacy, in: Keller/Ulfstein (eds.), UN Human Rights Treaty Bodies: Law and Legitimacy, 2012, p. 124.

[172] See *Tomuschat*, Human Rights: Between Idealism and Realism, Third Edition, 2014, p. 235, who observes that the Human Rights Committee first drew its experience only from the reporting procedure, but soon also took into consideration the views adopted under the individual complaints procedure.

[173] *Kälin/Künzli*, The Law of International Human Rights Protection, Second Edition, 2019, p. 213, who describe that the experiences of treaty bodies are "synthesized" in General Comments; *Neuman*, Giving Meaning and Effect to Human Rights, The Contribution of Human Rights Committee Members, in: Moeckli/Keller/Heri (eds.) The Human Rights Covenants at 50: Their Past, Present, and Future, 2018, p. 35, who states that General Comments "provide a synthesis or progressive codification of the HRC's interpretation of a particular substantive article of the ICCPR"; *Keller/Grover*, General Comments of the Human Rights Committee and their legitimacy, in: Keller/Ulfstein (eds.), UN Human Rights Treaty Bodies: Law and Legitimacy, 2012, p. 124.

[174] *Oette*, The UN Human Rights Treaty Bodies: Impact and Future, in: Oberleitner (ed.),

more, General Comments can serve a "policy recommendation function" in that treaty bodies share possible best practices with all State parties, or they inform about suitable strategies for preventing violations of rights.[175]

a) Committees with an explicit normative basis

Regarding the normative basis for the issuance of General Comments, provisions under the reporting procedure "can accommodate" this practice, at least as far as the Human Rights Committee is concerned.[176] The competence to adopt General Comments was the "most common denominator" during the early Committee's discussion on its mandate under article 40 ICCPR, and was supported by both members from socialist and western State parties.[177] The same finding applies to the CERD and CEDAW Committee. In both cases, the very wording of article 9(2) CERD and article 21(1) CEDAW respectively provides for the possibility to "make suggestions and general recommendations based on the examination of the reports and information received from the State Parties." The plural use of the terms "reports and recommendations" clearly indicates that these two Committees can issue recommendations addressed to all State parties.[178] Other similar provisions are article 45(d) CRC and article 39 CRPD, both of which enable their respective Committee to adopt General Comments.[179]

International Human Rights Institutions, Tribunals, and Courts, 2018, p. 103; *Seibert-Fohr*, The UN Human Rights Committee, in: Oberleitner (ed.), International Human Rights Institutions, Tribunals, and Courts, 2018, p. 127; see *Keller/Grover*, General Comments of the Human Rights Committee and their legitimacy, in: Keller/Ulfstein (eds.), UN Human Rights Treaty Bodies: Law and Legitimacy, 2012, p. 126, who detect a distinct "practice direction function" with a view to the interpretation of procedural provisions.

[175] *Keller/Grover*, General Comments of the Human Rights Committee and their legitimacy, in: Keller/Ulfstein (eds.), UN Human Rights Treaty Bodies: Law and Legitimacy, 2012, pp. 124–125.

[176] *Keller/Grover*, General Comments of the Human Rights Committee and their legitimacy, in: Keller/Ulfstein (eds.), UN Human Rights Treaty Bodies: Law and Legitimacy, 2012, p. 127.

[177] *Nowak*, CCPR Commentary, Second revised Edition, 2005, Article 40, State Reports, para. 63.

[178] *Tomuschat*, Human Rights: Between Idealism and Realism, Third Edition, 2014, p. 236; see also *Byrnes*, The Other Human Rights Treaty Body: The Work of the Committee on the Elimination of Discrimination against Women, Yale Journal of International Law 14 (1989), 1, 43, who argues that the term "suggestions" could possibly be understood to mean that the Committee can address them to individual States Parties, as they do not have to be general.

[179] *Treuthart*, Article 39, Report of the Committee, in: Bantekas/Stein/Anastasiou (eds.), The UN Convention on the Rights of Persons with Disabilities: A Commentary, 2018, p. 1124, with reference to *McGoldrick*, The United Nations Convention on the Rights of the Child, International Journal of Law and the Family 5 (1991), 132, 156, who identifies article 45(d) CRC as the legal basis for the adoption of State party-specific recommendations; affirming the CRC Committee's competence to adopt General Comments under article 45(d) CRC, *Kilkelly*, The CRC at 21: Assessing the Legal Impact, Northern Ireland Legal Quarterly 62 (2011), 143, 148.

b) CESCR Committee

The provisions under ICESCR are less clear in terms of vesting a supervisory body with the competence to issue General Comments. However, article 21 ICESCR obliges ECOSOC to submit "reports with recommendations of a general nature" to the General Assembly. Since the CESCR Committee replaced ECOSOC in its supervisory function under the reporting procedure, it can be taken to be entitled to issue such "recommendations of a general nature", a term which can cover the adoption of General Comments.[180] Furthermore, ECOSOC expressly invited the CESCR Committee to start the drafting of General Comments in 1987.[181]

c) Committee against Torture, the CMW and the CED Committee

The provisions of CAT, CMW and CED pose more interpretative challenges. Article 19(3) CAT empowers the Committee against Torture to "make such general comments on the report as it may consider appropriate and shall forward these to the State Party concerned." A text-based interpretation, focusing on the singular use of "report" and "State party concerned", arguably results in the Committee only being able to adopt country-specific comments.[182] Such a reading of the Convention might have prompted at least one State party to challenge the Committee against Torture's mandate in this domain,[183] which remains a very rare example of open critique, however.[184] On the other hand, article 19(3) CAT also refers to "general comments", from which it follows that treaty bodies have competence to make General Comments under other treaties.[185] A closer look at

---

[180] *Tomuschat*, Human Rights: Between Idealism and Realism, Third Edition, 2014, p. 235.
[181] ECOSOC, Resolution 1987/5, International Covenant on Economic, Social and Cultural Rights, UN Doc. E/RES/1987/5, 26.05.1987; *Tomuschat*, Human Rights: Between Idealism and Realism, Third Edition, 2014, p. 236.
[182] *Monina*, Article 19, State Reporting Procedure, in: Nowak/Birk/Monina (eds.), The United Nations Convention Against Torture and its Optional Protocol: A Commentary, Second Edition, 2019, para. 63; *Ingelse*, The UN Committee against Torture: An Assessment, 2001, p. 151; *Burgers/Danelius*, The United Nations Convention against Torture, 1988, p. 159, who argue that the wording of article 19(3) CAT can be taken to mean that the Committee cannot address comments to State parties in their entirety.
[183] In its written submission to General Comment No. 4, China noted that the Committee had not been authorized to do so, as article 19 CAT was the only legal basis for making any comments vis-à-vis State parties. The Committee should furthermore become aware of its mandate under the Convention and should "avoid liberal interpretation of Convention provisions" and should "avert imposing extra obligations on State parties", Written submissions by China in reaction to General Comment No. 4, https://www.ohchr.org/Documents/HRBodies/CAT/GCArticle3/China_en.pdf (last access: 21.08.2023).
[184] *Keller/Grover*, General Comments of the Human Rights Committee and their legitimacy, in: Keller/Ulfstein (eds.), UN Human Rights Treaty Bodies: Law and Legitimacy, 2012, p. 127, observing that no State party has ever raised formal objections to the Human Rights Committee's power to adopt General Comments.
[185] *Monina*, Article 19, State Reporting Procedure, in: Nowak/Birk/Monina (eds.), The

the *travaux préparatoires* also reveals that the drafters did not intend to bar the Committee against Torture from adopting General Comments.[186]

In the absence of any explicit and unequivocal basis for the Committee's power to pronounce general recommendations addressed to all State parties, scholars have pointed to the possible invocation of the implied powers doctrine.[187] Others proposed that it was "inherent" to the Committee against Torture to adopt General Comments in the performance of its supervisory mandate.[188]

However, another possible interpretation proposed here can lead to the same result of allowing the Committee against Torture to adopt General Comments. As previously mentioned, General Comments capture a treaty body's position in the interpretation of treaty provisions. These comments are developed in light of the experience gained under the reporting and individual complaints procedure. Since each State party is obliged to submit periodic reports, the Committee against Torture logically discharges its function under article 19(3) CAT in a multitude of cases. If the Committee then were to detect in each or in most State reports the same difficulty in implementation, each of these State parties would be equally concerned with regard to the widespread implementation obstacle. In such a case, General Comments would be derived from the sum of the individual reports submitted by State parties which encounter the same problem. Consequently, each State party would be the addressee of the General Comment that summarizes the treaty body's experience.

The same approach could be applied to the CMW Committee, which is vested by article 74(1) CMW, a similar provision to article 19(3) CAT, with the power to "transmit such comments as it may consider appropriate to the State party concerned." This finding might have led commentators to the conclusion that the CMW Committee enjoys an "implicit power" to draft and adopt General Comments.[189] One could, however, alternatively argue that the CMW Committee

---

United Nations Convention Against Torture and its Optional Protocol: A Commentary, Second Edition, 2019, paras. 63–64.

[186] *Ingelse*, The UN Committee against Torture: An Assessment, 2001, p. 152; see also *Monina*, Article 19, State Reporting Procedure, in: Nowak/Birk/Monina (eds.), The United Nations Convention Against Torture and its Optional Protocol: A Commentary, Second Edition, 2019, para. 62, who even considers the possibility that the *travaux préparatoires* provide evidence that the Committee against Torture can only adopt General Comments under article 19(3) CAT and not country-specific concluding observations.

[187] *Keller/Grover*, General Comments of the Human Rights Committee and their legitimacy, in: Keller/Ulfstein (eds.), UN Human Rights Treaty Bodies: Law and Legitimacy, 2012, pp. 127–128, who refer to ICJ's advisory opinion in Reparations for Injuries, but who nevertheless write of an "inherent" competence to issue General Comments; *Byrnes*, The Committee against Torture, in: Alston (ed.), The United Nations and Human Rights: A Critical Appraisal, First Edition, 1992, p. 530.

[188] *Ingelse*, The UN Committee against Torture: An Assessment, 2001, p. 151.

[189] See *Chetail*, The Committee on the Protection of the Rights of All Migrant Workers and Members of Their Families, in: Mégret/Alston (eds.), The United Nations and Human Rights: A Critical Appraisal, Second Edition, 2020, p. 620.

derives its competence in this domain from article 74(7) CMW. Said provision obliges the CMW Committee to submit its annual reports to the General Assembly and to include therein the "considerations and recommendations, based, in particular, on the examination of the reports and any observations presented by State parties." The plural use of "considerations and recommendations" is at least indicative of the power to address General Comments to the entirety of State parties.

Article 29(3) CED vests the CED Committee with the power to issue "such comments, observations or recommendations as it may deem appropriate", which could be considered the Committee's legal basis for the adoption of General Comments. Yet, the provision clarifies that the Committee shall communicate these comments, observations or recommendations to the State party concerned.[190] In case of the CED, even the reporting duty to the General Assembly under article 36(2) CED stipulates that the Committee shall inform the State party concerned before "an observation on a State party is published in the annual report", thus leaving less room for a textual interpretation. In practice, the CMW Committee has issued four General Comments so far, while the CED Committee is the only treaty body that has not yet adopted a single General Comment.

3. Follow-up under the reporting procedure

Possibly one of the greatest institutional and procedural weaknesses of human rights treaty bodies is their limited mandate in the enforcement of concluding observations and views adopted under the complaints procedure.[191] In order to supervise and monitor more closely the implementation of recommendations, eight out of nine UN human rights treaty bodies have developed a written and formalized follow-up procedure to concluding observations.[192]

Underlying rationales for follow-up procedures to concluding observations are that they enable treaty bodies and State parties under review to keep up the

---

[190] For the Committee's own understanding, see article 51(1) RoP, which determines that the Committee can adopt concluding observations vis-à-vis the State party under review in accordance with article 29(3) CED, CED Committee, Rules of Procedure, UN Doc. CED/C/1, 22.06.2012.

[191] *Gaer*, Implementing Treaty Body Recommendations: Establishing Better Follow-Up Procedures, in: Bassiouni/Schabas (eds.), New Challenges for the UN Human Rights Machinery, 2011, p. 107; *Schmidt*, Follow-up Mechanisms Before UN Human Rights Treaty Bodies and the UN Mechanisms Beyond, in: Bayefsky (ed.), The UN Human Rights Treaty System in the 21st Century, 2000, p. 233.

[192] For an overview of the various approaches developed by human rights treaty bodies as of 2017, see Procedures of the human rights treaty bodies for following up on concluding observations, decisions and Views, UN Doc. HRI/MC/2017/4, 08.05.2017, with the CRC Committee being the only human rights treaty body currently not deploying a written follow-up procedure.

dialogue in between the reporting intervals.¹⁹³ Additionally, the follow-up procedure is considered of "central importance for the effectiveness" of the reporting procedure, as it can foster the implementation of recommendations.¹⁹⁴

Nevertheless, the allegedly weaker mandate of treaty bodies, with fewer competencies than regional human rights courts, has raised the question as to whether treaty bodies are ultimately entitled to initiate this kind of implementation procedure. As indicated above, some members of the cross-regional group intervening in the multi-stakeholder review process in 2011 and 2012 held that follow-up activities were beyond a treaty body's legal mandate. Indeed, any explicit normative basis for the establishment of formalized follow-up procedures to concluding observations is missing under the treaties.¹⁹⁵ This observation might have prompted a range of scholars to conclude that follow-up activities are covered by Committees' implied powers,¹⁹⁶ but without specifying in more detail how these powers are eventually constructed.

a) Normative basis for follow-up activities

As a matter of fact, all human rights treaty bodies, except for the CESCR Committee, can either require additional reports or additional information by virtue of treaty provisions governing the reporting procedure.¹⁹⁷ The request to provide

---

¹⁹³ *Rodley*, The Role and Impact of Treaty Bodies, in: Shelton (ed.), The Oxford Handbook of International Human Rights Law, 2013, p. 638.

¹⁹⁴ *O'Flaherty*, The Concluding Observations of United Nations Human Rights Treaty Bodies, Human Rights Law Review 6 (2006), 27, 47; *Schmidt*, Follow-up Mechanisms Before UN Human Rights Treaty Bodies and the UN Mechanisms Beyond, in: Bayefsky (ed.), The UN Human Rights Treaty System in the 21st Century, 2000, p. 249, who argues that the effectiveness of the treaty body system will erode in the absence of follow-up procedures; *Bank*, Country-orientated procedures under the Convention against Torture: Towards a new dynamism, in: Alston/Crawford (eds.), The Future of UN Human Rights Treaty Monitoring, 2000, p. 161 with the observation that follow-up procedures are crucial to achieve any impact at all under the reporting procedure.

¹⁹⁵ *Rodley*, The Role and Impact of Treaty Bodies, in: Shelton (ed.), The Oxford Handbook of International Human Rights Law, 2013, p. 638; *Gaer*, Implementing Treaty Body Recommendations: Establishing Better Follow-Up Procedures, in: Bassiouni/Schabas (eds.), New Challenges for the UN Human Rights Machinery, 2011, p. 111.

¹⁹⁶ *Rodley*, The Role and Impact of Treaty Bodies, in: Shelton (ed.), The Oxford Handbook of International Human Rights Law, 2013, p. 638, who refers to both follow-up activities to concluding observations and to views; see also *Schmidt*, Follow-Up Activities by UN Human Rights Treaty Bodies and Special Procedures Mechanisms of the Human Rights Council – Recent Developments, in: Alfredsson et al. (eds.), International Human Rights Monitoring Mechanisms, Second Revised Edition, 2009, pp. 28–29, highlighting the importance of "establishing and effectively implementing procedures for follow-up to [concluding observations]", but who only invokes implied powers as the legal basis for the follow-up procedure to adopted views and who leaves it thus open where the treaty bodies exactly derive their mandate from.

¹⁹⁷ Vesting their Committee with the power to request additional reports: article 40(1)(b) ICCPR, article 9(1)(b) CERD, article 18(1)(b) CEDAW, article 19(1) CAT, article 73(1)(b)

information on the implementation of precisely identified recommendations could consequently be subsumed under these provisions. In practice, treaty bodies use said power when they consider a State report insufficient or outdated with regard to its information.[198] Recourse is also taken to these provisions when treaty bodies request exceptional or "ad hoc" reports in cases of serious and grave human rights violations which require immediate action.[199] Despite their use for exceptional reports, these provisions nevertheless allow for a literal and text-based interpretation resulting in the Committees being able to request follow-up reports.

Another possible justification for follow-up activities under the reporting procedure could alternatively be based on provisions that establish the treaty bodies and assign them the task of reviewing the progress made by State parties.[200] Some of these provisions explicitly require the Committees to consider the progress made in the implementation,[201] to examine the progress by State parties,[202] or to review the application of the Convention.[203] These articles alone may imply that the respective Committees have a "wider mandate" in terms of ongoing monitoring with regard to the implementation of recommendations.[204] The terms "steps taken" or "progress made" are thereby able to cover requests for additional follow-up information, though stronger emphasis on teleological interpretation might be needed here.

Finally, the practice of the CERD Committee demonstrates its own understanding of the provision from which it derives its power in the matter. It regular-

---

CMW; article 35(2) CRPD; vesting their Committees with the power to request additional information: article 44(4) CRC, article 29(4) CED.

[198] Concerning CAT, see *Monina*, Article 19, State Reporting Procedure, in: Nowak/Birk/Monina (eds.), The United Nations Convention Against Torture and its Optional Protocol: A Commentary, Second Edition, 2019, para. 40.

[199] *Monina*, Article 19, State Reporting Procedure, in: Nowak/Birk/Monina (eds.), The United Nations Convention Against Torture and its Optional Protocol: A Commentary, Second Edition, 2019, para. 40; *Boerefijn*, Article 18, in: Freeman/Chinkin/Rudolf (eds.) The UN Convention on the Elimination of All Forms of Discrimination Against Women: A Commentary, 2012, p. 500; *Nowak*, CCPR Commentary, Second revised Edition, 2005, Article 40, State Reports, para. 8.

[200] *Gaer*, Implementing Treaty Body Recommendations: Establishing Better Follow-Up Procedures, in: Bassiouni/Schabas (eds.), New Challenges for the UN Human Rights Machinery, 2011, p. 111, who simultaneously states that the respective normative basis remains weak.

[201] Article 17(1) CEDAW; *Hellum/Ikdahl*, Committee on the Elimination of Discrimination Against Women (CEDAW), in: Ruiz Fabri/Wolfrum (eds.), Max Planck Encyclopedia of International Procedural Law, Online version, January 2019, para. 10, considering the Committee's mandate therefore as "broad".

[202] Article 43(1) CRC.

[203] Article 72(1)(a) CMW.

[204] *Oette*, The UN Human Rights Treaty Bodies: Impact and Future, in: Oberleitner (ed.), International Human Rights Institutions, Tribunals, and Courts, 2018, p. 99.

ly formulates its request for follow-up reports with a reference to article 9(1) CERD.[205] Albeit the absence of similar references in other Committees' concluding observations or Rules of Procedure,[206] it can be assumed that they do equally consider the normatively similar or even congruent provisions under their respective treaties as the legal basis for follow-up activities.[207]

b) The CESCR Committee as the exception

More interpretative challenges are raised by the ICESCR, as it does not contain any comparable provision. However, in 1999, at its 21st session, the CESCR Committee decided to establish a follow-up procedure to concluding observations as well.[208] Noteworthy is the fact that the Committee considered itself competent to undertake missions to the State party concerned, if the latter should rest non-compliant with a view to its obligations under the follow-up procedure. While missions to the State party under review are not the question under consideration here, the legal arguments put forward in the justification can nevertheless support the Committee's competence to request follow-up reports. According to the Committee, on-site visits would provide for the necessary information required by the Committee to carry out its functions under article 22 and article 23 ICESCR.[209] If on-site visits, as a substitute for the submission of follow-up reports, shall enable the Committee to discharge its mandate under articles 22 and 23 ICESCR, the same must logically also hold true for follow-up procedures. Furthermore, as socio-economic rights, by their very nature, are to be realized progressively,[210] the Committee must be able to monitor their implementation

---

[205] For the Committee's request for follow-up reports, see for instance CERD Committee, Concluding observations on the combined fourteenth to seventeenth reports of Cambodia, UN Doc. CERD/C/KHM/CO/14–17, 30.01.2020, para. 49; Concluding observations on the combined seventeenth to nineteenth reports of Israel, UN Doc. CERD/C/ISR/CO/17–19, 27.01.2020, para. 54; Concluding observations on the combined tenth to twelfth reports of Uzbekistan, UN Doc. CERD/C/UZB/CO/10–12, 27.01.2020, para. 31.

[206] The CRPD Committee indicated in a report on its activities under the follow-up procedure that it is allowed to request reports whenever it deems their request appropriate under article 35(2) CRPD, CRPD Committee, Follow-up to concluding observations on State party reports, UN Doc. CRPD/C/19/3, 19.04.2019, para. 3; the CEDAW Committee indicated in its "Assessment of the follow-up procedure adopted on 6 November 2019" that the request for follow-up information was based on article 18(1)(b) of the Convention, https://tbinternet.ohc hr.org/_layouts/15/treatybodyexternal/Download.aspx?symbolno=INT%2fCEDAW%2fF GD%2f8161&Lang=en (last access: 21.08.2023).

[207] For the respective provisions that enable the Committees to request further reports, see *supra* footnote 504.

[208] Report of the Committee on Economic, Social and Cultural Rights (20th and 21st session), UN Doc. E/2000/22 (2000), paras. 38–41.

[209] Report of the Committee on Economic, Social and Cultural Rights (20th and 21st session), UN Doc. E/2000/22 (2000), para. 39.

[210] For the term "progressive realization" and some of its legal components, see *Corkery/ Saiz*, Progressive realization using maximum available resources: the accountability chal-

4. Follow-up under the individual complaints procedure

Under the individual complaints procedure, it was the Human Rights Committee which first initiated a formalized follow-up procedure in 1990 by appointing a "Special Rapporteur for the Follow-Up of Views".[211] Thereby it departed from previous practice, which was to engage in dialogue with State parties by sending notes verbales, or raising questions on the status of implementation during the constructive dialogue under the reporting procedure.[212] In line with follow-up activities to concluding observations, neither the Covenant nor the First Optional Protocol to the Covenant provide for an express enforcement mechanism.[213] The same applies to the Convention against Torture,[214] the CERD, CMW and CED and to the Optional Protocol to the CRPD.

Regarding the legal basis for follow-up activities to views adopted, several authors invoke implied powers here as well.[215] Others simply state that the follow-up mechanism was to be qualified as an implicit power of a treaty body by

---

lenge, in: Dugard et al. (eds.), Research Handbook on Economic, Social and Cultural Rights as Human Rights, 2020, pp. 278–290; on the concept of progressive realization, with an account of the drafting history of the ICESCR, see *Alston/Quinn*, The Nature and Scope of States Parties' Obligations under the International Covenant on Economic, Social and Cultural Rights, Human Rights Quarterly 9 (1987), 156, 172–181.

[211] *Schabas*, U.N. International Covenant on Civil and Political Rights, Nowak's CCPR Commentary, Third revised Edition, 2019, Art. 5 First OP, Adjudication of Communications, para. 40.

[212] *Egan*, The United Nations Human Rights Treaty System: Law and Procedure, 2011, pp. 263–264.

[213] *Nowak*, CCPR Commentary, Second revised Edition, 2005, Article 5 First OP, para. 42.

[214] *Monina*, Article 22, Individual Complaints Procedure, in: Nowak/Birk/Monina (eds.), The United Nations Convention Against Torture and its Optional Protocol: A Commentary, Second Edition, 2019, para. 174.

[215] *van Staden*, Monitoring Second-Order Compliance: The Follow-Up Procedures of the UN Human Rights Treaty Bodies, Czeck Yearbook of International Law 9 (2018), 329, 332; Rodley, The Role and Impact of Treaty Bodies, in: Shelton (ed.), The Oxford Handbook of International Human Rights Law, 2013, p. 638; *Ulfstein*, Individual Complaints, in: Keller/Ulfstein (eds.), UN Human Rights Treaty Bodies, UN Human Rights Treaty Bodies: Law and Legitimacy, 2012, p. 107; *Schmidt*, Follow-Up Activities by UN Human Rights Treaty Bodies and Special Procedures Mechanisms of the Human Rights Council – Recent Developments, in: Alfredsson et al. (eds.), International Human Rights Monitoring Mechanisms, Second Revised Edition, 2009, p. 26; *de Zayas*, Petitions before the United Nations Treaty Bodies: Focus on the Human Rights Committee's Optional Protocol Procedure, in: Alfredsson et al. (eds.), International Human Rights Monitoring Mechanisms, Second Revised Edition, 2009, p. 75, who refers to the implied powers doctrine as one of several possible sources of legitimacy.

means of which it "may enhance the effectiveness of the Convention".[216] Indeed, a complaints procedure that results in the adoption of views, which are nonetheless left unimplemented and disregarded by the State party concerned, does not fulfil the intended purpose of providing protection for individuals. The establishment of a follow-up procedure to views thus seeks to foster the overall object and purpose of the treaty provisions governing the complaints procedure or the respective Optional Protocol.[217]

But there are more arguments in favour of follow-up procedures to views adopted than mere considerations of effectiveness. Some of them were already raised in the discussions among Human Rights Committee members during the Committee's seventeenth session.[218] Some members felt that the request for follow-up information was beyond the Committee's powers, given that neither the Covenant nor the first Optional Protocol provided a legal basis in this matter.[219] In their opinion, the Human Rights Committee could leave the implementation of views only to the "good-will" of State parties.[220] In addition, any petitioner unsatisfied with the implementation of views could submit another subsequent communication. Furthermore, any monitoring activity in the implementation was considered to be incompatible with article 2(7) UNCh, and any further reaching power enjoyed by the Committee had to come into existence via treaty amendments under article 11 1st OP ICCPR.[221]

Proponents of the establishment of follow-up to views emphasized first that the procedure under the 1st Optional Protocol could not let be degenerated into an exercise in futility, and stressed that due consideration had to be paid to both the letter and the spirit of the Covenant.[222] They thereby relied on effectiveness-orientated considerations, comparable to scholars who invoke the implied powers doctrine as a possible justification. Moreover, proponents reasoned with

---

[216] *Monina*, Article 22, Individual Complaints Procedure, in: Nowak/Birk/Monina (eds.), The United Nations Convention Against Torture and its Optional Protocol: A Commentary, Second Edition, 2019, para. 174; *Ingelse*, The UN Committee against Torture: An Assessment, 2001, p. 193, who detects this implicit power in relation to the Committee against Torture.

[217] *McGoldrick*, The Human Rights Committee: Its Role in the Development of the International Covenant on Civil and Political Rights, 1991, p. 200.

[218] *de Zayas*, Petitions before the United Nations Treaty Bodies: Focus on the Human Rights Committee's Optional Protocol Procedure, in: Alfredsson et al. (eds.), International Human Rights Monitoring Mechanisms, Second Revised Edition, 2009, p. 75.

[219] Cf. Report of the Human Rights Committee (17th, 18th and 19th session), UN Doc. A/38/40 (1983), para. 392, where it was also stated that "the Committee could have no inherent powers that had not been given to it explicitly by State parties".

[220] Report of the Human Rights Committee (17th, 18th and 19th session), UN Doc. A/38/40 (1983), para. 392.

[221] Report of the Human Rights Committee (17th, 18th and 19th session), UN Doc. A/38/40 (1983), para. 392.

[222] Report of the Human Rights Committee (17th, 18th and 19th session), UN Doc. A/38/40 (1983), para. 393.

the preamble to the 1st Optional Protocol and the wording of article 2(3) ICCPR. The will to implement the Convention, the argument went, would equally entail the will to implement the views adopted. Interestingly, Committee members stressed the fact that follow-up to views "was not expressly prohibited" by the treaties and that the 1st Optional Protocol itself allowed considerable "latitude for interpretation".[223] This assumption is quite instructive and might indicate that Committee members considered an extensive interpretation to be suited to the 1st Optional Protocol and their statement is reminiscent of the "Lotus principle".

Another argument for vesting the treaty bodies with the power to request follow-up information under the complaints procedure can be directly drawn from the wording of articles 1 and 5(1) 1st Optional Protocol, which require the Committee to consider communications received. Broadly construed, the provisions could be taken to mean that the Committee does not only consider the admissibility and merits of communications, but also the measures taken by the State party to address the violations in the aftermath.[224] Given that the procedure serves to redress and remedy treaty violations, it is compelling to assume that the consideration of any communication is only terminated once the recommended measures have been implemented.[225] Such an interpretation extends the term "consideration" in its temporal dimension beyond the communication's actual examination. Thereby, the effectiveness-driven result of treaty bodies, being entitled to initiate follow-up procedures, is further bolstered by arguments drawing upon the wording and context of the 1st Optional Protocol and the Covenant. It has also been argued that State parties are obliged to consider adopted views in good faith, which requires them to at least "react at all to a finding" by the Committee.[226]

Lastly, though not being a legal argument in a strict sense, the drafters of more recently adopted Optional Protocols took into consideration the inclusion of provisions that *explicitly* vest treaty bodies with the power to request follow-up

---

[223] Report of the Human Rights Committee (17th, 18th and 19th session), UN Doc. A/38/40 (1983), para. 393.

[224] *de Zayas*, Petitions before the United Nations Treaty Bodies: Focus on the Human Rights Committee's Optional Protocol Procedure, in: Alfredsson et al. (eds.), International Human Rights Monitoring Mechanisms, Second Revised Edition, 2009, p. 75; *Schmidt*, Follow-up Mechanisms Before UN Human Rights Treaty Bodies and the UN Mechanisms Beyond, in: Bayefsky (ed.), The UN Human Rights Treaty System in the 21st Century, 2000, p. 235.

[225] *Monina*, Article 22, Individual Complaints Procedure, in: Nowak/Birk/Monina (eds.), The United Nations Convention Against Torture and its Optional Protocol: A Commentary, Second Edition, 2019, para. 174.

[226] *Tomuschat*, The Human Rights Committee, in: Peters (ed.), Max Planck Encyclopedia of Public International Law, Online version, April 2019, para. 14; see also *Shelton*, The Legal Status of Normative Pronouncements of Human Rights Treaty Bodies, in: Hestermeyer et al. (eds.), Coexistence, Cooperation and Solidarity, Liber Amicorum Rüdiger Wolfrum Volume I, 2012, p. 571.

information on the implementation of views.[227] Their inclusion is at least indicative of the acceptance of follow-up procedures. For instance, during the negotiations of the OP CEDAW, delegates welcomed the inclusion of such explicit power and considered the proposal a "positive contribution [...] to the progressive development of international law".[228] On the other hand, the drafters of the OP CRPD did not consider it necessary to include a comparable provision, although its drafting process only commenced after the OP CEDAW had entered into force. Nevertheless, considering the inclusion of the power to request follow-up information to views adopted in the two most recently adopted Optional Protocols, which are the 3rd OP CRC and the OP ICESCR, one can assume that the progressive development of international law has continued and the power to request follow-up information is now being included more regularly in international texts.

5. Adoption of interim measures

Another example of the extension of powers is the request for interim measures in cases of filed, but not yet examined, individual communications. The ultimate objective of interim measures is to preserve the *status quo* and, most importantly, to preserve the "equal rights of the parties pending the examination of a case in order to ensure the effectiveness and integrity of a final decision."[229] Furthermore, interim measures are accorded a strong protective character, as a State party is called to refrain from any action which could result in irreparable damage or injury to the individual having filed the communication.[230]

a) Competence to adopt interim measures

Despite being an "important weapon in the armoury of any tribunal",[231] the Human Rights Committee, the CERD Committee and the Committee against Torture are not *expressis verbis* vested with the power to issue provisional measures by virtue of their respective constituent treaties or Optional Protocol re-

---

[227] Article 7(4) OP CEDAW, article 11(1) 3rd OP CRC and article 9(2) OP ICESCR all provide for the express power to request follow-up information.

[228] See *Connors*, Optional Protocol, in: Freeman/Chinkin/Rudolf (eds.), The UN Convention on the Elimination of All Forms of Discrimination Against Women: A Commentary, 2012, pp. 656–659, with a detailed account of the genesis of the follow-up procedure under the Optional Protocol to CEDAW.

[229] *Keller/Marti*, Interim Relief Compared: Use of Interim Measures by the UN Human Rights Committee and the European Court of Human Rights, ZaöRV 73 (2013), 325, 327.

[230] *Pasqualucci*, Interim Measures in International Human Rights: Evolution and Harmonization, Vanderbilt Journal of Transnational Law 38 (2005), 1, 4.

[231] *Ghandhi*, The Human Rights Committee and Interim Measures of Relief, Canterbury Law Review 13 (2007), 203.

A. Interpretation of human rights treaties

gulating the individual complaints procedure. An explicit basis for the issuance of interim measures is only found in their respective Rules of Procedure.[232]

Rules of Procedure, however, determine internal affairs and do not create any legal obligations or legal effects at the external level in the first place. Nevertheless, as noted by the Human Rights Committee, the power to order interim measures is "essential to the Committee's role under the Protocol."[233] Interim measures are essential insofar as the possibility and the right of individuals to have their cases heard and settled by a human rights treaty body is ultimately frustrated if the adoption of views comes too late and the alleged violation has already led to irreparable and irreversible harm.[234]

The assertion is possibly best reflected by the fact that most interim measures are ordered in cases of persons awaiting execution or in non-refoulement cases.[235] Consequently, interim measures serve to secure and foster the overall object and purpose of the First Optional Protocol to the ICCPR, or of those provisions providing for the individual complaints procedure under CAT and CERD respectively.[236] Today, the power to order interim measures enjoyed by international courts, tribunals or the human rights treaty bodies is almost commonly accepted and no explicit legal basis seems to be required.[237]

---

[232] See *Pasqualucci*, Interim Measures in International Human Rights: Evolution and Harmonization, Vanderbilt Journal of Transnational Law 38 (2005), 1, 11–16, who differentiates between express authority by virtue of the treaty concerned, inherent, and implied authority to order interim measures.

[233] Human Rights Committee, *Piandiong et al. v. The Philippines*, Communication No. 869/1999, UN Doc. CCPR/C/70/D/869/1999, 19.10.2000, para. 5.4.

[234] *Pasqualucci*, Interim Measures in International Human Rights: Evolution and Harmonization, Vanderbilt Journal of Transnational Law 38 (2005), 1, 15.

[235] *Keller/Marti*, Interim Relief Compared: Use of Interim Measures by the UN Human Rights Committee and the European Court of Human Rights, ZaöRV 73 (2013), 325, 346–360, with a "typology" of interim measures ordered by the ECtHR and the Human Rights Committee; *Naldi*, Interim Measures in the UN Human Rights Committee, International and Comparative Law Quarterly 53 (2004), 445, 447.

[236] *Keller/Marti*, Interim Relief Compared: Use of Interim Measures by the UN Human Rights Committee and the European Court of Human Rights, ZaöRV 73 (2013), 325, 330; *Pasqualucci*, Interim Measures in International Human Rights: Evolution and Harmonization, Vanderbilt Journal of Transnational Law 38 (2005), 1, 15–16.

[237] *Keller/Marti*, Interim Relief Compared: Use of Interim Measures by the UN Human Rights Committee and the European Court of Human Rights, ZaöRV 73 (2013), 325, 330, who argue that not even an explicit provision is necessary for a treaty body's competence to order interim measures; with regard to international courts in general, see *Brown*, A Common Law of International Adjudication, 2007, p. 128, who considers the power to be inherent to international courts as it is necessary for their performance; compare, however, *Rosenne*, Provisional Measures in International Law: The International Court of Justice and the International Tribunal for the Law of the Sea, 2004, p. 7, who argues that "every international court or tribunal requires a specific provision in its constituent instrument to empower it to order provisional measures."

Said power is either implicitly read into the treaty as such or into the provisions providing for the individual complaints procedure,[238] which is the position shared by the Human Rights Committee.[239] Alternatively, it is accorded to them by reference to their implied or inherent powers.[240] Furthermore, each Optional Protocol vesting an already existing treaty body with the power to adopt views on individual communications contains an express legal basis for ordering interim measures. In the case of the CED, a similar provision was included in the treaty.[241] The only exception among the later adopted UN human rights treaties is the CMW. However, mirroring the common acceptance of interim measures, the CMW Committee is not considered to be prevented from requesting provisional measures once the procedure under article 77 CMW enters into force.[242]

b) Binding force of interim measures

However, there is another aspect that is much more contested by States Parties in relation to the interim measures ordered by UN human rights treaty bodies, namely the legal status accorded to them.[243]

---

[238] *Pasqualucci*, Interim Measures in International Human Rights: Evolution and Harmonization, Vanderbilt Journal of Transnational Law 38 (2005), 1, 16.

[239] Human Rights Committee, *Piandiong et al. v. The Philippines*, Communication No. 869/1999, UN Doc. CCPR/C/70/D/869/1999, 19.10.2000, para. 5.1, where the Committee held that "[implicit] in a State's adherence to the Protocol is an undertaking to cooperate with the Committee in good faith so as to permit and enable it to consider such communications, and after examination to forward its views to the State party and to the individual [...]."; *Naldi*, Interim Measures in the UN Human Rights Committee, International and Comparative Law Quarterly 53 (2004), 445, 448.

[240] *de Schutter*, The Formation of a Common Law of Human Rights, in: Bribosia/Rorive (eds.), Human Rights Tectonics: Global Dynamics of Integration and Fragmentation, 2018, p. 19, speaking of "inherent"; *Ulfstein*, Individual Complaints, in: Keller/Ulfstein (eds.), UN Human Rights Treaty Bodies: Law and Legitimacy, 2012, p. 101; with regard to the powers of regional human rights tribunals, see *Shelton*, Inherent and Implied Powers of Regional Human Rights Tribunals, in: Buckley/Donald/Leach (eds.), Towards Convergence in International Human Rights Law: Approaches of Regional and International Systems, 2016, pp. 479–484.

[241] Article 5(1) OP CEDAW, article 6(1) 3rd OP CRC, article 5(1) OP CESCR, article 4(1) OP CRPD, article 31(4) CED; see also *Tomuschat*, Human Rights: Between Idealism and Realism, Third Edition, 2014, pp. 264–265, who observes with regard to article 31(4) CED a variation in language, as the State party concerned will take interim measures; *Flinterman/Liu*, CEDAW and the Optional Protocol: First Experiences, in: Alfredsson et al. (eds.), International Human Rights Monitoring Mechanisms, Second Revised Edition, 2009, p. 93, evaluating the inclusion of the explicit power to order interim measures as the "progressive development of international law".

[242] *Egan*, The United Nations Human Rights Treaty System: Law and Procedure, 2011, p. 401.

[243] See for instance *Tomuschat*, Human Rights: Between Idealism and Realism, Third Edition, 2014, p. 264, who observes that "[even] well-intentioned countries" challenged the assertion that interim measures had binding force; *Ulfstein*, Individual Complaints, in: Kel-

A. Interpretation of human rights treaties

aa) Evolving practice by treaty bodies

The first communication in which the Human Rights Committee explicitly addressed the legal nature of interim measures was *Piandiong et al. v. The Philippines*.[244] The complainants, having been sentenced to death, submitted a communication to the Human Rights Committee by which they alleged violations of articles 6 and 14 ICCPR. The Committee subsequently requested the Philippines to refrain from executing the death penalty until the communication could be examined. Nevertheless, the State party did not comply with the request and executed the death penalty. In the merits, the Human Rights Committee found the State Party having committed "grave breaches of its obligations under the Optional Protocol if it acts to prevent or frustrate consideration by the Committee of a communication alleging a violation of the Covenant, or to render examination by the Committee moot and the expression of its Views nugatory and futile."[245] Thus, non-compliance with interim measures, in the view of the Human Rights Committee, amounts to an "autonomous treaty violation", even though the Committee did not expressly use the term "binding".[246] This specific finding has been repeated ever since by the Committee whenever a State party did not respect the request for interim relief.[247]

Similar, but less determined, reads the Committee against Torture's reasoning in *Núñez Chipana v. Venezuela*.[248] By extraditing the author, despite the Com-

---

ler/Ulfstein (eds.), UN Human Rights Treaty Bodies, UN Human Rights Treaty Bodies: Law and Legitimacy, 2012, p. 101.

[244] Human Rights Committee, *Piandiong et al. v. The Philippines*, Communication No. 869/1999, UN Doc. CCPR/C/70/D/869/1999, 19.10.2000; *Naldi*, Interim Measures in the UN Human Rights Committee, International and Comparative Law Quarterly 53 (2004), 445, 447–450.

[245] Human Rights Committee, *Piandiong et al. v. The Philippines*, Communication No. 869/1999, UN Doc. CCPR/C/70/D/869/1999, 19.10.2000, para. 5.2.

[246] *Keller/Marti*, Interim Relief Compared: Use of Interim Measures by the UN Human Rights Committee and the European Court of Human Rights, ZaöRV 73 (2013), 325, 345; see also *Rodley*, The Role and Impact of Treaty Bodies, in: Shelton (ed.), The Oxford Handbook of International Human Rights Law, 2013, p. 635, who observes that this is the only example where the Human Rights Committee considers non-compliance as "being *ipso jure* a violation of a binding obligation."

[247] *Keller/Marti*, Interim Relief Compared: Use of Interim Measures by the UN Human Rights Committee and the European Court of Human Rights, ZaöRV 73 (2013), 325, 364, with further examples from the Human Rights Committee's case law; *Ghandhi*, The Human Rights Committee and Interim Measures of Relief, Canterbury Law Review 13 (2007), 203, 219.

[248] *Keller/Marti*, Interim Relief Compared: Use of Interim Measures by the UN Human Rights Committee and the European Court of Human Rights, ZaöRV 73 (2013), 325, 344, footnote 92, said communication was the first time an international adjudicator unequivocally mentioned the obligation of State parties to respect interim measures; the same finding was repeated in Committee against Torture, *TPS v. Canada*, Communication No. 99/1997, UN Doc. CAT/C/24/D/99/1997, 16.05.1999, para. 15.6.; *Naldi*, Interim Measures in the UN

mittee's request to refrain from any such action, the State party "failed to comply with the spirit of the Convention."[249] The Committee furthermore noted that upon ratification and with acceptance of the procedure under article 22 CAT, a State party "undertook to cooperate with it in good faith in applying the procedure."

More recently adopted views, however, reveal that the Committee against Torture now also finds an independent violation if a State party does not abide by the Committee's request for interim measures. In *Cevdet Ayaz v. Serbia*, the Committee noted that "[by] failing to respect the request for interim measures [...] the State party violated its obligations under article 22 of the Convention [...]."[250] Other treaty bodies, such as the CRC and CESCR Committee, both of which have only quite recently begun to receive and consider individual communications, immediately took the position that a failure to implement interim measures constituted a violation of the respective provisions under their Optional Protocols.[251]

bb) Criticism by State parties

In response to interim measures ordered by human rights treaty bodies, however, several State parties argued that these were non-binding. For instance, Canada levelled criticism against the Committee against Torture that an interim measure was only a "recommendation to a State to take certain measures, not an order".[252] It reiterated that, though "given serious consideration", requests for interim measures were of a "non-binding nature".[253] Akin criticism was expressed by other State parties. Austria, for instance, argued that requests for interim measures by

---

Human Rights Committee, International and Comparative Law Quarterly 53 (2004), 445, 452–453.

[249] Committee against Torture, *Núñez Chipana v. Venezuela*, Communication No. 110/1998, UN Doc. CAT/C/21/D/110/1998, 10.11.1998, para. 8.

[250] Committee against Torture, *Cevdet Ayaz v. Serbia*, Communication No. 857/2017, UN Doc. CAT/C/67/D/857/2017, 02.08.2019, para. 7.3; see also *Thirugnanasampanthar v. Australia*, Communication No. 614/2014, UN Doc. CAT/C/61/D/614/2014, 09.08.2017, para. 6.3; and *Tursunov v. Kazakhstan*, Communication No. 538/2013, UN Doc. CAT/C54/D/538/2013, 08.05.2015, para. 7.2, in both communications, the Committee against Torture noted a serious failure of the respondent State party in its obligation under article 22 CAT.

[251] CRC Committee, *R.K. v. Spain*, Communication No. 27/2017, UN Doc. CRC/C/82/D/27/2017, 18.09.2019, para. 9.13; and *N.B.F. v. Spain*, Communication No. 11/2017, UN Doc. CRC/C/79/D/11/2017, 27.09.2018, para. 12.11; CESCR Committee, *López Albán v. Spain*, Communication No. 37/2018, UN Doc. E/C.12/66/D/37/2018, 11.10.2019, para. 13.3; and *S.S.R. v. Spain*, Communication No. 51/2018, UN Doc. E/C.12/66/D/51/2018, 11.10.2019, para. 7.8.

[252] Committee against Torture, *TPS v. Canada*, Communication No. 99/1997, UN Doc. CAT/C/24/D/99/1997, 16.05.1999, para. 8.2.

[253] Committee against Torture, *TPS v. Canada*, Communication No. 99/1997, UN Doc. CAT/C/24/D/99/1997, 16.05.1999, para. 8.4.

the Human Rights Committee did not "have any binding effect".[254] Belarus did not only oppose the binding nature of interim measures, but also questioned the Committee's very power to request them.[255] The drafting of both Committees' General Comments on the issue also caused controversy. The draft of the Human Rights Committee's General Comment No. 33 originally contained the passage that the failure to comply with the request for interim measures would constitute a grave breach of a State party's obligation under the Optional Protocol, thereby reflecting the language used in its views adopted. However, due to criticism by commenting State parties, the passage was eventually deleted and replaced with the formulation that the "[failure] to implement such interim or provisional measures is incompatible with the obligation to respect in good faith the procedure of individual communication".[256]

Noteworthy in this regard is General Comment No. 4 issued by the Committee Against Torture, which expressly states that a State party is in breach with its obligations under article 22 CAT whenever it does not abide by interim measures.[257] Unlike the Human Rights Committee, the Committee against Torture did not refrain from adopting the just-cited passage, notwithstanding repeated criticism by commenting State parties during the drafting process.[258]

---

[254] Human Rights Committee, *Weiss v. Austria*, Communication No. 1086/2002, UN Doc. CCPR/C/77/D/1086/2002, 03.04.2004, para. 5.3; *Naldi*, Interim Measures in the UN Human Rights Committee, International and Comparative Law Quarterly 53 (2004), 445, 450.

[255] Human Rights Committee, *Kovaleva and Kozyar v. Belarus*, Communication No. 2120/2011, UN Doc. CCPR/C/106/D/2120/2011, 29.10.2012, para. 6.3; *Keller/Marti*, Interim Relief Compared: Use of Interim Measures by the UN Human Rights Committee and the European Court of Human Rights, ZaöRV 73 (2013), 325, 345.

[256] Human Rights Committee, General Comment No. 33, Obligations of States parties under the Optional Protocol to the International Covenant on Civil and Political Rights, UN Doc. CCPR/C/GC/33, 25.06.2009, para. 19; see also *Ulfstein*, Individual Complaints, in: Keller/Ulfstein (eds.), UN Human Rights Treaty Bodies: Law and Legitimacy, 2012, p. 101; see further Human Rights Committee, General Comment No. 36, Article 6: right to life, UN Doc. CCPR/C/GC/36, 03.09.2019, para. 46, where the Committee reiterated almost *verbatim* the passus contained in General Comment No. 33.

[257] Committee against Torture, General Comment No. 4 (2017) on the implementation of article 3 of the Convention in the context of article 22, UN Doc. CAT/C/GC/4, 04.09.2018, para. 37.

[258] Canada reiterated that "interim measures are not legally binding in international law", https://www.ohchr.org/Documents/HRBodies/CAT/GCArticle3/Canada.pdf (last access: 21.08.2023); France argued that the requests were based on Rules of Procedure which could not create obligations at the external level and were thus void of any legal character, https://www.ohchr.org/Documents/HRBodies/CAT/GCArticle3/France.pdf (last access: 21.08.2023); and China took the position that, since the Committee Against Torture was not "explicitly authorized by the Convention to request interim measures", it should make clear that the Committees' requests were of recommendatory nature only, https://www.ohchr.org/Documents/HRBodies/CAT/GCArticle3/China_en.pdf (last access: 21.08.2023).

cc) Arguments in favour of interim measures' binding force

Even though views adopted and concluding observations are non-binding, this does not necessarily lead to the same result as far as interim measures are concerned.[259] A treaty body vested with the competence to receive and consider individual complaints must be able to effectively perform its function.[260] Where a State party could otherwise easily frustrate the communication procedure as such by ignoring the request for interim measures and causing irreparable harm to the individual concerned, treaty bodies would have no chance at all to influence the situation.[261] The competence to issue binding interim measures, which are "intimately tied to the object and purpose of human rights treaties",[262] thus bolsters the procedure's protective character for individuals in situations of distress. The initially paradoxical result that interim measures carry more weight than views can also be justified by the fact that they are only of a "temporary and not final character."[263] Thus, an effectiveness orientated interpretation of the treaty or optional protocol regulating the complaints procedure leads to the result that interim measures possess binding force.[264]

With a view to the normative basis being adduced for said interpretative result, the Committee against Torture takes recourse to article 22 CAT. While the Human Rights Committee did not clarify which articles exactly were violated by a non-compliant State party for a long time and only generally referred to a State party's obligation to "cooperate in good faith",[265] more recently adopted views

---

[259] *Ulfstein*, Individual Complaints, in: Keller/Ulfstein (eds.), UN Human Rights Treaty Bodies, UN Human Rights Treaty Bodies: Law and Legitimacy, 2012, p. 102.

[260] *Pasqualucci*, Interim Measures in International Human Rights: Evolution and Harmonization, Vanderbilt Journal of Transnational Law 38 (2005), 1, 25; *Naldi*, Interim Measures in the UN Human Rights Committee, International and Comparative Law Quarterly 53 (2004), 445, 449.

[261] *Ulfstein*, Individual Complaints, in: Keller/Ulfstein (eds.), UN Human Rights Treaty Bodies, UN Human Rights Treaty Bodies: Law and Legitimacy, 2012, p. 102.

[262] *Krsticevic/Griffey*, Interim Measures, in: Langford et al. (eds.), The Optional Protocol to the International Covenant on Economic, Social and Cultural Rights: A Commentary, 2016, p. 323.

[263] *Ulfstein*, Individual Complaints, in: Keller/Ulfstein (eds.), UN Human Rights Treaty Bodies, UN Human Rights Treaty Bodies: Law and Legitimacy, 2012, p. 102.

[264] *Tomuschat*, Human Rights: Between Idealism and Realism, Third Edition, 2014, p. 265, who points out that the ICJ deployed similar arguments of effectiveness when ruling that its provisional measures under article 41 of its own Statute carry binding force; *La Grand (Germany v. United States of America)*, Judgment, I.C.J. Reports 2001, p. 466, 506; for an overview of the ICJ's jurisprudence and the binding effect of its provisional measures, see *Oellers-Frahm/Zimmermann*, Article 41, in: Zimmermann/Tams (eds.), The Statute of the International Court of Justice: A Commentary, Third Edition, 2019, paras. 93–115, who also note that the "theory of institutional effectiveness" to justify the binding force of provisional measures has gained increasing support in legal literature.

[265] *Keller/Marti*, Interim Relief Compared: Use of Interim Measures by the UN Human Rights Committee and the European Court of Human Rights, ZaöRV 73 (2013), 325, 365.

A. Interpretation of human rights treaties

demonstrate the tendency to consider a disregard of interim measures as constituting a violation of article 1 of the First Optional Protocol.[266]

6. Reservations to human rights treaties

Even more controversially discussed was the power of treaty bodies to decide on the permissibility of reservations submitted by State parties. As with other multilateral international treaties, State parties can enter reservations to human rights treaties with the intention to exclude or to modify the legal effect of certain provisions of the treaty in their application.[267]

As far as the topic of reservations to human rights treaties is concerned, three closely connected, yet distinct, problems can be discerned. First, the question arises as to whether the rules provided for in articles 19 to 23 VCLT are applicable to human rights treaties, which also hinges on the more general allegation of human rights treaties forming a distinct category of treaties and requiring different treatment.[268] Second, the problem arises as to which entity is competent to decide on the permissibility of reservations.[269] Third, and closely related to the former, what are the legal consequences of an impermissible reservation, since the VCLT remains silent at this point.[270] As this thesis is about the powers enjoyed by treaty bodies, only the second and third questions shall merit closer attention here.

a) Developing positions by treaty bodies

While the CERD Committee originally held in 1978 that it had to accept the reservations submitted by State parties, as it had "no authority to do otherwise",[271] and while the CEDAW Committee only requested State parties to con-

---

[266] Human Rights Committee, *K.B. v. Russian Federation*, Communication No. 2193/2012, UN Doc. CCPR/C/116/D/2193/2012, 10.03.2016, para. 8.3; *N.S. v. Russian Federation*, Communication No. 2192/2012, UN Doc. CCPR/C/113/D/2192/2012, 27.03.2015, para. 8.3.

[267] Article 21(1) VCLT.

[268] *Ziemele/Liede*, Reservations to Human Rights Treaties: From Draft Guideline 3.1.12 to Guideline 3.1.5.6, European Journal of International Law 24 (2013), 1135, 1136–1137, with short reference to the position of the Human Rights Committee and the European Commission and Court of Human Rights on this matter; see also *Baylis*, General Comment 24: Confronting the Problem of Reservations to Human Rights Treaties, Berkeley Journal of International Law 17 (1999), 277, 293.

[269] *Boerefijn*, Impact on the Law on Treaty Reservations, in: Kamminga/Scheinin (eds.), The Impact of Human Rights Law on General International Law, 2009, p. 64.

[270] *Simma/Hernandez*, Legal Consequences of an Impermissible Reservation to a Human Rights Treaty: Where Do We Stand?, in: Cannizzaro (ed.), The Law of Treaties Beyond the Vienna Convention, 2011, p. 64.

[271] Report of the Committee on the Elimination of Racial Discrimination (17th and 18th session), UN Doc. A/33/18 (1978), para. 374; *Kjærum*, Approaches to Reservations by the Committee on the Elimination of Racial Discrimination, in: Ziemele (ed.), Reservations to Human Rights Treaties and the Vienna Convention Regime: Conflict, Harmony or Reconciliation, 2004, p. 73.

sider the withdrawal of seemingly impermissible reservations,[272] it was the Human Rights Committee in 1994 which expressed a much firmer view on the topic of reservations than any of the other treaty bodies before. Its "revolutionary policy on reservations"[273] caused vocal opposition by State parties and sparked a discussion on treaty bodies' competencies in this domain, which still does not seem to be conclusively settled today.

Principally, its General Comment No. 24 contained two features "of a human rights approach to reservations that are in tension with the Vienna Convention regime".[274] These are the competence to take views on a reservation's compatibility with the object and purpose of the Covenant, and the legal consequences of an impermissible reservation, with the severability approach as the solution proposed by the Human Rights Committee.[275]

According to the Human Rights Committee, it was "inappropriate" to leave the assessment of reservations to State parties because of the characteristics of human rights treaties. Decisive in the Committee's line of argumentation was the finding that human rights treaties formed a distinct category of multilateral treaties with individuals as third party beneficiaries and that, in deviation from the VCLT, State parties could not be taken as competent stakeholders to assess a reservation's validity.[276] With a view to the legal consequences of an invalid reservation, the Human Rights Committee held that these would be severed, which

---

[272] CEDAW Committee, General Recommendation No. 4, Sixth session, 1987; *McCall-Smith*, Reservations and the Determinative Function of the Human Rights Treaty Bodies, German Yearbook of International Law 54 (2011), 521, 536; the Committee repeated its request in 1992, CEDAW Committee, General Recommendation No. 20: Reservations to the Convention, 1992; for the CEDAW Committee's position on the issue of reservations up until 1993, see also *Schöpp-Schilling*, Reservations to the Convention on the Elimination of All Forms of Discrimination against Women: An Unresolved Issue or (No) New Developments?, in: Ziemele (ed.), Reservations to Human Rights Treaties and the Vienna Convention Regime: Conflict, Harmony or Reconciliation, 2004, pp. 12–18.

[273] *Engström*, Understanding Powers of International Organizations: A Study of the Doctrines of Attributed Powers, Implied Powers and Constitutionalism – with a Special Focus on the Human Rights Committee, Åbo 2009, p. 17.

[274] *Scheinin*, Reservations by States under the International Covenant on Civil and Political Rights and its Optional Protocols, and the Practice of the Human Rights Committee, in: Ziemele (ed.), Reservations to Human Rights Treaties and the Vienna Convention Regime: Conflict, Harmony or Reconciliation, 2004, p. 42.

[275] Early examples from the European context are *Belilos v. Switzerland (Merits and Just Satisfaction)*, Application No. 10328/83, judgment of 29 April 1988, Series A No. 132; *Loizidou v. Turkey (Preliminary Objection)* [GC], Application No. 15318/89, judgment of 23 March 1995, Series A No. 310.

[276] *McCall-Smith*, Reservations and the Determinative Function of the Human Rights Treaty Bodies, German Yearbook of International Law 54 (2011), 521, 537–538; Human Rights Committee, General Comment No. 24: Issues Relating to Reservations Made upon Ratification or Accession to the Covenant or the Optional Protocols thereto, or in Relation to Declarations under Article 41 of the Covenant, UN Doc. CCPR/C/21/Rev. 1/Add.6, 04.11.1994, paras. 17–18.

ultimately resulted in the treaty being in force for the respective State party without the benefit of the invalid reservation in question.[277] The latter was arguably the most disputed implication coming along with General Comment No. 24.[278]

b) Criticism of General Comment No. 24

According to the United States, the Human Rights Committee had neither the legal authority to make determinations concerning the permissibility of specific reservations,[279] nor were its positions in accordance with the Covenant scheme and international law in general, since the Committee appeared to deny State parties any role in the assessment of a reservation's permissibility.[280] Concerning the severability of invalid reservations, the United States made it abundantly clear that this was in their opinion "completely at odds with established legal practice and principles". Since the commitment to a treaty and its specific provisions was consent-based, it could not be "presumed, on the basis of some legal fiction, to be bound by it."[281]

The British comment on General Comment No. 24 differed slightly, and though disagreeing with some of the positions advanced by the Human Rights Committee, the United Kingdom principally acknowledged that "the Committee must necessarily be able to take a view of the status and effect of a reservation".[282] Notwithstanding these concessions, the United Kingdom expressed its concerns on the determinative nature of the Committee's statements in relation to impermissible reservations.[283] As far as the severability approach was concerned, the United Kingdom shared the position advanced by the United States. It held that

---

[277] Human Rights Committee, General Comment No. 24: Issues Relating to Reservations Made upon Ratification or Accession to the Covenant or the Optional Protocols thereto, or in Relation to Declarations under Article 41 of the Covenant, UN Doc. CCPR/C/21/Rev. 1/Add.6, 04.11.1994, paras. 17–18.

[278] *Boerefijn*, Impact on the Law on Treaty Reservations, in: Kamminga/Scheinin (eds.), The Impact of Human Rights Law on General International Law, 2009, p. 87, who refers to the severability approach as the "most controversial aspect".

[279] Report of the Human Rights Committee (52nd, 53rd and 54th session), UN Doc. A/50/40 Vol. I (1996), pp. 126–127; *Engström*, Understanding Powers of International Organizations: A Study of the Doctrines of Attributed Powers, Implied Powers and Constitutionalism – with a Special Focus on the Human Rights Committee, Åbo 2009, pp. 221–222.

[280] Report of the Human Rights Committee (52nd, 53rd and 54th session), UN Doc. A/50/40 Vol. I (1996), p. 127.

[281] Report of the Human Rights Committee (52nd, 53rd and 54th session), UN Doc. A/50/40 Vol. I (1996), pp. 129–130.

[282] Report of the Human Rights Committee (52nd, 53rd and 54th session), UN Doc. A/50/40 Vol. I (1996), p. 132.

[283] Report of the Human Rights Committee (52nd, 53rd and 54th session), UN Doc. A/50/40 Vol. I (1996), pp. 132–133; the criticism was mainly rooted in the fact that the formulation in General Comment No. 24 evoked the impression of the Human Rights Committee declaring its decisions on the admissibility of a reservation to be binding.

a State party which had submitted a reservation "fundamentally incompatible with participation in the treaty regime", would not become a party to the respective treaty.[284]

France, in turn, expressed much more stringent criticism. It rejected the entirety of paragraph 18 of General Comment No. 24, stressing that the Committee owed its existence solely to its constituent treaty, and that it would not possess any other powers than those provided for in it.[285] With a view to the severability of reservations, France pointed out that any participation in the treaty was contingent on state consent. Where the consent was not valid due to an impermissible reservation, the only possible consequence was not having become a party to the treaty in question.[286]

c) Question of competence

However, an important distinction must be drawn at this juncture. As indicated above, the power to adjudicate on reservations and the legal effects thereof are two different, yet very closely related, legal problems. According to some members of the ILC, the functions of treaty bodies must be viewed through an institutionalist lens, whereas the reservation regime, which is to entail the legal effects of invalid reservations, had to be viewed through the lens of treaty law, and, most importantly, these "two basically different aspects should not be confused".[287]

In practice, no problem arises without the other. Ruling a reservation impermissible is only of use to the respective monitoring body if it can proceed thereafter to exercise its functions with regard to the provisions that have been subjected to invalid reservations. Unless treaty bodies sever the invalid reservation from a State party's ratification, the State party would either not be bound at all or would be bound by all provisions subjected to none or only valid reservations.[288] Severing invalid reservations thus gives rise to the question whether, and

---

[284] Report of the Human Rights Committee (52nd, 53rd and 54th session), UN Doc. A/50/40 Vol. I (1996), p. 134.

[285] Report of the Human Rights Committee (55th, 56th and 57th session), UN Doc. A/51/40 Vol. I (1997), p. 106.

[286] Report of the Human Rights Committee (55th, 56th and 57th session), UN Doc. A/51/40 Vol. I (1997), p. 106.

[287] Report of the International Law Commission on the work of its forty-ninth session (12 May–18 July 1997), UN Doc. A/52/10 (1997), Chapter V, Reservations to Treaties, para. 138.

[288] *Nowak*, CCPR Commentary, Second revised Edition, 2005, Introduction, para. 27; see also *Goodman*, Human Rights Treaties, Invalid Reservations, and State Consent, American Journal of International Law 96 (2002), 531.

at what point exactly, the respective monitoring body acts *ultra vires*,[289] and when treaty bodies' actions amount to the exercise of "creeping jurisdiction".[290]

Hence, as proposed by scholars, the power to assess the validity of reservations, or at least to formulate recommendations in this matter, and to base its jurisdiction notwithstanding, or precisely because of, an invalid reservation are two different features,[291] both of which will be analysed more closely in the following.

aa) Competence to formulate recommendations as regards reservations

In its General Comment No. 24, the Human Rights Committee stressed that it was inappropriate to leave the assessment of reservations to State parties. It justified its view by pointing to the restricted principle of reciprocity in the realm of human rights treaties and the inconsistent pattern of objections raised by States as regards other State parties' reservations.[292] Moreover, the Human Rights Committee considered itself "particularly placed well" to objectively determine the compatibility of reservations with the object and purpose of the Covenant.[293]

Indeed, at first glance, these might be compelling arguments. State parties have only limited time to submit their objections within one year after ratification, and new State parties to the treaty concerned cannot object to reservations submitted by others who are already a party to the treaty.[294] Furthermore, the low

---

[289] Report of the International Law Commission on the work of its forty-ninth session (12 May–18 July 1997), UN Doc. A/52/10 (1997), Chapter V, Reservations to Treaties, para. 139.

[290] Report of the International Law Commission on the work of its forty-ninth session (12 May–18 July 1997), UN Doc. A/52/10 (1997), Chapter V, Reservations to Treaties, para. 144.

[291] *Boerefijn*, Impact on the Law on Treaty Reservations, in: Kamminga/Scheinin (eds.), The Impact of Human Rights Law on General International Law, 2009, pp. 84–92, who differentiates between the competence to examine reservations and formulate recommendations and the competence to determine the validity of a reservations and the consequences thereof; *Korkelia*, New Challenges to the Regime of Reservations under the International Covenant on Civil and Political Rights, European Journal of International Law 13 (2002), 437, 450, who distinguishes between the competence to determine the compatibility of a reservation with the object and purpose of a treaty and the competence to determine the consequences of an incompatible reservation; *Baratta*, Should Invalid Reservations to Human Rights Treaties be Disregarded?, European Journal of International Law 11 (2000), 413, 416.

[292] Human Rights Committee, General Comment No. 24: Issues Relating to Reservations Made upon Ratification or Accession to the Covenant or the Optional Protocols thereto, or in Relation to Declarations under Article 41 of the Covenant, UN Doc. CCPR/C/21/Rev. 1/Add.6, 04.11.1994, para. 17.

[293] Human Rights Committee, General Comment No. 24: Issues Relating to Reservations Made upon Ratification or Accession to the Covenant or the Optional Protocols thereto, or in Relation to Declarations under Article 41 of the Covenant, UN Doc. CCPR/C/21/Rev. 1/Add.6, 04.11.1994, para. 18.

[294] *Boerefijn*, Impact on the Law on Treaty Reservations, in: Kamminga/Scheinin (eds.), The Impact of Human Rights Law on General International Law, 2009, p. 84.

number of objections raised in human rights treaty regimes is explained by the fact that State parties are supposedly more interested in the right to submit reservations themselves than to object to reservations.[295] Nevertheless, these are rather functional arguments,[296] or at the very least, an assessment of the state of affairs.[297]

But the Committee made another point that seems stronger in legal terms. It argued that assessing the permissibility of reservations was "a task that the Committee cannot avoid in the performance of its functions" and that it had to know the exact scope of its obligations under the reporting procedure or the individual complaints procedure.[298] While some commentators consider this argument belonging to the realm of necessity and functionality too,[299] it should rather be understood as an attempt to derive the power in question from the provisions governing the reporting procedure,[300] or individual complaints procedure. Especially when taking into consideration a State party's obligation to report on factors and difficulties in the implementation of a treaty, a human rights treaty body must at least be able to comment on a reservation, the latter indicating difficulties in implementation.[301]

---

[295] *Boerefijn*, Impact on the Law on Treaty Reservations, in: Kamminga/Scheinin (eds.), The Impact of Human Rights Law on General International Law, 2009, p. 85; *McGrory*, Reservations of Virtue? Lessons from Trinidad and Tobago's Reservation to the First Optional Protocol, Human Rights Quarterly 23 (2001), 769, 822, who states that objections to reservations often "reflect nonlegal determinations by states"; *Lijnzaad*, Reservations to UN-Human Rights Treaties: Ratify and Ruin?, 1995, p. 414, arguing for a more proactive approach by the Committee in light of the "inertia" of State parties.

[296] *Baylis*, General Comment 24: Confronting the Problem of Reservations to Human Rights Treaties, Berkeley Journal of International Law 17 (1999), 277, 298.

[297] ILC, Second report on reservations to treaties, by Mr. Alain Pellet, Special Rapporteur, UN Doc. A/CN.4/477 & Corr.1 & 2 and Add.1 & Corr.1–4 (1996), para. 205.

[298] Human Rights Committee, General Comment No. 24: Issues Relating to Reservations Made upon Ratification or Accession to the Covenant or the Optional Protocols thereto, or in Relation to Declarations under Article 41 of the Covenant, UN Doc. CCPR/C/21/Rev. 1/Add.6, 04.11.1994, para. 18.

[299] *McCall-Smith*, Reservations and the Determinative Function of the Human Rights Treaty Bodies, German Yearbook of International Law 54 (2011), 521, 538; *Korkelia*, New Challenges to the Regime of Reservations under the International Covenant on Civil and Political Rights, European Journal of International Law 13 (2002), 437, 454, who sees the Committee's position supported "by its functional necessity."

[300] *Boerefijn*, Impact on the Law on Treaty Reservations, in: Kamminga/Scheinin (eds.), The Impact of Human Rights Law on General International Law, 2009, p. 86; *Baylis*, General Comment 24: Confronting the Problem of Reservations to Human Rights Treaties, Berkeley Journal of International Law 17 (1999), 277, 314, who arrives at the same solution but arguing that the Committee is bound by article 31(2)(b) VCLT when evaluating a State party's compliance.

[301] *Boerefijn*, Impact on the Law on Treaty Reservations, in: Kamminga/Scheinin (eds.), The Impact of Human Rights Law on General International Law, 2009, p. 86.

Therefore, criticism that treaty bodies lacked the express power to deal with the issue of reservations,[302] or that their respective legal basis in that matter was weak,[303] can be refuted in so far as the evaluation of reservations forms an integral part of their monitoring and quasi-judicial functions.[304] Their power could either be read into the respective provisions regulating a treaty body's mandate under the reporting procedure, or, alternatively, be taken as "inherent" in a treaty body's concept,[305] or considered an implied power.[306] Also the ILC Guide to Practice on Reservations considers treaty bodies to be "necessarily competent" to assess the permissibility of reservations.[307] However, it was equally stated by the ILC that other entities, such as State parties, are not excluded from making any assessment, as their powers are not mutually exclusive, but cumulative.[308]

---

[302] As articulated by the US for instance in reaction to General Comment No. 24; cf. Report of the International Law Commission on the work of its forty-ninth session (12 May–18 July 1997), UN Doc. A/52/10 (1997), Chapter V, Reservations to Treaties, paras. 134–135, according to some members of the ILC, treaty bodies could not assess the permissibility of reservation unless an explicit treaty provision would provide for this power. Furthermore, they argued that the broader powers of regional bodies could not easily be transferred to UN human rights treaty bodies.

[303] *Baylis*, General Comment 24: Confronting the Problem of Reservations to Human Rights Treaties, Berkeley Journal of International Law 17 (1999), 277, 296.

[304] *McCall-Smith*, Mind the Gaps: The ILC Guide to Practice on Reservations to Human Rights Treaties, International Community Law Review 16 (2014), 263, 303; see in relation to the CRC Committee *Schabas*, Reservations to the Convention on the Rights of the Child, Human Rights Quarterly 18 (1996), 472, 488.

[305] *Walter*, Article 19, Formulation of reservations, in: Dörr/Schmalenbach (eds.), Vienna Convention on the Law of Treaties: A Commentary, Second Edition, 2018, para. 129; *Baratta*, Should Invalid Reservations to Human Rights Treaties be Disregarded?, European Journal of International Law 11 (2000), 413, 415; *Lijnzaad*, Reservations to UN-Human Rights Treaties: Ratify and Ruin?, 1995, p. 413, who considers the "integral treaty" as the basis for the Committee's actions in this matter; generally accepting said competence, *Chinkin*, Reservations and Objections to the Convention on the Elimination of All Forms of Discrimination against Women, in: Gardner (ed.), Human Rights as general Norms and a State's Right to opt out: Reservations and Objections to Human Rights Conventions, 1997, p. 79.

[306] *Giegerich*, Vorbehalte zu Menschenrechtsabkommen: Zulässigkeit, Gültigkeit und Prüfungskompetenzen von Vertragsgremien: Ein konstitutioneller Ansatz, ZaöRV 55 (1995), 713, 767–768, who also refers to the competence as an "Annexkompetenz".

[307] Report of the International Law Commission, Sixty-third session (26 April–3 June and 4 July–12 August 2011), UN Doc. A/66/10/Add.1 (2011), Guide to Practice on Reservations to Treaties, Commentary to Guideline 3.2.1, para. 4; said position was already included in the Special Rapporteur's second report, ILC, Second report on reservations to treaties, by Mr. Alain Pellet, Special Rapporteur, UN Doc. A/CN.4/477 & Corr.1 & 2 and Add.1 & Corr.1–4 (1996), para. 206.

[308] Report of the International Law Commission, Sixty-third session (26 April–3 June and 4 July–12 August 2011), UN Doc. A/66/10/Add.1 (2011), Guide to Practice on Reservations to Treaties, Commentary to Guideline 3.2, para. 1; see in this context *McCall-Smith*, Mind the Gaps: The ILC Guide to Practice on Reservations to Human Rights Treaties, International Community Law Review 16 (2014), 263, 303, who rightly criticizes that the ILC Guidelines do

bb) Competence to determine the legal consequences of invalid reservations

The effect of an invalid reservation, first and foremost, touches upon the crucial question of whether the rules in the VCLT provide an adequate solution to this problem and whether the State party concerned remains bound by the treaty and if so, to what extent.[309] It is therefore not initially an issue of competence. However, if the severability approach promoted by the Human Rights Committee and regional human rights courts is followed, it overrides State consent in cases of doubt. Severing reservations entails considering individual complaints which exactly relate to those rights which have been subjected to (inadmissible) reservations, and where the State party has thus deliberately excluded the treaty body's jurisdiction to the extent provided for in its respective reservations.[310] Only the latter is ultimately a question of competence, namely the competence of the treaty body to determine its own jurisdiction, which is the logical consequence of assuming a reservation's severability.

One important example where the Human Rights Committee found it had jurisdiction precisely because of an invalid reservation was the communication *Kennedy v. Trinidad and Tobago*.[311] Prior to the submission of the complaint, Trinidad and Tobago had denounced the First Optional Protocol and then re-acceded to it by simultaneously entering a reservation which excluded the Human Rights Committee's competence to receive and consider communications from individuals having been sentenced to death.[312]

The majority of the Committee members found the reservation in question to be incompatible with the object and purpose of the First Optional Protocol as it would "[run] counter to some of the basic principles embodied in the Covenant and its Protocols".[313] The Committee then concluded that it was not barred from examining the communication, and thus applied the severability approach

---

not provide a solution to possible contradictory assessments undertaken by State parties and treaty bodies.

[309] *Reservations to the Genocide Convention*, Advisory Opinion, I.C.J. Reports 1951, p. 15, 29, with the "total invalidity" option, which denotes that the State party did not become a party at all if the reservation proves to be incompatible with the object and purpose of the treaty concerned.

[310] *Bradley/Goldsmith*, Treaties, Human Rights, and Conditional Consent, University of Pennsylvania Law Review 149 (2000), 399, 436, arguing that it is "incorrect" of the Human Rights Committee to conclude that a State party remains bound.

[311] Human Rights Committee, *Kennedy v. Trinidad and Tobago*, Communication No. 845/1998, UN Doc. CCPR/C/74/D/845/1998, 28.03.2002.

[312] *Scheinin*, Reservations by States under the International Covenant on Civil and Political Rights and its Optional Protocols, and the Practice of the Human Rights Committee, in: Ziemele (ed.), Reservations to Human Rights Treaties and the Vienna Convention Regime: Conflict, Harmony or Reconciliation, 2004, p. 49.

[313] The Committee considered the admissibility and the merits of the communication separately, for the decision on the admissibility, see Report of the Human Rights Committee (67th, 68th and 69th session), UN Doc. A/55/40 Vol. II (2000), Annex XI.A, para. 6.7.

developed in General Comment No. 24.[314] Arguments in favour of the Committee's approach have been the allegedly special nature of human rights treaties, with individuals as the real beneficiaries, what should consequently guide any of the Committee's actions. Another argument for the severability approach was that a treaty body should consider a State party as a member to the treaty concerned as long as the State party has not indicated differently.[315]

Others criticized the Human Rights Committee for having gone too far in the application of the severability approach, especially regarding the communication at hand, where the State party's actions clearly indicated that it only had the intention to be bound by the First Option Protocol to the extent provided for by its reservation.[316] Provided that reliance on the unrestricted State consent constitutes the prerequisite for participation in a treaty regime, a State party shall not be bound in the case of entering an impermissible reservation, as the latter was a precondition for being bound at all.[317] Besides, to sever the reservation in question might potentially have the unwanted negative side-effect of State parties denouncing the treaty concerned with subsequent re-accession, possibily coupled with another reservation.[318]

A solution to this delicate dilemma may be provided by the ILC Guide to Practice on Reservations to Treaties. Its Guideline 3.2.1 provides that "[the] assessment made by such a body in the exercise of this competence has no greater legal effect than that of the act which contains it."[319] Put differently, the finding of an invalid reservation does not amount to a binding decision as to the extent to which a State party remains bound by the treaty. With respect to treaty bodies' quasi-judicial powers, this seems to be a mediating and adequate position.[320] As with adopted views and concluding observations, a State party is obliged to

---

[314] *Korkelia*, New Challenges to the Regime of Reservations under the International Covenant on Civil and Political Rights, European Journal of International Law 13 (2002), 437, 464–468.

[315] *Scheinin*, Reservations by States under the International Covenant on Civil and Political Rights and its Optional Protocols, and the Practice of the Human Rights Committee, in: Ziemele (ed.), Reservations to Human Rights Treaties and the Vienna Convention Regime: Conflict, Harmony or Reconciliation, 2004, p. 51.

[316] *McGrory*, Reservations of Virtue? Lessons from Trinidad and Tobago's Reservation to the First Optional Protocol, Human Rights Quarterly 23 (2001), 769, 826.

[317] *Bradley/Goldsmith*, Treaties, Human Rights, and Conditional Consent, University of Pennsylvania Law Review 149 (2000), 399, 436–437.

[318] *Helfer*, Not Fully Committed? Reservations, Risk, and Treaty Design, Yale Journal of International Law 31 (2002), 367, 381.

[319] Report of the International Law Commission, Sixty-third session (26 April–3 June and 4 July–12 August 2011), UN Doc. A/66/10/Add.1 (2011), Guide to Practice on Reservations to Treaties, Guideline 3.2.1.

[320] *Salem*, Sharia Reservations to Human Rights Treaties, in: Peters (ed.), Max Planck Encyclopaedia of International Public Law, Online version, March 2020, para. 24; *Aust*, Modern Treaty Law and Practice, Third Edition, 2013, p. 135, who underlines the differences between human rights treaty bodies and international courts or tribunals.

respect and consider treaty body pronouncements in good faith, but it is ultimately not bound by them in a strict legal sense. Furthermore, praised as possibly one of the most important parts of the ILC Guidelines,[321] Guideline 4.5.3 establishes a presumption of severability by which effect the State party, as long as it has not indicated a contrary position, is bound by the treaty without the benefit of the impermissible reservation. The ILC therefore "acknowledged"[322] the approach developed by the Human Rights Committee and regional human rights courts with the inclusion of the severability approach as the default rule unless the assumption is rebutted by the State party concerned. The solution proposed by the ILC is thus able to strike a balance between the two extremes of either total severance, or the effect of not being a member to the treaty anymore.[323]

cc) Interim conclusion on the topic of reservations

Even if this does not conclusively answer the question of whether treaty bodies are permitted to adopt views or concluding observations related to treaty guarantees State parties tried to exempt from their scrutiny by means of impermissible reservations, the example of reservations very clearly demonstrates what problems treaty bodies face due to their sometimes not precisely defined powers. That the topic of legal powers with regard to the assessment of reservations remains contentious is further mirrored by more recent Committee practice. Although the position developed by the Human Rights Committee seems to have prevailed and has been accepted by treaty body representatives at the sixth Inter-Committee Meeting in 2007,[324] the Committees proceed in a more cooperative fashion, as opposed to a confrontational one.[325] Taking for instance the CERD Committee, originally little or not at all inclined towards making any statements on the permissibility of reservations, it now prefers "fruitful dialogue" over "legal struggle".[326] The same has been noted with a view to the Human Rights Com-

---

[321] *Ziemele/Liede*, Reservations to Human Rights Treaties: From Draft Guideline 3.1.12 to Guideline 3.1.5.6, European Journal of International Law 24 (2013), 1135, 1150.

[322] *Ziemele/Liede*, Reservations to Human Rights Treaties: From Draft Guideline 3.1.12 to Guideline 3.1.5.6, European Journal of International Law 24 (2013), 1135, 1151–1152, who consider this as an inclusion of "progressive development of international law".

[323] *Swaine*, Treaty Reservations, in: Hollis (ed.), The Oxford Guide to Treaties, Second Edition, 2020, p. 302, stating that a presumption of severability "is certainly more moderate" than the other solutions in the extreme.

[324] Report of the chairpersons of the human rights treaty bodies on their nineteenth meeting, UN Doc. A/62/224, 13.08.2007, Annex, Report of the sixth inter-committee meeting of human rights treaty bodies, para. 48(v), with reference to the Report of the Working Group on Reservations, UN Doc. HRI/MC/2007/5, 09.02.2007, para. 16; *Boerefijn*, Impact on the Law on Treaty Reservations, in: Kamminga/Scheinin (eds.), The Impact of Human Rights Law on General International Law, 2009, p. 90.

[325] *Giegerich*, Treaties, Multilateral, Reservations to, in: Peters (ed.), Max Planck Encyclopedia of Public International Law, Online version, September 2020, para. 58, referring to the Committee practice as a "soft approach".

[326] *Thornberry*, The International Convention on the Elimination of All Forms of Racial

mittee, which rather seeks to persuade State parties to withdraw their problematic reservations.[327]

7. Conclusion on past extensions of powers

The preceding analysis has confirmed to a great extent the hypothesis established above. Treaty bodies, as well as academic literature, have been relying on considerations of effectiveness in the extension of powers of treaty bodies.

While the very competence to adopt concluding observations now constitutes a part of the reporting procedure without which it is hardly possible to think of it, their introduction provides an early and very instructive example of diverging positions on the respective treaty body's mandate. Particularly the discussions within the Human Rights Committee and the CEDAW Committee demonstrate the two major approaches in the delineation of powers, either focusing on the treaty's text or focusing on a more effectiveness-related interpretation. As far as the adoption of concluding observations is concerned, said practice is clearly covered by the wording of all treaties and their introduction is in conformity with the criteria established above.[328]

As far as General Comments are concerned, despite dispersed critiques of the mandate to issue them, their drafting and adoption can be subsumed under the relevant provisions governing the reporting procedure. What is more, the practice does not impose new obligations as such on State parties. While their content is more likely to be challenged for allegedly too progressive interpretations,[329] the

---

Discrimination: A Commentary, 2016, Article 20: Reservations, p. 464; see also *Helfer*, Not Fully Committed? Reservations, Risk, and Treaty Design, Yale Journal of International Law 31 (2006), 367, 381 proposing a "reservation dialogue" with government officials; see further *Lijnzaad*, Reservations to UN-Human Rights Treaties: Ratify and Ruin?, 1995, p. 417, where it is stated that "fruitful discussion" is given preference over a completely confrontational approach.

[327] *Swaine*, Treaty Reservations, in: Hollis (ed.), The Oxford Guide to Treaties, Second Edition, 2020, p. 304; see also *Schlütter*, Aspects of human rights interpretation by the UN treaty bodies, in: Keller/Ulfstein (eds.), UN Human Rights Treaty Bodies: Law and Legitimacy, 2012, pp. 285–286, who observes that treaty bodies only rarely assess the "material content of a reservation"; see also *Salem*, Sharia Reservations to Human Rights Treaties, in: Peters (ed.), Max Planck Encyclopaedia of International Public Law, Online version, March 2020, para. 23, who notes that the CEDAW Committee, next to other treaty bodies, has never declared a single reservation impermissible, though it has regularly indicated its concerns to State parties.

[328] See, however, the rare position of *Pedone/Kloster*, New Proposals for Human Rights Treaty Body Reform, Journal of Transnational Law & Policy 22 (2012–2013), 29, 41–42, who argue that the practice of adopting concluding observations is beyond a treaty body's mandate. Nevertheless, their critique seems to be motivated more by the content of the concluding observations and not by their adoption as such.

[329] Instructive in this manner are the comments of the United States in reaction to draft General Comment No. 36, where it "expressed concerns with the Committee's interpretive practice generally", but what seems to have been mostly motivated by the content of the

very competence to adopt General Comments is thus covered by the mandate of treaty bodies.[330]

With a view to the introduction of follow-up procedures, both to concluding observations and views adopted, new obligations have been imposed on State parties. Nevertheless, it can be safely assumed that sufficient normative bases under the treaties exist, and that a treaty body's power in this matter is ultimately not grounded on pure considerations of effectiveness, contrary to what the sole reference to the implied powers doctrine would suggest. Particularly follow-up requests to concluding observations can be easily subsumed under the provisions allowing Committees to request further information. Under the individual complaints procedure, it is the interplay between the broad interpretation of the provisions authorising treaty bodies to consider communications, and the undeniable need to ensure that the procedure is protective and effective for individuals, that may outweigh the fact that the follow-up procedure imposed another obligation on State parties.

As far as the issuance of interim measures and their legal weight are concerned, each extension of powers has been motivated to a great extent by considerations of effectiveness and has caused more controversy. Nevertheless, as has also been demonstrated, a normative basis could be identified. Specifically, the binding character of interim measures must be considered indispensable for the effective dischargement of the individual complaints procedure. Similar reasons have been invoked in the justification of treaty bodies being able to assess a reservation's permissibility.

Against the backdrop of both current and past attempts at reform and the preceding analysis, discussions on the role of treaty bodies will very likely oscillate between two extremes: either focusing exclusively on the text of the treaty or on considerations of maximum effectiveness.[331] The determinants proposed

---

specific General Comments. Indicative of such assumption is the State party's further remark that "[in] keeping with its advisory mandate, the Committee should refrain from providing its recommendations in imperative ('must') or mandatory ('required') terms", Observations of the United States of America On the Human Rights Committee's Draft General Comment No. 36 On Article 6 – Right to Life, October 6, 2017, https://www.ohchr.org/en/calls-for-input/general-comment-no-36-article-6-right-life (last access: 21.08.2023); see also *Reiners*, Transnational Lawmaking Coalitions for Human Rights, 2021, p. 34, who aptly states that "the line separating a treaty body interpreting norms from one creating new ones is thin but crucial."

[330] See in this regard *Ulfstein*, Law-making by human rights treaty bodies, in: Liivoja/Petman (eds.), International Law-making, 2014, p. 252, who aptly notes that the question is rather how the competence to adopt General Comments is eventually exercised, thus it is the content of General Comments that gives rise to criticism by State parties; see for a similar reasoning, *Klein/Kretzmer*, The UN Human Rights Committee: The General Comments – The Evolution of an Autonomous Monitoring Instrument, German Yearbook of International Law 58 (2015), 189, 204, who observe that it is not the competence that is controversial, but the normative status of General Comments.

[331] See in this context, *Opsahl*, The Human Rights Committee, in: Alston (ed.), The United Nations and Human Rights: A Critical Appraisal, First Edition, 1992, p. 397, who notes that

above and confirmed in the preceding section can ensure that a balance is struck, and thus provide a legal framework in the delineation of treaty bodies' powers. Each extension of powers has been grounded on an existing normative basis provided for in the treaties, at least indirectly. Whenever the normative basis appears weak, more effectiveness-orientated interpretation has been brought into play, but only to the extent that the extension of powers has been indispensable for the exercise of functions already conferred on treaty bodies. What is more, new and additional legal obligations may also only be imposed when they prove to be equally indispensable for the performance of mandates. Finally, it makes a difference whether the extension of powers involves purely internal matters or affects the relationship with State parties.

B. Broadening of competencies with the involvement of State parties

Despite the main focus on treaty bodies' own legal possibilities, two further avenues for vesting the Committees with additional powers shall be illustrated, both of which include the action of State parties to the treaties.

These are first, subsequent practice within the meaning of article 31(3)(b) VCLT and second, the General Assembly's authority in the context of the treaty body strengthening process and its (legal) relationship to human rights treaty bodies.

I. Subsequent practice

Even though subsequent practice constitutes one of several bases for, or gives rise to, evolutive interpretation,[332] it is considered here as an independent interpretative method in the extension of treaty bodies' powers. The interpretative method of subsequent practice is a means by which State parties can exert decisive influence in altering or even modifying the treaty concerned without formal treaty amendments.[333] A considerable advantage of subsequent practice, in contrast to

---

the room for initiatives by the Committee is "probably less limited by legal barriers than by the Committee's resources and other practical constraints."

[332] Report of the International Law Commission, Seventieth session (30 April–1 June and 2 July–10 August 2018), UN Doc. A/73/10 (2018), Text of the draft conclusions on subsequent agreements and subsequent practice in relation to the interpretation of treaties, commentary to draft conclusion 8, paras. 14–16 with specific focus on human rights courts and bodies and their use of article 31(3)(b) VCLT in the context of evolutive interpretation.

[333] *Roberts*, Subsequent Agreements and Practice: The Battle over Interpretive Power, in: Nolte (ed.), Treaties and Subsequent Practice, 2013, p. 95.

the "living-instrument" approach, lies in the fact that it can be applied to provisions which were not intended to be of evolutionary character.[334]

1. Relevant authors of subsequent practice

Read strictly, article 31(3)(b) VCLT only qualifies the parties to the treaty concerned as authors of subsequent practice.[335] However, with specific regard to human rights treaty bodies, it has been argued that their findings, views and pronouncements could possibly constitute subsequent practice under article 31(3)(b) VCLT in their own right as well.[336]

One vigorous proponent of such a broad understanding of who is entitled to contribute to relevant practice was the Human Rights Committee itself. It included in its draft General Comment No. 33 that its own body of jurisprudence constituted subsequent practice within the meaning of article 31(3)(b) VCLT. In the alternative, it held that at least the acquiescence of State parties to its pronouncements constituted relevant practice.[337]

Following criticism from several State parties, the Human Rights Committee finally refrained from including explicit reference to article 31(3)(b) VCLT and adopted its final version of General Comment No. 33 without the controversial passage.[338] The United Kingdom rejected the Committee's assertion that its body

---

[334] See *Gardiner*, Treaty Interpretation, Second Edition, 2015, p. 275, who observes of "more limited potential" of evolutive interpretation when compared to subsequent practice; *Arato*, Subsequent Practice and Evolutive Interpretation: Techniques of Treaty Interpretation over Time and Their Diverse Consequences, The Law and Practice of International Courts and Tribunals 9 (2010), 443, 452.

[335] For a short enumeration of who might be a relevant actor in a treaty's application, see *Kohen*, Keeping Subsequent Agreements and Practice in Their Right Limits, in: Nolte (ed.), Treaties and Subsequent Practice, 2013, pp. 41–42.

[336] Cf. generally *McGrogan*, On the Interpretation of Human Rights Treaties and Subsequent Practice, Netherlands Quarterly of Human Rights 32 (2014), 347; ILA, Committee on International Human Rights Law and Practice, Final Report on the Impact of the Findings of the United Nations Human Rights Treaty Bodies, Conference 2004, p. 7, cited in: *Keller/Grover*, General Comments of the Human Rights Committee and their legitimacy, in: Keller/Ulfstein (eds.), UN Human Rights Treaty Bodies: Law and Legitimacy, 2012, p. 131, *Keller* and *Grover* seem at least convinced, as they refer to the report's suggestion as compelling; see also *Mechlem*, Treaty Bodies and the Interpretation of Human Rights, Vanderbilt Journal of Transnational Law 42 (2009), 905, 920, who equally acknowledges, however, that the role of State parties cannot be completely ignored in the interpretation of treaties; *Hall*, The Duty of States Parties to the Convention against Torture to Provide Procedures Permitting Victims to Recover Reparations for Torture Committed Abroad, European Journal of International Law 18 (2007), 921, 927.

[337] Human Rights Committee, Draft General Comment No. 33, Second revised Edition as of 18 August 2008, UN Doc. CCPR/C/GC/33/CRP.3, para. 17.

[338] Report of the International Law Commission, Seventieth session (30 April–1 June and 2 July–10 August 2018), UN Doc. A/73/10 (2018), Text of the draft conclusions on subsequent agreements and subsequent practice in relation to the interpretation of treaties, commentary to draft conclusion 13, para. 10.

of jurisprudence would constitute subsequent practice under article 31(3)(b) VCLT. It argued that the Committee was composed of independent experts, serving in their personal capacity, who were thus not considered as acting on behalf of State parties. Furthermore, the UK disagreed with the Committee's alternative assertion. It argued that missing actions or comments on the Committee's pronouncements could not qualify as "acquiescence with the content of those statements."[339]

The United States reacted similarly, if not even more critically and "strongly [disagreed] with this extraordinary assertion". Only the consistent practice by all State parties, or at least common acceptance, could fulfil the criteria under article 31(3)(b) VCLT. Secondly, the United States questioned whether acquiescence of State parties could reflect established practice, as silence to treaty bodies' statements could not imply acquiescence of the conclusion contained therein.[340] Australia also rejected the Committee's first assertion, but reacted less critically to the "acquiescence-position", agreeing in principle to such a possibility. Nevertheless, it simultaneously held that any such agreement could only be reached via gradual development over time, which would need to involve all State parties to the treaty concerned, and that rejections and expressions of disagreements would have to be given equal consideration.[341]

The above portrayed criticism by State parties to draft General Comment No. 33 was considered evidence by the ILC that pronouncements of expert treaty bodies do not qualify as subsequent practice under article 31(3)(b) VCLT.[342] These critiques are justified in that, contrary to acts by international organizations, which are entitled to discharge their actions in lieu of contracting parties and whose actions are hence attributable to State parties, treaty body members serve independently in their personal capacity.[343] Yet, according to the ILC, a "pronouncement of an expert treaty body may give rise to, or refer to, a subse-

---

[339] Comments of the Government of the United Kingdom of Great Britain and Northern Ireland on draft General Comment 33: "The Obligations of States Parties under the Optional Protocol to the International Covenant on Civil and Political Rights", 17 October 2008, available from: https://www.ohchr.org/EN/HRBodies/CCPR/Pages/GC33-ObligationsofStatesParties.aspx (last access: 21.08.2023).

[340] Comments of the United States of America on the Human Rights Committee's "Draft General Comment 33: The Obligations of States Parties Under the Optional Protocol to the International Covenant Civil and Political Rights", 17 October 2020.

[341] Views of the Australian Government on draft General Comment No. 33: "The Obligations of States Parties Under the Optional Protocol to the International Covenant Civil and Political Rights", 03 October 2008.

[342] Report of the International Law Commission, Seventieth session (30 April–1 June and 2 July–10 August 2018), UN Doc. A/73/10 (2018), Text of the draft conclusions on subsequent agreements and subsequent practice in relation to the interpretation of treaties, Commentary to draft conclusion 13, para. 10.

[343] *Dörr*, Article 31, General rule of interpretation, in: Dörr/Schmalenbach (eds.), Vienna Convention on the Law of Treaties: A Commentary, Second Edition, 2018, para. 85.

quent agreement or subsequent practice by parties under article 31, paragraph 3, or subsequent practice under article 32."[344]

But even if one were to opt for a broader interpretation of article 31(3)(b) VCLT, whereby treaty bodies' pronouncements would themselves amount to conduct in the interpretation of the treaty concerned,[345] the question still remains whether there is an agreement between the contracting parties. In that regard the ILC held, in conformity with opposing State parties to draft General Comment No. 33, that "[silence] by a party shall not be presumed to constitute subsequent practice under article 31, paragraph 3 (b), accepting an interpretation of a treaty as expressed in a pronouncement of an expert treaty body."[346]

It appears that the relevant question is ultimately what weight is to be accorded to the silence on the part of State parties. While the ILC established a presumption against silence constituting acceptance of treaty body pronouncements, it has been noted elsewhere that the legal situation in the sphere of human rights treaties should be the reverse, with an agreement having been reached by silence, unless "explicit disagreement" is articulated by State parties.[347] Nevertheless, this specific assertion can be challenged on various grounds.

A State party to the treaty under interpretation will simply not be able to react to and comment on each pronouncement.[348] This holds particularly true for the

---

[344] Report of the International Law Commission, Seventieth session (30 April–1 June and 2 July–10 August 2018), UN Doc. A/73/10 (2018), Text of the draft conclusions on subsequent agreements and subsequent practice in relation to the interpretation of treaties, draft conclusion 13(3).

[345] *McGrogan*, On the Interpretation of Human Rights Treaties and Subsequent Practice, Netherlands Quarterly of Human Rights 32 (2014), 347, 369–370.

[346] Reaching the same conclusion in legal literature, *Kanetake*, UN human rights treaty monitoring bodies before domestic courts, International and Comparative Law Quarterly 67 (2018), 201, 218; *Klein/Kretzmer*, The UN Human Rights Committee: The General Comments – The Evolution of an Autonomous Monitoring Instrument, German Yearbook of International Law 58 (2015), 189, 205–206; *Kohen*, Keeping Subsequent Agreements and Practice in Their Right Limits, in: Nolte (ed.), Treaties and Subsequent Practice, 2013, p. 42, who states that treaty body practice "will certainly be of particular importance in the interpretation of the treaties concerned"; *Mechlem*, Treaty Bodies and the Interpretation of Human Rights, Vanderbilt Journal of Transnational Law 42 (2009), 905, 921, arguing that treaty body pronouncements may "induce and reflect" subsequent practice under article 31(3)(b) VCLT; *Meron*, Human Rights Law-Making in the United Nations: A Critique of Instruments and Process, 1986, p. 10.

[347] *McGrogan*, On the Interpretation of Human Rights Treaties and Subsequent Practice, Netherlands Quarterly of Human Rights 32 (2014), 347, 370.

[348] Report of the International Law Commission, Seventieth session (30 April–1 June and 2 July–10 August 2018), UN Doc. A/73/10 (2018), Text of the draft conclusions on subsequent agreements and subsequent practice in relation to the interpretation of treaties, commentary to draft conclusion 13, para. 19; *Moeckli*, Interpretation of the ICESCR: Between Morality and State Consent, in: Moeckli/Keller/Heri (eds.), The Human Rights Covenants at 50: Their Past, Present, and Future, 2018, p. 69; see also *van Alebeek/Nollkaemper*, The legal status of decisions by human rights treaty bodies in national law, in: Keller/Ulfstein (eds.), UN Human

B. Broadening of competencies with the involvement of State parties

adoption of views under the individual complaints procedure. Here, the reasoning might also entail progressive interpretation of treaty guarantees and could thereby set precedents which would call for reaction by State parties.[349] In contrast to General Comments, however, views are not circulated to all State parties, and for some years now, treaty bodies have no longer included adopted views in their annual reports submitted to the General Assembly, which further impedes their dissemination. But even reacting to other documents adopted by treaty bodies alone, which might bear interpretative value, presents itself as challenging, if not nearly insurmountable.

While the ILC draft conclusions on the pronouncement of expert treaty bodies hence pose a mediatory solution, by which the output of treaty bodies is still given due consideration,[350] the additional question arises as to whether the idea of resorting to practice by treaty bodies themselves in the course of delineating their own mandates would be appropriate after all. Presupposed that treaty bodies would qualify as authors of subsequent practice, an application to the interpretation of procedural provisions would render the interpretative method a vehicle for possible self-empowerment. Such a method would be completely detached from any interaction with State parties. In relation to General Comments, it has been observed that treaty bodies might be at risk of engaging in "circular reasoning" when references to concluding observations and General Comments are made back and forth without attaching the findings to the agreement of State parties.[351] Logically, the same must hold all the more true for the determination of new procedural powers.

Thus, the adherence to subsequent practice in the form of treaty bodies' own actions, without attaching any meaning to the conduct or consent by State parties, is not helpful in further clarifying their powers. This finding, nevertheless, does not equate with subsequent practice being irrelevant at all in the strengthening process. Actions by State parties under the reporting procedure, for instance, might meet all necessary criteria pursuant to article 31(3)(b) VCLT, and could thereby lead to the reinterpretation of procedural provisions. The next section shall therefore briefly shed light on the three criteria necessary for inter-

---

Rights Treaty Bodies: Law and Legitimacy, 2012, p. 410, noting that "the interpretation of a treaty may not always be clearly publicised".

[349] *McGrogan*, On the Interpretation of Human Rights Treaties and Subsequent Practice, Netherlands Quarterly of Human Rights 32 (2014), 347, 368, who excludes adopted views from the determination of subsequent practice by treaty bodies on the same grounds.

[350] *Azaria*, The Legal Significance of Expert Treaty Bodies Pronouncements for the Purpose of the Interpretation of Treaties, International Community Law Review 22 (2020), 33, 59–60.

[351] *Moeckli*, Interpretation of the ICESCR: Between Morality and State Consent, in: Moeckli/Keller/Heri (eds.), The Human Rights Covenants at 50: Their Past, Present, and Future, 2018, p. 69; *Schlütter*, Aspects of human rights interpretation by the UN treaty bodies, in: Keller/Ulfstein (eds.), UN Human Rights Treaty Bodies: Law and Legitimacy, 2012, p. 292.

pretation via subsequent practice under article 31(3)(b) VCLT. The section will also briefly analyse whether there are any particularities concerning their application in the context of human rights treaties.

2. Constituent elements of subsequent practice under article 31(3)(b) VCLT

The first and objective criterion is the practice by State parties, which can arise in form of legislative, executive, or judicial actions, as long as these actions are attributable to the State party concerned.[352] Practice is, however, not limited to actions by organs belonging to the classical branches of power, but can take a variety of other forms.[353]

In terms of quantity and repetition, subsequent practice under article 31(3)(b) VCLT requires a consistent, common and concordant practice by all State parties, or at least acceptance, either explicit or implicit by those State parties not participating in or actively contributing to the relevant practice.[354] Hence, to amount to an interpretation under article 31(3)(b) VCLT, no strict evidence of all State parties actually participating in the relevant practice is necessary.[355]

In addition to the objective element of sufficient and consistent State practice, two further subjective elements are required. The first prescribes that the relevant practice must take place in the application of the treaty.[356] Subsequent practice hence "requires, in particular, a determination whether the parties have taken a position regarding the interpretation of the treaty."[357]

Conduct which is not motivated by the conscious implementation of treaty obligations does not fall under article 31(3)(b) VCLT, as is the same with "volun-

---

[352] *Buga*, Modification of Treaties by Subsequent Practice, 2018, p. 32; *Gardiner*, Treaty Interpretation, Second Edition, 2015, pp. 257–258.

[353] Report of the International Law Commission, Seventieth session (30 April–1 June and 2 July–10 August 2018), UN Doc. A/73/10 (2018), Text of the draft conclusions on subsequent agreements and subsequent practice in relation to the interpretation of treaties, commentary to draft conclusion 5, para. 2; *Gardiner*, Treaty Interpretation, Second Edition, 2015, p. 257; *Buga*, Modification of Treaties by Subsequent Practice, 2018, p. 50, who reaches the conclusion that a "broader concept" of practice has to be applied; *Dörr*, Article 31, General rule of interpretation, in: Dörr/Schmalenbach (eds.), Vienna Convention on the Law of Treaties: A Commentary, Second Edition, 2018, para. 79.

[354] *Dörr*, Article 31, General rule of interpretation, in: Dörr/Schmalenbach (eds.), Vienna Convention on the Law of Treaties: A Commentary, Second Edition, 2018, para. 80; *Gardiner*, Treaty Interpretation, Second Edition, 2015, pp. 266–267.

[355] *Aust*, Modern Treaty Law and Practice, Third Edition, 2013, p. 216; compare also *Gardiner*, Treaty Interpretation, Second Edition, 2015, p. 257, who proposes to move along a "sliding scale" in the assessment of whether sufficient State practice is prevalent.

[356] *Dörr*, Article 31, General rule of interpretation, in: Dörr/Schmalenbach (eds.), Vienna Convention on the Law of Treaties: A Commentary, Second Edition, 2018, para. 81.

[357] Report of the International Law Commission, Seventieth session (30 April–1 June and 2 July–10 August 2018), UN Doc. A/73/10 (2018), Text of the draft conclusions on subsequent agreements and subsequent practice in relation to the interpretation of treaties, draft conclusion 6.

tary practice".³⁵⁸ As with any other case in which the presence of a subjective element has to be proven, providing evidence that the State parties apply the treaty in question by taking a position regarding its interpretation poses challenges.³⁵⁹ One indication can be how "specifically" the practice is related to the treaty.³⁶⁰ Furthermore, the character of the treaty under scrutiny may suggest that its parties are taking a position regarding its interpretation, with particular reference having been made to the European Convention on Human Rights in this context.³⁶¹ At least with a view to the ECHR, there exists a presumption that State parties "are mindful of their obligations" stemming from the Convention, and any differentiation between domestic legislation and the implementation of the treaty concerned may seem "artificial".³⁶²

The second subjective element requires the establishment of an agreement regarding the treaty's interpretation between all parties.³⁶³ While silence, acquiescence, and the principle of estoppel all may play a crucial role in establishing such an agreement,³⁶⁴ it must be recalled here that things lay differently in the sphere of UN human rights treaties. Silence to treaty body pronouncements cannot easily be regarded as acquiescence or subsequent practice under article 31(3)(b) VCLT.³⁶⁵

---

³⁵⁸ Voluntary practice might lead to the same factual situation as the application of the treaty concerned would implicate, but is eventually not motivated by its conscious application or implementation, see Report of the International Law Commission, Seventieth session (30 April–1 June and 2 July–10 August 2018), UN Doc. A/73/10 (2018), Text of the draft conclusions on subsequent agreements and subsequent practice in relation to the interpretation of treaties, commentary to draft conclusion 6, para. 9.

³⁵⁹ *Buga*, Modification of Treaties by Subsequent Practice, 2018, p. 57; *Arato*, Subsequent Practice and Evolutive Interpretation: Techniques of Treaty Interpretation over Time and Their Diverse Consequences, The Law and Practice of International Courts and Tribunals 9 (2010), 443, 459.

³⁶⁰ Report of the International Law Commission, Seventieth session (30 April–1 June and 2 July–10 August 2018), UN Doc. A/73/10 (2018), Text of the draft conclusions on subsequent agreements and subsequent practice in relation to the interpretation of treaties, commentary to draft conclusion 6, para. 10; *Buga*, Modification of Treaties by Subsequent Practice, 2018, p. 57.

³⁶¹ Report of the International Law Commission, Seventieth session (30 April–1 June and 2 July–10 August 2018), UN Doc. A/73/10 (2018), Text of the draft conclusions on subsequent agreements and subsequent practice in relation to the interpretation of treaties, commentary to draft conclusion 6, para. 14.

³⁶² *Seibert-Fohr*, The Effect of Subsequent Practice on the European Convention on Human Rights, Considerations from a General International Law Perspective, in: van Aaken/Mutoc (eds.), The European Convention on Human Rights and General International Law, 2018, p. 74.

³⁶³ *Dörr*, Article 31, General rule of interpretation, in: Dörr/Schmalenbach (eds.), Vienna Convention on the Law of Treaties: A Commentary, Second Edition, 2018, para. 84.

³⁶⁴ For a detailed analysis of relevant case law, see *Buga*, Modification of Treaties by Subsequent Practice, 2018, pp. 63–70.

³⁶⁵ Report of the International Law Commission, Seventieth session (30 April–1 June and

Probative value for an agreement on the interpretation of UN human rights treaties may be accorded to resolutions adopted by Conferences of State parties or resolutions adopted by organs of international organizations.[366] However, their probative value is subject to the restriction that resolutions adopted by consensus require further consideration to determine whether an agreement has been reached.[367] To provide such evidence in cases of doubt, recourse can be taken again to the relevant practice. The more the latter proves to be of a concordant, common and consistent character, the "less corroborative evidence" is required to determine whether an agreement has been reached.[368] "Participation in the practice is obviously the clearest evidence" when seeking to induce an agreement regarding a treaty's interpretation.[369]

In conformity with the presumption of human rights treaties being applied intentionally, the respective treaty's character "can impact the scope and degree of practice necessary to evidence agreement."[370] Most notably in the context of human rights treaties, the ECtHR does not engage in detailed analysis as to whether an agreement has been reached by all members; it rather relies on observing a sufficiently consistent practice by a majority of State parties.[371] If this

---

2 July–10 August 2018), UN Doc. A/73/10 (2018), Text of the draft conclusions on subsequent agreements and subsequent practice in relation to the interpretation of treaties, draft conclusion 13(3).

[366] Report of the International Law Commission, Seventieth session (30 April–1 June and 2 July–10 August 2018), UN Doc. A/73/10 (2018), Text of the draft conclusions on subsequent agreements and subsequent practice in relation to the interpretation of treaties, commentary to draft conclusion 13, para. 13.

[367] Report of the International Law Commission, Seventieth session (30 April–1 June and 2 July–10 August 2018), UN Doc. A/73/10 (2018), Text of the draft conclusions on subsequent agreements and subsequent practice in relation to the interpretation of treaties, commentary to draft conclusion 13, para. 14; for the probative value of resolutions adopted by consensus within Conferences of State parties, see Report of the International Law Commission, Seventieth session (30 April–1 June and 2 July–10 August 2018), UN Doc. A/73/10 (2018), Text of the draft conclusions on subsequent agreements and subsequent practice in relation to the interpretation of treaties, commentary to draft conclusion 11, paras. 31–38.

[368] *Buga*, Modification of Treaties by Subsequent Practice, 2018, p. 71.

[369] *Gardiner*, Treaty Interpretation, Second Edition, 2015, p. 267.

[370] *Buga*, Modification of Treaties by Subsequent Practice, 2018, p. 74.

[371] *Seibert-Fohr*, The Effect of Subsequent Practice on the European Convention on Human Rights, Considerations from a General International Law Perspective, in: van Aaken/Mutoc (eds.), The European Convention on Human Rights and General International Law, 2018, pp. 73–74; see also *Sorel/Boré Eveno*, Article 31, Convention of 1969, in: Corten/Klein (eds.), The Vienna Conventions on the Law of Treaties: A Commentary, 2011, para. 45, who observe that the ECtHR "remains fairly flexible" with its evaluation of subsequent practice under article 31(3)(b) VCLT; Report of the International Law Commission, Seventieth session (30 April–1 June and 2 July–10 August 2018), UN Doc. A/73/10 (2018), Text of the draft conclusions on subsequent agreements and subsequent practice in relation to the interpretation of treaties, commentary to draft conclusion 10, para. 6, where it is stated that the ECtHR seems to "possess some margin" in the determination of an agreement established by the parties.

condition is met, an agreement in the interpretation of the Convention is presumed.[372] In correspondence to the "context-dependent nature" of subsequent practice,[373] it has also been proposed to differentiate between State practice as a supplementary means under article 32 VCLT, subsequent practice as part of the general rule of interpretation when interpreting substantive guarantees, subsequent practice in the interpretation of procedural rules and subsequent practice with respect to treaty modification.[374] Interpretation of procedural provisions, according to the proposed differentiation, requires State practice which is "sufficiently consistent, consolidated over time and shared by a plurality of Contracting states to presume the respective agreement by the Contracting States" under article 31(3)(b) VCLT.

If existent and considered relevant, actions by State parties to the treaties will be analysed in the third main section of the thesis at hand regarding their classification as subsequent practice, which could possibly lead to the broadening of the treaty bodies' mandates.

II. Authority of the United Nations General Assembly

As has been demonstrated above, the discourse on the treaty body strengthening process mainly originated from within the United Nations. In light of General Assembly Resolution 68/268, by which the Assembly called on treaty bodies to implement certain proposals, the question arises as to what authority the General Assembly has over the treaty bodies and what legal weight can be attached to its actions and statements.

1. Involvement in treaty amendments

As with any other international multilateral treaty, UN human rights treaties can be altered by amendment procedures, which are in principle the "formal legal device for making changes"[375] and which applies to both substantive and procedural provisions. All UN human rights core treaties, with the exception of the Convention against Torture, assign a decisive role to the General Assembly under

---

[372] *Seibert-Fohr*, The Effect of Subsequent Practice on the European Convention on Human Rights, Considerations from a General International Law Perspective, in: van Aaken/Motoc (eds.), The European Convention on Human Rights and General International Law, 2018, p. 74.

[373] *Buga*, Modification of Treaties by Subsequent Practice, 2018, p. 74.

[374] *Seibert-Fohr*, The Effect of Subsequent Practice on the European Convention on Human Rights, Considerations from a General International Law Perspective, in: van Aaken/Motoc (eds.), The European Convention on Human Rights and General International Law, 2018, pp. 79–80.

[375] *Brunnée*, Treaty Amendments, in: Hollis (ed.), The Oxford Guide to Treaties, Second Edition, 2020, p. 336.

their amendment procedures. Under the more "complex"[376] procedure,[377] found in article 51 ICCPR, article 29 ICESCR, article 29 CAT, article 50 CRC, article 90 CMW, article 44 CED and article 47 CRPD, an amendment will only come into force if it has been approved by the General Assembly. Under the less detailed amendment procedure, provided for by article 23 CERD and article 26 CEDAW, it is upon the General Assembly to decide which steps shall be taken when a State party has notified the Secretary-General with its request for revision of the respective treaty.[378]

However, both legal and practical arguments render this avenue for vesting treaty bodies with additional powers less convincing and appealing. First, the General Assembly Resolution 68/268 and the preceding intergovernmental process, as well as the follow-up activities to said resolution, do not qualify as treaty amendments. Neither of them was initiated in accordance with the relevant treaty provisions. In addition, though not differentiating between substantive and procedural provisions as such, the vehicle of a formal amendment might prove unsuitable for certain treaty changes anyways, particularly for those affecting the institutional design of treaty bodies.[379] Pursuant to provisions present in many of the UN human rights treaty,[380] an amendment shall only be binding on those State parties that have agreed to it.[381] All other State parties remain bound to the unamended version of the treaty.

In practice, this would lead to obscure results. The increase in the number of Committee members or the alteration of annual meeting time, for instance, cannot logically be amended individually, but only for all State parties.[382] To avoid

---

[376] *Nowak*, CCPR Commentary, Second revised Edition, 2005, Article 51, Amendment of the Covenant, para. 1.

[377] See *Bowman*, Towards a Unified Treaty Body for Monitoring Compliance with UN Human Rights Conventions? Legal Mechanisms for Treaty Reform, Human Rights Law Review 7 (2007), 225, 236, who differentiates between two "basic models"

[378] The choice to place the General Assembly as the entity competent to direct the amendment procedure might have been driven by the intention to create a "universal regime", *Kroworsch*, Article 26, in: Freeman/Chinkin/Rudolf (eds.), The UN Convention on the Elimination of All Forms of Discrimination Against Women: A Commentary, 2012, p. 559.

[379] *Monina*, Article 29, Amendment, in: Nowak/Birk/Monina (eds.), The United Nations Convention Against Torture and its Optional Protocol: A Commentary, Second Edition, 2019, para. 14; *Nowak*, CCPR Commentary, Second revised Edition, 2005, Article 51, Amendment of the Covenant, para. 7.

[380] Article 51(3) ICCPR, article 29(3) ICESCR, article 29(3) CAT, article 50(3) CRC, article 90(3) CMW, article 44(4) CED; under CERD and CEDAW no comparable provisions exist, for the situation under CRPD see further below.

[381] The provisions under the UN human rights treaties mirror the general rule provided for by article 40(4) VCLT.

[382] See *Monina*, Article 29, Amendment, in: Nowak/Birk/Monina (eds.), The United Nations Convention Against Torture and its Optional Protocol: A Commentary, Second Edition, 2019, para. 15, who states that the respective provisions "simply [do] not make sense for certain procedural amendments"; or *Nowak*, CCPR Commentary, Second revised Edition, 2005, Article 51, Amendment of the Covenant, para. 7, who considers this an "absurd result".

B. Broadening of competencies with the involvement of State parties

any such paradoxical situation, article 47(3) CRPD offers an innovative and, so far, unique solution among the UN human rights core treaties.[383] The Conference of State parties to CRPD can decide by consensus that an amendment, relating exclusively to article 34, 38, 39 or 40 CRPD, shall be binding upon all State parties the thirtieth day after having reached the required acceptance by two-thirds of members to the treaty. While this proves helpful in circumventing the high threshold of acceptance, it has been rightly criticized that opposing State parties would eventually be at a disadvantage, and that the question of an amendment's binding force can be revisited after having undergone the procedure provided for in article 47(1) and (2) CPRD.[384]

Given these difficulties arising from the strict application of formal amendment procedures under UN human rights core treaties, it comes as no surprise that their overall evaluation presents a rather negative picture.[385] In practice, four amendments have been initiated by State parties, all more or less unsuccessful though. In January 1992, the Australian delegate proposed an amendment to articles 17(7) and 18(5) CAT, and article 8(6) CERD respectively, whereby the two Committees would receive their future funding from the regular UN budget and not as they previously did, directly from the State parties to the Conventions.[386] In 1995, another amendment was initiated in relation to CEDAW and sought to increase the Committee's meeting time, which is by virtue of article 20(1) CEDAW limited to two weeks per year only.[387]

---

[383] *Magliveras*, Article 47, Amendments, in: Bantekas/Stein/Anastasiou (eds.), The UN Convention on the Rights of Persons with Disabilities: A Commentary, 2018, p. 1191, footnote 19.

[384] *Magliveras*, Article 47, Amendments, in: Bantekas/Stein/Anastasiou (eds.), The UN Convention on the Rights of Persons with Disabilities: A Commentary, 2018, pp. 1196–1197.

[385] *Monina*, Article 29, Amendment, in: Nowak/Birk/Monina (eds.), The United Nations Convention Against Torture and its Optional Protocol: A Commentary, Second Edition, 2019, para. 1, who refers to the procedure under article 29 CAT as "fairly complicated and impractical"; *Magliveras*, Article 47, Amendments, in: Bantekas/Stein/Anastasiou (eds.), The UN Convention on the Rights of Persons with Disabilities: A Commentary, 2018, p. 1191, who describes the amendment procedure under article 47 CPRD as "cumbrous"; see as well *Kroworsch*, Article 26, in: Freeman/Chinkin/Rudolf (eds.), The UN Convention on the Elimination of All Forms of Discrimination Against Women: A Commentary, 2012, p. 559, who describes the procedure under CEDAW as "cumbersome"; *Bowman*, Towards a Unified Treaty Body for Monitoring Compliance with UN Human Rights Conventions? Legal Mechanisms for Treaty Reform, Human Rights Law Review 7 (2007), 225, 239 who also considers the use of amendment procedures a "cumbersome and protracted process".

[386] *Monina*, Article 17, Committee against Torture, in: Nowak/Birk/Monina (eds.), The United Nations Convention Against Torture and its Optional Protocol: A Commentary, Second Edition, 2019, p. 494.

[387] CEDAW, Report of the State Parties (8th Meeting), UN Doc. CEDAW/SP/1995/2, 02.06.1995, para. 8; interestingly, at variance with article 26 CEDAW, the amendment was adopted at the 8th Meeting of State parties to the Convention in 1995, and subsequently approved by the General Assembly, thus not in accordance with the steps foreseen under article 26 CEDAW, *Kroworsch*, Article 26, in: Freeman/Chinkin/Rudolf (eds.), The UN Con-

Curiously, all three amendments have not yet come into force, as the required two-third quorum of acceptance by State parties has not been reached.[388] While the endorsement by General Assembly resolutions of the amended versions of the Convention against Torture and the CERD was originally intended to serve as a temporary solution to guarantee the Committees' funding,[389] it has now instead become a quasi-permanent replacement for the last step in the amendment procedure.[390]

The only successful amendment so far is an amendment to article 43(2) CRC to increase the number of Committee members from 10 to 18. It was proposed and filed to the Secretary-General by Costa Rica on 17 April 1995 in accordance with article 50(1) CRC.[391] The proposed amendment was adopted at the subsequently convened Conference of State parties, approved by General Assembly Resolution 50/155 and entered into force on 18 November 2002 after having reached the threshold of a two-third acceptance by State parties pursuant to article 50(2) CRC.[392] As regards article 50(3) CRC, which stipulates that the amendment shall only enter into force for those State parties that have formally accepted it, State parties "simply ignored" this provision and considered the amendment having entered into force for all State parties to the Convention.[393]

---

vention on the Elimination of All Forms of Discrimination Against Women: A Commentary, 2012, p. 558.

[388] So far, only 31 out of 170 State parties have formally accepted the amendment to the Convention against Torture, https://treaties.un.org/Pages/ViewDetails.aspx?src=TREATY&mtdsg_no=IV-9-a&chapter=4&clang=_en (last access: 21.08.2023); only 54 out of 182 State parties have formally accepted the amendment to the CERD, https://treaties.un.org/Pages/ViewDetails.aspx?src=TREATY&mtdsg_no=IV-2-a&chapter=4&clang=_en (last access: 21.08.2023); 81 out of 189 State parties have accepted the amendment to the CEDAW, https://treaties.un.org/pages/ViewDetails.aspx?src=TREATY&mtdsg_no=IV-8-a&chapter=4&clang=_en (last access: 21.08.2023).

[389] UN General Assembly, Resolution 47/111, UN Doc. A/RES/47/111, 16.12.992, paras. 9(a) and (b).

[390] *Monina*, Article 29, Amendment, in: Nowak/Birk/Monina (eds.), The United Nations Convention Against Torture and its Optional Protocol: A Commentary, Second Edition, 2019, para. 13, with specific focus on the CAT amendment; with a view to the CERD amendment, *Monina*, Article 17, Committee against Torture, in: Nowak/Birk/Monina (eds.), The United Nations Convention Against Torture and its Optional Protocol: A Commentary, Second Edition, 2019, p. 494; *Kroworsch*, Article 26, in: Freeman/Chinkin/Rudolf (eds.), The UN Convention on the Elimination of All Forms of Discrimination Against Women: A Commentary, 2012, p. 558.

[391] CRC, Conference of State Parties under Article 50 of the Convention, UN Doc. CRC/SP/18/Rev. 1, 01.11.1995, para. 4.

[392] *Verheyde/Goedertier*, A Commentary on the United Nations Convention on the Rights of the Child, Articles 43–45: The UN Committee on the Rights of the Child, 2006, p. 9.

[393] *Monina*, Article 29, Amendment, in: Nowak/Birk/Monina (eds.), The United Nations Convention Against Torture and its Optional Protocol: A Commentary, Second Edition, 2019, para. 15; *Nowak*, CCPR Commentary, Second revised Edition, 2005, Article 51, Amendment of the Covenant, para. 7.

2. Endorsement/authorization of Committee activities

In light of the previous section, it appears that the General Assembly stands in for missing ratification and acceptance whenever State parties could not surmount the thresholds for amending the treaties in accordance with the relevant provisions. Furthermore, some of the Committees have explicitly asked the General Assembly to authorize certain measures they planned to implement. For instance, the CEDAW Committee has gradually expanded its annual meeting time by requesting the General Assembly first for authorization to meet twice annually (1995–2005), and then to meet three times a year from 2006 onwards.[394] In 2002, the Committee was also authorized by General Assembly Resolution 56/229 to hold an additional and exceptional three-weeks session, completely devoted to the elimination of the backlog of reports awaiting consideration.[395] Nevertheless, authorization by the General Assembly in these cases does not qualify as legal authorization in the sense of treaty amendments, nor does it vest Committees with new powers. Additional meeting time requires first and foremost concomitant additional financial and human resources.

Next to the authorization of additional meeting time, the General Assembly reacted to another type of request which might raise more questions concerning its authority and its legal relationship with the human rights treaty bodies. Another means of handling the backlog of reports awaiting consideration is to split up into parallel working chambers,[396] which ideally results in almost twice as many examined State reports per session. Specifically, both the CRC[397] and CEDAW[398] Committee considered this option viable and requested the General Assembly for authorization, but also other treaty bodies, such as the Human Rights Committee,[399] have already trialled and applied this method. The General Assembly, in turn, often responded positively to such requests and granted the

---

[394] *Boerefijn*, Article 20, in: Freeman/Chinkin/Rudolf (eds.), The UN Convention on the Elimination of All Forms of Discrimination Against Women: A Commentary, 2012, p. 516.

[395] UN General Assembly, Resolution 56/229, Convention on the Elimination of All Forms of Discrimination against Women, UN Doc. A/RES/56/229, 01.02.2002, para. 13.

[396] *Smith*, Monitoring the CRC, in: Alfredsson et al. (eds.), International Human Rights Monitoring Mechanisms, 2009, p. 112.

[397] *Akthar/Nyamutata*, International Child Law, Fourth Edition, 2020, p. 104; *Verheyde/Goedertier*, A Commentary on the United Nations Convention on the Rights of the Child, Articles 43–45: The UN Committee on the Rights of the Child, 2006, pp. 9–10; requests have been made in 2003, CRC Committee, Report on the thirty-fourth Session, UN Doc. CRC/C/133, 14.01.2004, p. 5; in 2008, CRC Committee, Report on the forty-eighth session, UN Doc. CRC/C/48/3, 16.11.2009, Annex II; and in 2011, Report of the Committee on the Rights of the Child (54th–59th session), UN Doc. A/67/41, Annex III.

[398] *Boerefijn*, Article 20, in: Freeman/Chinkin/Rudolf (eds.), The UN Convention on the Elimination of All Forms of Discrimination Against Women: A Commentary, 2012, p. 516.

[399] For example, see Report of the Human Rights Committee (117th, 118th and 119th session), UN Doc. A/72/40 (2017), para. 52.

Committees additional meeting time, though sometimes not meeting all the requests posed by the Committees.[400]

The interesting aspect about the requests for working in parallel chambers is that their authorization arguably goes beyond the mere grant of additional meeting time. It touches on the working methods of Committees and deviates from what is provided for in the treaties. These make mention of a single Committee, composed of the entirety of Committee members, and do not mention parallel working chambers.[401] Here, involvement of the General Assembly would prove at least problematic. It has neither the power to prescribe nor to prevent Committees from taking decisions relating to their working methods, since this lies with their internal autonomy.[402] In practice, however, the Committees still adopt their concluding observations in closed plenary meetings after having conducted the pre-sessional work and the constructive dialogue in split-up chambers.[403] Thus, authorization in the aforementioned cases has to be considered as well as a budgetary approval of the additional costs coming along with working in parallel chambers.

3. General Assembly as a Conference of State parties

A last option to lend legal weight to the actions of the General Assembly in the context of the treaty body strengthening process offers its possible consideration as a proxy for a Conference of State parties to the various human rights treaties. Among the United Nations human rights treaties, only article 40 CRPD establishes a Conference of State parties. All other treaties are silent on the topic of a plenary body consisting of the parties to the respective treaty.[404] The Conference of State parties under CRPD serves as a "formal collectivity of member states", which takes action in matters that require the participation of all State parties.[405] Given that the amendment procedures have proven themselves cumbersome and

---

[400] See for instance in reaction to the 2003 request by the CRC Committee, UN General Assembly, Resolution 59/261, Rights of the child, UN Doc. A/RES/59/261, 23.12.2004, para. 9, whereby working in parallel chambers was approved as "an exceptional and temporary measure, for a period of two years".

[401] *Callejon et al.*, Optimizing the UN Treaty Body System, p. 20, footnote 22 and p. 42.

[402] *Gaer*, A Voice Not an Echo: Universal Periodic Review and the UN Treaty Body System, Human Rights Law Review 7 (2007), 109, 118.

[403] With regard to CEDAW, *Boerefijn*, Article 18, in: Freeman/Chinkin/Rudolf (eds.) The UN Convention on the Elimination of All Forms of Discrimination Against Women: A Commentary, 2012, p. 503.

[404] See *Bantekas*, Article 40, Conference of State Parties, in: Bantekas/Stein/Anastasiou (eds.), The UN Convention on the Rights of Persons with Disabilities: A Commentary, 2018, pp. 1135–1138 with the background and the *travaux préparatoires* for the inclusion of such an organ under the CRPD.

[405] *Bantekas*, Article 40, Conference of State Parties, in: Bantekas/Stein/Anastasiou (eds.), The UN Convention on the Rights of Persons with Disabilities: A Commentary, 2018, p. 1142.

B. Broadening of competencies with the involvement of State parties

mostly unsuitable, decisions taken at a possible Conference of State parties might be an alternative and more feasible avenue when contracting parties wish to change the way things are.

Article 40 CRPD can serve as an illustrative starting point for possible impacts of a Conference of State parties, providing for the Conference's competence to "consider any matter with regard to the implementation of the present Convention".[406] Therefore, the Conference of State parties to CRPD is theoretically entitled to adopt measures relating to the Committee and its mandate under the reporting procedure. At first glance, however, this seems to be incompatible with the autonomy of the CRPD Committee and its power to independently establish its own Rules of Procedure. Yet, the powers of said Conference of State parties find their limits within the general rules of international law, and particularly within the CRPD framework.[407] It follows that any measure that aims at undermining the Committee's autonomy or independence in the exercise of its functions and duties would contradict the CRPD itself and is not covered by the Conference's mandate.

In line with the antagonistic relationship between treaty bodies and State parties, the CRPD type of Conference of State parties poses both possibilities and risks. On the one hand, it provides an opportunity for discussion on the implementation of the Convention,[408] could possibly take an active role in the implementation of recommendations and views adopted by the Committee,[409] and might help clarify and develop normative standards further, just as Conferences of State parties did in the context of arms control and environment treaties.[410] On the other hand, as noted by scholars, a Conference of State parties could potentially control and ultimately unduly inhibit treaty bodies in the effective perfor-

---

[406] *Bantekas*, Article 40, Conference of State Parties, in: Bantekas/Stein/Anastasiou (eds.), The UN Convention on the Rights of Persons with Disabilities: A Commentary, 2018, p. 1143, who favours a broad interpretation of article 40(1) CPRD under recourse to the implied powers doctrine.

[407] *Bantekas*, Article 40, Conference of State Parties, in: Bantekas/Stein/Anastasiou (eds.), The UN Convention on the Rights of Persons with Disabilities: A Commentary, 2018, p. 1143.

[408] *Stein/Lord*, Monitoring the Convention on the Rights of Persons with Disabilities: Innovations, Lost Opportunities, and Future Potential, Human Rights Quarterly 32 (2010), 689, 700.

[409] See *Bantekas*, Article 40, Conference of State Parties, in: Bantekas/Stein/Anastasiou (eds.), The UN Convention on the Rights of Persons with Disabilities: A Commentary, 2018, p. 1137 with the more far-reaching Mexican proposal empowering the Conference of State parties inter alia with "an active role in overviewing the implementation".

[410] *Stein/Lord*, Monitoring the Convention on the Rights of Persons with Disabilities: Innovations, Lost Opportunities, and Future Potential, Human Rights Quarterly 32 (2010), 689, 714; for a short overview of possible functions of the Conference of State parties under article 40 CRPD, see also *Lord/Stein*, The Committee on the Rights of Persons with Disabilities, in: Mégret/Alston (eds.), The United Nations and Human Rights: A Critical Appraisal, Second Edition, 2020, p. 566.

mance of their powers. For instance, the Conference could adopt decisions that would contravene decisions by the treaty bodies, as allegedly being *ultra vires*.[411]

In practice, the Conference of State parties under CRPD has neither tended to one side nor the other. During its first six annual sessions between 2008 and 2013, it took no formal decisions and only conducted round-tables, held informal meetings on certain selected topics, such as the right to work and employment[412] or women with disabilities,[413] and regularly held interactive dialogues on the implementation of the Convention by the United Nations system. At its 7th session in 2014, the Conference adopted official decisions for the first time, all of which, however, pertained to internal procedural and organizational aspects related to the Conference itself and did not concern any implementation-related activities by the Committee.[414] Hypothetically, CPRD provides for a mechanism which could serve in the treaty body strengthening process, but which has not yet been deployed.[415] What appears more problematic is that none of the other UN human rights treaty does exhibit any comparable provisions to article 40 CRPD. However, nothing bars State parties from convening any such conference.

In the context of creating a unified and single treaty body, a possible General Assembly resolution or other non-binding documents were considered a "slightly more promising route to reform", though not being a "legally watertight option"[416] either. It has been argued that State parties to a human rights treaty could express their decision via a resolution, formally adopted by a meeting to which all

---

[411] *Bantekas*, Article 40, Conference of State Parties, in: Bantekas/Stein/Anastasiou (eds.), The UN Convention on the Rights of Persons with Disabilities: A Commentary, Oxford, p. 1138; *Stein/Lord*, Monitoring the Convention on the Rights of Persons with Disabilities: Innovations, Lost Opportunities, and Future Potential, Human Rights Quarterly 32 (2010), 689, 700.

[412] Report of the fourth session of the Conference of States Parties to the Convention on the Rights of Persons with Disabilities (07–09 September 2011), UN Doc. CRPD/CSP/2011/2, 08.12.2011, para. 14.

[413] Report of the fifth session of the Conference of States Parties to the Convention on the Rights of Persons with Disabilities (12–14 September 2012), UN Doc. CRPD/CSP/2012/2, 25.10.2012, para. 16.

[414] Report of the seventh session of the Conference of States Parties to the Convention on the Rights of Persons with Disabilities (10–12 June 2014) UN Doc. CRPD/CSP/2014/5, 31.07.2014, para. 17 and Annex I.

[415] Interestingly, article 15(5) and (6) of the current third revised draft (17.08.2021) on a treaty on business and human rights provides for a Conference of State parties, which shall "consider any matter with regard to the implementation of the (Legally Binding Instrument), including any further development needed towards fulfilling its purposes." The wording is decisively similar to article 40(1) CRPD, if not even more precise as to the task of a Conference of State parties under the future treaty, https://www.ohchr.org/Documents/HRBodies/HRCouncil/WGTransCorp/Session6/LBI3rdDRAFT.pdf (last access: 21.08.2023).

[416] *Bowman*, Towards a Unified Treaty Body for Monitoring Compliance with UN Human Rights Conventions? Legal Mechanisms for Treaty Reform, Human Rights Law Review 7 (2007), 225, 243.

B. Broadening of competencies with the involvement of State parties   131

State parties have been invited.[417] Nevertheless, this is not easily transferrable to resolutions such as General Assembly Resolution 68/268. Resolution 68/268 addresses the treaty bodies in their entirety, but from the perspective of treaty law, it is necessary to adopt a formal decision with regard to each single treaty. Despite belonging to a system of partially interacting treaty bodies, each treaty body is ultimately established by its own treaty regime. Any modification or implementation-related decision requires the participation of the respective State parties and excludes non-parties in the decision-making process which have no voting rights. An overall General Assembly resolution thus presents itself as too undifferentiated.

It must therefore be assumed that the General Assembly cannot exercise power over human rights treaty bodies in a legal sense, but its decisions, mainly of budgetary character, still do affect the treaty bodies to a great extent.[418]

---

[417] *Bowman*, Towards a Unified Treaty Body for Monitoring Compliance with UN Human Rights Conventions? Legal Mechanisms for Treaty Reform, Human Rights Law Review 7 (2007), 225, 241, who equally acknowledges that such an approach entails practical obstacles and would circumvent the formal amendment procedures.

[418] *Boerefijn*, The Reporting Procedure under the Covenant on Civil and Political Rights: Practice and Procedures of the Human Rights Committee, 1999, pp. 109–110, who notes that the relationship between the Human Rights Committee and the General Assembly "is a delicate one". This finding is transferrable to all other treaty bodies.

Part IV

Reform proposals under the reporting procedure and their implementation

The reporting procedure under the nine human rights core treaties is often referred to as the "key mechanism"[1] or as the "centerpiece"[2] among the various functions discharged by UN human rights treaty bodies. It is the only manatory mechanism each State party is obliged to comply with, regardless of the specific treaty.[3] The standard reporting procedure consists of four steps. First, a State party is supposed to submit its initial or periodic report, in accordance with the periodicity prescribed by the respective treaty or, if the treaty does not provide for any express periodicity, in accordance with the reporting intervals as determined by the respective Committee. In a next step, the treaty body prepares a List of Issues, by which it specifies the topics it would like to discuss during the following constructive dialogue. Third, the State party submits in reaction to the List of Issues its written replies and fourth, the constructive dialogue is conducted on the basis of the information exchanged.[4] A reporting cycle comes to an end with the adoption of concluding observations, which are made public and disseminated among State parties. Most treaty bodies include therein the request for the submission of follow-up reports, which are expected to be submitted before the next reporting cycle begins.

The following section will shed light on reform proposals, all of which might potentially fall within the powers of the treaty bodies in terms of their realization

---

[1] *Kälin*, Examination of state reports, in: Keller/Ulfstein (eds.), UN Human Rights Treaty Bodies: Law and Legitimacy, 2012, p. 16; *Rodley*, The United Nations Human Rights Council, Its Special Procedures, and Its Relationship with the Treaty Bodies: Complementarity or Competition?, in: Boyle (ed.), New Institutions for Human Rights Protection, 2009, p. 57, who refers to the reporting procedure as the "core function".

[2] *Kretzmer/Klein*, The Human Rights Committee: Monitoring State Parties' Reports, Israel Yearbook on Human Rights 45 (2015), 133, 139; see, however, *Seibert-Fohr*, The UN Human Rights Committee, in: Oberleitner (ed.), International Human Rights Institutions, Tribunals, and Courts, 2018, p. 137, who detects the interpretation of the Covenant as the Human Rights Committee's "essential role".

[3] *Rodley*, The Role and Impact of Treaty Bodies, in: Shelton (ed.), The Oxford Handbook of International Human Rights Law, 2013, p. 626.

[4] See for example *Pillay*, Strengthening the United Nations human rights treaty body system, p. 49; or for a graphic overview of the procedure, Human Rights Committee, Simplified reporting procedure, Report of the Working Group, UN Doc. CCPR/C/123/3, 06.12.2018, para. 32.

and implementation. These are the application of the simplified reporting procedure to initial and periodic State reports, the introduction of a comprehensive reporting calendar, which aligns reporting periodicities among all UN human rights core treaties, and the shift to regular reviews in the absence of reports vis-à-vis non-compliant State parties. Furthermore, with specific view to the steps after the constructive dialogue, the state of follow-up procedures will be subject to closer scrutiny, coupled with a proposal that could avoid very broad reporting gaps in the event of establishing a comprehensive reporting calendar.

The overarching premise is that the various proposals are considered contingent on each other. Although each of them could be implemented alone, it is argued here that greater gains of efficiency and effectiveness are realized when setting the uniform application of the simplified reporting procedure as a condition for the establishment of a comprehensive reporting calendar. Regular reviews in the absence of a report, in turn, presuppose the existence of a master calendar. Each proposal will be analysed in detail, by taking account of both current developments and treaty body practice. Finally, it will be analysed whether treaty bodies have the legal mandate to implement the various proposals on their own, hence without State consent.

A. Object and purpose of human rights reporting

Before starting to describe and analyse the reform proposals that rest in the hands of the treaty bodies, it is of great importance to spell out the purposes of State reporting to human rights treaty bodies. Only those reform proposals will be considered suitable and feasible which eventually enable the treaty bodies to better discharge their mandate and to fulfil the purposes of State reporting. Given that any extension of powers derived from treaty interpretation might be based on a teleological approach of interpretation, it is all the more essential to identify the underlying rationales of human rights reporting.

First and foremost, the reporting procedure is neither of a judicial nor quasi-judicial character nor does it constitute an implementation mechanism with coercive elements.[5] Contrary to the individual complaints procedure before treaty bodies, State reporting is not an adversarial procedure and it is not comparable to human rights adjudication aimed at granting victims of violations possible remedies. It is thus said to be the most sovereign-friendly compliance mechanism in the protection of human rights.[6]

---

[5] *Kälin*, Examination of state reports, in: Keller/Ulfstein (eds.), UN Human Rights Treaty Bodies: Law and Legitimacy, 2012, p. 35

[6] *Devereux/Anderson*, Reporting under International Human Rights Treaties: Perspectives from Timor Leste's Experience of the Reformed Process, Human Rights Law Review 8 (2008), 69, 73, describing reporting as "relatively non-confrontational"; see also *Creamer/Simmons*, The Proof Is in the Process: Self-Reporting Under International Human Rights

Even though the purposes of human rights reporting have been portrayed as manifold,[7] it is questionable whether it is really necessary to dwell upon very nuanced classifications, especially with regard to the purpose of the project at hand. As will be demonstrated further below, the identification of fine-grained and more differentiated purposes might be of relevance when assessing treaty bodies' reform proposals. Nevertheless, on a more abstract level, two main objectives of human rights reporting can be identified in principle. These are, on the one hand, international monitoring and thus creating (international) accountability of a State party for its own human rights record,[8] and, on the other hand, enabling the State party under review to conduct a critical self-assessment of its own performance in the implementation of protected rights and treaty guarantees.[9] It is argued here that any other more nuanced or fine-grained objective can ultimately be attributed to one of these two main purposes, which can be aptly

---

Treaties, American Journal of International Law 114 (2020), 1, 50, who state that reporting procedures were often considered as the "bare minimum" enforcement mechanism.

[7] See for example *Oberleitner*, Menschenrechtsschutz durch Staatenberichte, 1998, pp. 55–67, who detects a dialogue function, an assessment function and the improvement of the human rights situation in the State party concerned as the reporting procedure's objectives; see also *Alston*, The Purposes of Reporting, in: Manual on Human Rights Reporting, HR/PUB/91/1 (Rev. 1), 1997, p. 24, who even determines seven different objectives of human rights reporting to UN human treaty bodies: the initial review function, monitoring function, policy formulation function, public scrutiny function, evaluation function, function of acknowledging problems and information exchange function.

[8] *Kretzmer/Klein*, The Human Rights Committee: Monitoring State Parties' Reports, Israel Yearbook on Human Rights 45 (2015), 133, 137–138 and 143; *Meier/Kim*, Human Rights Accountability through Treaty Bodies: Examining Human Rights Treaty Monitoring for Water and Sanitation, Duke Journal of Comparative and International Law 26 (2015), 139, 144, who consider the treaty body monitoring process as "an external check on state efforts to implement human rights obligations"; *Kälin*, Examination of state reports, in: Keller/Ulfstein (eds.), UN Human Rights Treaty Bodies: Law and Legitimacy, 2012, p. 37, reaching the conclusion that the reporting procedure "has essentially become a mechanism aimed at monitoring compliance"; *Rodley*, The United Nations Human Rights Council, Its Special Procedures, and Its Relationship with the Treaty Bodies: Complementarity or Competition?, in: Boyle (ed.), New Institutions for Human Rights Protection, 2009, p. 60, speaking of an "act of formal and public accountability".

[9] *Kälin*, Examination of state reports, in: Keller/Ulfstein (eds.), UN Human Rights Treaty Bodies: Law and Legitimacy, 2012, p. 39, who points to "awareness-raising" and "institutional learning" in the domestic system; *Rodley*, The United Nations Human Rights Council, Its Special Procedures, and Its Relationship with the Treaty Bodies: Complementarity or Competition?, in: Boyle (ed.), New Institutions for Human Rights Protection, 2009, p. 60; *Lansdown*, The reporting process under the Convention on the Rights of the Child, in: Alston/Crawford (eds.), The Future of UN Human Rights Treaty Monitoring, 2000, p. 114, who emphasizes that reporting serves as a means by which governments achieve a greater understanding of their own human rights record; *Oberleitner*, Menschenrechtsschutz durch Staatenberichte, 1998, p. 62; also the initial review function detected by *Alston* can be attributed to the general objective of self-evaluation, *Alston*, The Purposes of Reporting, in: Manual on Human Rights Reporting, HR/PUB/91/1 (Rev. 1), 1997, p. 21.

summed up as either "introspection at the national level or inspection at the international level".[10]

I. Initially perceived functions of reporting by treaty bodies

As far as the own understanding of treaty bodies is concerned, the two main functions identified above were not always considered to be on equal footing. Closely connected to or even intertwined with the discussion among Human Rights Committee members on whether the Committee was competent to adopt concluding observations vis-à-vis individual State parties,[11] was the question of what purpose to ascribe to the reporting procedure in its own right. The Human Rights Committee's first Reporting Guidelines stated that the "Committee's aim was to contribute to the development of friendly relations between States in accordance with the provisions of the Charter of the United Nations."[12] Additionally, in its first annual report to the General Assembly, the Committee identified assistance to State parties in the promotion and protection of the rights enshrined in the Covenant as the main purpose of the State reporting procedure.[13]

Comparable to the Human Rights Committee, the CESCR Committee clarified the objectives of human rights reporting in its first General Comment.[14] The Committee spelled out seven different purposes, but despite speaking of "public scrutiny of government policies", as did the fourth objective, General Comment No. 1 put strong emphasis on self-evaluation undertaken by State parties, assisting the State party under review in the awareness of its own human rights situation and the exchange of information among members to the Covenant, all of which strongly correspond to objectives as previously identified by the Human Rights Committee.

---

[10] Human Rights Committee, Simplified reporting procedure, Report of the Working Group, UN Doc. CCPR/C/123/3, 06.12.2018, para. 46.

[11] See *supra* Part III A.IV. 1.a).

[12] *Kretzmer*, The UN Human Rights Committee and International Human Rights Monitoring, Straus Institute Working Paper No. 12, 2010, p. 22.

[13] *Kretzmer*, The UN Human Rights Committee and International Human Rights Monitoring, Straus Institute Working Paper No. 12, 2010, p. 24.

[14] CESCR Committee, General Comment No. 1: Reporting by State Parties, 27.07.1989, contained in UN Doc. E/1989/22 (1989), Annex III, the seven objectives are: to conduct a "comprehensive review of national legislation, administrative rules and procedures and practices", regular monitoring of the implementation of the rights contained in the Covenant conducted by the State party itself, to provide an opportunity for the State party under revision to demonstrate that progress in the realization of socio-economic rights has been achieved, to "facilitate public scrutiny of government policies", to provide a basis for evaluation by which both the Committee and the State party can assess whether progress has been achieved in the realization of Covenant rights, to enable the State party under revision to develop a better understanding of "problems and shortcomings encountered" when implementing socio-economic rights and to "facilitate the exchange of information among States".

The Committees' main focus on the assistance of State parties and hence on a rather non-confrontational approach may be explained by the Cold War atmosphere during the 1980s. Greater emphasis on creating accountability would have been seen by many, especially Eastern bloc countries, as too much interference with national sovereignty.[15]

II. Changing perception of the functions attributed to reporting

Nevertheless, with the changing political climate after the end of the Cold War and in the context of the treaty body strengthening process, the Human Rights Committee and other treaty bodies took a firmer stance on their role under the reporting procedure.[16]

Especially the reporting guidelines developed as part of the second reform initiative at the beginning of the 2000s are instructive in this sense, as they reveal a different "and more comprehensive" perception of the reporting procedure and its functions than was the case in the 1980s.[17]

At the requests of the second Inter-Committee Meeting and the fifteenth Meeting of Chairpersons, the Secretariat began drafting harmonized reporting guidelines, applicable to each treaty.[18] The first draft contained four purposes attached to human rights reporting. The first one emphasized the holistic perspective on human rights. State parties "should consider the implementation of the rights protected in each treaty within the wider context of its implementation of all of their international human rights obligations".[19] Simultaneously, reference was made to the Universal Declaration of Human Rights and the connected concept of interrelatedness and interdependence.[20]

---

[15] *Hertig Randall*, The History of the Covenants: Looking Back Half a Century and Beyond, in: Moeckli/Keller/Heri (eds.), The Human Rights Covenants at 50: Their Past, Present, and Future, 2018, p. 24.

[16] *Kretzmer/Klein*, The Human Rights Committee: Monitoring State Parties' Reports, Israel Yearbook on Human Rights 45 (2015), 133, 141; *Kälin*, Examination of state reports, in: Keller/Ulfstein (eds.), UN Human Rights Treaty Bodies: Law and Legitimacy, 2012, p. 36; *O'Flaherty/Tsai*, Periodic Reporting: The Backbone of the UN Treaty Body Review Procedure, in: Bassiouni/Schabas (eds.), New Challenges for the UN Human Rights Machinery, 2011, p. 42.

[17] *Kälin*, Examination of state reports, in: Keller/Ulfstein (eds.), UN Human Rights Treaty Bodies: Law and Legitimacy, 2012, p. 39.

[18] Guidelines on an expanded core document and treaty-specific targeted reports and harmonized guidelines on reporting under the international human rights treaties, Report of the secretariat, UN Doc. HRI/MC/2004/3, 09.06.2004; see also *Kälin*, Examination of state reports, in: Keller/Ulfstein (eds.), UN Human Rights Treaty Bodies: Law and Legitimacy, 2012, p. 38 with a short description and summary of the purposes listed in the draft guidelines.

[19] Guidelines on an expanded core document and treaty-specific targeted reports and harmonized guidelines on reporting under the international human rights treaties, Report of the secretariat, UN Doc. HRI/MC/2004/3, 09.06.2004, Annex, para. 7.

[20] Guidelines on an expanded core document and treaty-specific targeted reports and

The second purpose was of a more general nature and about "commitment to treaties", which could be considered a reaffirmation that a State party is obliged to give effect to treaty provisions and to participate in the reporting procedure.[21]

Third, the guidelines addressed the "opportunity to take stock of the state of human rights protection within their jurisdiction", which clearly corresponds to the main function of self-evaluation as identified above.[22]

The fourth purpose underlined that reporting would create a framework for the constructive dialogue between treaty bodies and State parties, in which treaty bodies carry out their "supportive role in fostering effective implementation of the international human rights instruments and in encouraging international cooperation in the promotion and protection of human rights in general."[23]

The final guidelines adopted by the treaty bodies incorporated the last three purposes almost *verbatim*, but did not explicitly mention the holistic perspective on the implementation and realization of human rights as a distinct purpose.[24] However, the lack of direct reference to the concept must not obscure the fact that it found its way into the reporting guidelines anyway, though with less straightforward language. A State party's "commitment should be viewed within the wider context of the obligation of all States to promote respect for the rights and freedoms, set out in the Universal Declaration of Human Rights and international human rights instruments".[25] Given that the treaty body reform aims at closer cooperation in substantive matters too, the objective of enabling State parties to understand their human rights obligations as belonging to a wider and interconnected system of human rights treaties might be of crucial relevance.[26]

Despite the focus on self-evaluation and the aim of assisting State parties in understanding their own human rights situation, the Harmonized Reporting

---

harmonized guidelines on reporting under the international human rights treaties, Report of the secretariat, UN Doc. HRI/MC/2004/3, 09.06.2004, Annex, para. 7.

[21] Guidelines on an expanded core document and treaty-specific targeted reports and harmonized guidelines on reporting under the international human rights treaties, Report of the secretariat, UN Doc. HRI/MC/2004/3, 09.06.2004, Annex, para. 8.

[22] Guidelines on an expanded core document and treaty-specific targeted reports and harmonized guidelines on reporting under the international human rights treaties, Report of the secretariat, UN Doc. HRI/MC/2004/3, 09.06.2004, Annex, para. 9, where it is also stated that the reporting procedure shall facilitate further discussion at the national level, "conducted in a spirit of cooperation and mutual respect", at para. 10 in the same document.

[23] Guidelines on an expanded core document and treaty-specific targeted reports and harmonized guidelines on reporting under the international human rights treaties, Report of the secretariat, UN Doc. HRI/MC/2004/3, 09.06.2004, Annex, para. 11.

[24] Compilation of Guidelines on the Form and Content of Reports to be submitted by State Parties to the International Human Rights Treaties, Report of the Secretary-General, UN Doc. HRI/GEN/2/Rev. 6, 03.06.2009.

[25] Compilation of Guidelines on the Form and Content of Reports to be submitted by State Parties to the International Human Rights Treaties, Report of the Secretary-General, UN Doc. HRI/GEN/2/Rev. 6, 03.06.2009 para. 8.

[26] See for the cooperation among treaty bodies, *infra* Part V.

Guidelines must not obscure that treaty bodies consider themselves in a stronger monitoring position nowadays. Instructive is for instance article 48(2) RoP CED adopted by the Committee on Enforced Disappearance at its first and second sessions in 2011 and 2012 respectively. The provision stipulates that the Committee "shall examine the implementation of the obligations of State parties under the Convention".[27] The provision thus clearly demonstrates that the Committee considers itself as a body with a supervisory function. Even though other treaty bodies' documents are less explicit in assigning themselves a strong monitoring mandate, treaty bodies do perceive themselves as bodies "monitoring state compliance".[28]

In sum, beginning as bodies who considered their main task helping State parties to understand and take stock of their human rights situation, treaty bodies now obviously monitor compliance and thus fulfil both main purposes ascribed to human rights reporting.[29] It must therefore be stated that any effectiveness-orientated or teleological interpretation of treaty provisions governing the State reporting procedure must duly take into account these two main objectives.

B. Simplified Reporting Procedure

The reform proposal which will most likely be implemented first by all treaty bodies is the simplified reporting procedure. In the following chapter, the procedure shall be analysed in detail. The first section seeks to delineate the procedure's origin and dissemination throughout the treaty body system. Thereby it will take account of developments both within the individual Committees and within the Meeting of Chairpersons. The second section will then shed light on the current situation regarding procedural alignments and focus on possible "best practices" in the drafting of Lists of Issues Prior to Reporting, the latter being the key factor for the implementation of the simplified reporting procedure. Furthermore, given the fragmented status of the treaty body system, this chapter will also focus on ways and means to mitigate unnecessary overlap under the simplified

---

[27] Committee on Enforced Disappearance, Rules of Procedure, UN Doc. CED/C/1, 22.06.2012; Report of the Committee on Enforced Disappearances (1st and 2nd session), UN Doc. A/67/56, Annex IV.

[28] *Kretzmer*, The UN Human Rights Committee and International Human Rights Monitoring, Straus Institute Working Paper No. 12, 2010, p. 39, who detects a "radical change" in the functions of the reporting procedure with the Human Rights Committee beginning to review non-reporting State parties. An argument which can be transferred to all other treaty bodies.

[29] See for instance Human Rights Committee, Simplified reporting procedure, Report of the Working Group, UN Doc. CCPR/C/123/3, 06.12.2018, para. 46, where it is stated that reporting serves two "interrelated goals", which are "introspection" and "inspection", the latter especially conducted by the Committee itself.

reporting procedure. Finally, the chapter will conclude with an examination on how far the legal mandate of treaty bodies extends when they seek to impose the uniform application of the simplified reporting procedure on all State parties. It will specifically be analysed whether the various treaty bodies can *oblige* State parties to adhere exclusively to the procedure.

I. Simplified and standard reporting procedure compared

The simplified reporting procedure, in contrast to the standard reporting procedure, only consists of three steps. It is the treaty bodies that initiate the upcoming reporting cycle by sending a questionnaire to the respective State party (the List of Issues Prior to Reporting or LOIPR). The latter is mainly based on previous concluding observations adopted vis-à-vis the State party under review, where available.[30] The State party then submits its answers, which count as the report required under the respective treaty obligation. Based on the State party's written replies to the LOIPR, the constructive dialogue is conducted and, similar to the standard reporting procedure, concluding observations are eventually adopted and circulated.[31] The major difference between the two procedures hence resides in omitting the first step under the standard reporting procedure and by letting the Committees select the topics for the constructive dialogue first.[32] According to the Human Rights Committee, the application of the simplified reporting procedure "changes the dynamics of the reporting process", as the procedure is "question-driven" and focuses on the most important topics right from the beginning.[33]

II. Origins and dissemination of the simplified reporting procedure

1. Committee against Torture

The first treaty body to introduce the simplified reporting procedure in application to periodic reports was the Committee against Torture, which introduced the procedure at its thirty-eighth session in 2007. The adoption was motivated by the belief that the simplified reporting procedure would assist State parties "in preparing focused reports", since the issuance of Lists of Issues Prior to Reporting could offer both guidance on the content of periodic reports and could

---

[30] For possible sources of information in the preparation of LOIPRs, see Human Rights Committee, Focused reports based on replies to lists of issues prior to reporting (LOIPR): Implementation of the new optional reporting procedure (LOIPR procedure), UN Doc. CCPR/C/99/4, 29.09.2010, para. 12.

[31] *Pillay*, Strengthening the United Nations human rights treaty body system, p. 49.

[32] Cf. *Giegling*, Challenges and Chances of a Written State Report: Analysis and Improvement of a Monitoring Instrument on the Implementation of Human Rights, 2021, p. 38.

[33] Human Rights Committee, Simplified reporting procedure, Report of the Working Group, UN Doc. CCPR/C/123/3, 06.12.2018, para. 30.

B. Simplified Reporting Procedure

equally enable State parties to fulfil their reporting obligations in a "timely and effective manner."[34]

Two years after the procedure's introduction and after having completed first reviews, the Committee against Torture decided to continue the issuance of Lists of Issues Prior to Reporting on a regular basis and justified its decision with the positive feedback received from State parties.[35] At its 46th session in 2011, the Committee conducted a preliminary evaluation and reached the conclusion that the simplified reporting procedure was a "positive step" and hence kept using it.[36]

Added to this, further proposals on how to render the simplified reporting procedure more effective were included in the Committee's preliminary assessment,[37] most of which were taken up again for discussion at the Committee's fifty-third session in 2014.[38] Despite the high rate of acceptance among State parties,[39] the adherence to the simplified reporting procedure remained optional until recently and State parties are invited to accept the procedure by notes verbales or by respective invitations integrated in the latest concluding observations.[40]

---

[34] Report of the Committee against Torture (37th and 38th session), UN Doc. A/62/44 (2007), para. 23; *Kälin*, Examination of state reports, in: Keller/Ulfstein (eds.), UN Human Rights Treaty Bodies: Law and Legitimacy, 2012, p. 29.

[35] Report of the Committee against Torture (41st and 42nd session), UN Doc. A/64/44 (2009), para. 27.

[36] Report of the Committee against Torture (45th and 46th session), UN Doc. A/66/44 (2011), paras. 36–38.

[37] Committee against Torture, Status of the optional reporting procedure of the Committee against Torture and proposals for its revision, Report by the Secretariat, UN Doc. CAT/C/47/2, 27.09.2011, para. 38; for a brief summary of those proposals, see *Monina*, Article 19, State Reporting Procedure, in: Nowak/Birk/Monina (eds.), The United Nations Convention Against Torture and its Optional Protocol: A Commentary, Second Edition, 2019, para. 92.

[38] Report of the Committee against Torture (55th, 56th and 57th session), UN Doc. A/71/44 (2016), para. 30; *Monina*, Article 19, State Reporting Procedure, in: Nowak/Birk/Monina (eds.), The United Nations Convention Against Torture and its Optional Protocol: A Commentary, Second Edition, 2019, para. 92.

[39] As far as apparent from the Committee against Torture's latest annual report, only four out of 137 State parties declined the invitation to report under the simplified reporting procedure. Of the 133 State parties, 105 State parties have expressly accepted to adhere to the simplified reporting procedure, whereas the other 28 did not yet respond or did not have been invited yet, Report of the Committee against Torture (67th and 68th session), UN Doc. A/75/44 (2020), para. 28.

[40] *Monina*, Article 19, State Reporting Procedure, in: Nowak/Birk/Monina (eds.), The United Nations Convention Against Torture and its Optional Protocol: A Commentary, Second Edition, 2019, para. 89; this still holds true when considering the 2022 annual report, Report of the Committee against Torture (71st, 72nd and 73rd session), UN Doc. A/77/44, paras. 26–29; for developments in 2022 see *infra* Part IV., II., 11.

2. Human Rights Committee

The next treaty body to consider the adoption of the simplified reporting procedure was the Human Rights Committee. At its ninety-seventh session in October 2009, it decided to commence with the drafting of Lists of Issues Prior to Reporting.[41] Comparable to the Committee against Torture, the Human Rights Committee considered the adoption of the simplified reporting procedure an opportunity to alleviate the reporting burden imposed on State parties. According to the Committee, the simplified reporting procedure would both provide more detailed guidance on the expected content of a State report and be speedier, as reports under the simplified reporting procedure would be given priority and should be examined within one year of their submission.[42]

First utilizing LOIPRs on a pilot basis only, a limited number of five State parties per session were invited by the Human Rights Committee to avail themselves of the simplified reporting procedure.[43] However, the Committee revised its initial approach at its 111th session in 2014 to the effect that the simplified reporting procedure would henceforth be offered to all States Parties, but only for the submission of periodic and not initial reports.[44] In complement to this decision, the Human Rights Committee established at its 116th session in 2016 that concluding observations should contain a standard paragraph by which State parties would be invited to accept the simplified reporting procedure.[45]

The latest steps by the Human Rights Committee in relation to the application of the simplified reporting procedure were taken on the basis of a Working Group's report, presented to the Committee at its 123rd session.[46] Probably the most important decision among those taken by the Committee in this matter is the use of the simplified reporting procedure as the default procedure under

---

[41] Report of the Human Rights Committee (97th, 98th and 99th session) UN Doc. A/65/40 (Vol. I) (2010), para. 40, with further reference to Human Rights Committee, Focused reports based on replies to lists of issues prior to reporting (LOIPR): Implementation of the new optional reporting procedure (LOIPR procedure), UN Doc. CCPR/C/99/4, 29.09.2010.

[42] Human Rights Committee, Focused reports based on replies to lists of issues prior to reporting (LOIPR): Implementation of the new optional reporting procedure (LOIPR procedure), UN Doc. CCPR/C/99/4, 29.09.2010, paras. 2–3.

[43] *Schabas*, U.N. International Covenant on Civil and Political Rights, Nowak's CCPR Commentary, Third revised Edition, 2019, Art. 40 CCPR, para. 8.

[44] Report of the Human Rights Committee (111th, 112th and 113th session), UN Doc. A/70/40 (2015), para. 56(a); *Schabas*, U.N. International Covenant on Civil and Political Rights, Nowak's CCPR Commentary, Third revised Edition, 2019, Art. 40 CCPR, para. 8.

[45] Report of the Human Rights Committee (114th, 115th and 116th session), UN Doc. A/71/40 (2016), para. 52.

[46] Human Rights Committee, Simplified reporting procedure, Report of the Working Group, UN Doc. CCPR/C/123/3, 06.12.2018; the Committee established the Working Group at its 120th session, see in that regard, Report of the Human Rights Committee (120th, 121st and 122nd session), UN Doc. A/73/40, (2018), para. 52(b).

article 40(4) ICCPR.[47] In order to achieve a swift implementation of its decision, the Committee amended its Rules of Procedure to the effect that it now uses the simplified reporting procedure as an opt-out model.[48] The amendment implicates that unless a State party indicates that it would like to maintain its review under the former standard reporting procedure, the simplified reporting procedure applies automatically.[49]

3. CMW Committee

The third treaty body to adopt the simplified reporting procedure was the Committee on the Protection of the Rights of All Migrant Workers and Members of Their Families in 2011.[50] Similar to the Committee against Torture and comparable to the original usage by the Human Rights Committee, the CMW Committee offered the simplified reporting procedure as an additional option and made its use contingent on the respective State party's acceptance.[51] Remarkable about the CMW Committee's application of the procedure is the fact that it creates a direct nexus between the procedure and the introduction of a comprehensive five-year reporting calendar. The offer addressed to State parties to avail themselves of the simplified reporting procedure is meant to constitute a means by which to secure compliance with the calendar.[52]

4. CRPD Committee

Next in line was the Committee on the Rights of Persons with Disabilities, which took the respective decision to offer the simplified reporting procedure for periodic State reports at its tenth session in 2013.[53] Apart from revising its reporting guidelines in 2016, by taking account of the simplified reporting procedure,[54] no further significant developments are discernable under the CRPD.

---

[47] Report of the Human Rights Committee (123rd, 124th and 125th session), UN Doc. A/74/40 (2019), Annex II, para. 2.

[48] Human Rights Committee, Rules of procedure of the Human Rights Committee, UN Doc. CCPR/C/3/Rev. 12, 04.01.2021, article 73(2) RoP which states that State parties have to opt out, if they wish to be reviewed under the former standard reporting procedure.

[49] Report of the Human Rights Committee (126th, 127th and 128th session), UN Doc. A/75/40 (2020), Annex II, para. 2(b).

[50] Report of the Committee on the Protection of the Rights of All Migrant Workers and Members of Their Families (13th and 14th session), UN Doc. A/66/48 (2011), para. 26.

[51] Report of the Committee on the Protection of the Rights of All Migrant Workers and Members of Their Families (15th and 16th session), UN Doc. A/67/48 (2012), para. 25.

[52] Report of the Committee on the Protection of the Rights of All Migrant Workers and Members of Their Families (15th and 16th session), UN Doc. A/67/48 (2012), para. 25; see also, CMW Committee, Rules of Procedure, CMW/C/2, 08.02.2019, article 33(2) RoP.

[53] Report of the Committee on the Rights of Persons with Disabilities on its tenth session, UN Doc. CRPD/C/10/2, 13.05.2014, para. 10(c); *Combrinck*, Article 36, Consideration of Reports, in: Bantekas/Stein/Anastasiou (eds.), The UN Convention on the Rights of Persons with Disabilities: A Commentary, 2018, p. 1070.

[54] Compare the revised Guidelines, CRPD Committee, Guidelines on periodic reporting

5. CERD Committee

At its fifty-eighth session in 2014, the Committee on the Elimination of Racial Discrimination also decided to provide State parties with long overdue reports with the simplified reporting procedure from 2015 onwards.[55] The Committee's main rationale for the introduction of the procedure are its possible incentives it can set for State parties that have been long absent from the reporting machinery, and to let them re-enter into a dialogue with the Committee.[56] While this was initially limited to those State parties whose periodic reports were overdue for more than ten years, the Committee extended the procedure's application in 2017 to State parties that have been overdue for more than five years.[57] As becomes apparent from the available documentation, one can tentatively conclude that the simplified reporting procedure has already partially been living up to the Committee's expectations. State parties like Afghanistan, overdue since 1986 with its second to sixteenth periodic report, or Botswana, overdue since 2009, have submitted combined reports under the simplified reporting procedure and thus re-entered into a dialogue with the Committee.[58] In addition, discussions within the Committee indicate that the application of the simplified reporting procedure for all State parties has also been taken into consideration.[59]

6. CEDAW Committee

The next treaty body to follow suit and apply the simplified reporting procedure on a pilot basis was the Committee on the Elimination of Discrimination against Women at its 58th session in 2014.[60] It offered the procedure, however, only to

---

to the Committee on the Rights of Persons with Disabilities, including under the simplified reporting procedures, UN Doc. CRPD/C/3, 02.09.2016; *Combrinck*, Article 36, Consideration of Reports, in: Bantekas/Stein/Anastasiou (eds.), The UN Convention on the Rights of Persons with Disabilities: A Commentary, 2018, p. 1070.

[55] Report of the Committee on the Elimination of Racial Discrimination (85th and 86th session), UN Doc. A/70/18 (2015), paras. 28 and 56.

[56] Human Rights Committee, Simplified reporting procedure, Report of the Working Group, UN Doc. CCPR/C/123/3, 06.12.2018, para. 35(e).

[57] Report of the Committee on the Elimination of Racial Discrimination (93rd, 94th and 95th session), UN Doc. A/73/18 (2018), para. 38.

[58] Report of the Committee on the Elimination of Racial Discrimination (99th and 100th session), UN Doc. A/75/18 (2020), para. 52; CERD Committee, Combined second to sixteenth periodic reports submitted by Afghanistan under article 9 of the Convention, due since 1986, UN Doc. CERD/C/AFG/2–16, 27.07.2020; Combined seventeenth to twenty-second periodic reports submitted by Botswana under article 9 of the Convention, due since 2009, UN Doc. CERD/C/BWA/17–22.

[59] Report of the Committee on the Elimination of Racial Discrimination (99th and 100th session), UN Doc. A/75/18 (2020), para. 51, but no decision has been reached yet; see also Report of the Committee on the Elimination of Racial Discrimination (104th, 105th and 106th session), UN Doc. A/77/18 (2022), paras. 56–58.

[60] Report of the Committee on the Elimination of Discrimination against Women (58th, 59th and 60th session), UN Doc. A/70/38 (2015), Part one, decision 58/II.

those State parties with overdue reports and which met the additional criterion of having submitted an updated Common Core Document in accordance with the harmonized Reporting Guidelines. The document should not date back more than five years. A possible substitute of the latter was whether the State party had experienced "significant political and/or socioeconomic changes" within the last five years.[61]

After having suspended the application of the simplified reporting procedure in 2016 for evaluation purposes,[62] the Committee reinstated it by simultaneously amending its previously established criteria for State parties to be eligible to participate. From now on, *each* State party that had submitted an initial report under the standard procedure and a Common Core Document not dating back more than five years could request to be reviewed under the simplified reporting procedure.[63] Despite popular demand by State parties, the Committee continued to consider only up to three State parties per session under the simplified reporting procedure, due to resource constraints and the extra workload imposed by the drafting of LOIPRs while simultaneously operating under the standard reporting procedure.[64]

In 2020, the Committee further alleviated the criteria for reviews under the simplified reporting procedure, abandoning the requirement of the submission of a Common Core Document. The decision seemed to be motivated by aligning working methods with those of other treaty bodies in this domain.[65] In 2021, the Committee decided to rescind its decision by which the number of LOIPRs per session was limited to three.

7. CESCR Committee

At its 54th session in 2015, the Committee on Economic Social and Cultural Rights decided to offer Lists of Issues Prior to Reporting to those nine State

---

[61] Report of the Committee on the Elimination of Discrimination against Women (58th, 59th and 60th session), UN Doc. A/70/38 (2015), Part one, decision 58/II; *Byrnes*, The Committee on the Elimination of Discrimination Against Women, in: Mégret/Alston (eds.), The United Nations and Human Rights: A Critical Appraisal, Second Edition, 2020, p. 406.

[62] Report of the Committee on the Elimination of Discrimination against Women (64th, 65th and 66th session), UN Doc. A/72/38 (2017), Part two, decision 65/V; *Byrnes*, The Committee on the Elimination of Discrimination Against Women, in: Mégret/Alston (eds.), The United Nations and Human Rights: A Critical Appraisal, Second Edition, 2020, p. 407.

[63] Report of the Committee on the Elimination of Discrimination against Women (67th, 68th and 69th session), UN Doc. A/73/38 (2018), Part three, decision 69/V.

[64] Report of the Committee on the Elimination of Discrimination against Women (70th, 71st and 72nd session), UN Doc. A/74/38 (2019), Part one, decision 70/VI; *Byrnes*, The Committee on the Elimination of Discrimination Against Women, in: Mégret/Alston (eds.), The United Nations and Human Rights: A Critical Appraisal, Second Edition, 2020, p. 407.

[65] Report of the Committee on the Elimination of Discrimination against Women (73rd, 74th and 75th session), UN Doc. A/75/38 (2020), Part one, decision 73/III.

parties whose third periodic reports were due in 2017.[66] After having conducted the first constructive dialogues under the new procedure and in reaction to the "positive outcome", as perceived by the Committee itself, it was decided to prolong the pilot period in 2018, and the Committee invited 13 other State parties to participate.[67]

In light of the parallel discussions on the subject matter, which were increasingly taking place at the Meeting of Chairpersons,[68] the Committee decided in October 2019 to offer Lists of Issues Prior to Reporting to all State parties on a regular basis, while giving priority to those having "the longest reporting history."[69] Most recently, the Committee took the decision to follow the Human Rights Committee. Starting in 2022, it shifted to a predictable review cycle based on an eight-year calendar. The transition equally entailed the application of the simplified reporting procedure as the default mode, and requires State parties to actively opt out when they wish to be reviewed under the standard reporting procedure.[70]

8. CRC Committee

The last Committee to introduce the simplified reporting procedure was the CRC Committee in 2016. Pursuant to a decision dating back to 2014, the Committee made the procedure available to State parties whose periodic reports were due from 1 September 2019 onwards.[71] Comparable to most other treaty bodies, the CRC Committee invited State parties to avail themselves of the simplified reporting procedure, but also amended its criteria: starting in February 2020, State parties with overdue periodic reports have been equally entitled to participate.[72]

9. CED Committee as the exception

The only Committee which has not yet adopted a comparable simplified reporting procedure is the Committee on Enforced Disappearances. This circumstance might be owed to the fact that, in contrast to all other eight human rights treaty

---

[66] CESCR Committee, Report on the fifty-fourth, fifty-fifth and fifty-sixth sessions, UN Doc. E/2016/22 (2016), paras. 75–76.
[67] CESCR Committee, Report on the sixty-third and sixty-fourth sessions, UN Doc. E/2019/22 (2019), para. 90.
[68] See *infra* Part IV B.II.10.
[69] CESCR Committee, Report on the sixty-fifth and sixty-sixth sessions, UN Doc. E/2020/22 (2020), para. 21.
[70] CESCR Committee, Report on the sixty-seventh and sixty-eighth sessions, UN Doc. E/2021/22 (2021), para. 22.
[71] Report of the Committee on the Rights of the Child (72nd to 77th session), UN Doc. A/73/41 (2018), para. 18.
[72] Report of the Committee on the Rights of the Child (78th to 84th session), UN Doc. A/75/41 (2020), para. 20.

B. Simplified Reporting Procedure 147

bodies,[73] it does not require State parties to submit periodic reports. This particularity has led commentators to the assumption that the Committee on Enforced Disappearances was "somewhat different from the other treaties in this regard since State Parties are not required to submit general reports."[74]

Article 29(1) CED does only require State parties to submit an initial report within two years after the entry into force of the Convention for the State Party concerned. Other than that, there are no provisions providing for regular periodic reporting activities comparable to other human rights core treaties. Rather, article 29(4) CED enables the Committee on Enforced Disappearance to request States Parties to submit additional information on the implementation of the Convention, which is not comparable to provisions enshrined in other treaties.

The omission of periodic reporting duties can be explained by the drafter's intention to ease the reporting burden imposed on contracting parties,[75] and is further explained by numerous voices in the drafting process which considered periodic reporting an ill-fitting means to react to the phenomenon of enforced disappearances, which eventually led to the incorporation of the urgent action procedure under article 30 CED, and the on-site visiting procedure under article 33 CED.[76]

Recent steps taken by the Committee and its own understanding of article 29(1) and article 29(4) CED strongly suggest the assumption, however, that the Committee's practice still bears strong resemblance to periodic reporting under other UN human rights core treaties. As a matter of fact, the Committee principally distinguishes between a formalized follow-up procedure similar to those established by other treaty bodies, on the one hand, and requests for additional information pursuant to article 29(4) CED, on the other hand.[77] As far as the latter is concerned, the Committee regularly includes in its concluding observations a paragraph by which it requests the State party concerned to submit "specific and updated information on the implementation of all its recommendations

---

[73] Identifying progress achieved in aligning the working methods and practices of the treaty bodies Note by the Secretariat, HRI/MC/2018/3, 23.03.2018, para. 8, with an overview as at 2018.

[74] *Kjærum*, State Reports, in: Alfredsson et al. (eds.), International Human Rights Monitoring Mechanisms, Second Revised Edition, 2009, p. 18.

[75] *de Frouville*, The Committee on Enforced Disappearances, in: Mégret/Alston (eds.), The United Nations and Human Rights: A Critical Appraisal, Second Edition, 2020, p. 592.

[76] *Egan*, The United Nations Human Rights Treaty System: Law and Procedure, 2011, p. 170.

[77] *de Frouville*, The Committee on Enforced Disappearances, in: Mégret/Alston (eds.), The United Nations and Human Rights: A Critical Appraisal, Second Edition, 2020, p. 592; see also CED Committee, Rules of Procedure, UN Doc. CED/C/1, 22.06.2012 with article 49 RoP providing for the additional information procedure and article 54 RoP providing for the follow-up procedure to concluding observations; *Citroni*, Committee on Enforced Disappearances (CED), in: Ruiz Fabri/Wolfrum (eds.), Max Planck Encyclopedia of International Procedural Law, Online version, December 2018, para. 18.

and any other new information on the fulfilment of the obligations contained in the Convention".[78] The common time frame for the submission of this "additional information" is normally six years, but has been occasionally narrowed down to three years in cases of serious violations.[79] Thus, the Committee's practice corresponds quite strongly to periodic reporting. This holds even more true given recent refinements developed by the Committee in relation to the additional information procedure pursuant to article 29(4) CED.

Depending on a case-by-case analysis, the Committee will first evaluate the status of implementation of its recommendations, and subsequently send a list of topics to the State party concerned. The State party is then required to submit its answers within a time frame determined by the Committee. Contingent on the "specific circumstances of the situation at stake and the stakeholders involved", the Committee will then either conduct a dialogue with the State party, or it will conduct a desk review of the information received pursuant to article 29(4) CED.[80]

This approach thus clearly incorporates decisive features of the simplified reporting procedure as applied by other treaty bodies. Taking account of the Committee's main rationales for the introduction of its additional information procedure, which are "thorough monitoring" and making the best use of restrained available resources to situations most urgently requiring action,[81] it becomes even more apparent that the newly developed procedure is in its essence very similar to the simplified reporting procedure.

---

[78] See for instance CED Committee, Concluding observations on the report submitted by the Plurinational State of Bolivia under article 29 (1) of the Convention, UN Doc. CED/C/BOL/CO/1, 24.10.2019, para. 46; Concluding observations on the report submitted by Slovakia under article 29 (1) of the Convention, UN Doc. CED/C/SVK/CO/1, 24.10.2019, para. 32.

[79] *de Frouville*, The Committee on Enforced Disappearances, in: Mégret/Alston (eds.), The United Nations and Human Rights: A Critical Appraisal, Second Edition, 2020, p. 592.

[80] Letter of the Committee on Enforced Disappearances, p. 4, https://www.ohchr.org/Documents/HRBodies/TB/HRTD/CoFacilitationProcess/outcomes/Letter-CED.pdf (last access: 21.08.2023); in 2022, the CED Committee modified the additional information procedure, but it still decides on a case-by-case analysis whether and when it will require additional information, "CED REPORTING PROCEDURE UNDER ARTICLE 29(4), CHAIRS MEETING JUNE 2022", available at: https://tbinternet.ohchr.org/_layouts/15/treatybodyexternal/Download.aspx?symbolno=INT%2FCHAIRPERSONS%2FGED%2F34%2F4036&Lang=en (last access: 21.08.2023).

[81] Letter of the Committee on Enforced Disappearances, p. 4, available at: https://www.ohchr.org/Documents/HRBodies/TB/HRTD/CoFacilitationProcess/outcomes/Letter-CED.pdf (last access: 21.08.2023).

10. Developments at the 2019 Meeting of Chairpersons

Key developments concerning the adoption of the simplified reporting procedure among all treaty bodies took place at the 31st Meeting of Chairpersons in 2019. Besides agreeing on offering the simplified reporting procedure to all State parties for periodic reports,[82] the Chairs further elaborated on a background paper on possible elements of a common aligned procedure in the application of the simplified reporting procedure.[83] The following elements were endorsed:[84] first, the Chairs agreed on the usefulness of an aligned methodology combined with predictable deadlines, including both deadlines for the submissions and for the reviews of reports. Additionally, the Committees should reflect on what kind of Common Core Document they would need under the simplified reporting procedure and what kind of template they would prefer for LOIPRs. The Chairs also opted for the development of internal guidelines applicable to the drafting of LOIPRs and concluding observations, and recommended that individual Committees consider the introduction of minimum and maximum numbers of questions, and, correspondingly, minimum and maximum numbers of concluding observations.[85] Furthermore, there should be an opportunity for stakeholders to provide further input just prior to the date of the dialogue, whereas Committees should also clarify that other topics than those addressed in the List of Issues Prior to Reporting could be raised during the constructive dialogue, so as to allow Committee members to retain a degree of flexibility.

Moreover, the individual Committees were encouraged to discuss the possibility of reviewing State parties in the absence of a report and to align their working methods in this matter accordingly. With a view to the substantive overlap of treaty provisions and the corresponding duplication of questions raised, the Chairs endorsed the proposal to coordinate the drafting of LOIPRs to ensure avoidance of "unnecessary and unintentional duplication or overlap". At the same time, they also stressed the importance of the use of "positive and intentional reinforcement or repetition in cases when something needs to be highlighted repeatedly". However, the Chairs neither clarified the notion of unnecessary duplication, nor explained when exactly an issue would need to be addressed more than once.

---

[82] Report of the Chairs of the human rights treaty bodies on their thirty-first annual meeting, UN Doc. A/74/256, 30.07.2019, Annex II, para. (b).

[83] Simplified reporting procedure: possible elements of a common aligned procedure, Note by the Secretariat, UN Doc. HRI/MC/2019/3, 15.04.2019.

[84] Report of the Chairs of the human rights treaty bodies on their thirty-first annual meeting, UN Doc. A/74/256, 30.07.2019, Annex II.

[85] In 2014, the Chairs had already discussed a possible common format for LOIPRs but rejected a common application among all treaty bodies. They were of the opinion that the individual treaty bodies "should retain the flexibility to structure the lists of issues in accordance with their needs and the situation in the State party under review", Report of the Chairs of the human rights treaty bodies on their twenty-sixth meeting, UN Doc. A/69/285, 11.08.2014, para. 40.

11. Interim conclusion

The preceding section has revealed that each treaty body has taken steps to offer the simplified reporting procedure to the State parties whose implementation activities it is monitoring. Given the current usage by those treaty bodies that have gained the most experience so far, such as the Committee against Torture or the Human Rights Committee, with the latter having shifted from an opt-in to an opt-out model, these developments might bode the reporting procedure's future design among all human rights treaty bodies.

Other developments, such as reducing the criteria which State parties must fulfil to avail themselves of the simplified reporting procedure, or the transition from the pilot use of LOIPRs to their regular application, point to the same direction. Finally, and most importantly, the Chairs reached in 2022 the conclusion to apply the simplified reporting procedure to all initial and periodic reports.[86] Despite the procedure's general acceptance among Chairpersons, it remains to be seen how slow or fast-paced the actual implementation will proceed in the near future. Some Committees already implemented the decision. For example, the CEDAW Committee now also applies the simplified reporting procedure under the opt-out system,[87] as well as the CMW Committee.[88] The same will apply to periodic reports under the CRC from 2024.[89]

At the same time, the distribution of the simplified reporting procedure within the human rights treaty body system and the velocity with which it is being implemented are a good example of how slow-paced progress can be. Since its introduction in 2007 by the Committee against Torture, almost 16 years later, the procedure's application and the related coordination have only now come to the fore, as increasing attention is being devoted to the topic by the Meeting of Chairpersons.[90]

Clearly, the application of the simplified reporting procedure bears several advantages, such as the possible incentives it may set for a more structured, targeted and precisely conducted monitoring by treaty bodies,[91] not to mention its possible long-term cost-savings effects.[92] In focusing solely on fewer selected

---

[86] Report of the Chairs of the human rights treaty bodies on their thirty-fourth annual meeting, UN Doc. A/77/228, 26.07.2022, para. 55, No. 1, para. (d).

[87] CEDAW Committee, CEDAW/C/2022/II/CRP, decision 82/3.

[88] Report of the Committee on the Protection of the Rights of All Migrant Workers and Members of Their Families (33rd and 34th session), UN Doc. A/77/48 (2022), para 14.

[89] https://www.ohchr.org/en/treaty-bodies/crc/reporting-guidelines (last access: 21.08.2023).

[90] Already at their 2020 meeting, the Chairs confirmed the further implementation of the simplified reporting procedure and further attempts at harmonizing working methods in that regard, Report of the Chairs of the human rights treaty bodies on their thirty-second annual meeting, UN Doc. A/75/346, 14.09.2020, para. 46(b) and (d).

[91] See for instance Human Rights Committee, Simplified reporting procedure, Report of the Working Group, UN Doc. CCPR/C/123/3, 06.12.2018, para. 59.

[92] See for a preliminary calculation, *Pillay*, Strengthening the United Nations human

issues, the reporting burden resting on State parties could be alleviated and over the long term, the workload imposed on treaty bodies is expected to "progressively diminish".[93]

Furthermore, the application of the simplified reporting procedure may nudge State parties to submit their long overdue reports and allows them to re-enter into dialogue with treaty bodies.[94] On the other hand, deploying Lists of Issues Prior to Reporting does mean including fewer issues in a State party's report and review.[95] Even though many State parties responded positively to the procedure's application, others remarked that the procedure would bar them from presenting a comprehensive picture,[96] or that they preferred the standard review procedure.[97] The inclusion of fewer topics can alternatively be framed as "reducing the thoroughness of the process", which possibly leads to a rather superfluous treatment of State parties, and could do more harm than good.[98]

Despite possible concessions to this critique, under the current *modus operandi* it is not possible to conduct a thorough and comprehensive review of an entire treaty, ultimately resulting in a superficial review as well. It appears impossible to address the implementation of each treaty guarantee during the limited time available for the constructive dialogue. Against the background of the prevailing lack of necessary resources, treaty bodies should hence focus on fewer issues, try to be more selective and address those issues which present themselves as the most urging.[99] In this respect, the procedure proves to be a suitable means.

---

rights treaty body system, pp. 49–50; therefore, clearly speaking positively of the procedure, *Egan*, Strengthening the United Nations Human Rights Treaty Body System, Human Rights Law Review 13 (2013), 209, 218.

[93] Human Rights Committee, Simplified reporting procedure, Report of the Working Group, UN Doc. CCPR/C/123/3, 06.12.2018, para. 56(d).

[94] Which is the underlying assumption of the CERD Committee.

[95] For considerations on limiting the number of questions, see Report of the Chairs of the human rights treaty bodies on their thirty-first annual meeting, UN Doc. A/74/256, 30.07.2019, Annex II, para. (j), with the Chairs, however, not determining concrete limits in numbers.

[96] Human Rights Committee, Simplified reporting procedure, Report of the Working Group, UN Doc. CCPR/C/123/3, 06.12.2018, para. 43.

[97] UN General Assembly, Status of the human rights treaty body system, Report of the Secretary-General, UN Doc. A/73/309, 06.08.2018, para. 14; *Abashidze/Koneva*, The Process of Strengthening the Human Rights Treaty Body System: The Road towards Effectiveness or Inefficiency?, Netherlands International Law Review 66 (2019), 357, 377.

[98] *Sarkin*, The 2020 United Nations human rights treaty body review process: prioritising resources, independence and the domestic state reporting process over rationalising and streamlining treaty bodies, The International Journal of Human Rights 25 (2021), 1301, 1308, who also writes of "worrying" and "disturbing" suggestions with a view to a more streamlined and focused reporting procedure.

[99] *Krommendijk*, Less is more: Proposals for how UN human rights treaty bodies can be more selective, Netherlands Quarterly of Human Rights 38 (2020), 5, 7–8.

III. Further alignment of the simplified reporting procedure

Under the premise that further harmonization in procedural matters is beneficial, as it can eradicate what are perceived as burdensome particularities under the various treaties, the following sections shall shed light on the current practice of treaty bodies with regard to the usage of LOIPRs to initial reports (1), whether there are any "good or best practices" to adhere to,[100] which justifies a closer look at the individual application by treaty bodies (2), and finally, whether treaty bodies have taken into consideration how to handle the prevailing risk of substantial overlap and possible negative repetition of issues raised in LOIPRs before two or more Committees (3).

1. Application to initial reports

Initial reports serve a slightly different purpose than subsequent periodic reports. They mark the very starting point of the reporting procedure and should ideally enable the treaty body to gain a comprehensive and "in-depth understanding" of the situation in the State party under initial review.[101]

The problem with applying the simplified reporting procedure to initial reports as well appears to be that the contracting parties will never be able to complete any reporting cycle with the drafting of such a comprehensive report. Consequently, adherence to the simplified reporting procedure from the very beginning means that the Committees determine each issue raised. Thereby, the objective of conducting a thorough self-evaluation, at least as far as initial reports are concerned, would fade into the background.

Originally not applying the simplified reporting procedure to initial reports, the Committee against Torture revised its position at its fifty-third session and subsequently decided to offer the simplified reporting procedure to State parties that were required to submit their initial reports, but on condition that those State parties were long overdue in submitting their reports, and that the Committee would only offer this opportunity to two State parties per year.[102]

In 2011, when the CMW Committee took the decision to introduce the simplified reporting procedure, it expressly held that the procedure did not apply to

---

[100] See for example Human Rights Committee, Simplified reporting procedure, Report of the Working Group, UN Doc. CCPR/C/123/3, 06.12.2018, para. 120 (e), where it is recommended to "ensure that the way in which the simplified reporting procedure is implemented is consistent between the various treaty bodies."

[101] *Kjærum*, State Reports, in: Alfredsson et al. (eds.), International Human Rights Monitoring Mechanisms, Second Revised Edition, 2009, p. 18; *O'Flaherty*, The United Nations Human Rights Treaty Bodies as Diplomatic Actors, in: O'Flaherty et al. (eds.), Human Rights Diplomacy: Contemporary Perspectives, 2011, p. 158; article 44(3) CRC and article 35(4) CRPD explicitly stipulate that an initial report must be comprehensive.

[102] Report of the Committee against Torture (53rd and 54th session), UN Doc. A/70/44 (2015), para. 25 and 26(a).

B. Simplified Reporting Procedure

initial reports and that the Committee was to continue requesting comprehensive initial reports.[103] Interestingly, at its eighteenth session in 2013, the Committee however adopted LOIPRs vis-à-vis two State parties which were excessively overdue with the submission of their initial report, though without any further explanation.[104]

Conscious of the ongoing strengthening process and against the background of the common elements for a uniform application of the simplified reporting procedure, the Human Rights Committee also took the decision to apply the simplified reporting procedure to initial reports.[105] It appears that the Human Rights Committee does not differentiate between overdue or timely submitted initial reports.

As far as is apparent from the available documentation, other treaty bodies have not yet applied the procedure to initial reports.[106] Their reluctance may well be explained by the above-mentioned purpose of initial reports to deliver a thorough and comprehensive picture of the situation in the State party concerned, upon which subsequent reporting cycles can rely. In view of the 2022 decision, however, other Committees are likely to follow soon.

2. Format of Lists of Issues Prior to Reporting

In order to alleviate the reporting burden resting on State parties, at least with a view to treaty-specific particularities, the adherence to a common template for the adoption of LOIPRs seems to be of added value.[107] The following section will thus shed light on the various approaches among the Committees, and will seek to detect best practices which could form part of a common template each human rights treaty body might use.

---

[103] Report of the Committee on the Protection of the Rights of All Migrant Workers and Members of Their Families (13th and 14th session), UN Doc. A/66/48 (2011), para. 26.

[104] Report of the Committee on the Protection of the Rights of All Migrant Workers and Members of Their Families (17th and 18th session), UN Doc. A/68/48 (2013), para. 40.

[105] Report of the Human Rights Committee (126th, 127th and 128th session), UN Doc. A/75/40 (2020), Annex III, para. 15.

[106] See, however, Aide-mémoire on tracking the implementation status of decisions and recommendations of the Chairs of the treaty bodies, UN Doc. HRI/MC/2022/2, 18.03.2022, para. 13 with an enumeration of six Committees that have offered or "agreed to offer" the procedure in relation to initial reports.

[107] See Conclusions of the Chairs of the human rights treaty bodies on the OHCHR Working Paper – Options and guiding questions for the development of an implementation plan for the conclusions of the human rights treaty body Chairs at their 34th meeting in June 2022 (A/77/228, paras. 55–56), paras. 7–11 as one of the most recent examples where the Committees articulate the need for further harmonisation of working methods.

a) Format of LOIPRs under CAT

The Lists of Issues Prior to Reporting generated by the Committee against Torture can generally be divided into three parts. The first and main section focuses on the "[specific] information on the implementation of articles 1–16 of the Convention, including with regard to the Committee's previous recommendations", which is followed by two minor sections addressing "other issues" and "[general] information on other measures and developments relating to the implementation of the Convention in the State party".[108]

The Committee normally includes an introductory passage in which it refers to the issues chosen for the follow-up procedure under the preceding cycle and indicates whether the State party has provided information in response to the follow-up request,[109] notifies a State party if it has not complied with its follow-up obligations,[110] and indicates to what extent the State party under review has implemented the recommendations chosen.[111]

The introductory passage is followed by the topics the Committee wants to address in the upcoming reporting cycle. On a general note, the Committee has adopted an article-by-article approach, which means that it poses questions in relation to each of the substantive provisions of the Convention separately. Under the section labelled "other issues", the Committee refers to topics which do not fall solely under one article of the Conventions, but rather addresses topics of general importance which pertain to the Convention and its implementation *in toto*.[112]

---

[108] For recently adopted LOIPRs by the Committee against Torture, see List of issues prior to submission of the sixth periodic report of Belarus, UN Doc. CAT/C/BLR/QPR/6, 17.06.2021; List of issues prior to submission of the ninth periodic report of Norway, UN Doc. CAT/C/NOR/QPR/9, 16.06.2021.

[109] See for instance Committee against Torture, List of issues prior to submission of the seventh periodic report of Argentina, UN Doc. CAT/C/ARG/QPR/7, 05.06.2020, para. 1.

[110] Committee against Torture, List of issues prior to submission of the fourth periodic report of the Philippines, UN Doc. CAT/C/PHL/QPR/4, 16.01.2019, para. 1.

[111] Committee against Torture, List of issues prior to submission of the sixth periodic report of Belarus, UN Doc. CAT/C/BLR/QPR/6, 17.06.2021, para. 1; List of issues prior to submission of the seventh periodic report of Chile, UN Doc. CAT/C/CHL/QPR/7, 17.05.2021, para. 1; List of issues prior to submission of the sixth periodic report of the Republic of Korea, UN Doc. CAT/C/KOR/QPR/6, 09.06.202, para. 1.

[112] A reoccurring item is the steps taken by the respective State party to respond to terrorist threats and whether these might have affected human rights safeguards in law or in practice, see for instance Committee against Torture, List of issues prior to submission of the seventh periodic report of the Russian Federation, UN Doc. CAT/C/RUS/QPR/7, 21.06.2021, para. 33; List of issues prior to submission of the third periodic report of Afghanistan, UN Doc. CAT/C/AFG/QPR/3, 05.06.2020, para. 35. In terms of more recent developments, especially in light of the COVID-19 pandemic, the Committee uses the "other issue-section" to remind State parties of the non-derogable nature of the prohibition of torture and that State parties are asked to provide information on how their steps taken during the pandemic comply with the framework established by the Convention, Committee against Torture, List

In the last section, the Committee normally requests State parties to "provide detailed information on any other relevant legislative, administrative, judicial or other measures taken since the consideration of the previous report to implement the provisions of the Convention or the Committee's recommendations, [...]."[113] With respect to the motivation for the application of the simplified reporting procedure, which is to enable treaty bodies and State parties to engage in a more focused and detailed dialogue, it is questionable, however, whether such a broadly-framed demand proves helpful in meeting this objective.

b) Format of LOIPRs under the ICCPR

The Human Rights Committee divides its Lists of Issues Prior to Reporting in two sections. First, under part A, the Committee requests general information on the domestic human rights situation, including new measures and developments relating to the implementation of the Covenant. Second, under section B, it asks for specific information on the implementation of articles 1 to 27 ICCPR, which also makes up the significantly larger part of the document.[114]

Whereas the Committee against Torture uses the section headed "other issues" to address topics which relate to the general implementation of the Convention, the Human Rights Committee raises these issues in its introductory section. It requests State parties to report on the progress made in the ratification of the Optional Protocols to the Covenant,[115] or demands information on procedures which are in place to implement the Committee's views under the individual complaints procedure.[116] The introductory section additionally serves to address exceptional circumstances which might require increased attention due to their urgency or gravity.[117]

---

of issues prior to submission of the fifth periodic report of Senegal, UN Doc. CAT/C/SEN/QPR/5, 25.05.2021, para. 29; List of issues prior to submission of the ninth periodic report of Norway, UN Doc. CAT/C/NOR/QPR/9, 16.06.2021, para. 29.

[113] See for example Committee against Torture, List of issues prior to submission of the seventh periodic report of Czechia, UN Doc. CAT/C/CZE/QPR/7, 10.06.2021, para. 30; List of issues prior to submission of the seventh periodic report of the Russian Federation, UN Doc. CAT/C/RUS/QPR/7, 21.06.2021, para. 35.

[114] See exemplarily for recently adopted LOIPR, Human Rights Committee, List of issues prior to submission of the seventh periodic report of Canada, UN Doc. CCPR/C/CAN/QPR/7, 24.08.2021.

[115] Human Rights Committee, List of issues prior to the submission of the third periodic report of the Congo, UN Doc. CCPR/C/COG/QPR/3, 01.09.2020, para. 1; List of issues prior to submission of the second periodic report of Indonesia, UN Doc. CCPR/C/IDN/QPR/2, 02.09.2020, para. 1; List of issues prior to submission of the eighth periodic report of the United Kingdom of Great Britain and Northern Ireland, UN Doc. CCPR/C/GBR/QPR/8, 05.05.2020, para. 1.

[116] Human Rights Committee, List of issues prior to submission of the seventh periodic report of Canada, UN Doc. CCPR/C/CAN/QPR/7, 24.08.2021, para 1.

[117] Great Britain, for example, was requested to "provide information on the implications of the withdrawal from the Charter of Fundamental Rights of the European Union and the

Next to these rather exceptional requests, a common feature found in almost every List of Issues Prior to Reporting is the request to provide information on "any significant developments in the legal and institutional framework within which human rights are promoted and protected"[118] since the last reporting cycle. In addition, State parties are frequently asked to deliver information on measures or steps taken to implement the recommendations contained in the Committee's previous concluding observations.[119] Again, it is doubt worthy if such a practice is of added value. It seems that State parties are thereby required to report on *all* measures taken to comply with the preceding concluding observations from the last reporting cycle. De facto, this might be tantamount to the drafting of a comprehensive report under the standard reporting procedure and leaves the State party in uncertainty how to meet this demand. In some of the most recently adopted LOIPRs, however, the Committee seems to have narrowed its focus to a single topic which requires priority, and which formed part of the preceding concluding observations.[120] These requests resemble the Committee against Torture's practice to indicate the progress achieved under the follow-up procedure.

Concerning the specific information on the implementation of the specific treaty provisions, the Committee does not follow an article-by-article approach, but raises thematic issues which are connected to the respective treaty provisions. In this regard, the Committee indicates which articles of the Covenant relate to the specific question.

---

loss of funding from the European Union for human rights projects", Human Rights Committee, List of issues prior to submission of the eighth periodic report of the United Kingdom of Great Britain and Northern Ireland, UN Doc. CCPR/C/GBR/QPR/8, 05.05.2020, para. 2; Somalia received the question to what extent the State party was in the position to secure the Covenant rights in those territories not being under its effective control (with reference to Somaliland and Puntland), Human Rights Committee, List of issues prior to submission of the initial report of Somalia, UN Doc. CCPR/C/SOM/QPR/1, 05.05.2020, para. 2.

[118] See for instance, Human Rights Committee, List of issues prior to submission of the third periodic report of Albania, UN Doc. CCPR/C/ALB/QPR/3, 19.08.2021, para. 1; List of issues prior to submission of the second periodic report of Turkey, UN Doc. CCPR/C/TUR/QPR/2, 25.08.2021, para. 1; List of issues prior to submission of the second periodic report of Burkina Faso, UN Doc. CCPR/C/BFA/QPR/2, 01.09.2020, para. 1.

[119] See for instance, Human Rights Committee, List of issues prior to submission of the third periodic report of Nepal, UN Doc. CCPR/C/NPL/QPR/3, 27.05.2021, para. 1; List of issues prior to submission of the fifth periodic report of the United Republic of Tanzania, UN Doc. CCPR/C/TZA/QPR/5, 20.08.2021, para. 1; List of issues prior to submission of the third report of Guyana, UN Doc. CCPR/C/GUY/QPR/3, 31.08.2020, para. 1; List of issues prior to submission of the second periodic report of Montenegro, UN Doc. CCPR/C/MNE/QPR/2, 06.05.2020, para. 1; List of issues prior to submission of the eighth periodic report of the United Kingdom of Great Britain and Northern Ireland, UN Doc. CCPR/C/GBR/QPR/8, 05.05.2020, para. 1.

[120] Human Rights Committee, List of issues prior to submission of the second periodic report of Turkey, UN Doc. CCPR/C/TUR/QPR/2, 25.08.2021 para. 1; List of issues prior to the submission of the third periodic report of the Democratic People's Republic of Korea, UN Doc. CCPR/C/PRK/QPR/3, 22.06.2021, para. 1.

c) Format of LOIPRs under CMW

The Lists of Issues Prior to Reporting adopted by the CMW Committee are structured into three sections.[121] The first section deals with the implementation of the Convention and is further divided into questions concerning "general information" and questions pertaining to the implementation of specific treaty provisions. The provision-specific questions are structured along the Convention. The Committee has thus opted for an article-by-article approach.

In the second section, the Committee normally requests the State party to submit within a maximum of three pages information on, inter alia, new laws or regulations that concern the interests and rights of migrant workers, policies or policy programmes, or the ratification of further international agreements related to the protection of migrant workers. Particular reference is often made to ILO Conventions, such as the ILO Domestic Workers Convention 2011 (No. 189), for example.[122]

In the third and last section headed "[data], official estimates, statistics and other information, if available", the CMW Committee requires State parties to deliver this kind of information with respect to certain very vulnerable groups among migrant workers, such as migrant workers in detention,[123] or unaccompanied children or migrant children separated from their parents.[124]

---

[121] See for the most recently adopted LOIPRs, CMW Committee, List of issues prior to submission of the initial report of the Congo, UN Doc. CMW/C/COG/QPR/1, 23.02.2021; List of issues prior to submission of the third periodic report of El Salvador, UN Doc. CMW/C/SLV/QPR/3, 23.02.2021.

[122] CMW Committee, List of issues prior to submission of the second periodic report of Burkina Faso, UN Doc. CMW/C/BFA/QPR/2, 11.10.2019, para. 35; List of issues prior to submission of the combined initial to third periodic reports of Belize, UN Doc. CMW/C/BLZ/QPR/1-3, 03.10.2019, para. 33; List of issues prior to submission of the initial report of Sao Tome and Principe, UN Doc. CMW/C/STP/QPR/1, 10.05.2019, para. 31; List of issues prior to submission of the third periodic report of Azerbaijan, UN Doc. CMW/C/AZE/QPR/3, 09.10.2018, para. 27.

[123] CMW Committee, List of issues prior to submission of the second periodic report of Burkina Faso, UN Doc. CMW/C/BFA/QPR/2, 11.10.2019, para. 36(b); List of issues prior to submission of the combined initial to third periodic reports of Belize, UN Doc. CMW/C/BLZ/QPR/1-3, 03.10.2019, para. 34(b); List of issues prior to submission of the initial report of Sao Tome and Principe, UN Doc. CMW/C/STP/QPR/1, 10.05.2019, para. 32(b).

[124] CMW Committee, List of issues prior to submission of the second periodic report of Burkina Faso, UN Doc. CMW/C/BFA/QPR/2, 11.10.2019, para. 36(d); List of issues prior to submission of the combined initial to third periodic reports of Belize, UN Doc. CMW/C/BLZ/QPR/1-3, 03.10.2019, para. 34(d); List of issues prior to submission of the initial report of Sao Tome and Principe, UN Doc. CMW/C/STP/QPR/1, 10.05.2019, para. 32(d).

d) Format of LOIPRs under CRPD

The Committee on the Rights of Persons with Disabilities structures its Lists of Issues Prior to Reporting along the Convention provisions which means that section A is devoted to information relating to "purpose and general obligations (arts. 1–4)", section B deals with "specific rights (arts. 5–30)" and the last section C is devoted to "specific obligations" arising from articles 31 to 33 CRPD.[125] The first section often contains the request to provide information "on the measures taken to implement the recommendations issued by the Committee in its previous concluding observations".[126] At times, the Committee also requests information "on the implementation of each previous recommendation".[127]

Yet again, the adequacy of such a request in the context of a procedure that supposedly aims at more focused and precise scrutiny of human rights implementation is highly debatable. At least, the Committee seems to limit its very broad approach to a certain degree. It sometimes indicates which recommendations should be considered in particular, which are nonetheless very far-reaching and could possibly encompass a variety of measures to report on. For example, reference can be made to recommendations such as to "[ensure] concepts of reasonable accommodation and universal design are regulated in areas such as education, health, transportation and construction"[128] or to report on measures to "[review] its domestic legislation and bring it into line with the Convention".[129]

e) Format of LOIPRs under CERD

To date, the Committee on the Elimination of All Forms of Racial Discrimination has adopted only twelve Lists of Issues of Prior to Reporting, which is due to the fact that the Committee understands the simplified reporting procedure primarily as a means to encourage State parties that have remained absent from the reporting procedure for a long time to "rejoin the system."

In terms of structure, the Committee applies an article-by-article approach, comparable to the Committee against Torture, the CMW and the CRPD Committee. First, it requires general information, which in most documents comprises

---

[125] See for example, CRPD Committee, List of issues prior to submission of the combined second to fourth reports of Chile, UN Doc. CRPD/C/CHL/QPR/2–4, 13.10.2020.

[126] CRPD Committee, List of issues prior to submission of the combined second to fourth periodic reports of Croatia, UN Doc. CRPD/C/HRV/QPR/2–4, 30.04.2020, para. 1; List of issues prior to submission of the combined second and third periodic reports of Slovakia, UN Doc. CRPD/C/SVK/QPR/2–3, 23.10.2019, para. 1.

[127] CPRD Committee, List of issues prior to the submission of the combined second and third periodic reports of the Cook Islands, UN Doc. CPRD/C/COK/QPR/2–3, 29.04.2019, para. 1.

[128] CRPD Committee, List of issues prior to submission of the combined second to fourth periodic reports of Croatia, UN Doc. CRPD/C/HRV/QPR/2–4, 30.04.2020, para. 1(b).

[129] CRPD Committee, List of issues prior to submission of the combined second and third periodic reports of Slovakia, UN Doc. CRPD/C/SVK/QPR/2–3, 23.10.2019, para. 1(b).

questions relating to the general legal framework and recent developments relevant to the rights enshrined in the Convention. Afterwards, the Committee poses questions in numerical order from article 1 to article 7 CERD.[130]

f) Format of LOIPRs under CEDAW

Common to almost every List of Issues Prior to Reporting adopted by the CEDAW Committee is the introductory paragraph. The Committee requires the State party under review to "provide information and statistics, disaggregated by age, disability, ethnicity, minority status and nationality" or other distinction criteria "on the current situation of women in the State party, to enable monitoring of the implementation of the Convention."[131]

Next, the Committee formulates the questions it wants to raise during the constructive dialogue, but it does not proceed in an article-by-article manner, nor does it indicate which articles are related to the specific questions. Instead, it proceeds in a topic-orientated fashion and poses its questions in relation to issues such as "access to justice,"[132] "gender-based violence against women",[133] "education"[134] or "marriage and family relations",[135] just to mention a few reoccurring topics raised by the Committee.

The last paragraph usually requires the State party under review to "provide any additional information deemed relevant regarding legislative, policy, administrative and any other measures taken to implement the provisions of the Convention and the Committee's concluding observations since the consideration of the previous periodic report."[136] Once again, it seems questionable whether this very unspecific question is compatible with the underlying rationales of the simplified procedure.

---

[130] For examples of more recently adopted LOIPRs by the CERD Committee, see List of issues prior to submission of the twentieth and twenty-first combined periodic reports of India, UN Doc. CERD/C/IND/QPR/20–21, 30.08.2021; List of issues prior to submission of the fifteenth periodic report of Lesotho, UN Doc. CERD/C/LSO/QPR/15, 30.04.2021; List of issues prior to submission of the thirteenth to fifteenth periodic reports of Maldives, CERD/C/MDV/QPR/13–15, 30.04.2021.

[131] See exemplarily for this recurrent formulation in the first paragraph: CEDAW Committee, List of issues and questions prior to the submission of the seventh periodic report of Estonia, UN Doc. CEDAW/C/EST/QPR/7, 16.07.2021, para. 1; the specific distinction criteria may vary from State party to State party.

[132] CEDAW Committee, List of issues and questions prior to the submission of the seventh periodic report of the Netherlands, UN Doc. CEDAW/C/NLD/QPR/7, 21.07.2021, para. 4.

[133] CEDAW Committee, List of issues and questions prior to the submission of the fifth periodic report of the Niger, UN Doc. CEDAW/C/NER/QPR/5, 22.07.2021, para. 11.

[134] CEDAW Committee, List of issues and questions prior to the submission of the tenth periodic report of Bhutan, UN Doc. CEDAW/C/BTN/QPR/10, 10.03.2021, paras. 14–15.

[135] CEDAW Committee, List of issues and questions prior to the submission of the seventh periodic report of Estonia, UN Doc. CEDAW/C/EST/QPR/7, 16.07.2021, para. 23.

[136] CEDAW Committee, List of issues and questions prior to the submission of the fifth periodic report of the Niger, UN Doc. CEDAW/C/NER/QPR/5, 22.07.2021, para. 25.

g) Format of LOIPRs under the ICESCR

Generally, the CESCR Committee seems to divide its LOIPRs into three sections. These are: "issues of particular relevance", the "ongoing implementation of the Covenant" and "good practices" the State party has developed since the last constructive dialogue and which have contributed to the realization of economic, social and cultural rights, with particular focus on marginalized and disadvantaged individuals and groups.[137]

The section which addresses issues of particular relevance serves to highlight the importance of the selected topics and is also used to refer to topics which would fall under the "other issues-section" in LOIPRs adopted by the Committee against Torture or under the introductory passage as used by the Human Rights Committee.[138]

Concerning the LOIPR's structure under the main section, three "approaches" can be detected. In the List of Issues Prior to Reporting sent to New Zealand and Mongolia, the Committee applied an article-by-article approach and went in numeric order from article 1(2) ICESCR to articles 13 and 14 ICESCR.[139] These are, however, the only documents in which the Committee included headings with simultaneous reference to the respective provisions. Other documents contain a similar order, but they do not comprise headings which would indicate the normative basis for the pronouncements. Other Lists of Issues Prior to Reporting, in turn, do not even contain headings or any structural elements and thus simply enumerate the questions the Committee wants to raise.[140]

---

[137] See for one of the most recent examples, CESCR Committee, List of issues prior to submission of the seventh periodic report of Sweden, UN Doc. E/C.12/SWE/QPR/7, 16.11.2020.

[138] With regard to the Ukraine, the Committee asked for information on the situation in the Donetsk and Luhansk region for instance, CESCR Committee, List of issues prior to submission of the seventh periodic report of Ukraine, UN Doc. E/C.12/UKR/QPR/7, 14.11.2018, para. 3; it is also this section that the Committee choses to ask questions related to the COVID-pandemic, see for example, List of issues prior to submission of the seventh periodic report of Sweden, UN Doc. E/C.12/SWE/QPR/7, 16.11.2020, para. 3.

[139] CESCR Committee, List of issues prior to submission of the fifth periodic report of Mongolia, UN Doc. E/C.12/MNG/QPR/5, 21.11.2019; List of issues prior to the submission of the fourth periodic report of New Zealand, UN Doc. E/C.12/NZL/QPR/4, 12.04.2016.

[140] See for instance, CESCR Committee, List of issues prior to submission of the sixth periodic report of Italy, UN Doc. E/C.12/ITA/QPR/6, 16.04.2020; List of issues prior to submission of the fifth periodic report of Chile, UN Doc. E/C.12/CHL/QPR/5, 09.04.2020; List of issues prior to submission of the seventh periodic report of Canada, UN Doc. E/C.12/CAN/QPR/7, 07.04.2020; List of issues prior to submission of the fifth periodic report of France, UN Doc. E/C.12/FRA/QPR/5, 06.04.2020.

h) Format of LOIPRs under CRC

The CRC Committee first requests information concerning "new developments", which include, inter alia, the demand for "information on the adoption or reform of laws, policies and programmes, and any other type of measures taken […]",[141] or information related to the COVID pandemic.[142] The main section is composed of questions relating to the "rights under the Convention and its Optional Protocols" and concludes with questions that relate to the two Optional Protocols to the Convention. Normally, the Committee follows an issues-specific approach with the adherence to thematic clusters that correspond to those already developed by the Committee in the course of adopting concluding observations.[143]

i) Comparison and detection of best practices

As has become apparent, the various formats and templates deployed by treaty bodies differ to varying degrees, yet they roughly correspond to a common overall structure. Each treaty body devotes at least one section to more broadly framed topics, such as the general implementation of the respective treaty, exceptional circumstances requiring immediate attention, or necessary data which should be provided as soon as possible.

While requests for information on the implementation of all recommendations made under the preceding reporting cycle are arguably too undifferentiated, and contradict the very objective of rendering the reporting procedure more targeted, precise, and focused,[144] the Committee against Torture's introductory passage should be given due consideration by all treaty bodies. The Committee summarizes the results of the follow-up procedure, which logically entails a limited number of items. Additionally, and even more importantly, such an approach arguably creates links between the different reporting cycles, helps keep the follow-up procedure from ending up in futility, and makes the State party concerned aware of its progress already achieved.

Regarding the treaty-specific section, two approaches are discernable. A treaty body might either decide to work in an article-by-article manner, or it might follow an issue-specific approach, with the clustering of two or more substantive provisions under thematic headings. Both approaches are supported by solid reasoning. The group- and issue-specific Committees will, by their very nature,

---

[141] CRC Committee, List of issues prior to submission of the combined sixth and seventh periodic reports of Bulgaria, UN Doc. CRC/C/BGR/QPR/6–7, 09.07.2021, paras. 2–3.

[142] CRC Committee, List of issues prior to submission of the combined third and fourth periodic reports of Liechtenstein, UN Doc. CRC/C/LIE/QPR/3–4, 30.06.2021, para. 2(b).

[143] For those clusters, see *Evans*, The Committee on the Rights of the Child, in: Mégret/Alston (eds.), The United Nations and Human Rights: A Critical Appraisal, Second Edition, 2020, p. 525.

[144] *Krommendijk*, Less is more: Proposals for how UN human rights treaty bodies can be more selective, Netherlands Quarterly of Human Rights 38 (2020), 5, 8.

have a narrower focus and might thus work in an article-by-article manner. The Committee against Torture, for instance, has opted for the article-by-article approach, which seems reasonable as it confines its work to the prohibition of torture. The Covenant Committees, in turn, cover a broad set of rights and guarantees. It is in these cases that they should rather opt for a thematic approach, just as the Human Rights Committee does. While treaty bodies should retain the autonomy to structure the LOIPR's main section in such a way that suits best their constituent treaty, a distinct formal feature is worth considering and should ideally be applied by all treaty bodies.

The majority of treaty bodies link their questions to the specific treaty provisions which serve as the normative basis for the Committee's monitoring activity in the respective matter. With regard to the adoption of concluding observations, this methodology has been described as "best practice", since it "has the obvious merit of reinforcing the relationship between the concluding observations and the treaty itself."[145] In addition, citations of the relevant provisions have been identified as "a key tool to ensure that the HRC is not overstepping its competence to monitor implementation of the ICCPR."[146] What holds true for concluding observations can necessarily also only be true for LOPIRs. They constitute the starting point of a new reporting cycle, and the sooner abstract treaty provisions are put into a specific perspective, the greater the chances that the procedure will have any impact. Thus, the CEDAW Committee and the CESCR Committee, which do not yet seem to have developed any consistent practice in that regard, should fall into line with the other Committees and align their practices accordingly.

Another feature which has been identified as an indicator of the quality of concluding observations in terms of generating a long-term dialogue between the respective Committee and State parties is making references to previous concluding observations.[147] Next to explicitly mentioning the issues chosen for the follow-up procedure and assessing the progress achieved in their implementation, the inclusion of references to preceding concluding observations can serve as another principal means by which treaty bodies can create links between the various reporting cycles.

The Committee against Torture regularly refers back to concluding observations adopted during the preceding reporting cycle. It does so by indicating the precise paragraph of the former concluding observation and connects it to the specific question it wants to address for the upcoming cycle.[148] The Human Rights

---

[145] *O'Flaherty*, The Concluding Observations of United Nations Human Rights Treaty Bodies, Human Rights Law Review 6 (2006), 27, 43.

[146] *Kälin*, Examination of state reports, in: Keller/Ulfstein (eds.), UN Human Rights Treaty Bodies: Law and Legitimacy, 2012, p. 49.

[147] *O'Flaherty*, The Concluding Observations of United Nations Human Rights Treaty Bodies, Human Rights Law Review 6 (2006), 27, 40.

[148] For an instructive example with many references to previous concluding observations,

Committee proceeds similarly, and while tendencies in the CMW Committee's practice tentatively point to the same direction, no definite conclusion on its willingness to follow suit of the aforementioned Committees can be drawn at the moment, since many of its LOIPRs were sent to State parties which had to submit their initial reports. Other treaty bodies, such as the CESCR and the CRPD Committee include fewer references to preceding concluding observations.

However, it should be clarified that mere references to concluding observations adopted are far from being an indicator of, or a prerequisite for, an effective and efficient monitoring under the simplified reporting procedure. If the Committees consider it necessary to spontaneously address other issues during the constructive dialogue than those included in their LOIPRs, the addition of references is logically no longer possible, as these topics may not have been addressed at all in earlier concluding observations.

The merits of including references, presupposed that topics have been repeatedly raised before the respective Committee, lie above all in the possibility of creating continuity. With regard to issues that require long-term efforts, the treaty body and the State party concerned will engage in a lasting dialogue. Second, the inclusion of references has the obvious effect of reminding the State party under review that parts of previous dialogues had already revolved around the same subject. Ultimately, this might contribute to the State party's awareness and facilitates its self-evaluation process.

Last, as regards the formal design of LOIPRs, treaty bodies should be advised to include a standard paragraph which indicates that they might raise topics other than those included in their LOIPRs. The inclusion of such a reminder could counter possible criticism that the simplified reporting procedure is too narrowly focused and does not guarantee to cover a treaty's implementation exhaustively.[149]

Some Committees, such as the CRC Committee, already include such remarks in their LOIPRs. It regularly stresses in the introductory passage that it "may take up all aspects of children's rights set out in the Convention and its Optional Protocols during the dialogue with the State party."[150] Other treaty bodies, such

---

see Committee against Torture, List of issues prior to submission of the ninth periodic report of Norway, UN Doc. CAT/C/NOR/QPR/9, 16.06.2021.

[149] For such criticism, see *Sarkin*, The 2020 United Nations human rights treaty body review process: prioritising resources, independence and the domestic state reporting process over rationalising and streamlining treaty bodies, The International Journal of Human Rights 25 (2021), 1301, 1309; also rather critical *Abashidze/Koneva*, The Process of Strengthening the Human Rights Treaty Body System: The Road towards Effectiveness or Inefficiency?, Netherlands International Law Review 66 (2019), 357, 378.

[150] See among the more recently adopted LOIPRs, CRC Committee, List of issues prior to submission of the combined fifth and sixth periodic reports of Oman, UN Doc. CRC/C/OMN/QPR/5–6, 30.06.2021, para. 1; List of issues prior to submission of the combined sixth and seventh periodic reports of Sweden, UN Doc. CRC/C/SWE/QPR/6–7, 23.07.2020, para. 1.

as the CEDAW or CMW Committee, used to incorporate similar paragraphs in earlier adopted LOIPRs,[151] but ceased following this approach without apparent reason.

3. Solutions to the problem of substantive overlap

Possibly more important than adopting LOIPRs on the basis of a common structure and a common template are ways and means to address the overlapping mandates of several treaty bodies regarding substantive treaty provisions. Unless treaty bodies abide by a strict reporting calendar with fixed deadlines for both, the submission and consideration of LOIPRs/reports, they constantly run the risk of repeating topics that might have been discussed in detail between the State party under review and another Committee before.

Unnecessary duplications within a relatively short period of time have been identified as one of the major factors leading to the so-called "evaluation fatigue".[152] They should thus be avoided whenever possible. On the other hand, repetition of certain topics does not automatically equate with a waste of resources or an exercise in vain. Some topics might require increased attention through the lens of several human rights treaties on the grounds of their multi-layered discriminatory dimensions, or simply because these issues have their roots in fundamental structural problems, not easily overcome.

The human rights treaty bodies do not perceive the repetition of issues negative per se, as can be inferred from the inclusion of the terms "positive and intentional reinforcement or repetition"[153] in their common elements paper on the simplified reporting procedure. Despite the statement that positive and intentional reinforcement or repetition may be useful in cases "when something needs to be highlighted repeatedly",[154] they do not define any criteria as to when exactly a topic should receive repeated attention.

---

[151] See for instance CEDAW Committee, List of issues and questions prior to the submission of the combined sixth and seventh periodic reports of Ireland, UN Doc. CEDAW/C/IRL/QPR/6–7, 16.03.2016, para. 27; however, most recent Committee practice indicates that the Committee reinstated the inclusion of such a reminder, List of issues and questions prior to the submission of the tenth periodic report of Bhutan, UN Doc. CEDAW/C/BTN/QPR/10, 03.2021, para. 25; List of issues and questions prior to the submission of the eighth periodic report of Chile, UN Doc. CEDAW/C/CHL/QPR/8, 10.03.2021, para. 25; see also List of issues and questions prior to the submission of the eighth periodic report of Italy, UN Doc. CEDAW/C/ITA/QPR/8, 10.03.2021, para. 25.

[152] *Krommendijk*, Less is more: Proposals for how UN human rights treaty bodies can be more selective, Netherlands Quarterly of Human Rights 38 (2020), 5, 7; *Morijn*, Reforming United Nations Human Rights Treaty Monitoring Reform, Netherlands International Law Review 58 (2011), 295, 297.

[153] Report of the Chairs of the human rights treaty bodies on their thirty-first annual meeting, UN Doc. A/74/256, 30.07.2019, Annex II, para (i).

[154] Report of the Chairs of the human rights treaty bodies on their thirty-first annual meeting, UN Doc. A/74/256, 30.07.2019, Annex II, para (i).

The Committees speak of "intentional" repetition, which implies a conscious decision when deciding to reiterate questions another treaty body might just have recently raised on its own. Here it is relevant to note that the human rights situation is different in each State party. Being in one State party possibly the most serious and grave violation of rights, the same topic might represent only one among several similar shortfalls in the implementation of treaty guarantees in another State party. What is more, each treaty body, in particular the issue- and group-specific Committees, was set up to monitor the implementation of specific rights and guarantees. Accordingly, each issue- or group-specific treaty body might consider different issues worth repeating, depending on how much they correspond to the core of the respective treaty.[155]

Ultimately, it lies in the eye of the beholder to identify which occurrences of human rights violations specifically require increased and repeated attention. Hence, any decision rests with the various Committees. At this point, the way of addressing the overlap in the work of treaty bodies plays a more pivotal role than trying to avoid duplication and repetition at all costs, which is inevitable anyway due to the fragmented status of the human rights treaty body system.

In concreto, this would mean to consciously select and repeat those issues which present themselves as the most pressing in the view of the respective monitoring body. Perhaps even more importantly, treaty bodies could signalize to the State party under review why the issue has been placed on the agenda again. Whereas the introduction of a comprehensive reporting calendar,[156] encompassing each treaty, possibly mitigates much effort otherwise needed in avoiding unnecessary overlap and helps to create positive duplication, the following section shall shed light on three emerging trends/activities among treaty bodies which could enable them to implement the concept of positive and intentional repetition. Their implementation would render the introduction of a comprehensive reporting calendar to this end less indispensable.

a) Cross-references to external documents

Taking a closer look at the LOIPRs issued by the Committee against Torture, one can find many examples in which it included references to other treaty bodies' concluding observations. However, the referencing activities of the Committee are not limited to documents issued by UN human rights treaty bodies, but include other external sources, such as reports by special procedure mandate holders after their mission to the State party under review,[157] conclusions and/or

---

[155] Cf. *Payandeh*, Fragmentation within international human rights law, in: Andenas/Bjorge (eds.), A Farewell to Fragmentation: Reassertion and Convergence in International Law, 2015, p. 311.

[156] See *infra*, Part IV C.

[157] See, for instance, the LOIPR sent to Paraguay, Committee against Torture, List of issues prior to submission of the eighth periodic report of Paraguay, UN Doc. CAT/C/PRY/QPR/8, 11.06.2020, with repeated reference to the Report of the Special Rap-

recommendations as adopted under the Universal Periodic Review,[158] or judgments handed down by regional human rights courts,[159] with this enumeration being non-exhaustive. While these citations of sources outside the treaty body system might serve as an indicator of the Committee's "connectivity"[160] with other human rights institutions and monitoring processes, the following section shall only consider the interaction between UN human rights treaty bodies themselves.

aa) Rationales for including cross-references in LOIPRs

The citation of external sources stemming from reviews conducted by other treaty bodies or outcome documents as produced under other human rights review mechanisms bears strong resemblance to cross-referencing in international courts' and tribunals' decisions and judgments. The latter forms an integral part of what is commonly referred to as "transjudicial communication"[161] or "judicial dialogue"[162] between international courts and tribunals. Among the various rationales for international adjudicators to refer to other courts' decisions,[163] seek-

---

porteur on contemporary forms of slavery, including its causes and consequences, on her mission to Paraguay, UN Doc. A/HRC/39/52/Add.1, 20.07.2018; or the List of issues prior to submission of the sixth periodic report of Belarus, UN Doc. CAT/C/BLR/QPR/6, 17.06.2021, with reference to the Report of the Special Rapporteur on the situation of human rights in Belarus, UN Doc. A/HRC/41/52, 08.05.2019.

[158] See for instance the LOIPR sent to the Republic of Korea, Committee against Torture, List of issues prior to submission of the sixth periodic report of the Republic of Korea, UN Doc. CAT/C/KOR/QPR/6, 09.06.2020 with seven references to conclusions and/or recommendations contained in the report of the Working Group on the Universal Periodic Review, Republic of Korea, UN Doc. A/HRC/37/11, 27.12.2017.

[159] Committee against Torture, List of issues prior to submission of the eighth periodic report of France, UN Doc. CAT/C/FRA/QPR/8, 02.01.2019, with several references to judgments rendered by the ECtHR.

[160] See for the seldom used term "connectivity" *Cleveland*, Enhancing Human Rights Connectivity for the Treaty Body System, Document submitted for the Treaty Body Review Conference, Geneva, 8–9 December 2016, available, https://www.geneva-academy.ch/joomlatools-files/docman-files/Draft%20List%20of%20Submissions%20–%20Academic%20Platform%202020%20Review%20without%20Propositions%20.pdf (last access: 21.08.2023).

[161] *Voeten*, Borrowing and Nonborrowing among International Courts, The Journal of Legal Studies 39 (2010), 547, 549.

[162] *Boisson de Chazournes*, Plurality in the Fabric of International Courts and Tribunals: The Threads of a Managerial Approach, European Journal of International Law 28 (2017), 13, 36; *Peters*, The refinement of international law: From fragmentation to regime interaction and politicization, International Journal of Constitutional Law 15 (2017), 671, 695; *Helfer/Slaughter*, Toward a Theory of Effective Supranational Adjudication, Yale Law Journal 107 (1997), 273, 389.

[163] For a summary of arguments in favour and against the practice of cross-referencing, see *Cheeseman*, Harmonising the Jurisprudence of Regional and International Human Rights Bodies: A Literature Review, in: Buckley/Donald/Leach (eds.), Towards Convergence in International Human Rights Law: Approaches of Regional and International Systems, 2016, pp. 610–619.

ing to render their own judgments more persuasive, well-reasoned and legitimate is arguably one of the most prominent motives.[164] Nevertheless, before applying any methodology or theory developed in the context of judicial dialogue among international courts to LOIPRs as drafted by treaty bodies, two decisive distinctions must be drawn first. LOIPRs are neither judgments or decisions, nor do they form part of a contentious procedure at the end of which a binding decision is rendered.

On the contrary, LOIPRs do initiate the next round of State reporting, which is in theory a non-adversarial procedure, aiming to a great extent at allowing State parties to engage in a thorough self-assessment. The procedure comes to an end with the adoption of concluding observations, which are legally non-binding and are rather understood as recommendations. Therefore, persuasiveness in the sense as required in judgements is not necessary.

Keeping in mind that treaty bodies seek to create *intentional* duplication, and that the addressees of LOIPRs are State parties who otherwise might complain about fruitless and burdensome repetition of the same issues ever again, the indication of other Committees having discussed the same question serves in the first place as a signal device. The Committees can hereby demonstrate to State parties under review that they are aware of raising similar or even identical topics.[165] Quotations of other treaty bodies' documents thus signalize to the respective State party that the Committee has taken a deliberate decision on those topics for the upcoming reporting cycle.

Additionally, and by analogy with the motives for the usage of cross-references in judgments, citations in LOIPRs may indeed enhance the legitimacy of a treaty body's work in a twofold manner. First, the respective Committee is able to demonstrate that the question is worth addressing and can indicate that another Committee came across the same subject-matter.[166] Second, repetition signifies a

---

[164] *de Schutter*, The Formation of a Common Law of Human Rights, in: Bribosia/Rorive (eds.), Human Rights Tectonics: Global Dynamics of Integration and Fragmentation, 2018, p. 22; *Mac-Gregor*, What Do We Mean When We Talk about Judicial Dialogue: Reflections of a Judge of the Inter-American Court of Human Rights, Harvard Human Rights Journal 30 (2017), 89, 96; *Boisson de Chazournes*, Plurality in the Fabric of International Courts and Tribunals: The Threads of a Managerial Approach, European Journal of International Law 28 (2017), 13, 42, but who also detects coherence as the main motive for adding cross-references at 44; *Voeten*, Borrowing and Nonborrowing among International Courts, The Journal of Legal Studies 39 (2010), 547, 553; *Slaughter*, A Typology of Transjudicial Communication, University of Richmond Law Review 29 (1994), 99, 119.

[165] *Voeten*, Borrowing and Nonborrowing among International Courts, The Journal of Legal Studies 39 (2010), 547, 554, who observes that cross-references may serve as "strategic communication" vis-à-vis State parties.

[166] Cf. *Walker*, International Human Rights Law: Towards Pluralism or Harmony? The Opportunities and Challenges of Coexistence: The View from the UN Treaty Bodies, in: Buckley/Donald/Leach (eds.), Towards Convergence in International Human Rights Law: Approaches of Regional and International Systems, 2016, p. 501, who argues that references serve to support conclusions.

persistent need for improvement. References to other treaty bodies arguably lend also more weight the respective Committee's selection of topics for the upcoming review cycle, as the State party has not yet taken the decisive steps despite having been recommended to do so by other treaty bodies.

What is more, cross-referencing in LOIPRs may enable treaty bodies to pursue one of the reporting procedure's objectives, as has been defined by themselves. As indicated above, the harmonized Reporting Guidelines stated that the reporting procedure should enable State parties to better comprehend the concept of interdependent, indivisible and interrelated human rights.[167]

bb) Practice of the Committee against Torture

In practice, the latter is possibly best illustrated by the Committee against Torture's use of cross-references under articles 2, 11 and 16 CAT. These are the provisions under which many questions are accompanied by references to other treaty bodies' concluding observations. Especially articles 2 and 16 CAT are the broadest provisions of the Convention in that they establish the general obligation to take measures in order to prevent acts of torture or other acts of cruel, inhuman or degrading treatment or punishment which do not amount to torture.[168]

Reoccurring topics under articles 2, 11 and 16 CAT are, inter alia, domestic violence,[169] gender-based violence,[170] human trafficking,[171] or violence committed

---

[167] Compilation of Guidelines on the Form and Content of Reports to be submitted by State Parties to the International Human Rights Treaties, Report of the Secretary-General, UN Doc. HRI/GEN/2/Rev. 6, 03.06.2009, para. 8

[168] With regard to article 2 CAT, see *Zach*, Article 2, Obligation to Prevent Torture, in: Nowak/Birk/Monina (eds.), The United Nations Convention Against Torture and its Optional Protocol: A Commentary, Second Edition, 2019, para. 21, who refers to article 2(1) CAT as an umbrella clause that encompasses all obligations to prevent individual from torture, not necessarily limited to those explicitly enshrined in the Convention.

[169] Committee against Torture, List of issues prior to submission of the sixth periodic report of Belarus, UN Doc. CAT/C/BLR/QPR/6, 17.06.2021, para. 9; List of issues prior to submission of the initial report of Lesotho, UN Doc. CAT/C/LSO/QPR/1, 17.06.2019, para. 12; List of issues prior to submission of the fourth periodic report of Kuwait, UN Doc. CAT/C/KWT/QPR/4, 14.06.2019, para. 7; List of issues prior to submission of the initial report of Malawi, UN Doc. CAT/C/MWI/QPR/1, 27.12.2017, para. 4.

[170] Committee against Torture, List of issues prior to submission of the seventh periodic report of Czechia, UN Doc. CAT/C/CZE/QPR/7, 10.06.2021, para. 6; List of issues prior to submission of the initial report of Mali, UN Doc. CAT/C/MLI/QPR/1, 05.06.2020, para. 7; List of issues prior to submission of the fifth periodic report of Panama, UN Doc. CAT/C/PAN/QPR/5, 11.06.2020, para. 6; List of issues prior to submission of the eighth periodic report of Paraguay, UN Doc. CAT/C/PRY/QPR/8, 11.06.2020, para. 7.

[171] Committee against Torture, List of issues prior to submission of the seventh periodic report of Chile, UN Doc. CAT/C/CHL/QPR/7,17.05.2021, para. 7; List of issues prior to submission of the fifth periodic report of Panama, UN Doc. CAT/C/PAN/QPR/5, 11.06.2020, para. 7; List of issues prior to submission of the eighth periodic report of Ecuador, UN Doc. CAT/C/ECU/QPR/8, 26.12.2019, para. 9.

against children in the form of corporal punishment.[172] Common to all these questions is that the Committee approaches the general provisions in a more issue-specific or group-specific fashion. If the Committee requests a State party to explain, for example, what measures it has taken to prevent gender-based violence,[173] it narrows the scope of the provision concerned and exclusively focuses on a group of persons who are more at risk to be exposed to violence, or which are discriminated against more often. By construing the scope of application more narrowly, the issue raised moves closer to those rights and guarantees forming the core of the treaties quoted.

Such an approach additionally contributes to the awareness at the national level that certain vulnerable groups are affected by multiple forms of discrimination, which, in a next step, might also lead to the better understanding of multi-layered dimensions of human rights as such.[174] Given that the reporting procedure is not a monolith task, but a procedure which entails the participation of many officials at the domestic level, not to mention that State parties often assign different ministries to prepare reports,[175] citations become even more useful.

However, cross-referencing does not always follow a clear and consistent pattern and is rather arbitrary to a certain degree.[176] This assumption is exemplari-

---

[172] Committee against Torture, List of issues prior to submission of the fifth periodic report of Panama, UN Doc. CAT/C/PAN/QPR/5, 11.06.2020, para. 31; List of issues prior to submission of the eighth periodic report of Ecuador, UN Doc. CAT/C/ECU/QPR/8, 26.12.2019, para. 39; List of issues prior to submission of the initial report of Lesotho, UN Doc. CAT/C/LSO/QPR/1, 17.06.2019, para. 46.

[173] Committee against Torture, List of issues prior to submission of the eighth periodic report of Denmark, UN Doc. CAT/C/DNK/QPR/8, 13.06.2018, para. 6, with the Committee referring to concluding observations and recommendations adopted during the UPR and to concluding observations adopted by the Human Rights Committee, the CEDAW and CRC Committee.

[174] Such indication might particularly prove helpful to State parties having to submit their initial reports. The Committees can indicate from the very beginning which topics require a multidimensional perspective on implementation, see for LOIPRs of initial reports replete with external references, Committee against Torture, List of issues prior to submission of the initial report of Mali, UN Doc. CAT/C/MLI/QPR/1, 05.06.2020; List of issues prior to submission of the initial report of Lesotho, UN Doc. CAT/C/LSO/QPR/1, 17.06.2019; List of issues prior to submission of the initial report of Somalia, UN Doc. CAT/C/SOM/QPR/1, 09.01.2018; List of issues prior to submission of the initial report of Malawi, UN Doc. CAT/C/MWI/QPR/1, 27.12.2017.

[175] In Germany, under the 19th legislature, the Federal Ministry of Justice and Consumer Protection was in charge of drafting the reports under the ICCPR, CERD, CAT and CED, the Federal Ministry for Family Affairs, Senior Citizens, Women and Youth prepared reports under CEDAW and CRC, and the Federal Ministry of Labor and Social Affairs was tasked with the drafting of reports under the ICESCR and CRPD.

[176] *Mac-Gregor*, What Do We Mean When We Talk about Judicial Dialogue: Reflections of a Judge of the Inter-American Court of Human Rights, Harvard Human Rights Journal 30 (2017), 89, 122, who describes that to enter or not to enter into judicial dialogue is first and foremost a "political decision".

ly reflected by the mere amplitude of cross-citations found in the Committee's LOIPRs. For instance, the List of Issues Prior to Reporting addressed to Mongolia only contained two references to concluding observations adopted by the Human Rights Committee[177] whereas 66 references to external documents were included in the LOIPR sent to Argentina.[178] However, comparable to internal referencing, and once again in analogy to judicial dialogue, the omission of references does not necessarily signify arbitrariness. Treaty bodies might have good reasons to exercise restraint when adding references to their questions.

First, a lack of references to other treaty bodies' concluding observations could be explained by a corresponding lack of suitable and available documents. Simply put, the respective Committee might want to address issues that have not been dealt with by other treaty bodies vis-à-vis the State party under review. Moreover, the State party might not have ratified other treaties that would be a suitable subject for thematic cross-referencing. Second, the available documents issued by other treaty bodies might be outdated or do not entirely cover the precise aspects the treaty body wants to discuss with the State party concerned. Third, the respective treaty body may simply not deem it necessary to include any such references, even though suitable documents are existent.

b) Internal coordination

Preceding the adoption of LOIPRs, two further avenues are open to the Committees in avoiding unnecessary overlap in their work. These are the possibility of "back-to-back reviews", and providing each Committee with relevant information on whether other treaty bodies just recently raised a specific issue on their own.

Again, the introduction of a comprehensive reporting calendar would render these coordination activities less burdensome, but even without its establishment, they are likely to reduce negative repetition. As indicated in the Chairpersons' position paper on the ongoing strengthening process, the two Covenant Committees explore the possibility of conducting "back-to-back reviews".[179] According to the Human Rights Committee, these reviews could comprise the adoption of a joint set of LOIPRs,[180] which could result in reduced overlap of substantive issues.[181] Nevertheless, the List of Issues Prior to Reporting sent to Finland, which participated as the first subject of examination, did not exhibit any specific

---

[177] Committee against Torture, List of issues prior submission of the third report of Mongolia, UN Doc. CAT/C/MNG/QPR/3, 18.06.2019.

[178] Committee against Torture, List of issues prior to submission of the seventh periodic report of Argentina, UN Doc. CAT/C/ARG/QPR/7, 05.06.2020.

[179] Report of the Chairs of the human rights treaty bodies on their thirty-first annual meeting, UN Doc. A/74/256, 30.07.2019, Annex III.

[180] Human Rights Committee, Simplified reporting procedure, Report of the Working Group, UN Doc. CCPR/C/123/3, 06.12.2018, para. 108.

[181] *Callejon et al.*, Optimizing the UN Treaty Body System, p. 23.

features which would indicate any kind of increased coordination or consultation between the two Covenant Committees beforehand.[182]

Finally, and supposedly the more viable option for coordinating the issuance of LOIPRs, as no aligned reporting schedule is required, the Committee against Torture decided to provide its country rapporteurs with all Lists of Issues Prior to Reporting adopted by other treaty bodies for the same State party within the last year.[183] The Committee's underlying rationale is the better handling of overlapping questions and that country rapporteurs can better react to any overlaps by "deleting, adapting or reinforcing",[184] the latter clearly corresponding to the practice of cross-referencing as analysed above. In addition, the drafts of LOIPRs shall be sent to rapporteurs in other Committees with a five-day deadline for comments.[185] Taken together with a possible database containing all Lists of Issues Prior to Reporting,[186] any such attempts in seeking better coordination in the drafting process might mitigate to a great extent the problems caused by substantive overlap in the work of the Committees.

c) Interim conclusion on the avoidance of substantial overlap

The possible advantages of including references in LOIPRs notwithstanding, treaty bodies, of course, do not need to slavishly adhere to such an approach. On the other hand, cross-citations might serve as a key tool in mitigating the negative effects, and reinforcing the positive effects of, overlap in the performance of treaty bodies under the reporting procedure. Given that sooner or later the simplified reporting procedure is very likely to become the default procedure under all human rights core treaties, and additionally given that treaty bodies will possibly seek to reduce the number of questions to a maximum of 25 to 30,[187] the need

---

[182] Human Rights Committee, List of issues prior to submission of the seventh periodic report of Finland, UN Doc. CCPR/C/FIN/QPR/7, 16.04.2019; CESCR Committee, List of issues prior to submission of the seventh periodic reports of Finland, UN Doc. E/C.12/FIN/QPR/7, 09.04.2019.

[183] Report of the Committee against Torture (67th and 68th session), UN Doc. A/75/44 (2020), Annex III, para. 2.

[184] Report of the Committee against Torture (67th and 68th session), UN Doc. A/75/44 (2020), Annex III, para. 2.

[185] Report of the Committee against Torture (67th and 68th session), UN Doc. A/75/44 (2020), Annex III, para. 2; the CEDAW Committee, probably in correspondence to the practice developed by the Committee against Torture, took the decision to ask the Secretariat to circulate such requests among Committee members, Report of the Committee on the Elimination of Discrimination against Women (73rd, 74th and 75th session), UN Doc. A/75/38 (2020), Part three, decision 75/IV.

[186] Such a proposal was incorporated in the Chairs' elements for a common aligned procedure for the simplified reporting procedure, Report of the Chairs of the human rights treaty bodies on their thirty-first annual meeting, UN Doc. A/74/256, 30.07.2019, Annex II, para. (e).

[187] See for instance, Report of the Committee against Torture (67th and 68th session), UN Doc. A/75/44 (2020), Annex III, para. 3.

for consciously handling the overlapping mandates among the various Committees becomes even more imminent. In doing so, the various Committees are advised to check first whether suitable material for any referencing is available. Coupled with fortified coordination efforts and increased communication between the various Committees in the drafting process of LOIPRs, it seems possible to avoid futile repetition and to create positive duplication.

IV. Treaty bodies' mandates to implement the simplified reporting procedure

While in the long-term perspective the uniform application of the simplified reporting procedure among all treaty bodies will probably lead to both, a decrease in the workload of treaty bodies and a more efficient and effective State reporting procedure, the simultaneous application of the simplified and standard reporting procedure requires additional meeting time and more human and financial resources accordingly.[188] The parallel adherence to both procedures is due to the fact that not all Committees have already introduced the simplified reporting procedure as an opt-out model, and, State parties still *can* decide to opt out. Under the current system, State parties can thus yield a decisive influence and may ultimately restrain treaty bodies from applying the simplified reporting procedure in a coherent and standardized manner. Against the backdrop of the chronical lack of resources threatening to undermine the work of the United Nations human treaty bodies, the transitional phase during which both procedures are made available should hence be as short as possible.

A first step in the harmonization process would be to expressly include the simplified reporting procedure in all Committees' Rules of Procedure and to apply it as the default procedure. In this context, the question also arises as to whether it is possible for the treaty bodies to oblige State parties to adhere to the simplified reporting procedure exclusively and, correspondingly, to exclude any submission of reports under the standard procedure.

While the substitution of a standard report with answers to Lists of Issues Prior to Reporting "still complies with the legal duty of State reporting" imposed on State parties, as they continue to submit a document which can be considered as a *report*, but "just in a different shape",[189] two further questions arise. First, is the prescription of a certain reporting procedure covered by the treaty bodies' mandate and second, considering specifically the adherence to the simplified reporting procedure, are treaty bodies legally entitled to limit the content and information contained in a State party's report? In the ongoing strengthening

---

[188] Human Rights Committee, Simplified reporting procedure, Report of the Working Group, UN Doc. CCPR/C/123/3, 06.12.2018, para. 55(e).

[189] *Krommendijk*, Less is more: Proposals for how UN human rights treaty bodies can be more selective, Netherlands Quarterly of Human Rights 38 (2020), 5, 9.

process, various State parties have voiced that the simplified reporting procedure should remain optional and could not be "unilaterally" imposed by treaty bodies.[190] On the basis of the criteria established above, it will be thus analysed whether the various Committees possess the power to compulsorily introduce the simplified reporting procedure as the only reporting mode.

1. Sequence of actions under the standard reporting procedure

Given a strict textual reading of the relevant provisions, a reporting cycle is based on submitted reports, handed in by the respective State party which, accordingly, is the stakeholder to initiate the first or any subsequent reporting cycle.[191] For instance, article 40(1) ICCPR requires State parties to submit a report which, pursuant to article 40(2) ICCPR, is first submitted to the Secretary-General of the United Nations, who then forwards the report to the Human Rights Committee for consideration. All other UN human rights core treaties use a similar or identical structure, whereby the State party first submits the report, which is then eventually examined by the respective Committee.[192]

Therefore, a common feature is the placement of State parties as the entity that initiates every reporting cycle. This finding has led early commentators to the assumption that the issuance of questionnaires which State parties use to draft and submit their reports was beyond a treaty body's mandate.[193] In addition, and context-wise, all treaties devote different paragraphs or even different articles to the obligation to submit reports and to the consideration of reports submitted by the Committees. Arguably, these observations, taken as a systematical argument, reinforce the text-based interpretative result of treaty bodies being the stakeholders reacting to rather than initiating the submission of reports. It becomes evident that the treaty bodies are accorded a *secondary* role in the reporting proce-

---

[190] *Abashidze/Koneva*, The Process of Strengthening the Human Rights Treaty Body System: The Road towards Effectiveness or Inefficiency?, Netherlands International Law Review 66 (2019), 357, 377; see also "The Consideration of the State of the Human Rights Treaty Body System", submission by the "African Group and Bahrain" to the co-facilitation process on treaty body review 2020, para. 17; Cuban Contributions, Review of the Status of the Human Rights Treaty Body System, p. 5 with critical remarks on the "selectivity"; Pakistan's inputs for the Co-Facilitator's Report, para. 6; all are available under: https://www.ohchr.org/en/calls-for-input/co-facilitation-process-treaty-body-review-2020 (last access: 21.08.2023).

[191] See *Schmahl*, Kinderrechtskonventionen mit Zusatzprotokollen, Handkommentar, Zweite Auflage, 2017, Artikel 44/45, para. 3, who observes that the wording of the CRC clarifies that State parties are the primary initiators of a reporting cycle.

[192] Article 9(1) CERD, article 18(1) CEDAW, article 73(1) CMW, article 16(1) ICESCR, article 19(1) CAT, article 44(1) CRC, article 29(1) CED, article 35(1) CRPD.

[193] *Partsch*, The Racial Discrimination Committee, in: Alston (ed.), The United Nations and Human Rights: A Critical Appraisal, First Edition, 1992, p. 350; see also Human Rights Committee, Simplified reporting procedure, Report of the Working Group, UN Doc. CCPR/C/123/3, 06.12.2018, para. 30, with the statement that the simplified reporting procedure changes the dynamics of the reporting process.

dure, at least as far as the mere sequence of actions provided for in the treaties is concerned.

2. Content to include in reports according to treaty provisions

The simplified reporting procedure also raises questions of interpretation when it comes to the determination by treaty bodies of which issues to include or exclude from State parties' reports. In combination with treaty bodies being the stakeholders to initiate a reporting cycle under the simplified reporting procedure, this entails quite a reversal of the current system and would clearly put the Committees in a stronger position.[194]

A closer look at the provisions governing the reporting procedure reveals, however, that they neither provide for much guidance in terms of content to include, nor who might take decisions in that matter. Apart from requiring State parties to report on the measures taken to implement the treaty concerned,[195] or to report on "legislative, judicial, administrative or other measures" taken to give effect to the respective Convention,[196] the provisions governing the reporting procedure are not helpful in determining the expected content of a State party's report. Some treaties require State parties to include information on "the factors and difficulties, if any, affecting the implementation" of the treaty,[197] but this does not give a more precise indication of the expected content either.

At first sight article 44(2) CRC seems more helpful, as State parties shall provide "sufficient information" in order to enable the Committee to develop a "comprehensive understanding of the implementation of the Convention in the country concerned." Equally, article 35(1) CRPD requires a comprehensive report, which could indicate that each State report shall cover all aspects in depth. However, a comprehensive report could alternatively only cover certain rights or

---

[194] See in that regard UN General Assembly, Interim Report on Updated Study by Mr. Philipp Alston, UN Doc. A/CONF.157/PC/62/Add.11/Rev. 1, 22.04.1993, para. 179, the independent expert noted that the introduction of "specifically-focused reports" would reverse the existing reporting system.

[195] Article 40(1) ICCPR requires "reports on the measures they have adopted which give effect to the rights recognized herein and on the progress made in the enjoyment of those rights"; article 16(1) ICESCR asks State parties for "reports on the measures which they have adopted and the progress made in achieving the observance of the rights recognized herein"; article 19(1) CAT requests "reports on the measures they have taken to give effect to their undertakings under this Convention"; article 44(1) CRC mentions "reports on the measures they have adopted which give effect to the rights recognized herein and on the progress made on the enjoyment of those rights"; article 29(1) CED requires "a report on the measures taken to give effect to its obligations under this Convention"; and article 35(1) CRPD requires "a comprehensive report on measures taken to give effect to its obligations under the present Convention and on the progress made in that regard".

[196] Article 9(1) CERD, article 18(1) CEDAW, article 73(1) CMW.

[197] Article 40(2) ICCPR, article 17(2) ICESCR, article 44(2) CRC, article 73(2) CMW, article 35(5) CRPD.

guarantees, but in a very thorough and detailed manner.[198] Thus, after having scrutinized all relevant treaty provisions, it becomes obvious that they only contain vague information as to the expected content.[199] Overall, this rather confirms that a State report should be comprehensive and cover all areas of the respective treaty, especially considering the wording of article 44(2) CRC and article 35(1) CRPD.

a) Entity to define a report's content

aa) Article 17 ICESCR

One of the few treaty provisions that deals with the question of who is entitled to define a report's content is article 17(1) ICESCR. According to this provision, it is left to the Economic and Social Council to establish a programme concerning stages for State parties to furnish their reports accordingly. Due to Resolution 1985/17,[200] by which ECOSOC established the CESCR Committee and simultaneously transferred its monitoring function to the newly founded treaty body, the latter could arguably be vested with the power to define the content of State parties' reports. However, Resolution 1985/17 only expressly refers to the transferal of those responsibilities, and accordingly powers, arising from articles 21 and 22 ICESCR. Consequently, the power to establish a programme of reporting schemes as referred to under article 17(1) ICESCR was to be excluded from the Committee's competencies.

This can be opposed, in turn, with the fact that Resolution 1985/17 does not limit the transferal of powers to those arising from articles 21 and 22 ICESCR, as these are mentioned "in particular." On the other hand, the monitoring function and with it the power to establish the programme under article 17(1) ICESCR originally pertained to ECOSOC, a political body, composed of State parties' representatives.[201] Initially, the competence to determine the subject matter of reports hence fell to States being present in the Economic and Social Council. This is another argument that strongly supports the conclusion that it is the State parties which should determine the content of a report, and not the CESCR Committee.

---

[198] *Kanter*, Article 35, Reports by State Parties, in: Bantekas/Stein/Anastasiou (eds.), The UN Convention on the Rights of Persons with Disabilities: A Commentary, 2018, p. 1045; see for a similar observations concerning article 44(2) CRC, *Verheyde/Goedertier*, A Commentary on the United Nations Convention on the Rights of the Child, Articles 43–45: The UN Committee on the Rights of the Child, 2006, p. 17.

[199] *Boerefijn*, Article 18, in: Freeman/Chinkin/Rudolf (eds.), The UN Convention on the Elimination of All Forms of Discrimination Against Women: A Commentary, 2012, p. 495.

[200] Economic and Social Council, Resolution 1985/17, Review of the composition, organization and administrative arrangements of the Sessional Working Group of Governmental Experts on the Implementation of the International Covenant on Economic, Social and Cultural Rights, UN Doc. E/RES/1985/17, 28.05.1985.

[201] *Tomuschat*, Human Rights: Between Idealism and Realism, Third Edition, 2014, p. 221.

With regard to the Committee's practice, it has been observed that it soon abandoned the three-year reporting intervals on different thematic clusters, as established prior to its coming into existence, and introduced a single report to be submitted every five years.[202] A closer look into the decision reveals, however, that the CESCR Committee only recommended to ECOSOC that the latter should "take the necessary steps with a view to amending the reporting programme previously adopted by the Council in its resolution 1988 (LX)."[203] The fact that the Committee merely recommended that the Council take the necessary steps signifies nothing more than that it considered itself not competent in the matter, which indicates clearly that the Committee has not received the powers arising from Article 17 ICESCR. It must therefore be considered as not being empowered to compulsorily define the content of State reports under the ICESCR.

bb) Articles 73(3) CMW and 35(3) CRPD

Articles 73(3) CMW and 35(3) CRPD both provide that the respective Committee shall adopt guidelines applicable to the content of the reports, thereby even imposing a duty to adopt guidelines on these two Committees.[204] However, as the very term "guidelines" implies, these are legally non-binding and are rather intended to provide guidance to State parties in drafting their reports, and they do not determine the expected content of a State report in a legally binding manner.[205] The inclusion of the Committee's duty to adopt guidelines applicable to the content of reports submitted is furthermore a codification of long-standing treaty body practice, common among all Committees, and arguably mirrors their own understanding of whether being able to prescribe information to be definitely included in periodic reports.[206] The inclusion of article 35(3) CRPD in particular can be traced back to a suggested modification brought forward by the Israeli

---

[202] *Alston*, The Committee on Economic, Social and Cultural Rights, in: Mégret/Alston (eds.), The United Nations and Human Rights: A Critical Appraisal, Second Edition, 2020, p. 446.

[203] CESCR Committee, Report on the Second Session (8–25 February 1988), UN Doc. E/1988/14 (1988), para. 351.

[204] *Kanter*, Article 35, Reports by State Parties, in: Bantekas/Stein/Anastasiou (eds.), The UN Convention on the Rights of Persons with Disabilities: A Commentary, 2018, p. 1045.

[205] *Ferrajolo*, Articles 34 to 36 CPRD, in: Della Fina/Cera/Palmisano (eds.), The United Nations Convention on the Rights of Persons with Disabilities: A Commentary, Cham 2017, p. 624; *Verheyde/Goedertier*, A Commentary on the United Nations Convention on the Rights of the Child, Articles 43–45: The UN Committee on the Rights of the Child, 2006, p. 18.

[206] See Compilation of Guidelines on the Form and Content of Reports to be submitted by State Parties to the International Human Rights Treaties, Report of the Secretary-General, UN Doc. HRI/GEN/2/Rev. 6, 03.06.2009.

delegation during the drafting process.²⁰⁷ Unfortunately, no further explanation or discussion are available as to why the drafters specifically opted for the Committee to adopt guidelines. Furthermore, none of the other seven human rights core treaties do contain any comparable provision. Taken as *an argumentum e contrario*, the respective treaty bodies are not empowered to take any binding decisions, given that they are not even explicitly vested with the power to adopt guidelines.

On the other hand, the establishment of guidelines would appear somewhat futile if State parties were able to ignore them completely. In order to review the progress made in the implementation of treaty guarantees, treaty bodies logically need information to rely on when making their assessment. Any such evaluation seems only possible if there is a corresponding set of minimum information provided by the State party under review.²⁰⁸ Yet, establishing guidelines that cover a treaty comprehensively on the one hand and narrowing down the topics for the upcoming reporting cycle, as in the case of the simplified reporting procedure on the other, are two different aspects, not to be confused. Ultimately, the guidelines are intended to provide assistance to State parties in the drafting of their comprehensive reports that cover the entire treaty under review. Herein also lies the decisive difference to the preparation of LOIPRs under the simplified reporting procedure. The latter presupposes a narrower focus on issues determined by the Committees.

b) Rules governing the follow-up procedure

A last option for arriving at the Committee's power to prescribe authoritatively what to include in State reports can possibly be derived from those provisions that empower the Committees to request further reports or further information.²⁰⁹ However, first of all, these provisions provide for the submission of further reports only, without indicating their expected content or who might be entitled to determine their content.

In practice, treaty bodies have made use of such requests, for instance, in response to inadequate reports that only superfluously presented the human rights situation in the State party concerned, or when information provided by State parties became outdated again prior to the constructive dialogue.²¹⁰ With

---

²⁰⁷ *Kanter*, Article 35, Reports by State Parties, in: Bantekas/Stein/Anastasiou (eds.), The UN Convention on the Rights of Persons with Disabilities: A Commentary, 2018, p. 1043.

²⁰⁸ *Giegling*, Challenges and Chances of a Written State Report: Analysis and Improvement of a Monitoring Instrument on the Implementation of Human Rights, 2021, pp. 57–58, who reaches the conclusion that a report must contain in the minimum sufficient information. However, there is a difference between the requirement of submitting a minimum set of information and the power enjoyed by treaty bodies to determine each specific aspect of a State report.

²⁰⁹ These are: article 40(1)(b) ICCPR, article 9(1)(b), article 18(1)(b) CEDAW, article 19(1) CAT, article 44(4) CRC, article 73(1)(b) CMW, article 29(4) CED, article 35(2) CRPD.

²¹⁰ *Monina*, Article 19, State Reporting Procedure, in: Nowak/Birk/Monina (eds.), The

regard to such reports, Committees may indicate what to include.²¹¹ As a matter of fact, requesting additional reports or information would be futile if treaty bodies were not allowed to determine their expected content. Otherwise, they would have to continue requesting additional reports until the State party under review has delivered the expected information. Additional reports or additional information can thus only logically be requested by simultaneously clarifying which information the State party ought to include.

However, common to all these supplementary reports is the fact that their requests for submission were always made in response, and thus in secondary reaction, to reports already submitted. The sequence of actions thus corresponds to the one under the standard reporting procedure, under which Lists of Issues are sent back to the State party after receipt of its report. While the provisions at hand arguably enable treaty bodies to alter the periodicities provided for in the Conventions,²¹² they do not allow any deductions with respect to possible powers in the determination of a periodic or initial report's content.

Another argument supporting this finding can be directly drawn from the wording of article 19(1) CAT. The provision distinguishes between further supplementary reports, which are subsequent periodic reports under the standard reporting procedure, and other reports, a term which covers the above-mentioned additional and ad hoc reports.²¹³ These additional reports hence emerge as a distinct feature and must be distinguished from periodic reports. While being empowered to define an additional report's content, the Committees are ultimately not entitled to make definite statements on the information included in the next periodic report by virtue of the above scrutinized provisions.

3. Final evaluation

It has become obvious that the periodic reporting procedure, in accordance with the relevant treaty provisions, is primarily based on reports submitted by State parties. Only subsequently, in a second step, are they considered and examined by treaty bodies. A text-based and systematic interpretation of the treaty provisions governing the reporting procedure confirms the interpretative result of treaty bodies being the stakeholders to react second. What is more, the treaties are almost silent as to the content to include in initial and periodic State reports. Only three out of nine UN human rights core treaties provide for any provision that

---

United Nations Convention Against Torture and its Optional Protocol: A Commentary, Second Edition, 2019, para. 40; *Schabas*, U.N. International Covenant on Civil and Political Rights, Nowak's CCPR Commentary, Third revised Edition, 2019, Art. 40 CCPR, para. 5.

²¹¹ *Schabas*, U.N. International Covenant on Civil and Political Rights, Nowak's CCPR Commentary, Third revised Edition, 2019, Art. 40 CCPR, para. 5.

²¹² See *infra*, Part IV C.IV. 2.b).

²¹³ *Monina*, Article 19, State Reporting Procedure, in: Nowak/Birk/Monina (eds.), The United Nations Convention Against Torture and its Optional Protocol: A Commentary, Second Edition, 2019, para. 40.

even indicates which stakeholder is empowered to define the content. However, the treaties only further confirm that the Committees cannot take any binding decisions in this matter.

The only treaty provisions that vaguely allude to the power of defining the content are those which entitle the Committees to request further reports or information. Nevertheless, these specific reports are either asked for clarification in response to reports already submitted, or cover situations of grave and serious violations of human rights which require immediate and urgent action. Common to all these additional reports is that they are not to be confused with *regular* periodic reports. They solely focus on a particular issue or on a given situation in the State party concerned. The same applies to follow-up requests, which are based on the same provisions. They do not constitute periodic reports either and are asked for in response to the constructive dialogue and hence only represent a treaty body's reaction and not its initiation.

Even if these provisions could conceivably serve as a normative basis, though a rather weak and opaque one, for any further reaching and effectiveness-orientated interpretation, the question arises whether such an expansion of powers under the reporting procedure constitutes a *necessary* one. It is recalled at this point that any extension of powers on the basis of considerations of necessity and effectiveness shall be deemed only possible when the contentious power in question proves indispensable for the proper functioning of the reporting machinery.

Given that reporting serves both the aim of creating international accountability and to enable State parties to conduct a thorough self-assessment, two directions for an effectiveness-oriented interpretation emerge. The objective of creating accountability by seeking to conduct more targeted and focused reviews, as it is the case with the simplified reporting procedure, might allow treaty bodies to compulsorily introduce the simplified reporting procedure. The conscious selection of only those issues which present themselves as the most urgent and serious violations could generate closer scrutiny and more accountability. On the other hand, with regard to the aim of enabling State parties to conduct a thorough self-assessment, *Tomuschat* argues that "States cannot be compelled to comply with such a restriction of their sovereign right to present an overall picture of the human rights situation under their jurisdiction."[214] Hence, any determination of the items to be included in a report prior to its actual submission could possibly contradict the aim of enabling the State party to conduct a thorough self-assessment by preparing a comprehensive report, and might additionally deprive the State party of useful and comprehensive guidance in the implementation of all treaty provisions.

Finally, and in conformity with the criteria developed above, such an alteration of the reporting procedure, initiated by treaty bodies, touches on one of a State party's fundamental obligations and interferes to a great extent with the

---

[214] *Tomuschat*, Human Rights: Between Idealism and Realism, Third Edition, 2014, p. 228.

external relationship between treaty bodies and State parties. Since the textual basis under the treaties remains weak, especially when considering that newly established treaties only vest their Committees with the power to adopt legally non-binding guidelines, treaty bodies do not possess the power to make State parties exclusively adhere to the simplified reporting procedure.[215] However, this does not mean that the Committees cannot introduce the procedure as an opt-out model, just as the Human Rights Committee and CESCR Committee have done.

4. Introduction of LOIPRs via subsequent practice

A last option to change the reporting procedure to the permanent and compulsory application of the simplified reporting procedure lies with subsequent practice by State parties in accordance with article 31(3)(b) VCLT.

Taking into account the varying degrees to which treaty bodies have taken recourse to the simplified reporting procedure so far, a sufficiently consistent practice is most likely achieved under the Convention against Torture and the ICCPR. The more individual State parties accept the offer to participate, or the fewer State parties decide to opt out, the sooner a vast majority of parties will have submitted their reports in accordance with the simplified reporting procedure. The repeated submission of two or even more reports under the simplified reporting procedure will lead to a uniform appearance and thus to a sufficiently consistent practice. It is recalled that it is not a prerequisite that each contracting party participates in the relevant practice.[216] However, it must be noted here that opting-out is still possible for all State parties at any point in time, which means that a consistent practice is always subject to the caveat that State parties could submit subsequent reports under the standard procedure again. If, however, it should turn out that no State parties opt out, it could theoretically be assumed that the simplified reporting procedure will become the standard procedure and that the opt-out option will then no longer apply, provided that the two subjective elements under article 31(3)(b) VCLT are also fulfilled.

---

[215] Compare in this matter the decision under the European Social Charter, taken by the Committee of Ministers of the Council of Europe, to request annual reports on one of four thematic groups than to submit biennial comprehensive reports covering all Charter provisions, Governmental Committee of the European Social Charter, New system for the presentation of reports on the application of the European Social Charter, CoE Doc. CM/Del/Dec(2006)963/4.2, 03.05.2006; *Giegling*, Challenges and Chances of a Written State Report: Analysis and Improvement of a Monitoring Instrument on the Implementation of Human Rights, 2021, p. 41. However, it is not surprising that it was not the ESC Committee that decided on the introduction of reports focusing on thematic groups. According to article 21 ESC, the form of reports to be submitted is determined by the Committee of Ministers.

[216] See for the current state of affairs under the Convention against Torture https://tbinternet.ohchr.org/_layouts/15/TreatyBodyExternal/OptionalReporting.aspx?TreatyID=1&Lang=En (last access: 21.08.2023).

Many reports submitted refer precisely to the respective treaty provisions, and even indicate that the submission was made in accordance with the simplified reporting procedure.[217] The references to both the relevant treaty provisions and the simplified reporting procedure suggest a conscious application of the treaty in question, and that State parties are mindful of fulfilling their reporting obligations when submitting answers to LOIPRs. Such practice bears much probative evidence as to the acceptance of the simplified reporting procedure among State parties and thus fulfils the first subjective criterion under article 31(3)(b) VCLT.

Last, an agreement between *all* parties on the interpretation of the provision in question has to be concluded. Resolution 68/268 is of limited help, however, especially against the background that it was adopted by consensus. Its evidentiary strength is all the more questionable considering its vague language. Resolution 68/268 only recommends State parties to consider the possibility of accepting the simplified reporting procedure and does not expressly encourage State parties to take such steps.[218] Particularly those voices in the on-going treaty body 2020 review process which oppose the application of the simplified reporting procedure and criticize treaty bodies for imposing the procedure "unilaterally"[219] cast further doubts on the question whether an agreement between all parties can be achieved. Given the criticism articulated by certain State parties and the cautious language deployed in Resolution 68/268, it must currently be concluded that an interpretation in accordance with article 31(3)(b) VCLT does not prove possible due to the lack of an agreement on the part all of State parties. Therefore,

---

[217] Committee against Torture, Third periodic report submitted by Costa Rica under article 19 of the Convention pursuant to the simplified reporting procedure, due in 2012, UN Doc. CAT/C/CRI/3, 12.06.2020, paras. 1 and 5; Eighth periodic report submitted by Luxembourg under article 19 of the Convention pursuant to the simplified reporting procedure, due in 2019, UN Doc. CAT/C/LUX/8, 16.03.2020, paras. 1 and 2; Seventh periodic report submitted by New Zealand under article 19 of the Convention pursuant to the simplified reporting procedure, due in 2019, UN Doc. CAT/C/NZL/7, 16.03.2020, para. 1; Human Rights Committee, Seventh periodic report submitted by Germany under article 40 of the Covenant pursuant to the optional reporting procedure, due in 2019, UN Doc. CCPR/C/DEU/7, 23.04.2020, para. 2; Seventh periodic report submitted by Finland under article 40 of the Covenant pursuant to the optional reporting procedure, due in 2020, UN Doc. CCPR/C/FIN/7, 23.04.2020, para. 1; Sixth periodic report submitted by Peru under article 40 of the Covenant pursuant to the optional reporting procedure, due in 2018, UN Doc. CCPR/C/PER/6, 27.02.2020, para. 1.

[218] UN General Assembly, Resolution 68/268, Strengthening and enhancing the effective functioning of the human rights treaty body system, UN Doc. A/RES/68/268, 09.04.2014, para. 2.

[219] See as an example of such open critique, submission by the "African Group and Bahrain" to the co-facilitation process on treaty body review 2020, para. 17, https://www.ohchr.org/en/calls-for-input/co-facilitation-process-treaty-body-review-2020 (last access: 21.08.2023); cf. also *Abashidze/Koneva*, The Process of Strengthening the Human Rights Treaty Body System: The Road towards Effectiveness or Inefficiency?, Netherlands International Law Review 66 (2019), 357, 377.

it cannot also be assumed that subsequent practice, at least for now, leads to the exclusion of the possibility of opting out and the standard procedure.

V. Conclusion on the simplified reporting procedure and outlook

Applied for the first time in 2007 by the Committee against Torture, the simplified reporting procedure has now spread throughout the entire UN human rights treaty body system. Recent developments regarding its application, such as its introduction as the default mode, and the attention received by the Meeting of Chairpersons, followed by proposals contained in the "common elements paper", strongly indicate that the procedure will prevail. It remains to be seen, however, whether its hoped-for benefits will materialize, whether the Committees will make further efforts with a view to procedural alignments, and whether they will increase coordination activities to avoid the futile duplication of mandates. As far as the latter is concerned, coordination with regard to substantive issues is probably one of the most pressing topics to be addressed. Here in particular, it would be advantageous to develop a uniform reporting scheme in the form of a comprehensive calendar, which is also the subject of the following chapter.

Regarding the Committees' legal mandate in implementing the simplified reporting procedure, the interpretation of the provisions regulating the reporting procedure has revealed that treaty bodies are barred from establishing the simplified reporting procedure as the *only* option, thereby making it mandatory. It is the combination of several features that leads to this result, including the weak textual basis in the treaties that indicates otherwise, the fact that such a change would revert the sequence of actions as provided for by the treaties, and the further fact that the simplified reporting procedure modifies to a significant extent the reporting obligation incumbent on State parties and thus affects the external treaty body-State party relationship. This interpretative result notwithstanding, all treaty bodies could introduce the procedure as an opt-out model. Thereby, they could possibly achieve greater participation in a shorter time span. Moreover, silent acceptance on the part of State parties could indicate their acceptance and thus an agreement within the meaning of article 31(3)(b) VCLT. If treaty bodies are able to provide further evidence for such an agreement, the procedure could be said to become the default and only option.

Last but not least, from a more general and comprehensive point of view, the simplified reporting procedure is only a further step in the development of the State reporting procedure, which has "evolved considerably since it was introduced in the 1970s."[220] In this context, it is worth noting that yet another proposal has emerged that seeks to replace every second review with a focused review.[221]

---

[220] Human Rights Committee, Simplified reporting procedure, Report of the Working Group, UN Doc. CCPR/C/123/3, 06.12.2018, para. 50.

[221] See for the possible steps and modalities of "focused review", Submission by the Geneva Human Rights Platform to the 33rd annual Meeting of Chairpersons by Human Rights

These focused reviews could, according to the annual report of the 32nd Meeting of Chairpersons, consist of "an in situ visit by one member of the treaty body with one member of the Secretariat to engage with the State party"[222] and they would take up even fewer topics than is currently the case under the simplified reporting procedure.

Yet, its introduction seems to have met with some opposition from Chairpersons. In 2021, the Chairs discussed for the first time the disadvantages and advantages of such a procedure. The general consensus was that further discussions were needed.[223] The Chair of the Human Rights Committee stressed that focused reviews were a "strategic" and possible "long-term goal" for the strengthening process,[224] and the Chair of the Committee against Torture rightly pointed out that focused reviews in situ would require resources which are nonetheless limited.[225] Last but not least, the Chair of the CRC Committee remarked aptly that focused reviews in situ would confront treaty bodies with complex scheduling activities and, maybe even more importantly from a legal point of view, raised the question whether concluding observations would have to be adopted in plenary.[226] It remains to be seen whether this newly emerging proposal will gain further support.

C. Comprehensive reporting calendar

The most promising device to avoid unnecessary overlap in the performance of treaty bodies in the context of State reporting is the introduction of a comprehensive reporting calendar by which the various schedules and periodicities of each single treaty would be harmonized and aligned accordingly. Though characterized as the "most far-reaching"[227] proposal or the "most prominent"[228] one con-

---

Treaty Bodies, p. 3, available at: https://www.ohchr.org/EN/HRBodies/AnnualMeeting/Pages/Meetingchairpersons.aspx (last access: 21.08.2023).

[222] Report of the Chairs of the human rights treaty bodies on their thirty-second annual meeting, UN Doc. A/75/346, 14.09.2020, para. 46(h).

[223] Report of the Chairs of the human rights treaty bodies on their thirty-third annual meeting, UN Doc. A/76/254, 30.07.2021, para. 56.

[224] Report of the Chairs of the human rights treaty bodies on their thirty-third annual meeting, UN Doc. A/76/254, 30.07.2021, para. 49.

[225] Report of the Chairs of the human rights treaty bodies on their thirty-third annual meeting, UN Doc. A/76/254, 30.07.2021, para. 50.

[226] Report of the Chairs of the human rights treaty bodies on their thirty-third annual meeting, UN Doc. A/76/254, 30.07.2021, para. 47.

[227] *Egan*, Strengthening the United Nations Human Rights Treaty Body System, Human Rights Law Review 13 (2013), 209, 215.

[228] *Gaer*, The Institutional Future of the Covenants, A World Court for Human Rights?, in: Moeckli/Keller/Heri (eds.) The Human Rights Covenants at 50: Their Past, Present, and Future, 2018, p. 345.

tained in the report published by *Navanethem Pillay* in 2012, the idea has been rather lying dormant until now. It was not included in General Assembly Resolution 68/268 due to practical, financial and legal concerns raised by opposing State parties during the intergovernmental process.[229]

However, the idea of establishing fixed periodicities with simultaneous coordination among all treaty bodies seems compelling. The following chapter shall shed light on several questions related to the possible future establishment of a comprehensive reporting calendar. In the first part, the idea will be explained in more detail and several proposals with respect to the calendar's concrete design will be presented. Second, current treaty body practice with regard to reporting periodicities will be analysed. At least some treaty bodies have phased in their own reporting schedules, and consultations between treaty bodies have resumed recently. The idea of a master reporting calendar has also regained momentum lately. The chapter concludes with the discussion of whether the Committees possess the power to alter reporting periodicities prescribed in their constituent instruments.

I. Necessity of a comprehensive reporting calendar

Apart from the CED, all human rights core treaties at the United Nations level require State parties to submit periodic reports, however with varying periodicities from two to five years.[230] The two Covenants do not explicitly require any fixed periodicity. Article 40(1)(b) ICCPR establishes that a State party must submit periodic reports whenever the Human Rights Committee requests so, while article 16 ICESCR makes no mention of any periodic reporting obligations at all. In practice, the Committee on Economic, Social and Cultural Rights originally established a five-year reporting cycle, which has been reduced for some States since 2000,[231] but more recently adopted concluding observations reveal

---

[229] *Broecker/O'Flaherty*, The Outcome of the General Assembly's Treaty Body Strengthening Process, p. 21; see also *Shany/Cleveland*, Treaty Body Reform 2020: Has the time come for adopting a Global Review Calendar?, p. 2, who explain the rejection by State parties with increased overall costs for the system in the case of implementing the reporting calendar, https://www.geneva-academy.ch/joomlatools-files/docman-files/Draft%20List%20of%20Submissions%20-%20Academic%20Platform%202020%20Review%20without%20Propositions%20.pdf (last access: 21.08.2023).

[230] The highest frequency of reports to be submitted is established by article 9(1)(b) CERD, requiring State parties to submit reports every two years. A periodicity of four years is established by article 19(1) CAT, article 35(2) CRPD and article 19(1)(b) CEDAW respectively, whereas article 73(1)(b) CMW and article 44(1)(b) CRC require State parties to submit periodic reports only every five years.

[231] *Egan*, The United Nations Human Rights Treaty System: Law and Procedure, 2011, p. 141, the reduction of reporting cycles depended on factors such as timely submission of reports, the quality of information, the quality of the constructive dialogue, responses on the part of State parties in reaction to concluding observations and the compliance rate with regard to the Covenant's implementation.

C. Comprehensive reporting calendar

that the Committee still generally sticks to a five-year reporting pattern generally.[232] The Human Rights Committee first established a four-year circle, and later changed its periodicity into a more flexible scheme, with reporting frequencies between three to six years. State parties with less concerning human rights records are monitored with longer periods in between.[233]

Due to these varying frequencies, an unforeseeable and unbalanced reporting scheme has emerged which renders it burdensome for State parties to comply with their different reporting obligations.[234] In the absence of any coordination,[235] it may be very likely that State parties have to report to several Committees in the same year, and it is then "hardly surprising that even the most compliant States can fall behind their reporting obligations."[236]

The need for a fixed reporting calendar becomes even more obvious when taking into consideration that many State parties do not submit their reports within due time. Delayed submissions force the individual treaty bodies to reschedule their own reporting calendar. This, in turn, affects those State parties negatively who are willing to comply with their reporting obligations in a timely manner. Their submitted reports are either "pushed back to later sessions" or they are "suddenly called to an earlier treaty body session."[237]

Furthermore, as the next link in this chain, the problem of substantive overlap between two or even more treaties becomes virulent. First, given that each treaty body establishes its own reporting schedule without any further coordination and second, given that only a few non-compliant State parties can easily cause disorder, it is very likely for a State party to appear before different treaty bodies

---

[232] CESCR Committee, Concluding observations on the seventh periodic report of Finland, UN Doc. E/C.12/FIN/CO/7, 30.03.2021, para. 55; Concluding observations on the second periodic report of Latvia, UN Doc. E/C.12/LVA/CO/2, 30.03.2021, para. 54; Concluding observations on the seventh periodic report of Ukraine, UN Doc. E/C.12/UKR/CO/7, 02.04.2020, para. 54.

[233] *Rodley*, The Role and Impact of Treaty Bodies, in: Shelton (ed.), The Oxford Handbook of International Human Rights Law, 2013, p. 627.

[234] *Egan*, Reform of the UN Human Rights Treaty Body System, in: Mégret/Alston (eds.), The United Nations and Human Rights: A Critical Appraisal, Second Edition, 2020, p. 656, who describes the current situation as "unmanageable"; *Pillay*, Strengthening the United Nations human rights treaty body system, p. 37.

[235] See *O'Flaherty/Tsai*, Periodic Reporting: The Backbone of the UN Treaty Body Review Procedure, in: Bassiouni/Schabas (eds.), New Challenges for the UN Human Rights Machinery, 2011, p. 47, who label the need for better cooperation among treaty bodies as an "environment challenge".

[236] *Egan*, The United Nations Human Rights Treaty System: Law and Procedure, 2011, p. 173, who also stresses that non-compliance may not be explained by "political apathy" only but also by "financial or [...] structural incapacity" at the domestic level.

[237] *Pillay*, Strengthening the United Nations human rights treaty body system, p. 41; see also *Dimitrijevic*, State Reports, in: Alfredsson et al. (eds.), International Human Rights Monitoring Mechanism, First Edition, 2001, p. 194, who even argues that non-compliant State parties violate their "obligation *vis-à-vis* other State Parties."

in very short intervals, which intensifies the reporting burden.[238] In these cases it is very likely that a State party has to take a stand on the same issues before different treaty bodies several times.[239] It becomes obvious that the uncoordinated reporting activities lead to a waste of resources and capacity,[240] further disadvantages those States who are actually willing to comply with their obligations, and therefore significantly increases the reporting burden for all State parties.

II. Possible calendar schemes

1. Pairing of treaty bodies with annual reviews

During the strengthening process so far, various ideas on how to arrange a comprehensive reporting calendar have been advanced. In her strengthening report, *Pillay* suggested establishing a comprehensive reporting calendar with five pairs of treaty bodies, with reviews by one pair of treaty bodies each year.[241] Hence, a State party that has ratified all UN human rights core treaties would be monitored at maximum by two human rights treaty bodies a year, and completes a full reporting cycle of all treaties within five years. As regards the pairing of the treaty bodies, *Pillay* proposed to combine the monitoring of the Covenants in the first year and to pair the other treaty bodies pursuant to "maximum commonality between the two reports due each year."[242] Despite arguing that the combination of the ICCPR and ICESCR would prove beneficial, *Pillay* left other options open as to how to pair the more specialized treaty bodies.

---

[238] *Egan*, Strengthening the United Nations Human Rights Treaty Body System, Human Rights Law Review 13 (2013), 209, 216.

[239] *Krommendijk*, Less is more: Proposals for how UN human rights treaty bodies can be more selective, Netherlands Quarterly of Human Rights 38 (2020), 5, 8; *Shany/Cleveland*, Treaty Body Reform 2020: Has the time come for adopting a Global Review Calendar?, p. 2, https://www.geneva-academy.ch/joomlatools-files/docman-files/Draft%20List%20of%20Submissions%20-%20Academic%20Platform%202020%20Review%20without%20Propositions%20.pdf (last access: 21.08.2023); see also *Callejon et al.*, Optimizing the UN Treaty Body System, p. 18, who point out that the "significant overlap" might increase coherence and consistency, but might also lead to repetition and thus potential incoherence.

[240] *Bernaz*, Continuing evolution of the United Nations treaty bodies system, in: Sheeran/Rodley (eds.), Routledge Handbook of International Human Rights Law, 2013, p. 713.

[241] *Pillay*, Strengthening the United Nations human rights treaty body system, p. 38, note that *Pillay* also included the two Optional Protocols to the CRC in her reporting schedule which means that in her model ten human rights treaty bodies are operating.

[242] *Pillay*, Strengthening the United Nations human rights treaty body system, p. 38, this results in her proposed model with the following pairs of treaty bodies: first year ICCPR and ICESCR, second year CRC and CRC OPs, third year CAT and CED, fourth year ICERD and ICEDAW and fifth year ICRMW and ICRPD.

2. Clustered reviews

A similar proposal, which opts for the pairing of various treaty bodies, was brought forward in the Academic Platform Report May 2018 under the auspices of the Geneva Academy. The report suggests to "hold clustered reviews every four years" which would mean dividing treaty bodies into two groups.[243] In intervals of four years, a State party would travel to Geneva and would be reviewed by each treaty body group in "clustered hearings lasting one week each".[244] Theoretically, this results in an overall eight-year cycle, during which the implementation of all human rights treaties is monitored.

Comparable to *Pillay's* suggestion, the "clustered review-proposal" also addresses the question of how to group the various treaty bodies. According to the authors, the pairing of the Covenants in one cluster, and the grouping of the more specialized treaties in a second cluster is preferable.[245] This specific conclusion is reached by taking into consideration the objective of generating more coherence among UN human rights treaty bodies. Since the two Covenants, as "general human rights instruments",[246] contain many provisions which are congruent to provisions under the group- and issue-specific treaties, such an arrangement poses the option of useful repetition and further synergies under the follow-up procedure.[247]

Finally, and thus different from *Pillay's* suggestion, the Geneva Academy Report explicitly mentions that State parties will be reviewed within one week by all the treaty bodies summed up in the respective cluster. This will lead to decreased traveling costs, might generate more synergies between the various Committees, and might additionally create awareness of interrelated and interdependent human rights provisions among State parties. The "clustered review-option" essentially builds upon a proposal brought forward by *Shany* and *Cleveland*. They also opt for the establishment of an overall eight-year cycle with clustered reviews by the two Covenant Committees and the more specialized Committees.[248] The review by the Human Rights Committee and the Committee on

---

[243] *Callejon et al.*, Optimizing the UN Treaty Body System, p. 21.
[244] *Callejon et al.*, Optimizing the UN Treaty Body System, p. 21.
[245] *Callejon et al.*, Optimizing the UN Treaty Body System, p. 22; cf. *Morijn*, Reforming United Nations Human Rights Treaty Monitoring Reform, Netherlands International Law Review 58 (2011), 295, 327–328, who also proposes to establish clusters, but four in total, combined with a five-year reporting periodicity.
[246] *Callejon et al.*, Optimizing the UN Treaty Body System, p. 22.
[247] *Callejon et al.*, Optimizing the UN Treaty Body System, p. 22; for possible synergies under the follow-up procedure, see *infra* Part IV F.2.
[248] *Shany/Cleveland*, Treaty Body Reform 2020: Has the time come for adopting a Global Review Calendar?, p. 3, https://www.geneva-academy.ch/joomlatools-files/docman-files/Draft%20List%20of%20Submissions%20–%20Academic%20Platform%202020%20Review%20without%20Propositions%20.pdf (last access: 21.08.2023); *Callejon et al.*, Optimizing the UN Treaty Body System, p. 23.

Economic, Social and Cultural Rights could be carried out in a "three-day back-to-back" fashion, and the specialized treaty bodies would conduct their monitoring in an "up to seven-day, back-to-back multi-door" review.[249]

In addition, their proposal does not solely focus on the monitoring process discharged by treaty bodies. Instead, it addresses the broader human rights mechanism architecture by extending the proposal to what would constitute a "global reporting calendar."[250] According to *Shany* and *Cleveland*, the in-between period of four years could be used to monitor State parties' human rights records via the Universal Periodic Review Mechanism.[251] This additional possibility is only mentioned in passing in the Geneva Academy Report,[252] and admittedly, as desirable it may be to align both monitoring procedures at the global level, such an undertaking appears to be even more complicated than coordinating the periodicities among all human rights treaty bodies.[253]

3. Single consolidated review

Next to the possibility of arranging clustered reviews, the Geneva Academy Report foresees a second option by which State parties would be reviewed only every seven to eight years by all treaty bodies within one week. Prior to this "single consolidated review", the respective State party would have to submit "a single state report", which would contain general and treaty-specific sections.[254] Alternatively, the authors also advance the option to hold a single consolidated review every four to five years, which however, would necessitate reduced meeting time for the constructive dialogues.[255] A similar proposal was developed by *Johnstone*, who advocates a "single periodic meeting" of all treaty bodies lasting two days. The first day, a plenary composed of members of all treaty bodies would meet the entire State delegation to discuss "cross-cutting issues", and on the second day

---

[249] *Shany/Cleveland*, Treaty Body Reform 2020: Has the time come for adopting a Global Review Calendar?, pp. 3–4, https://www.geneva-academy.ch/joomlatools-files/docman-files/Draft%20List%20of%20Submissions%20–%20Academic%20Platform%202020%20Review%20without%20Propositions%20.pdf (last access: 21.08.2023).

[250] *Shany/Cleveland*, Treaty Body Reform 2020: Has the time come for adopting a Global Review Calendar?, p. 3, https://www.geneva-academy.ch/joomlatools-files/docman-files/Draft%20List%20of%20Submissions%20–%20Academic%20Platform%202020%20Review%20without%20Propositions%20.pdf (last access: 21.08.2023).

[251] *Shany/Cleveland*, Treaty Body Reform 2020: Has the time come for adopting a Global Review Calendar?, pp. 3–4, https://www.geneva-academy.ch/joomlatools-files/docman-files/Draft%20List%20of%20Submissions%20–%20Academic%20Platform%202020%20Review%20without%20Propositions%20.pdf (last access: 21.08.2023).

[252] *Callejon et al.*, Optimizing the UN Treaty Body System, p. 24.

[253] See further below Part IV, C. IV. 2.

[254] *Callejon et al.*, Optimizing the UN Treaty Body System, p. 20.

[255] *Callejon et al.*, Optimizing the UN Treaty Body System, p. 20.

each single treaty body would meet State representatives to discuss the more topic and group-specific issues.[256]

4. Evaluation

Common to all these possible proposals is the expected increase of predictability.[257] The first major difference lies in the fact that the comprehensive five-year reporting calendar would require State parties to travel at least annually to Geneva, and to prepare several reports simultaneously. The clustered review and the single consolidated review would reduce the frequency in this regard.

Furthermore, both options presented by the Geneva Academy alleviate the reporting burden more effectively. Under both reporting schemes State parties would receive a "consolidated list of issues" and correspondingly, concluding observations "would be consolidated" as well.[258] It emerges that reporting obligations under two, several or even all UN human rights treaties could be fulfilled by preparing one set of documents at a time. In addition, said approach would "significantly reduce the complexity, overlap and redundancy of periodic reporting and repetitive oral reviews".[259] Here, treaty bodies could coordinate in advance which questions they would like to include in their LOIPRs.[260]

Of course, the comprehensive five-year reporting calendar could be combined with the simplified reporting procedure as well, and the five pairs of treaty bodies could also draft consolidated Lists of Issues Prior to Reporting. Still, State parties would have to prepare five consolidated reports, and taking into consideration the additional follow-up procedure, either the four-year clustered review cycle or the single consolidated review seem preferable in terms of decreased complexity and coordination among treaty bodies.

---

[256] *Johnstone*, Streamlining the Constructive Dialogue: Efficiency from States' Perspectives, in: Bassiouni/Schabas (eds.), New Challenges for the UN Human Rights Machinery, 2011, pp. 70–84.

[257] *Egan*, Reform of the UN Human Rights Treaty Body System, in: Mégret/Alston (eds.), The United Nations and Human Rights: A Critical Appraisal, Second Edition, 2020, p. 656 who considers the calendar a device that can eliminate the chaos under the current *modus operandi*; *Callejon et al.*, Optimizing the UN Treaty Body System, p. 23.

[258] *Callejon et al.*, Optimizing the UN Treaty Body System, p. 22; see also *Johnstone*, Streamlining the Constructive Dialogue: Efficiency from States' Perspectives, in: Bassiouni/Schabas (eds.), New Challenges for the UN Human Rights Machinery, 2011, p. 84, highlighting both difficulties, such as "extensive treaty body cooperation", and advantages, such as more congruent interpretations or the same status and visibility for all treaty bodies, coming along with consolidated concluding observations.

[259] *Shany/Cleveland*, Treaty Body Reform 2020: Has the time come for adopting a Global Review Calendar?, p. 4, https://www.geneva-academy.ch/joomlatools-files/docman-files/Draft%20List%20of%20Submissions%20–%20Academic%20Platform%202020%20Review%20without%20Propositions%20.pdf (last access: 21.08.2023).

[260] See above Part IV, B. III. 3.

Additionally, if all State parties were fully compliant with their reporting obligations, a treaty body such as the Human Rights Committee, with currently 169 State parties to monitor, would need eight years to conduct a review of all members to the ICCPR.[261] Compared to each other, the better arguments are therefore in favour of the four-year clustered review cycle. Particularly, the single review option could cause a "protection gap" and State parties would only need to present their human rights situation every eight years before all treaty bodies at once.[262]

Furthermore, the single or consolidated review presents itself as a "mammoth task for developed States and an impossible requirement on resource-poor ministries."[263] It should also be borne in mind that the single review option essentially corresponds to *Kofi Annan's* single State report-proposal.[264] The latter was mainly criticized because it was feared that State parties could possibly just focus on the two Covenants in the preparation of their reports, and already marginalized groups and more specific issues could be marginalized even further.[265]

One could argue that the division between the two Covenants and all other specialized treaties sets the same incentive to focus only on the ICCPR and ICESCR. However, a four-year clustered review allows more frequent review, and enables treaty bodies to "more contemporary" reviews.[266] Criticism can be further refuted by the fact that both, the Covenant Committees and the more specialized Committees can include references in their LOIPRs and concluding observations, by which they remind the State party under review of comparable recommendations through the lens of a more specialized treaty or *vice versa*.[267]

---

[261] *Seibert-Fohr*, The UN Human Rights Committee, in: Oberleitner (ed.), International Human Rights Institutions, Tribunals, and Courts, 2018, p. 134; *Shany/Cleveland*, Treaty Body Reform 2020: Has the time come for adopting a Global Review Calendar?, p. 5, https://www.geneva-academy.ch/joomlatools-files/docman-files/Draft%20List%20of%20Submissions%20-%20Academic%20Platform%202020%20Review%20without%20Propositions%20.pdf (last access: 21.08.2023).

[262] *Callejon et al.*, Optimizing the UN Treaty Body System, p. 23; *Creamer/Simmons*, The Proof Is in the Process: Self-Reporting Under International Human Rights Treaties, American Journal of International Law 114 (2020), 1, 49, who argue against an eight-year reporting gap because of the need to repeatedly address issues in order to achieve behavioural change by State parties.

[263] *Johnstone*, Streamlining the Constructive Dialogue: Efficiency from States' Perspectives, in: Bassiouni/Schabas (eds.), New Challenges for the UN Human Rights Machinery, 2011, p. 70, this becomes even more obvious when taking account of the four-year interval proposed by her, which seems very unrealistic against the background of the current status of the system.

[264] See *supra* Part II B.

[265] *O'Flaherty*, Reform of the UN Human Rights Treaty Body System: Locating the Dublin Statement, Human Rights Law Review 10 (2010), 319, 323.

[266] *Callejon et al.*, Optimizing the UN Treaty Body System, p. 22.

[267] Cf. *Creamer/Simmons*, The Proof Is in the Process: Self-Reporting Under International Human Rights Treaties, American Journal of International Law 114 (2020), 1, 49, who ba-

C. Comprehensive reporting calendar

This can thus be opposed to those who advocate a single periodic meeting in order to prevent treaty body experts from becoming "ever more specialized" and "ever more conceptually isolated."[268] At least current trends in the practice of the Committee against Torture, as identified above, argue against the presumption of Committees working in complete isolation from each other.

III. Discussions and practice among treaty bodies

The discussions among treaty bodies on the establishment of a comprehensive reporting calendar gained momentum at the 24th Meeting of Chairpersons in 2012. The treaty body Chairpersons "expressed [their] support for the valuable proposal" but made it clear that its implementation was first and foremost dependent on additional financial resources.[269] During the subsequent meeting in 2013, the Chairs resumed discussion on the suitable design of a comprehensive reporting calendar and decided on a timetable that would not exceed a five-year periodicity.[270]

Next to several advantages coming along with a fixed reporting schedule, the Chairs nevertheless drew attention to those State parties who "expressed concern about the possibility of a review in the absence of a report."[271] Indeed, when establishing a fixed and comprehensive calendar, covering the reporting requirements under all human rights core treaties, it becomes inevitable to review non-compliant State parties in the absence of a report on a regular basis. Otherwise, the maintenance of the fixed calendar could not be guaranteed.[272]

In addition, a non-reporting State party would be completely absent from the human rights treaty body system for at least four and at maximum eight years (depending on which model to select for the reporting calendar). Ultimately, the Chairs "endorsed in principle a common reporting calendar" but made its implementation contingent on several criteria. For instance, they held that "any scheduling of reports should follow as closely as possible the periodicity in the treaties, so as not to prejudice the legal reporting obligations of States parties,"[273]

---

sically opt for clustered reviews, but who propose to keep shorter reporting intervals with a view to the second cluster (the group- and issue-specific treaty bodies).

[268] *Johnstone*, Streamlining the Constructive Dialogue: Efficiency from States' Perspectives, in: Bassiouni/Schabas (eds.), New Challenges for the UN Human Rights Machinery, 2011, p. 71.

[269] Report of the Chairs of the human rights treaty bodies on their twenty-fourth meeting, UN Doc. A/67/222, 02.08.2012, paras. 32 a) and b).

[270] Report of the Chairs of the human rights treaty bodies on their twenty-fifth meeting, UN Doc. A/68/334, 19.08.2013, paras. 13 and 43; the timetable therefore corresponds to the idea advanced by High Commissioner *Pillay*.

[271] Report of the Chairs of the human rights treaty bodies on their twenty-fifth meeting, UN Doc. A/68/334, 19.08.2013, para. 23.

[272] *Callejon et al.*, Optimizing the UN Treaty Body System, p. 23.

[273] Report of the Chairs of the human rights treaty bodies on their twenty-fifth meeting, UN Doc. A/68/334, 19.08.2013, para. 43 c).

that non-reporting should be the exception, and that any calendar, regardless of its specific design, "should not be permissive as regards non-reporting."[274]

In the following years, the proposal lay dormant again and was eventually revisited for thorough discussion at the 31st Meeting of Chairpersons in 2019.[275] The topic's absence for several years can very probably be explained by the fact that Resolution 68/268 had not explicitly advocated the introduction of a comprehensive master calendar. Other features were brought into focus instead. In the meantime, some treaty bodies did take steps of their own as regards the establishment of reporting calendars, thus at least coordinating the reporting procedure under their own treaty.

1. Steps taken by the CMW Committee

The first treaty body to take measures in this matter was the CMW Committee, deciding in 2011 to examine all reports from 2014 onwards in accordance with a five-year comprehensive reporting calendar.[276] The calendar thus respects the Convention's periodicity pursuant to article 73(1)(b) CMW.

2. Steps taken by the Human Rights Committee

A couple of months prior to the 31st Meeting of Chairpersons in 2019, the Human Rights Committee revised its position paper, which was drafted in view of the upcoming discussion among Chairpersons and which was subsequently updated again at its 126th session.[277] In order to render the reporting procedure more predictable for all stakeholders involved, the Human Rights Committee decided to move in 2020 to a review cycle which "would be based on a 5-year review process, and a 3-year interval after one review process is concluded."[278] Such a schedule would consequently result in an overall eight-year cycle for State parties to complete one round of reporting.

The Human Rights Committee stressed in its updated position paper that existing capacity and financial resources would allow for the establishment of such a cycle. In practical terms, all State parties of the ICCPR would be divided into eight groups consisting of 21 or 22 States. In the first year, a State party would receive a List of Issues Prior to Reporting, and be expected to submit its

---

[274] Report of the Chairs of the human rights treaty bodies on their twenty-fifth meeting, UN Doc. A/68/334, 19.08.2013, para. 43 d).

[275] Report of the Chairs of the human rights treaty bodies on their thirty-first annual meeting, UN Doc. A/74/256, 30.07.2019, Annex III.

[276] Report of the Committee on the Protection of the Rights of All Migrant Workers and Members of Their Families (15th and 16th session), UN Doc. A/67/48 (2012), para. 25.

[277] Report of the Human Rights Committee (126th, 127th and 128th session), UN Doc. A/75/40 (2020), Annex III.

[278] Report of the Human Rights Committee (126th, 127th and 128th session), UN Doc. A/75/40 (2020), Annex III, para. 12.

written answers in the following year. During the third year, the constructive dialogue would take place, regardless of the submission of replies to the respective LOIPRs. According to the Committee, this would "ensure the regularity of reviews as provided for in the treaties".[279] It held further that this would allow for the maintenance of a fixed reporting scheme without the need to reschedule reviews of non-compliant State parties.[280] Followed by a two-year follow-up procedure on concluding observations, under which a State party is expected to submit its answers in the fifth year, the interaction between the Human Rights Committee and the State party under review ends, and after a three-year interval the next reporting cycle begins.[281]

3. Steps taken by the CESCR Committee

At its 68th session in October 2020, the CESCR Committee also opted for the introduction of an eight-year review calendar in order to improve the predictability of reporting.[282] Given that the CESCR Committee is planning to align its reporting activities with the Human Rights Committee, its decision comes as no surprise, even less so when taking into consideration the position paper on the future of the treaty body system adopted by the Chairs in 2019.[283]

4. Steps taken by the CED Committee

Together with its decision to introduce a refined version of its additional information procedure in accordance with article 29(4) CED, the CED Committee equally seeks to establish a comprehensive reporting calendar.[284] It is unclear, however, how this will unfold in concrete terms, as the CED Committee will determine the request for additional information by "varying from 1 to 8 years".[285] Strictly speaking, it is highly questionable if this concept even deserves the label "predictable".

---

[279] Report of the Chairs of the human rights treaty bodies on their thirty-first annual meeting, UN Doc. A/74/256, 30.07.2019, Annex III.

[280] *Shany/Cleveland*, Treaty Body Reform 2020: Has the time come for adopting a Global Review Calendar?, p. 4, https://www.geneva-academy.ch/joomlatools-files/docman-files/Draft%20List%20of%20Submissions%20–%20Academic%20Platform%202020%20Review%20without%20Propositions%20.pdf (last access: 21.08.2023).

[281] For a graphic depiction, see Report of the Human Rights Committee (126th, 127th and 128th session), UN Doc. A/75/40 (2020), Annex III, para. 16.

[282] CESCR Committee, Report on the sixty-seventh and sixty-eighth sessions, UN Doc. E/2021/22 (2021), para. 22.

[283] For their position paper, see two sections further below.

[284] Letter of the Committee on Enforced Disappearances of 24 July 2020, p. 8, https://www.ohchr.org/Documents/HRBodies/TB/HRTD/CoFacilitationProcess/TBExperts/CED_input_co-facilitators.pdf (last access: 21.08.2023).

[285] Letter of the Committee on Enforced Disappearances of 24 July 2020, p. 4, https://www.ohchr.org/Documents/HRBodies/TB/HRTD/CoFacilitationProcess/TBExperts/CED_input_co-facilitators.pdf (last access: 21.08.2023).

5. Treaty body position paper and 2022 Meeting of Chairpersons

In 2019, at the 31st Meeting of Chairpersons, discussions led to the adoption of a "Position paper of the Chairs of the human rights treaty bodies on the future of the treaty body system".[286] Inter alia, the paper addressed the questions of reporting cycles and timing of reviews. It took up several ideas previously developed by the Human Rights Committee as regards the possible design of a reporting calendar. Specifically, it took over the Human Rights Committee's proposal that the Covenant Committees will both move on to an eight-year review cycle. According to the paper, both will strive for synchronized timing of their reviews, which could entail a "single consolidated report" if the Committees choose to offer this as a possibility to State parties.[287]

Next to periodic monitoring discharged by the two Covenant Committees, the "Convention Committees will review countries on a four-year cycle, unless the provisions of a particular Convention provide otherwise."[288] While the proposals concerning the CESCR Committee and the Human Rights Committee are consistent with those who favour a single consolidated review or clustered review,[289] the position paper differs in that the specialized treaty bodies will review State parties every four years, unless treaty provisions provide otherwise. Since article 73(1)(b) CMW and article 44(1)(b) CRC provide for a five-year reporting cycle and article 9(1)(b) CERD requires State parties to submit reports every two years, at least those three Committees would not participate in an overall aligned reporting calendar.

Furthermore, the Chairs' position paper speaks of altering scheduled reviews in those cases where a "State party [should] be scheduled for review by a number of treaty bodies within a relatively short period".[290] Put differently, this means nothing else than that no final consensus on establishing a comprehensive reporting calendar could be reached among Chairpersons, covering all core treaties simultaneously. Particularly the Committee against Torture seems critical of the consolidated calendar. Despite its calls for more coordination, it held that a consolidated calendar "would be rigid and would lack the capacity to make late- or non-reporting States to report on time."[291] Furthermore, next to logistical issues, the Committee noted with concern that consolidated reports could pos-

---

[286] Report of the Chairs of the human rights treaty bodies on their thirty-first annual meeting, UN Doc. A/74/256, 30.07.2019, Annex III.

[287] Report of the Chairs of the human rights treaty bodies on their thirty-first annual meeting, UN Doc. A/74/256, 30.07.2019, Annex III.

[288] Report of the Chairs of the human rights treaty bodies on their thirty-first annual meeting, UN Doc. A/74/256, 30.07.2019, Annex III.

[289] See *supra* Part IV C.II.2. and 3.

[290] Report of the Chairs of the human rights treaty bodies on their thirty-first annual meeting, UN Doc. A/74/256, 30 July 2019, Annex III.

[291] Report of the Committee against Torture (64th, 65th and 66th session), UN Doc. A/74/44 (2019), Annex II, para. 4.

C. Comprehensive reporting calendar

sibly lead to "superficial treatment of the specific areas covered by the specialized treaties, [...]."[292]

It seems questionable whether this flexible solution ultimately represents any advantage. Apart from the two Covenant Committees, all specialized treaty bodies will continue to work on a four- or five-year basis. The caveat of being able to change scheduled review dates bears at the same time the risk of keeping the reporting procedure as nearly unpredictable and burdensome as it has been up to now.

These discussions among the Chairpersons gave the impression that an agreement on a general and uniform reporting periodicity among all Committees was still a long way off. During the discussions, a five-year reporting schedule has also re-entered the scene. However, it is also subject to possible exemptions, such as the eight-year reporting calendar introduced by the Human Rights Committee, or a different approach by the CRC Committee, which seems to consider a six-year periodicity more appropriate for its own purposes.[293]

Nevertheless, the Chairs performed another surprising turnaround. At the occasion of the 2022 Meeting of Chairpersons, the Chairs reached the conclusion that all treaty bodies with periodic reviews agree to "establish an eight-year review cycle for full reviews, with follow-up reviews in between".[294] As surprising as this decision may seem in the light of previous discussions, the proposed calendar is also intended to continue to guarantee the Committees a certain degree of flexibility.[295] Ultimately, much will depend on the individual treaty bodies' commitment and on the allocation of financial resources, which is a necessary prerequisite for the realisation of this ambitious project.[296] And although the Chairs seem to have reached a conclusion on the introduction of a comprehensive reporting calendar, there is still no definite idea regarding the ultimate design of such a calendar.[297]

---

[292] Report of the Committee against Torture (64th, 65th and 66th session), UN Doc. A/74/44 (2019), Annex II, para. 9.

[293] Report of the Chairs of the human rights treaty bodies on their thirty-third annual meeting, UN Doc. A/76/254, 30.07.2021, para. 41.

[294] Report of the Chairs of the human rights treaty bodies on their thirty-fourth annual meeting, UN Doc. A/77/228, 26.07.2022, para. 55, No. 1 (a).

[295] Report of the Chairs of the human rights treaty bodies on their thirty-fourth annual meeting, UN Doc. A/77/228, 26.07.2022, para. 55, No. 1 (c).

[296] See also Report of the Chairs of the human rights treaty bodies on their thirty-fourth annual meeting, UN Doc. A/77/228, 26.07.2022, para. 55, No. 1 (j).

[297] In the preparation for the 2023 Meeting of Chairpersons, a working paper proposed three options with different modalities for clustering treaty bodies and the conduct of back-to-back reviews, see Conclusions of the Chairs of the human rights treaty bodies on the OHCHR Working Paper – Options and guiding questions for the development of an implementation plan for the conclusions of the human rights treaty body Chairs at their 34th meeting in June 2022 (A/77/228, paras. 55–56), paras. 19–22. The modalities brought forward correspond to a great extent to those developed during the strengthening process so far.

IV. Legal questions concerning a reporting calendar

Irrespective of the final and concrete design of a possible comprehensive reporting calendar, treaty bodies will have to alter the periodicities provided for in the treaties, or must change the reporting intervals which have been established in constant practice. As aforementioned, the ICCPR leaves it to the Human Rights Committee's discretion to determine the frequency in which reports have to be submitted. The same applies to the CESCR and the CED Committee.

The crucial question is therefore whether all other specialized treaty bodies could decrease the reporting frequency contrary to what is stipulated in their constituent treaties. In another scenario, for example a single consolidated review every four to five years,[298] the question would be whether the periodicity of five years could be reduced to four years. Because of thus far unpredictable developments within the treaty body system, the following section shall analyse – detached from any concrete proposal – whether treaty bodies possess the power to reduce or increase reporting frequencies, even though this might be contrary to what is provided for in the treaties.[299]

1. Increase of reporting frequencies

The very wording of the treaty provisions that foresee fixed periodicities[300] reveals that the respective Committees are given leeway when it comes to the requests of further reports. Next to the periodic reporting obligation addressed at State parties in intervals of two, four or five years, a State party is additionally obliged to submit reports "whenever the Committee so requests".[301] The Committee against Torture is mandated in accordance with article 19(1) CAT to request not only supplementary reports every four years, but also "such other reports as it may request", and the Children's Rights Committee is vested with the competence to request further information relevant to the implementation of the Convention by article 44(4) CRC.

The latter is the only treaty provision which does not explicitly mention *reports*. It is, however, the existence of this provision which proves that the Com-

---

[298] See *Callejon et al.*, Optimizing the UN Treaty Body System, p. 20, who only mention this possibility in passing.

[299] *Shany/Cleveland*, Treaty Body Reform 2020: Has the time come for adopting a Global Review Calendar?, p. 5, who also address the "compatibility" of a comprehensive reporting calendar, https://www.geneva-academy.ch/joomlatools-files/docman-files/Draft%20List%20of%20Submissions%20–%20Academic%20Platform%202020%20Review%20without%20Propositions%20.pdf (last access: 21.08.2023).

[300] Article 19 CAT, article 18 CEDAW, article 9 CERD, article 73 CMW, article 44 CRC and article 35 CRPD.

[301] The exact same wording can be found under article 18(1)(b) CEDAW, article 19(1)(b) which additionally enables the Committee to request further information from State parties, article 73(1)(b) CMW and article 35(2) CRPD.

mittee is granted the same leeway as other treaty bodies. The requested information shall be relevant to the implementation of the Convention, which is essentially the same as monitoring the measures taken by a State party to give effect to the rights recognized in the Convention as prescribed by article 44(1) CRC. Accordingly, a purely text-based interpretation allows the conclusion that nothing bars the Committees from increasing the frequency of submitted reports.

Nevertheless, against the backdrop of the fact that many States do not comply in a timely manner with their reporting obligations under the various treaties, and that some treaty bodies have been unable to consider all reports submitted, it is utterly out of question that any treaty body would opt for a schedule with shorter reporting intervals. This conclusion is further bolstered by the fact that treaty bodies face an increasing workload in terms of individual communications, not to mention that the two Covenant Committees need approximately eight years to review all State parties based on the human and financial resources currently available.

2. Decrease of reporting frequencies

More likely and mirrored in the proposals developed by the Human Rights Committee and in several scholarly contributions, is the adoption of a fixed reporting calendar with reporting intervals of eight years. At this point, the question becomes more relevant whether the Committees also possess the competence to increase reporting intervals, since this raises issues of "compatibility [...] with the prescribed reporting obligations".[302] According to *Rodley*, the proposal of a comprehensive reporting calendar and its establishment "ignores the legal problem of the different periodicities for which the different treaties provide."[303] Especially with regard to the wording of CEDAW and CRPD, which require *at least* every four years a subsequent report, it becomes apparent that prolongments of reporting cycles are initially contrary to what is provided for in the treaties.

a) Practice by treaty bodies

Before addressing the legal problem itself, it is worth considering the practice established by treaty bodies, especially that of the Committee on the Elimination of Racial Discrimination. Article 9(1)(b) CERD provides for a two-year frequency and compliance with this reporting obligation alone appears to be burdensome, if not impossible.

---

[302] *Shany/Cleveland*, Treaty Body Reform 2020: Has the time come for adopting a Global Review Calendar?, p. 5, https://www.geneva-academy.ch/joomlatools-files/docman-files/Draft%20List%20of%20Submissions%20–%20Academic%20Platform%202020%20Review%20without%20Propositions%20.pdf (last access: 21.08.2023).

[303] *Rodley*, The Role and Impact of Treaty Bodies, in: Shelton (ed.), The Oxford Handbook of International Human Rights Law, 2013, p. 646.

aa) CERD Committee

Already in the late 1980s, the CERD Committee adopted measures, such as more flexible timetables, to reduce the reporting burden on State parties and to reduce its own workload.[304] Next to allowing non-compliant State parties to submit all overdue reports in one single document,[305] the Committee decided to request compliant State parties to submit a comprehensive report only every four years, and to hand in "brief updating reports" on each intervening occasion when the reports were due under the Convention.[306]

In 2001, the Committee changed its working methods again and introduced the possibility for State parties to submit two reports jointly if the period between the examination of the last periodic report and the scheduled date for the upcoming dialogue was less than two years.[307] De facto, the Committee thus extended the two-year periodicity provided for in article 9(1)(b) CERD to four years. This approach is still mirrored by Committee practice. In its concluding observations, the Committee regularly determines in the last paragraph when the next report is expected, and recommends to State parties to submit two,[308] three,[309] or even four[310] reports in one single document combined. Even though the CERD Committee *recommends* submitting joint reports, i.e., it is still at the discretion of State parties to submit a single periodic report every two years. To the author's best knowledge, such a submission has however never occurred.

---

[304] *Thornberry*, The International Convention on the Elimination of All Forms of Racial Discrimination: A Commentary, 2016, The Convention and the Committee, p. 46; *Egan*, The United Nations Human Rights Treaty System: Law and Procedure, 2011, p. 145.

[305] *Egan*, The UN Human Rights Treaty System: Law and Procedure, 2011, p. 145.

[306] Report of the Committee on the Elimination of Racial Discrimination (37th session), UN Doc. A/44/18 (1990), para. 38; *Egan*, The United Nations Human Rights Treaty System: Law and Procedure, 2011, p. 145; *Boerefijn*, The Reporting Procedure under the Covenant on Civil and Political Rights: Practice and Procedures of the Human Rights Committee, 1999, p. 241, noting that the CERD Committee is the treaty body which had to handle the situation of overdue reports longer than any other treaty body.

[307] Report of the Committee on the Elimination of Racial Discrimination (58th and 59th session), UN Doc. A/56/18 (2001), para. 477; *Thornberry*, The International Convention on the Elimination of All Forms of Racial Discrimination: A Commentary, 2016, The Convention and the Committee, p. 46, footnote 122.

[308] For more recently adopted concluding observations, see CERD Committee, Concluding observations on the combined tenth to twelfth reports of Uzbekistan, UN Doc. CERD/C/UZB/CO/10–12, 27.01.2020, para. 33; Concluding observations on the combined seventeenth to nineteenth reports of Columbia, UN Doc. CERD/C/COL/CO/17–19, 22.01.2020, para. 40.

[309] CERD Committee, Concluding observations on the combined fourteenth to seventeenth reports of Cambodia, UN Doc. CERD/C/KHM/CO/14–17, 30.01.2020, para. 51.

[310] CERD Committee, Concluding observations on the combined seventeenth to nineteenth reports of Israel, UN Doc. CERD/C/ISR/CO/17–19, 12.12.2019, para. 58.

bb) CEDAW Committee

Interesting to note is that in the case of CEDAW, it was not the Committee itself that initiated changes as regards more flexible reporting deadlines, but it was the General Assembly which requested in 1986 that the Committee adopt measures to eliminate the backlog of reports submitted for consideration.[311] For that purpose, the General Assembly encouraged the CEDAW Committee to discuss the "adjustment of the reporting system."[312] The Committee replied to this request by pointing out that, in its own view, the Convention would not allow alterations as regards the periodicity established by article 18(1)(b) CEDAW,[313] thereby relying on a strictly text-based reading of its constituent instrument.[314]

Nevertheless, over the years, the Committee gradually abandoned its reluctant position.[315] In order to handle the backlog of reports awaiting consideration more efficiently, it decided at its 16th session in 1997 to invite State parties to submit in maximum two overdue reports combined, "on an exceptional basis and as a temporary measure."[316] In 2000, at its 23rd session, the Committee then took the decision to invite State parties to combine all outstanding reports in one document.[317] In 2008, the Committee requested all State parties which had presented their reports during the 40th session to submit their subsequent two reports

---

[311] *Boerefijn*, Article 18, in: Freeman/Chinkin/Rudolf (eds.), The UN Convention on the Elimination of All Forms of Discrimination Against Women: A Commentary, 2012, p. 492.

[312] UN General Assembly, Resolution 41/108, Convention on the Elimination of All Forms of Discrimination Against Women, A/RES/41/108, 04.12.1986, para. 8.

[313] Report of the Committee on the Elimination of Discrimination against Women (Sixth session), UN Doc. A/42/38 (1987), para. 41; *Boerefijn*, Article 18, in: Freeman/Chinkin/Rudolf (eds.), The UN Convention on the Elimination of All Forms of Discrimination Against Women: A Commentary, 2012, p. 492.

[314] Report of the Committee on the Elimination of Discrimination against Women (Sixth session), UN Doc. A/42/38 (1987), para. 34, the Committee held that it had "no authority to extend the reporting periods set out in the Convention itself."

[315] *Egan*, The United Nations Human Rights Treaty System: Law and Procedure, 2011, p. 160, who notes that the Committee follows the practice of many of the other treaty bodies.

[316] Report of the Committee on the Elimination of Discrimination against Women (16th and 17th session), UN Doc. A/52/38/Rev. 1 (1997), Part one, decision 16/III; *Byrnes*, The Committee on the Elimination of Discrimination Against Women, in: Mégret/Alston (eds.), The United Nations and Human Rights: A Critical Appraisal, Second Edition, 2020, p. 406; *Boerefijn*, Article 18, in: Freeman/Chinkin/Rudolf (eds.), The UN Convention on the Elimination of All Forms of Discrimination Against Women: A Commentary, 2012, p. 492; see also *Bustelo*, The Committee on the Elimination of Discrimination Against Women at the Crossroads, in: Alston/Crawford (eds.), The Future of UN Human Rights Treaty Monitoring, 2000, p. 86, who notes that several Committee members objected to the decision. In their opinion, such practice could lead to State parties "evading their reporting obligation."

[317] Report of the Committee on the Elimination of Discrimination against Women (22nd and 23rd session), UN Doc. A/55/38 (2000), Part one, decision 23/II; *Boerefijn*, Article 18, in: Freeman/Chinkin/Rudolf (eds.), The UN Convention on the Elimination of All Forms of Discrimination Against Women: A Commentary, 2012, p. 492.

as combined reports.[318] Contrary to previous decisions in this matter, the Committee invited all State parties to submit combined reports, irrespective of their level of compliance. At the same time, the Committee made it abundantly clear that the allowance was intended as an exceptional measure only.

The general approach of only allowing a State party to submit combined reports to the effect of being compliant again with the periodicity under the Convention is also reflected in the Committee's Rules of Procedure. Article 49(3) RoP CEDAW stipulates that State parties may be allowed "to submit a combined report comprising no more than two overdue reports."[319] In practice, and despite the Committee's assertion that the submission of combined reports is only permitted in exceptional circumstances, by 2017 to 2018 about 40 per cent of all reports considered were combined reports.[320]

cc) Committee against Torture

The Committee against Torture has only accepted combined reports "on an exceptional basis",[321] but it is willing to adopt a "quasi-flexible approach" concerning due dates for the submission of periodic reports.[322] Correspondingly, articles 65(2) and 65(3) of its Rules of Procedure provide that the Committee "may recommend, at its discretion, that State parties consolidate their periodic reports" and that the "Committee may recommend, at its discretion, that State parties

---

[318] *Boerefijn*, Article 18, in: Freeman/Chinkin/Rudolf (eds.), The UN Convention on the Elimination of All Forms of Discrimination Against Women: A Commentary, 2012, p. 493; Report of the Committee on the Elimination of Discrimination against Women (40th and 41st session), UN Doc. A/63/38 (2008), Part one, decision 40/IV.

[319] Rules of Procedure of the Committee on the Elimination of Discrimination Against Women, UN Doc. HRI/GEN/3/Rev. 3, p. 111.

[320] *Byrnes*, The Committee on the Elimination of Discrimination Against Women, in: Mégret/Alston (eds.), The United Nations and Human Rights: A Critical Appraisal, Second Edition, 2020, p. 406, footnote 65; see, however, the concluding observations adopted vis-à-vis Kiribati and Latvia, CEDAW, Concluding observations on the combined initial, second and third periodic reports of Kiribati, UN Doc. CEDAW/C/KIR/CO/1–3, 11.03.2020, para. 61; and Concluding observations on the combined fourth to seventh periodic reports of Latvia, UN Doc. CEDAW/C/LVA/CO/4–7, 10.03.2020, para. 50, both State parties were requested to submit a single periodic report in four years, thus in accordance with the Convention's regular periodicity. Both of them had submitted a State report that combined three reports in total. This may underline the assumption that the Committee still seeks to respect the Convention's periodicity of four years.

[321] *Egan*, The United Nations Human Rights Treaty System: Law and Procedure, 2011, p. 152.

[322] *Egan*, The United Nations Human Rights Treaty System: Law and Procedure, 2011, p. 152.

present their periodic reports by a specified date."[323] However, the Committee normally does not invite State parties to submit combined reports.[324]

dd) CRC Committee

In the case of the CRC, the Committee adopted two recommendations concerning the reporting procedure and the issue of periodicity at its 29th session in 2002.[325] While "acknowledging the need to support States parties in an effort to ensure compliance with the strict time frame established by article 44, paragraph 1, of the Convention,"[326] the Committee decided to request State parties to submit two reports combined when the next periodic report was already due the year following the previous constructive dialogue, or, if the next periodic report was already due at the time of the upcoming dialogue.[327]

After having introduced these two recommendations, the Committee nevertheless stressed that "these rules apply only as an exceptional measure"[328] and that they would be only applied once in order to render State parties compliant again with the "strict reporting periodicity."[329]

However, Committee practice indicates that combined reports are the rule rather than the exception, and that the originally intended exceptional measure is now being used "more or less [continuously]".[330] The Committee's current *modus operandi* under the reporting procedure can further illustrate this assumption. All concluding observations adopted at the Committee's 88th session in September 2021 covered two periodic reports combined, and with regard to upcoming reporting cycles, some State parties were requested to submit combined reports again.[331]

---

[323] Committee against Torture, Rules of Procedure, UN Doc. CAT/C/3/Rev. 6, 01.09.2014.

[324] As far as could be determined, the last State party vis-à-vis which concluding observations were adopted in response to a combined report was Italy, Committee against Torture, Concluding observations on the combined fifth and sixth periodic reports of Italy, UN Doc. CAT/C/ITA/CO/5–6, 18.12.2017, para. 1, the State party was requested to submit its seventh report four years later in 2021, thus in accordance with the Convention's periodicity.

[325] *Akthar/Nyamutata*, International Child Law, Fourth Edition, 2020, p. 104.

[326] CRC Committee, Report on the Twenty-Ninth Session, UN Doc. CRC/C/114, 14.05.2002, p. 5.

[327] CRC Committee, Report on the Twenty-Ninth Session, UN Doc. CRC/C/114, 14.05.2002, p. 5.

[328] CRC Committee, Report on the Twenty-Ninth Session, UN Doc. CRC/C/114, 14.05.2002, p. 5.

[329] CRC Committee, Report on the Twenty-Ninth Session, UN Doc. CRC/C/114, 14.05.2002, p. 5.

[330] *Evans*, The Committee on the Rights of the Child, in: Mégret/Alston (eds.), The United Nations and Human Rights: A Critical Appraisal, Second Edition, 2020, p. 532.

[331] CRC Committee, Concluding observations on the combined fifth and sixth periodic reports of Czechia, UN Doc. CRC/C/CZE/CO/5–6, 27.09.2021, the State party was requested to submit its seventh report only, at para. 54; Concluding observations on the combined

ee) CRPD Committee

The CRPD Committee decided at its tenth session in September 2013 to offer State parties, whose initial reports were reviewed during the fifth, sixth, seventh and eighth sessions, to combine their second and third report in one document.[332] The request consequently encompassed both compliant and non-compliant State parties. The only criterion to avail oneself of this opportunity was the review of the initial report during one of the aforementioned sessions.

Interestingly, in relation to the simplified reporting procedure, the Committee introduced article 48ter in its Rules of Procedure at its sixteenth session in 2016, by which it offers State parties to adhere to the new procedure comprising the submission of both, single and combined periodic reports. However, the Committee does not clarify when exactly a State party should combine two reports under the simplified reporting procedure.[333] Recent practice suggests that the Committee tries to apply the simplified reporting procedure in conjunction with the submission of two periodic reports combined.[334]

ff) CMW Committee

The last Committee established by a Convention which provides for fixed periodicities, the CMW Committee, does neither seem to allow combined reports nor does it adjust the five-year cycle provided for under article 73(1)(b) CMW. In its recently adopted concluding observations, the Committee requests State parties to hand in their next periodic report in five years and offers them in addition the possibility to avail themselves of the simplified reporting procedure.[335] It is re-

---

second to fourth periodic reports of the Kingdom of Eswatini, UN Doc. CRC/C/SWZ/CO/2–4, 29.09.2021, the State party should submit its fifth and sixth report combined, at para. 74; Concluding observations on the combined fifth and sixth periodic reports of Switzerland, UN Doc. CRC/C/CHE/CO/5–6, 27.09.2021; Concluding observations on the combined fifth and sixth periodic reports of Poland, UN Doc. CRC/C/POL/CO/5–6, 27.09.2021.

[332] Report of the Committee on the Rights of Persons with Disabilities on its tenth session, UN Doc. CRPD/C/10/2, 13.05.2014, Annex IV, para. 1.

[333] CRPD Committee, Rules of Procedure, UN Doc. CRPD/C/1/Rev. 1, 10.10.2016.

[334] See for instance, CRPD Committee, Concluding observations on the initial report of Estonia, UN Doc. CRPD/C/EST/CO/1, 05.05.2021, para. 70 with the request addressed at the State party to submit its second to fourth periodic report with simultaneous application of the simplified reporting procedure. France was requested to submit its second to fifth report combined and to adhere to the simplified reporting procedure, CRPD Committee, Concluding observations on the initial report of France, UN Doc. CRPD/C/FRA/CO/1, 04.10.2021, para. 72. See also, for instance, the requests addressed to Australia and Ecuador to combine the next two periodic reports, both State parties had submitted their previous reports under the simplified reporting procedure, CRPD Committee, Concluding observations on the combined second and third periodic reports of Ecuador, UN Doc. CRPD/C/ECU/CO/2–3, 21.10.2019, para. 65; Concluding observations on the combined second and third periodic reports of Australia, UN Doc. CRPD/C/AUS/CO/2–3, 15.10.2019, para. 67.

[335] CMW Committee, Concluding observations on the second periodic report of Chile,

called here that the Committee took the decision to combine the possible adherence to the simplified reporting procedure with the establishment of a comprehensive reporting calendar.[336]

gg) General tendencies among the treaty bodies

The general practice of treaty bodies which monitor a Convention with express periodicities reveals that each Committee, apart from the CMW Committee, has at some point extended the reporting intervals. Reporting under CERD has long moved away from the two-year frequency provided by article 9(1)(b) CERD. Under CRC and CRPD, there are indications of similar developments. The CRPD Committee started to request State parties to combine two periodic reports, and the CRC Committee, even though it has stressed on previous occasions that the combination of two reports should remain "exceptional" and highlighted the Convention's "strict reporting periodicity",[337] generally seems to accept the submission of two reports combined.

The CEDAW Committee, originally disinclined to combined reports, only recommends to State parties with two overdue reports to combine them into one document. Thus, the CEDAW Committee normally tries to respect the four-year periodicity and the combination of two reports as provided for in article 49(3) RoP CEDAW is a means to let State parties re-enter the normal reporting schedule. Despite the repeated emphasis that combined reports remain an exception, in practice their requests occur frequently.

Almost every Committee has, acting from necessity, requested State parties to submit combined reports and thereby "disregarded" the respective treaty's periodicity. The underlying rationales may differ from Committee to Committee, but each treaty body reacted either to backlogs of reports awaiting review, or to non-compliant State parties, which should re-enter the reporting system on a regular basis.[338] Thus, purely practical considerations make it almost essential to decrease reporting intervals.[339]

The obvious need to reduce reporting frequencies is also not unique to the human rights treaty bodies. According to article 22 ILO, States are required to

---

UN Doc. CMW/C/CHL/CO/2, 11.05.2021, para. 66; Concluding observations on the third periodic report of Bosnia and Herzegovina, UN Doc. CMW/C/BIH/CO/3, 11 September 2019, para. 66; Concluding observations on the third periodic report of Colombia, UN Doc. CMW/C/COL/CO/3, 27.01.2020, para. 58.

[336] Report of the Committee on the Protection of the Rights of All Migrant Workers and Members of Their Families (15th and 16th session), UN Doc. A/67/48 (2012), para. 25.

[337] CRC Committee, Submission of Reports by State Parties, UN Doc. CRC/C/139, 02.04.2004, p. 3.

[338] A similar approach can be detected under the reporting system established by the ACHPR, see *Murray*, The African Charter on Human and Peoples' Rights: A Commentary, 2019, Article 62, State Reporting, p. 794.

[339] *Callejon et al.*, Optimizing the UN Treaty Body System, p. 43.

report every year on the implementation of those ILO conventions they have ratified. *De facto*, the reporting intervals under the ILO supervisory system, which is thought to be comparable to the monitoring undertaken by human rights treaty bodies,[340] have been "gradually relaxed".[341] Under the current *modus operandi*, States are expected to submit a report that covers certain key conventions every three years, and to deliver another report which focuses on all the other ILO conventions ratified every six years.[342] Furthermore, it should be borne in mind that the Committees fix the due dates for the submission of periodic reports in accordance with the time frame provided for in the treaties. However, after the submission, it takes on average 17 to 18 months until the report is finally examined, which creates "de facto [a] six-year period"[343] under the Convention against Torture. The same result can be observed with regard to all other Conventions and Committees.[344]

b) Legal arguments

This practice raises the question as to whether there are also legal arguments which could justify the extension of reporting intervals, possibly to a maximum of eight years.

In her strengthening report, *Pillay* argues that the comprehensive reporting calendar "would be consistent with the existing legal obligations to submit reports under the treaties, the original object and purpose of which is to ensure a periodic review […], without exception and without discrimination, in a way that

---

[340] *Helfer*, Pushback Against Supervisory Systems: Lessons for the ILO from International Human Rights Institutions, in: Politakis et al. (eds.), ILO100 – LAW FOR SOCIAL JUSTICE, 2019, p. 258.

[341] *van Alphen Fyfe/Fiti Sinclair*, Supervisory and Review Procedures: International Labour Organization (ILO), in: Peters (ed.), Max Planck Encyclopedia of Public International Law, Online version, April 2020, para. 25.

[342] *van Alphen Fyfe/Fiti Sinclair*, Supervisory and Review Procedures: International Labour Organization (ILO), in: Peters (ed.), Max Planck Encyclopedia of Public International Law, Online version, April 2020, paras. 25–27.

[343] *Nowak/McArthur*, The United Nations Convention Against Torture: A Commentary, First Edition, 2008, Article 19, State Reporting Procedure, para. 39.

[344] In relation to CEDAW, see *Byrnes*, The Committee on the Elimination of Discrimination against Women, in: Hellum/Aasen (eds.), Women's Human Rights: CEDAW in International, Regional and National Law, 2013, p. 34, who notes that State parties may have to wait two years until their report is considered; reaching a similar conclusion regarding CRC and noting that reports are considered "at best" two years after their submission, *Doek*, The CRC: Dynamics and Direction of Monitoring its Implementation, in: Invernizzi/Williams (eds.), The Human Rights of Children, From Vision to Implementation, 2011, p. 108; see also *Riedel*, Global Human Rights Protection at the Crossroads: Strengthening or Reforming the System, in: Breuer et al. (eds.), Der Staat im Recht, Festschrift für Eckart Klein zum 70. Geburtstag, 2013, p. 1299, who observes that reports are sometimes three years old when the constructive dialogue is finally taking place.

the current process is unable to guarantee."³⁴⁵ She thereby refers to the third element of article 31(1) VCLT, i.e. a teleological interpretation of the treaty concerned. Given that the reporting procedure serves to enable State parties to conduct a self-assessment in the implementation of treaty guarantees, and further given that each State party shall benefit in equal measure from a Committee's guidance, extending reporting intervals seems to constitute the only viable measure to ensure equal treatment of all parties while facing prevailing resource constraints and limited meeting time. However, as a matter of fact, six out of nine human rights core treaties stipulate an unequivocal time frame for the submission of reports, which contravenes the establishment of an eight-year periodicity in the first place.

To cast further doubts on the question whether any prolongment is permissible under the treaties, article 18(1)(b) CEDAW and article 35(2) CRPD both provide that State parties are obliged to submit further subsequent periodic reports "at least" every four years.³⁴⁶ Taken literally, reporting intervals are thus at maximum four years, and any longer period in between cannot be implemented.

On the other hand, first and foremost, these provisions impose reporting obligations on State parties – which are required to submit reports at least every four years – and they do not explicitly mention the Committees' competence to alter periodicities; the latter being the question at stake. However, such power could be derived from the fact that they are vested with the power to request additional reports whenever they consider this necessary.³⁴⁷

Both, article 18(1)(b) CEDAW and article 35(2) CRPD entail two features, the periodic reporting obligation and the respective Committee's power to request further supplementary reports. The two features are separated by the word "and". The decisive factor is therefore the reading of the word "and" and the related question of how the provision's two features, fixed periodicity and the Committee's power to request further reports, correlate with each other.

A first possible reading could suggest that the power to request additional and supplement reports cannot interfere with the strict reporting obligation. The word "and" would indicate that the Committee's power in that matter is subordinate to the time frame provided for in the first part of the provision. It would therefore only be possible to *shorten* the reporting intervals by requesting supplementary reports in between.

---

[345] *Pillay*, Strengthening the United Nations human rights treaty body system, p. 41.

[346] Article 18(1)(b) CEDAW reads: "Thereafter at least every four years and further whenever the Committee so requests." Article 35(2) CRPD reads: "Thereafter, States Parties shall submit subsequent reports at least every four years and further whenever the Committee so requests."

[347] Next to article 18(1)(b) CEDAW and article 35(2) CRPD, article 19(1) CAT second sentence, article 73(1)(b) CMW and article 9(1)(b) CERD provide for the submission of reports when the Committees request so. Article 44(4) CRC states that the Committee may "request from States Parties further information relevant to the implementation of the Convention."

On the other hand, "and" could as well mean that the two features provided for by article 18(1)(b) CEDAW and article 35(2) CRPD must be read separately. The first part of these two provisions stipulates the reporting obligation of the State parties, the second part, on the contrary, establishes the treaty body's power to request further reports. An alternative reading could denote that the word "and" does not subordinate the second feature, but that it coordinates both of them. Consequently, the request for further reports could be considered in isolation from the reporting periodicity. Such a reading allows for the conclusion that the reporting obligation, often perceived as burdensome, could be alleviated by treaty bodies via the extension of reporting intervals whenever this may be *necessary*, thus when the treaty bodies so request. Said power would then be an expression of the discretion granted to the Committees by the second part of article 18(1)(b) CEDAW and article 35(2) CRPD respectively.

Though the textual basis may still be considered rather weak, a more effectiveness-orientated argumentation can be brought into play, namely in that extending the periodicities presents itself as the only means to ensure the equal treatment of all State parties. Taking up the argument advanced by *Pillay*, moving from a four-year cycle to any longer period in between the submission of reports is *indispensable* within the meaning of the "necessary-requirement" when interpreting the treaties in a progressive manner. As aforementioned, such a step constitutes the only viable means to uphold regular reporting activities vis-à-vis all State parties to one of the UN human rights treaties. Arriving at such competence in relation to CERD, CAT, CRC and CMW would be all the more possible as these treaties do not provide for a comparably rigid reporting schedule. In their cases, there is no mention of "at least" under the treaties with regard to periodic reporting by State parties.

On the other hand, it could be objected that, similar to the arguments raised in the context of the simplified reporting procedure,[348] a *right* to submit a report could also arise as a mirror image of the obligation to submit such a report "at least every four years." If treaty bodies were to alter the periodicity to eight years, for example, a State party could possibly be deprived of its right to assistance and guidance in implementation of the respective human rights treaty. Nevertheless, even if one were to assume such a corresponding entitlement of State parties to exist, its enforcement must not have repercussions on other State parties' rights under the same treaty, let alone the possible effects on the respective treaty body, which is also charged with other treaty-based tasks.

Over time, treaty bodies have been accorded with additional tasks. Starting off with periodic reporting of the CRC only, the CRC Committee, for instance, was first given the task to also monitor the implementation of two further Optional Protocols, and it is now further tasked with the examination of individual communications by virtue of the 3rd Optional Protocol. However, what is striking

---

[348] See *supra* Part III B.V. 3.

is that none of these treaties have defined how to allocate resources or meeting time devoted when discharging the various mandates imposed by several legal sources.

In the absence of any distribution formula, each duty imposed on the Committee must be considered equal. This, in turn, would mean giving equal attention to each task, which would ultimately lead to less time being spent on the State reporting procedure. Yet, in practical terms, most of the individual complaints before UN human rights treaty bodies are filed with the Human Rights Committee and the Committee against Torture. But as the number of complaints filed with each treaty body is generally expected to increase, their workload will increase accordingly, and the question arises if one task should be given preference over the other. All these arguments are strongly in favour of human rights treaty bodies possessing the competence to extend the reporting periodicities under their treaties.

c) Extending reporting intervals via subsequent practice

Another option in the realization of a comprehensive reporting calendar, or at least the decrease of reporting frequencies, rests with the reliance on subsequent practice pursuant to article 31(3)(b) VCLT.

As observed above, the CERD Committee regularly invites State parties to submit combined reports and State parties regularly comply with the Committee's request. Said practice is in existence since the 1990s. It follows that most of the State parties to the Convention have submitted two or even more reports combined. It can therefore be assumed that a sufficiently consistent practice with a view to the submission of joint reports has emerged, and it may also be well assumed that State parties have submitted their combined reports with the intention to fulfil their respective reporting obligations, covering all of their biennial reports at once.

Furthermore, this practice seems to be followed by each State party, and in the absence of any objections to the request for the submission of combined reports, an agreement as to the treaty's interpretation might be presumed to exist. Said assumption can be bolstered by the fact that reporting at two-year intervals under CERD appears to be very burdensome, and that the alleviation of reporting duties is very likely to be endorsed by State parties.

Ultimately, the crucial question is what the precise legal consequences are. Some State parties have combined two reports, others have combined three reports and others haven even covered a timespan of ten or more years with the submission of five or more reports in one single document. The legal consequences of possible subsequent practice could either be that, at minimum, an extension to a four-year reporting interval is reached or, constituting the more far-reaching option, the CERD Committee could be considered vested with the power to determine how many reports a State party should combine.

As the Committee seems from time to time to request combined reports as early as three years after the adoption of the last concluding observations, it is almost impossible to pin down an exact time frame which would be the common dominator in extending the periodicity under article 9(1) CERD. The more far-reaching result, which is at the same time the one that seems normatively more convincing, as it provides legal certainty, is that the Committee is vested with the power to determine the reporting period for each State party individually. Despite the solution's far-reaching consequences, this kind of interpretative result appears possible as subsequent practice can even lead to the modification of the treaty under interpretation.[349] The latter only requires a more consistent practice, shared by most or all members to the treaty.[350] As far as vesting the CERD Committee with the power to determine the reporting intervals is concerned, it is also not necessary to assume that such interpretation qualifies as a modification of the treaty. Indeed, article 9(1)(b) CERD vests the Committee with the power to request reports whenever it wishes so. Hence, the treaty provides for some discretion granted to the Committee when determining reporting intervals, and the interpretation of article 9(1)(b) CERD by means of subsequent practice would not amount to a modification of the Convention.

The avenue described here for vesting the CERD Committee with the power to shorten reporting intervals also seems possible with a view to other Committees, especially the CRC Committee or the CRPD Committee, where most State parties follow equal requests to submit two reports combined. A sufficiently consistent practice might have been already achieved, or may be achieved in the near future.

IV. Possible synergies with the UPR

In any way, there is yet another way in which a reporting gap could be closed in the event of the introduction of an eight-year periodicity. Next to the monitoring undertaken by treaty bodies, all State parties regularly take part in the Universal Periodic Review (UPR) at the Human Rights Council.

In light of the UPR's intended complementary nature to the activities carried out by UN human rights treaty bodies,[351] and the fact that both mechanisms are

---

[349] *Buga*, Modification of Treaties by Subsequent Practice, 2018, pp. 133–137 with a definition of the term "modification"; see also *Hafner*, Subsequent Agreements and Practice: Between Interpretation, Informal Modification, and Formal Amendment, in: Nolte (ed.), Treaties and Subsequent Practice, 2013, pp. 114–117.

[350] Cf. *Seibert-Fohr*, The Effect of Subsequent Practice on the European Convention on Human Rights, Considerations from a General International Law Perspective, in: van Aaken/Mutoc (eds.), The European Convention on Human Rights and General International Law, 2018, pp. 79–80, exploring possibilities of treaty modification via subsequent practice under the ECHR.

[351] UN General Assembly, Resolution 60/251, Human Rights Council, UN Doc. A/RES/60/251, 15.03.2006, para. 5(e), where it is stated that the UPR shall complement and not duplicate the work of treaty bodies.

"highly comparable in their functioning",[352] it seems reasonable to consider the UPR as a kind of possible intermediate follow-up process to the recommendations adopted by human rights treaty bodies.[353] Such an undertaking appears even more convincing, given that a significant number of recommendations adopted under the UPR expressly refer to concluding observations and views adopted by UN treaty bodies,[354] and additionally provided that all State parties to the human rights core treaties participate in the UPR.[355] This solution for reviewing State parties in between a possible comprehensive eight-year reporting cycle under the UPR is however not as simple and convincing as it may look like at first glance. Although the UPR is intended to complement the Committees, its establishment has caused controversy about whether the new reporting mechanism might not ultimately pose a threat to the work and authority of human rights treaty bodies.[356]

Together with the replacement of the Commission of Human Rights by the Human Rights Council,[357] the UPR was created in order to "give more visibility and emphasis to human rights"[358] and was intended to put an end to the prevailing selectivity and politicization prevalent in the former Commission on Human Rights.[359] While duplication of treaty body recommendations under the UPR

---

[352] *Carraro*, Promoting Compliance with Human Rights: The Performance of the United Nations' Universal Periodic Review and Treaty Bodies, International Studies Quarterly 63 (2019), 1079, 1080.

[353] See *Ramcharan*, Modernizing the UN Human Rights System, 2019, pp. 174–175, who suggests that treaty body members should participate in the various stages of the UPR when the respective State report is considered, ultimately leading to "greater synergy between the two procedures."

[354] *Shah/Sivakumaran*, The Use of International Human Rights Law in the Universal Periodic Review, Human Rights Law Review 21 (2021), 265, 277–279 with a detailed overview, aggregated by the various UN human rights core treaties; *Rodley*, UN treaty bodies and the Human Rights Council, in: Keller/Ulfstein (eds.), UN Human Rights Treaty Bodies: Law and Legitimacy, 2012, p. 329, observing a "substantial reliance" on recommendations by treaty bodies; *Dominguez-Redondo*, The Universal Periodic Review – Is There Life beyond Naming and Shaming in Human Rights Implementation?, New Zealand Law Review 4 (2012), 673, 696.

[355] *Rodley*, UN treaty bodies and the Human Rights Council, in: Keller/Ulfstein (eds.), UN Human Rights Treaty Bodies: Law and Legitimacy, 2012, p. 325.

[356] *Collister*, Rituals and implementation in the Universal Periodic Review and the human rights treaty bodies, in: Charlesworth/Larking (eds.), Human Rights and the Universal Periodic Review, 2014, p. 109; *Gaer*, A Voice Not an Echo: Universal Periodic Review and the UN Treaty Body System, Human Rights Law Review 7 (2007), 109.

[357] For the history and the development of the Commission on Human Rights, see *Pace*, The United Nations Commission on Human Rights: 'A Very Great Enterprise', 2020.

[358] *Chauville*, The Universal Periodic Review's first cycle: successes and failures, in: Charlesworth/Larking (eds.), Human Rights and the Universal Periodic Review, 2014, pp. 89–90.

[359] *Rivera*, The UN Human Rights Council: Achievements and Challenges in Its First Decade, in: Oberleitner (ed.), International Human Rights Institutions, Tribunals, and Courts, 2018, pp. 56–57.

does not necessarily have to be considered negative, it is the persisting, highly political character of the UPR that might pose a risk to the work of treaty bodies.[360] In this sense it has been argued that recommendations adopted by human rights treaty bodies might be re-evaluated during the UPR, which may ultimately lead to the adoption of weaker recommendations, or those being contradictory to concluding observations formerly adopted by the Committees.[361] Obviously, the State-centred, highly political and diplomatic[362] UPR review process could result in State parties accepting and relying only on such recommendations that would present them in the more favourable light. Thereby, they could easily criticize treaty bodies for excessive and overly severe scrutiny. In this scenario, reliance on the UPR as an intermediate follow-up procedure would turn out to provide a disservice to the treaty bodies. Contradictory recommendations under the UPR could be taken as evidence to prove treaty bodies wrong, ultimately undermining their legitimacy and authority.[363] In addition, State parties might also reject the recommendations made by their peer reviewers, and could thereby indirectly reject concluding observations, presupposed that they formed the basis for the respective recommendation.[364]

On the other hand, from the perspective of treaty bodies, the UPR shall by no means constitute a fully integrated follow-up procedure, and it is not intended to closely scrutinize each of the recommendations adopted by treaty bodies. Despite possible repercussions on certain recommendations adopted by treaty bodies and the procedure's highly political character, the UPR serves as another forum in which all UN Member States are reviewed in their implementation of *all* UN human rights core treaties.[365] It also bears the considerable advantage of render-

---

[360] *Ramcharan*, Modernizing the UN Human Rights System, 2019, pp. 173–174.

[361] *Limon/Montoya*, The Universal Periodic Review, Treaty Bodies and Special Procedures: A connectivity study, June 2019, p. 22; *Collister*, Rituals and implementation in the Universal Periodic Review and the human rights treaty bodies, in: Charlesworth/Larking (eds.), Human Rights and the Universal Periodic Review, 2014, p. 116; *Rodley*, Duplication and Divergence in the Work of the United Nations Human Rights Treaty Bodies: A Perspective from a Treaty Body Member, American Society of International Law Proceedings 105 (2011), 512, 514; *O'Flaherty*, The United Nations Human Rights Treaty Bodies as Diplomatic Actors, in: O'Flaherty et al. (eds.), Human Rights Diplomacy: Contemporary Perspectives, 2011, p. 164, who notes that the UPR may also bring to the fore that the quality of treaty bodies' concluding observations is not always high.

[362] Which is owed to the fact that States are represented by their diplomatic delegates during the review, *Carraro*, The United Nations Treaty Bodies and Universal Periodic Review: Advancing Human Rights by Preventing Politicization?, Human Rights Quarterly, 39 (2017), 943, 944.

[363] *Collister*, Rituals and implementation in the Universal Periodic Review and the human rights treaty bodies, in: Charlesworth/Larking (eds.), Human Rights and the Universal Periodic Review, 2015, p. 116; *Gaer*, A Voice Not an Echo: Universal Periodic Review and the UN Treaty Body System, Human Rights Law Review 7 (2007), 109, 125.

[364] *Rodley*, UN treaty bodies and the Human Rights Council, in: Keller/Ulfstein (eds.), UN Human Rights Treaty Bodies: Law and Legitimacy, 2012, p. 328.

[365] *Rivera*, The UN Human Rights Council: Achievements and Challenges in Its First

ing recommendations adopted by treaty bodies more visible at both, the national and the international level.[366] While a politicized atmosphere may not seem quite appropriate for a forum dedicated to the implementation of human rights, its positive side-effect is that State parties apparently are more willing to participate in the process.[367]

With a view to possible rejections of recommendations previously adopted by treaty bodies, it has been rightly stated that a State remains bound by its international treaty obligations, and, from a purely legal point of view, discussions in the UPR cannot lead to the invalidation of treaty body pronouncements.[368] In addition, it is one thing for State parties to potentially undermine the authority of treaty bodies, but it is another for them to seize every opportunity to do so. Ultimately, it is also not essential that all treaty body recommendations are congruently repeated under the UPR, but that a further mechanism exists which can close, or at least shorten, reporting gaps before the monitoring bodies in the event of establishing an eight-year reporting calendar. In this sense, the UPR lives up to its complementary role to the work of the Committees.

V. Conclusion on the comprehensive reporting calendar

As has become apparent from the discussions among the various Committees, the introduction of a comprehensive reporting calendar with fixed and aligned periodicities across the whole treaty body system seems to be a project that causes more controversies than one might have guessed. Even though all Committees have at some point allowed State parties to combine several outstanding reports, postponed reviews and have thereby de facto extended reporting periodicities, it seems that a definite commitment to realistic reporting intervals, i.e. of seven to eight years, was for a long time still a long way off; this might change when treaty bodies will continue to discuss modalities for the proposed eight-year calendar.

With a view to the treaty bodies' powers in this matter, the extension of reporting intervals is covered by their mandate, although at first glance treaty provisions in their literal meaning indicate exactly the opposite. Admittedly, any extension to seven or eight years could result in very broad reporting gaps, let

---

Decade, in: Oberleitner (ed.), International Human Rights Institutions, Tribunals, and Courts, 2018, p. 59.

[366] *Ramcharan*, Modernizing the UN Human Rights System, 2019, p. 174.

[367] *Carraro*, The United Nations Treaty Bodies and Universal Periodic Review: Advancing Human Rights by Preventing Politicization?, Human Rights Quarterly, 39 (2017), 943, 967; *Chauville*, The Universal Periodic Review's first cycle: successes and failures, in: Charlesworth/Larking (eds.), Human Rights and the Universal Periodic Review, 2014, p. 91, who observes that the UPR may also serve to encourage State parties to report to treaty bodies.

[368] *Collister*, Rituals and implementation in the Universal Periodic Review and the human rights treaty bodies, in: Charlesworth/Larking (eds.), Human Rights and the Universal Periodic Review, 2014, p. 119.

alone the fact that non-reporting and thus delinquent State parties would be completely absent for a considerable period of time. However, the grouping of treaty bodies in two clusters, coupled with possible synergies under the UPR, and additionally provided that the follow-up procedure offers another possibility for State parties and Committees to enter in dialogue, the risk already seems to be less relevant. Particularly with a view to non-compliant State parties, treaty bodies need to develop a more robust approach if they would like to uphold any possible comprehensive calendar scheme. The following section will thus analyse one promising path in this matter.

D. Reviews in the absence of a report

In the case of introducing a comprehensive reporting calendar, it is of great importance to secure abidance by State parties. Non-compliance by State parties in the past has caused disruption and can easily render any careful coordination undertaken in advance futile. It is therefore essential to explore ways and means how to uphold a comprehensive reporting calendar in the quite likely event of non-compliance by State parties with regard to their periodic reporting obligations. The most promising device in this matter appears to be reviews in the absence of a report.

By now, all treaty bodies have added provisions to their Rules of Procedure which deal with constantly delinquent State parties that have not submitted their reports in due time. Nevertheless, the various codifications and procedures developed differ among the various human rights treaty bodies and do not provide a particularly consistent overall picture. As a bottom-line, each Committee requires the Secretariat to provide information on all cases of non-submitted reports prior to the respective Committee session. Another common denominator is that each treaty body may transmit a reminder to the State parties concerned, by which they are called on to submit the outstanding reports. Beyond this, the procedures are varying and arguably reflect different evolutionary stages as regards reviews of State parties in the absence of a report.

Before turning to legal arguments which might argue for or against regularly conducted reviews in the absence of a report, the practice by treaty bodies and its development shall be explored in more detail. The Committees' practice merits closer attention, as it sometimes does not correspond to the procedures provided for by the respective Rules of Procedure, and only closer scrutiny will allow to portray the slightly varying approaches.

I. Practice by treaty bodies

1. CERD Committee

The first treaty body to introduce the possibility of monitoring State parties in absence of a report was the CERD Committee in 1991.[369] According to the Committee's decision, those State parties whose periodic reports were "excessively overdue" would be reviewed on the basis of the last reports submitted and the resulting considerations made by the Committee.[370]

In 1996, the Committee extended the approach to initial reports which were overdue for more than five years. Representatives of a non-compliant State party should be invited to participate in the considerations and the review would be based on all information submitted by the respective State party "to other organs of the United Nations", or, if these neither non-available, be based on "reports and information prepared by organs of the United Nations."[371]

While the Committee has quite regularly *considered* State parties in the absence of a report, concluding observations as such were only adopted in a few cases. Between the introduction of its method in reaction to non-compliant State parties and the end of 1998, 53 State parties were considered in the absence of a report.[372] However, as the outcome of these considerations, State parties were only invited to submit their overdue reports within a specified time frame and were additionally advised to avail themselves of technical assistance provided by the advisory service of the High Commissioner for Human Rights.[373]

It was not until 2004 that the Committee adopted for the first time *provisional* concluding observations vis-à-vis a delinquent State party. The case of Saint Lucia, which had ratified the Convention in 1990 and failed to submit its initial report ever since, led the Committee to the decision to adopt provisional concluding observations. These were made public and bore great resemblance to concluding observations under the standard reporting procedure. They contained both elements of approval and areas of concern.[374] In 2007, the Committee adopt-

---

[369] Report of the Committee on the Elimination of Racial Discrimination (39th and 40th session), UN Doc. A/46/18 (1992), para. 27; *Egan*, The United Nations Human Rights Treaty System: Law and Procedure, 2011, p. 149.

[370] Report of the Committee on the Elimination of Racial Discrimination (39th and 40th session), UN Doc. A/46/18 (1992), para. 27.

[371] Report of the Committee on the Elimination of Racial Discrimination (48th and 49th session), UN Doc. A/51/18 (1996), para. 608.

[372] *Vandenhole*, The Procedures Before the UN Human Rights Treaty Bodies: Divergence or Convergence?, 2004, p. 84; Report of the Committee on the Elimination of Racial Discrimination (54th and 55th session), UN Doc. A/54/18 (1999), Letter of transmittal.

[373] See for three sets of very similar considerations adopted vis-à-vis State parties in the absence of a report, Report of the Committee on the Elimination of Racial Discrimination (50th and 51st session), UN Doc. A/52/18 (1997), for Rwanda paras. 370–373, for the Seychelles paras. 374–376 and for Mongolia paras. 377–379.

[374] Report of the Committee on the Elimination of Racial Discrimination (64th and 65th session), UN Doc. A/59/18 (2004), paras. 434–458.

ed concluding observations on Ethiopia in the absence of a report, which were modelled after regular concluding observations[375] and in 2012 the Committee proceeded in the same vein as regards Belize,[376] yet without labelling these two sets of concluding observations as being provisional.

2. CESCR Committee

The first State party to be reviewed in the absence of a report under the ICESCR was Kenya in 1993.[377] At its sixth session, the Committee decided to introduce a review procedure for persistent non-reporting State parties, applicable to both initial and periodic reports.[378] Priority would be given to State parties whose reports were "considerably overdue on the basis of the length of time involved".[379]

At its thirty-sixth session, the Committee further accentuated its approach by dividing overdue State parties in three groups:[380] State parties whose reports were due within the past eight years, due from eight to twelve years ago, and State parties with reports due more than twelve years. Each State party, regardless of its classification, would receive a maximum up to three reminders before the review in the absence of a report would take place "in light of all available information."[381]

In practice, the examination of State parties in the absence of a report has remained a rare exception. More recent activities indicate an even more regressive attitude towards reviews without having received a State report beforehand. The consensus among Committee members now seems to be rather to seek other ways and means by which to secure reporting compliance, such as deriving possible benefit from the universal periodic review or to strengthen national mechanisms.[382]

---

[375] CERD Committee, Concluding Observations of the Committee on the Elimination of Racial Discrimination on Ethiopia, UN Doc. CERD/C/ETH/CO/15, 09.03.2007.

[376] CERD Committee, Concluding observations on Belize, adopted by the Committee under the review procedure at its eighty-first session, CERD/C/BLZ/CO/1, 03.05.2013.

[377] *Kretzmer*, The UN Human Rights Committee and International Human Rights Monitoring, Straus Institute Working Paper No. 12, 2010, p. 37.

[378] CESCR Committee, Report on the Seventh Session, UN Doc. E/1993/22 (1993), para. 40.

[379] CESCR Committee, Report on the Seventh Session, UN Doc. E/1993/22 (1993), para. 41.

[380] *Odello/Seatzu*, The UN Committee on Economic, Social and Cultural Rights: The Law, Process and Practice, 2013, p. 163.

[381] CESCR Committee, Report on the thirty-sixth and thirty-seventh sessions, UN Doc. E/2007/22 (2007), para. 42.

[382] CESCR Committee, Sixty-fifth session, Summary record (partial) of the 29th meeting, 8 March 2019, at 11.40 a.m., UN Doc. E/C.12/2019/SR.29, 15.03.2019, para. 10; *Alston*, The Committee on Economic, Social and Cultural Rights, in: Mégret/Alston (eds.), The United Nations and Human Rights: A Critical Appraisal, Second Edition, 2020, p. 451; this assumption is further bolstered by the 2021 annual report of the Committee, which leaves the impression that the Committee is following a cooperative rather than a confrontational ap-

3. CRC Committee

At its seventh session in 1994, the CRC Committee provided an overview of its reporting procedure and included the statement that "the Committee may decide to consider the situation in the country in the absence of a report, but on the basis of all available information."[383] Although the Committee has in the past occasionally sent reminders and "warned" State parties that their examination would take place in the absence of a report,[384] it never resorted to such a measure.[385] Somewhat opaque are the CRC Committee's Rules of Procedure. Pursuant to article 71(2) RoP CRC, it "shall consider the situation as it deems necessary". This could either signify that the Committee will thoroughly examine the situation in the State party concerned, with the eventual adoption of concluding observations, or, alternatively, that it will further seek the submission of reports by invoking other means. Given the Committee's reluctance to resort to reviews in the absence of a report, article 71(2) RoP CRC very likely refers to other means to persuade State parties to submit overdue report.

4. Committee against Torture

Even though already deliberating on the possibility of reviewing State parties in the absence of a report in 1998,[386] the Committee against Torture first amended its Rules of Procedure at its 28th session in 2002. Thereby it established a "mechanism" to handle non-reporting States and those who failed to send a delegation to the Committee's meetings.[387] The then newly adopted article 65(3) RoP CAT[388] provided that the Committee might notify State parties in "appropriate cases" that it intends "to examine the measures taken by the State party to protect or

---

proach, with Committee members entering in dialogue with delinquent State parties, CESCR Committee, Report on the sixty-seventh and sixty-eighth sessions, UN Doc. E/2021/22 (2021), paras. 44–45.

[383] CRC Committee, Overview of the reporting procedures, UN Doc. CRC/C/33, 24.10.1994, para. 32.

[384] *Vandenhole*, The Procedures before the UN Human Rights Treaty Bodies: Divergence or Convergence?, 2004, p. 150.

[385] *Evans*, The Committee on the Rights of the Child, in: Mégret/Alston (eds.), The United Nations and Human Rights: A Critical Appraisal, Second Edition, 2020, p. 530.

[386] *Byrnes*, The Committee against Torture and the Subcommittee for the Prevention of Torture, in: Mégret/Alston (eds.), The United Nations and Human Rights: A Critical Appraisal, Second Edition, 2020, p. 483.

[387] Report of the Committee against Torture (27th and 28th session), UN Doc. A/57/44, (2002), paras. 15 and 16; *Monina*, Article 19, State Reporting Procedure, in: Nowak/Birk/Monina (eds.), The United Nations Convention Against Torture and its Optional Protocol: A Commentary, Second Edition, 2019, paras. 103–105.

[388] Committee against Torture, Rules of Procedure, UN Doc. CAT/C/3/Rev.4, 09.08.2002; in its most recent Rules of Procedure the procedure is provided by article RoP 67(3), Committee against Torture, Rules of Procedure, UN Doc. CAT/C/3/Rev.6, 01.09.2014.

give effect to the rights recognized in the Convention, and make such general comments as it deems appropriate in the circumstances." It took the Committee, however, another 14 years until the procedure was eventually applied with regard to an initial periodic report.[389] So far, the Committee has reviewed only four State parties in the absence of a report[390] and it appears that the Committee is more inclined to keep on sending reminders, or to seek other ways and means by which to ensure the submission of periodic and initial State reports. Notably, the Committee offers long overdue State parties the adherence to the simplified reporting procedure in order to avoid reviews in the absence of a report.[391]

5. Human Rights Committee

The same year as the Committee against Torture, the Human Rights Committee amended its Rules of Procedure and introduced a procedure for dealing with non-reporting State parties and State parties who required a postponement of their scheduled appearance before the Committee at short notice.[392] The newly adopted Rule of Procedure provided for the possibility to monitor a State party's implementation measures in private session, and to adopt provisional concluding observations. A precondition was that the State party had remained constantly non-compliant despite having received reminders to finally submit the required report.[393] These provisional concluding observations would subsequently be transmitted to the State party concerned for possible comments.

The procedure has undergone several changes since then. While originally foreseeing the possibility of adopting provisional concluding observations in private sessions and submitted to the State party concerned only, the Committee first introduced the option of turning provisional concluding observations into final concluding observations made public, with the possibility that State parties

---

[389] *Byrnes*, The Committee against Torture and the Subcommittee for the Prevention of Torture, in: Mégret/Alston (eds.), The United Nations and Human Rights: A Critical Appraisal, Second Edition, 2020, p. 484; in 2012, however, the Committee had already reviewed Syria in the absence of report, although not in relation to a periodic report, but in relation to a special report, Committee against Torture, Consideration by the Committee against Torture of the implementation of the Convention in the Syrian Arab Republic in the absence of a special report requested pursuant to article 19, paragraph 1, UN Doc. CAT/C/SYR/CO/1/Add.2, 29.06.2012.

[390] Report of the Committee against Torture (71st, 72nd and 73rd session), UN Doc. A/77/44 (2022), para. 31, with a short overview of the Committee's practice in that matter so far.

[391] Report of the Committee against Torture (69th and 70th session), UN Doc. A/76/44 (2021), para. 29.

[392] *Schabas*, U.N. International Covenant on Civil and Political Rights, Nowak's CCPR Commentary, Third revised Edition, 2019, Article 40, State Reports, para 7; Report of the Human Rights Committee (73rd, 74th and 75th session), UN Doc. A/57/40 Vol. I (2002), paras. 53–54.

[393] Article 69A RoP, Human Rights Committee, Rules of Procedure, UN Doc. CCPR/C/3/Rev. 6, 24.04.2001.

could first submit comments on the provisional concluding observations.[394] In 2011, the Human Rights Committee then moved on to conduct public reviews in the absence of a report, with the adoption of concluding observations as public documents immediately afterwards.[395]

This development represents a significant step. The Committee did not wait anymore for a State party's response before publishing its findings as conclusive outcome documents. The approach is in line with the general assertion that the Committees consider themselves as robust and strong monitoring bodies. Since 2019, the Human Rights Committee links the simplified reporting procedure to possible reviews in the absence of a report. Non-compliant State parties will receive a list of issues with topics the Committee will examine and to which the State party can react, thus allowing State parties one last chance to submit their information.[396] As of March 2019, the Human Rights Committee has initiated 24 State reviews in the absence of report, and several review in absence procedures are either pending or have been recently initiated by the Committee.[397]

6. CEDAW Committee

The CEDAW Committee was initially "hesitant" to adopt similar measures in cases of chronically non-reporting State parties, but revised its position at its 31st session. It decided to follow suit of other Committees.[398] This, however, only as a measure of last resort and in the presence of a delegation.[399] The Committee further clarified that it would decide on an individual case-by-case basis which State party to review in the absence of a report and that other efforts, such as notifications and further invitations should proceed this ultima ratio.[400] In 2009, the Committee monitored the Convention's implementation for the first time in the absence of a report but with a delegation being present.[401] In other cases of long overdue reports, the Committee sought first to persuade State parties to submit reports by other means, which is in conformity with its "last-resort-ap-

---

[394] Article 70(3) RoP, Human Rights Committee, Rules of Procedure, UN Doc. CCPR/C/3/Rev. 7, 04.08.2004.

[395] Article 70, RoP, Human Rights Committee, Rules of Procedure UN Doc. CCPR/C/3/Rev. 10, 11.01.2012.

[396] Article 71(2) RoP, Human Rights Committee, Rules of Procedure, UN Doc. CCPR/C/3/Rev. 11, 09.01.2019.

[397] Report of the Human Rights Committee (123rd, 124th and 125th session), UN Doc. A/74/40 (2019), paras. 65–67.

[398] *Boerefijn*, Article 18, in: Freeman/Chinkin/Rudolf (eds.), The UN Convention on the Elimination of All Forms of Discrimination Against Women: A Commentary, 2012, p. 493.

[399] *Boerefijn*, Article 18, in: Freeman/Chinkin/Rudolf (eds.), The UN Convention on the Elimination of All Forms of Discrimination Against Women: A Commentary, 2012, p. 493.

[400] Report of the Committee on the Elimination of Discrimination Against Women (30th and 31st session), UN Doc. A/59/38 (2004), para. 439.

[401] *Egan*, The United Nations Human Rights Treaty System: Law and Procedure, 2011, pp. 163–164.

proach". Generally, it seems little inclined to eventually proceed with the examination of a State party in the absence of a report.[402]

7. CMW Committee

In 2012, the CMW Committee changed its Rules of Procedure and also established a mechanism to consider State parties in the absence of a report.[403] Article 31bis of its Rules of Procedure at the time stipulated that the Committee might notify a non-compliant State party that it would conduct a review in the absence of report in public session, and that the resulting concluding observations would be made public afterwards.[404] Furthermore, the Committee combines the simplified reporting procedure with the examination of State parties in the absence of a report. According to its current Rules of Procedure, a State party may also receive a list of issues as to the main matters to be examined which then shall be considered as the requested report.[405] Hence, the Committee seemed to draw upon experience by other treaty bodies and directly adopted the procedure deployed by the Human Rights Committee without a similar evolutionary process as portrayed above.

So far, the CMW Committee has examined five countries in the absence of a report.[406] Taking into account the relatively short period of time during which the Committee has used the newly developed review procedure to date, and the fact that significantly fewer countries are members to the CMW, as compared to the ICCPR or ICESCR for example, it becomes obvious that the CMW Committee is less hesitant in examining State parties in the absence of a report.

8. CED Committee

The CED Committee, to the best of the author's knowledge, has not yet examined State parties in the absence of a report, though the Committee's Rules of Procedure provide for this specific review procedure as well.[407] Interesting to note

---

[402] See *Byrnes*, The Committee on the Elimination of Discrimination Against Women, in: Mégret/Alston (eds.), The United Nations and Human Rights: A Critical Appraisal, Second Edition, 2020, p. 407, who observes that most State parties were prompted to submit their overdue reports or that the Committee did not review them in the absence of a report in the final analysis.

[403] Report of the Committee on the Protection of the Rights of All Migrant Workers and Members of Their Families (15th and 16th session), UN Doc. A/67/48 (2012), para. 26.

[404] The rule corresponds to the currently existing rule in this matter.

[405] Article 34(2) RoP, CMW Committee, Rules of Procedure, UN Doc. CMW/C/2, 08.02.2019.

[406] These countries are Belize, Cabo Verde, Jamaica, Nigeria and Saint Vincent and the Grenadines, Report of the Committee on the Protection of the Rights of All Migrant Workers and Members of Their Families (33rd and 34th session), UN Doc. A/77/48 (2022), Annex II.

[407] Article 50 RoP, Committee on Enforced Disappearances, Rules of Procedure, UN Doc. CED/C/1, 22.06.2012.

D. Reviews in the absence of a report 219

is that the Committee decided to initiate examinations of State parties in the absence of a report only when reports were five years overdue.[408] Furthermore, it follows the approach developed by other treaty bodies in sending specific list of issues to the State parties as a last means of ensuring the submission of any kind of written statement.[409]

9. CRPD Committee

Finally, the CRPD Committee is already vested, by virtue of its treaty, with the power to monitor a State party in the absence of a report. Article 36(2) CRPD establishes that whenever a State party is "significantly overdue" in the submission of a report, the Committee may notify the State party that it is going to examine the implementation of the Convention on the basis of reliable information available to the Committee if the State party does not submit the requested report within three months following the notification. Thus, the treaty itself authorizes the Committee "to take a more proactive role in addressing delinquency in reporting by state parties"[410] and what may be an effective means in terms of making State parties to respect their reporting obligations.[411] Nevertheless, no use of the procedure has been reported yet.[412]

10. Evaluation

Common to the practice among all treaty bodies is that examinations in the absence of a report are rather the exception than the rule.[413] All Committees first seek to persuade State parties to submit a report, on the basis of which the review process should primarily take place. This is done for example either by means of sending notifications, further reminders, or by the offer to avail oneself of the simplified reporting procedure. When initiating reviews in the absence of a re-

---

[408] Report of the Committee on Enforced Disappearances (13th and 14th session), UN Doc. A/73/56 (2018), para. 13(g).

[409] See for instance, CED Committee, List of issues in the absence of the report of Mali due under article 29 (1) of the Convention, UN Doc. CED/C/MLI/QAR/1, 25.09.2020; List of issues in the absence of the report of Nigeria due under article 29 (1) of the Convention, UN Doc. CED/C/NGA/QAR/1, 13.11.2019.

[410] *Stein/Lord*, Monitoring the Convention on the Rights of Persons with Disabilities: Innovations, Lost Opportunities, and Future Potential, Human Rights Quarterly 32 (2010), 689, 724.

[411] *Combrinck*, Article 36, Consideration of Reports, in: Bantekas/Stein/Anastasiou (eds.), The UN Convention on the Rights of Persons with Disabilities: A Commentary, 2018, p. 1079.

[412] *Combrinck*, Article 36, Consideration of Reports, in: Bantekas/Stein/Anastasiou (eds.), The UN Convention on the Rights of Persons with Disabilities: A Commentary, 2018, p. 1079, to the best of the author's knowledge, this still holds true.

[413] *Combrinck*, Article 36, Consideration of Reports, in: Bantekas/Stein/Anastasiou (eds.), The UN Convention on the Rights of Persons with Disabilities: A Commentary, 2018, p. 1079.

port, most of the Committees focus on long-overdue State parties.[414] Nevertheless, there seems to be a tendency, at least among the Human Rights Committee and the CMW Committee, to make more frequent use of the procedure. Other treaty bodies, such as the Committee against Torture or the CESCR Committee, on the other hand, seem less inclined towards monitoring implementation in the absence of a report. These Committees rely on softer measures and cooperative approaches when confronted with delinquent State parties.[415]

Particularly revealing for the evolution of the process are the changes made to the Rules of Procedure of the Human Rights Committee. Its rules gradually evolved from providing for the consideration of a State party in closed sessions only, to the adoption of standard concluding observations and making them publicly available. The Human Rights Committee can thus be taken as a front-runner in the development of a more pro-active approach in dealing with the problem of persistently non-compliant State parties. With a view to the alignment of working methods, other treaty bodies should be advised to amend their Rules of Procedure accordingly.

II. Developments at the Meeting of Chairpersons

This overall reticent attitude by treaty bodies is further reflected by discussions at the inter-Committee level. The topic of reviews in the absence of a report has recently only sporadically surfaced at Meetings of Chairpersons.[416] Besides agreeing on the procedure's positive impact on long overdue State parties in submitting their outstanding reports,[417] the topic was not examined or discussed in any detail.

---

[414] Inter-Committee Meeting, Report on the working methods of the human rights treaty bodies relating to the State party reporting process, UN Doc. HRI/ICM/2011/4, 23.05.2011, para. 91.

[415] Interestingly, when Israel failed to participate in the universal periodic review on the scheduled date, the Human Rights Council called upon Israel to participate and decided to reschedule its review. Explicit mention of possible reviews in the absence of a State party is not included in the decision, Human Rights Council, Report of the Human Rights Council on its seventh organizational meeting, OM/7/101, Non-cooperation of a State under review with the universal periodic review mechanism, UN Doc. A/HRC/OM/7/1, 04.04.2013.

[416] See, however, as far as earlier meetings are concerned, Report of the chairpersons of the human rights treaty bodies on their twenty-first meeting, UN Doc. A/64/276, 10.08.2009, Annex II, Report of the ninth inter-committee meeting of human rights treaty bodies, para. 11, where the participating treaty body members highlighted the procedure's impact on non-reporting State parties, with the simultaneous remark that its application should remain a measure of last resort.

[417] See for instance, Report of the Chairs of the human rights treaty bodies on their twenty-seventh meeting, UN Doc. A/70/302, 07.08.2015, para. 28; Report of the Chairs of the human rights treaty bodies on their 29th meeting, UN Doc. A/72/177, 20.07.2017, para. 8.

In 2016, the Chairs adopted their first recent decision concerning reviews in the absence of a report. It was recommended that treaty bodies consider the introduction of said review procedure, but only in relation to *very long overdue* reports.[418] Interestingly, the 2019 adopted position paper of the Chairs on the future of the treaty body system provides for regular reviews in the absence of a report conducted by both Covenant Committees.[419]

Yet, the proposal appears to be at odds with the observation made above that the CESCR Committee takes a hesitant position in this matter. It also somewhat contradicts the recommendation contained in the possible elements for a common aligned procedure for the simplified reporting procedure. According to the latter, "Committees should discuss whether to consider the activities of States parties in the field of human rights in the absence of a report and should consider aligning their practices in that regard".[420] But then again, what is surprising is that in 2020 the Chairs proposed that both, Covenant and Convention Committees establish a review cycle with review schedules, "whether reporting or not reporting".[421] Taking into consideration these diverging and to a certain extent contradicting statements, it must be assumed that the Chairs have not yet reached any definite conclusion in this matter and that reviews in the absence of a report are a delicate topic that is rather reluctantly tackled.[422]

III. Legal mandate of treaty bodies with regard to reviews in the absence of a report

As analysed in the previous section, reviews in the absence of a report constitute currently rather the exception than the rule. Treaty bodies proceed only very carefully when they intend to monitor a State party's human rights record without having received a report beforehand. In the event of establishing a comprehensive reporting calendar, regardless of its ultimate design, treaty bodies would probably need to apply this specific review procedure more often, since postpone-

---

[418] Report of the Chairs of the human rights treaty bodies on their twenty-eighth meeting, UN Doc. A/71/270, 02.08.2016, para. 82.

[419] Report of the Chairs of the human rights treaty bodies on their thirty-first annual meeting, UN Doc. A/74/256, 30.07.2019, Annex III, Position paper of the Chairs of the human rights treaty bodies on the future of the treaty body system.

[420] Report of the Chairs of the human rights treaty bodies on their thirty-first annual meeting, UN Doc. A/74/256, 30.07.2019, Annex II, para. (h).

[421] Report of the Chairs of the human rights treaty bodies on their thirty-second annual meeting, UN Doc. A/75/346, 14.09.2020, paras. 46(g) and (h).

[422] In this context, it is also interesting to note that the 2022 conclusions only indirectly refer to regular reviews in the absence of a report, see Report of the Chairs of the human rights treaty bodies on their thirty-fourth annual meeting, UN Doc. A/77/228, 26.07.2022, para. 55 No. 1 (g).

ments and rescheduling of State parties' examinations would cause the collapse of a comprehensive reporting calendar.[423]

This gives rise to the question of whether treaty bodies possess, in addition to the power of changing the periodicities provided for in the treaties, the additional power to review a non-compliant State party without having access to the respective State report, not as a means of last resort, but as a means to ensure *regular monitoring* of all State parties.[424]

In this regard, it has been critically noted that such an approach would contradict the "current normative basis of the Committees' work, since there is no mention of the possibility of a review in the absence of a report in the human rights treaties, [except for the CRPD]."[425] Less explicit, but still alluding to criticism of reviews in the absence of a report, are various voices in the ongoing strengthening process. For instance, the submission of the African Group and Bahrain stated that the "principle of genuine cooperation and dialogue with State parties" constituted one of the main pillars of a functional and efficient treaty body system.[426] Other State parties even took a firmer stance and criticized treaty bodies for operating beyond their mandate, as they did not give due consideration to a State party's report.[427]

1. Text-based interpretation

First and foremost, the finding that the wording does not provide for any such competence is incontestable.[428] Even article 36(2) CRPD might not necessarily

---

[423] See *supra* Part IV C.I.

[424] Noting as well that the procedure has raised questions, *Boerefijn*, Article 18, in: Freeman/Chinkin/Rudolf (eds.), The UN Convention on the Elimination of All Forms of Discrimination Against Women: A Commentary, 2012, p. 493; see also *Kretzmer*, Human Rights, State Reports, in: Peters (ed.), Max Planck Encyclopedia of Public International Law, Online version, October 2008, para. 32, who observes that "it is not at all clear that treaty bodies […] are authorized by the conventions" to review State parties in the absence of a report.

[425] *Abashidze/Koneva*, The Process of Strengthening the Human Rights Treaty Body System: The Road towards Effectiveness or Inefficiency?, Netherlands International Law Review 66 (2019), 357, 380.

[426] Submission of the African Group and Bahrain, The Consideration of the State of the Human Rights Treaty Body System, para. 2, https://www.ohchr.org/en/calls-for-input/co-facilitation-process-treaty-body-review-2020 (last access: 21.08.2023); see also the Position of the Russian Federation regarding the review of the implementation of provisions of UN GA Resolutions 68/268 on Strengthening and Enhancing the Effective Functioning of the Human Rights Treaty Body System, available under the same link as cited above.

[427] Submission by the Government of People's Republic of China, On the Consideration of the State of the UN Human Rights Treaty Body System, https://www.ohchr.org/en/calls-for-input/co-facilitation-process-treaty-body-review-2020 (last access: 21.08.2023); see also the Pakistani submission, available under the same link, in which it is stated that "State parties responses should be considered with particular status, respect and responsibility."

[428] In this regard, *Crawford* has noted that non-compliant State parties cannot be "cen-

enable the CRPD Committee to conduct *regular* reviews in the absence of a report. The provision only vests the Committee with the power to apply the procedure vis-à-vis State parties which are "significantly overdue". The latter presents itself as a vague legal term and leaves the Committee with discretion in its interpretation.[429] Given the very wording, "significantly overdue" corresponds rather to a situation in which a State party has been non-compliant for several years. The treaty provision in its literal meaning hence does not vest the Committee with the power to examine a State party in the absence of report on a regular basis. Besides, and in analogy to the discussion on the simplified reporting procedure's application, other treaty provisions governing the State reporting procedure might bar treaty bodies from conducting reviews in the absence of a report on a regular basis.

a) Sources of information according to treaty provisions

Common to many UN human rights core treaties is the fact that concluding observations are adopted in reaction to, and are hence based on, the examination of the reports and information received from State parties.[430] A strict reading of these provisions may thus suggest that the treaty bodies lack the necessary mandate to conduct reviews without any report at hand, or that State parties must at least have submitted an initial report.[431] Less rigid in terms of basing recommendations on State parties' reports are article 40(4) ICCPR, article 29(3) CED and article 74(1) CMW, all of which provide for the Committees to review reports, but do not explicitly link the transmission of comments to the reports studied beforehand. However, of course, here too, the primary basis for the respective recommendations are the reports received from State parties. Additionally, and context-wise, the above-mentioned sequence of actions under the reporting procedure, with treaty bodies reacting, must be borne in mind.

---

sored" by means other than notifying the delays in the Committees' annual reports or by calls made by the UN General Assembly, *Crawford*, The UN human rights treaty system: A system in crisis?, in: Alston/Crawford (eds.), The Future of UN Human Rights Treaty Monitoring, 2000, p. 4.

[429] *Combrinck*, Article 36, Consideration of Reports, in: Bantekas/Stein/Anastasiou (eds.), The UN Convention on the Rights of Persons with Disabilities: A Commentary, 2018, p. 1079.

[430] Article 9(2) CERD and article 21(1) CEDAW *verbatim*: "The Committee [...] may make suggestions and general recommendations based on the examination of the reports and information received from the States Parties."; article 19(3) CAT: "Each report shall be considered by the Committee which may make such general comments on the report as it may consider appropriate and shall forward these to the State Party concerned." Article 36(1) CRPD: "Each report shall be considered by the Committee, which shall make such suggestions and general recommendations on the report as it may consider appropriate and shall forward these to the State Party concerned."

[431] *Thornberry*, Confronting Racial Discrimination: A CERD Perspective, Human Rights Law Review 5 (2005), 239, 245 with further reference to *Banton*, International Action Against Racial Discrimination, 1996, p. 151.

b) Committees with a wider mandate

Interesting to note is article 74(7) CMW,[432] which obliges the CMW Committee to present an annual report to the General Assembly of the United Nations, and which bears strong textual resemblance to article 9(2) CERD and article 21(1) CEDAW. The latter two are those provisions which are invoked to justify the respective Committee's mandate to adopt concluding observations, whereas the CMW Committee derives its authority in this domain from article 74(1) CMW. Nevertheless, the specific feature about article 74(7) CMW is that the Committee is required to include in its annual reports its own considerations and recommendations, based, *in particular*,[433] on the examination of the reports and any observations presented by State parties. In other words, the Committee is asked to report on its monitoring activities, and to include concluding observations. These, in turn, are to be based on reports and observations received from State parties, but only "in particular", which implies nothing else than that they could possibly be also based on any other source of information.

Finally, the CRC Committee is probably by virtue of its constituent treaty the Committee with the widest mandate to base concluding observations on other sources of information. Article 45(d) CRC authorizes the Committee to make suggestions and general recommendations based on information received pursuant to articles 44 and 45 CRC. Whereas article 44 CRC stipulates the standard reporting procedure, information received pursuant to article 45 CRC contains expert advice given by specialized agencies, the United Nations Children's Fund and other competent bodies. Especially the notion of "other competent bodies" could be construed quite broadly. In practice, it already comprises information from NGOs and regional organizations, such as the Council of Europe or the African Union.[434] Interestingly, even though its constituent treaty provides the CRC Committee with more possible sources of information to rely on, it is the only treaty body which has never resorted to reviews in the absence of a report so far.[435]

---

[432] The wording of article 74(7) CMW is as follows: The Committee shall present an annual report to the General Assembly of the United Nations on the implementation of the present Convention, containing its own considerations and recommendations, based, in particular, on the examination of the reports and any observations presented by States Parties.

[433] Emphasis added by the author.

[434] *Schmahl*, Kinderrechtskonventionen mit Zusatzprotokollen, Handkommentar, Zweite Auflage, 2017, Artikel 44/45, para. 18; *Verheyde/Goedertier*, A Commentary on the United Nations Convention on the Rights of the Child, Articles 43–45: The UN Committee on the Rights of the Child, 2006, p. 32; *Lansdown*, The reporting process under the Convention on the Rights of the Child, in: Alston/Crawford (eds.), The Future of UN Human Rights Treaty Monitoring, 2000, p. 119, who notes that the Committee actively makes use of this option and thereby receives more critical information from NGOs.

[435] See *supra* Part IV D.I.3.

In conclusion, those who highlight the missing legal basis for reviews in the absence of a report might be correct at first sight, though with some restrictions as regards the CMW and the CRC. What is more, State parties participating under the reporting procedure might also be entitled to be heard and to present their progress achieved in the implementation of the respective treaty.[436] This is in line with the argument that possible regular reviews of a State party in the absence of a report "[undermine] the principle of constructive cooperation between the treaty bodies and States."[437] Indeed, under the premise that the two main objectives of State reporting are self-evaluation and the creation of international accountability, self-evaluation under the guidance of treaty bodies would recede into the background if treaty bodies were to realize a comprehensive reporting calendar with regular reviews in the absence of a report.

2. Effectiveness-orientated interpretation

On the other hand, focusing on a cooperative approach should not come at the expense of any monitoring activity at all. It would be absurd if non-compliant States, who are in constant breach of their reporting obligations, were ultimately able to block and thwart the entire reporting procedure.[438] In this sense, concluding observations in the absence of a report should not be understood as coercive measures or even sanctions.[439] Quite the opposite, they continue to be of crucial importance to State parties, as they provide the basis for any future reporting cycle. To this end, they serve as a basis for possible self-evaluation conducted by the delinquent party, not to mention their particular importance for other stakeholders, such as NGOs.

Furthermore, in light of the fact that all treaty bodies have established formalized follow-up procedures, States parties are continuously able to comment on the observations adopted in the absence of a report and thereby remain in

---

[436] *Ferrajolo*, Articles 34–36, in: Della Fina/Cera/Palmisano (eds.), The United Convention on the Rights of Persons with Disabilities: A Commentary, Cham 2017, p. 629.

[437] *Abashidze/Koneva*, The Process of Strengthening the Human Rights Treaty Body System: The Road towards Effectiveness or Inefficiency?, Netherlands International Law Review 66 (2019), 357, 380.

[438] See *Chetail*, Committee on the Protection of the Rights of All Migrant Workers and Members of their Families (CMW), in: Ruiz Fabri (ed.), Max Planck Encyclopedia of International Procedural Law, Online version, August 2018, para. 20, noting that the failure to submit reports "undermines the primary function" of the Committee on Migrant Workers.

[439] See *Giegling*, Challenges and Chances of a Written State Report: Analysis and Improvement of a Monitoring Instrument on the Implementation of Human Rights, 2021, p. 138, who does not seem to consider reviews in the absence as sanctions, but does not conclusively answer this question either; *Boerefijn*, The Reporting Procedure under the Covenant on Civil and Political Rights: Practice and Procedures of the Human Rights Committee, 1999, p. 253, describing reviews in the absence of a report as "a more severe measure", but she questions at the same time whether delinquent State parties will be "genuinely impressed" by such an approach.

dialogue with treaty bodies. The independent expert *Alston* argued in a similar vein in his final report on the treaty body system.[440] He reached the conclusion that the adoption of concluding observation in the absence of a report was "the only viable option open to the treaty bodies"[441] to handle the situation of overdue reports. Regarding the legal basis for such an approach, *Alston* added that "the principal foundation is to be found in a teleological approach to interpretation".[442] Otherwise, non-compliant State parties would be able to "to defeat the object and purpose of the implementation provisions."[443] Others levelled criticism against such an approach because of the "centrality of the state report" and the "lack of textual support".[444] However, in keeping with the criteria established above, focusing on teleological lines of argumentation seems compelling and possible.

First, reviewing State parties in the absence of a report does not impose new obligations on contracting parties. Second, though the explicit normative basis appears to be weak, this must not obscure the fact that the very existence of treaty bodies is owed to their review and assistance function in the implementation of treaty guarantees. The State reporting procedure is the only mandatory supervisory mechanism among all UN human rights core treaties. It forms the minimum standard in terms of monitoring a treaty's implementation. Ratifying and acceding to human rights treaties logically entails accepting the procedure.

In addition, the introduction of regular reviews in the absence of a report must be considered in conjunction with the introduction of a comprehensive reporting calendar. Non-compliant State parties possibly deprive compliant State parties of their scheduled review dates, and thus of their assistance in implementation.

---

[440] Economic and Social Council, Final report on enhancing the long-term effectiveness of the United Nations human rights treaty system, UN Doc. E/CN.4/1997/74, 27.03.1997.

[441] Economic and Social Council, Final report on enhancing the long-term effectiveness of the United Nations human rights treaty system, UN Doc. E/CN.4/1997/74, 27.03.1997, para. 45; see also *Abashidze*, The Complementary Role of General Comments, in: Bassiouni/Schabas (eds.), New Challenges for the UN Human Rights Machinery, 2011, p. 141, who argues that treaty bodies "have the legitimate right to [...] review the performance of the State in question on the basis of any available information", however without clarifying on which basis exactly.

[442] Economic and Social Council, Final report on enhancing the long-term effectiveness of the United Nations human rights treaty system, UN Doc. E/CN.4/1997/74, 27.03.1997, para. 46; see also *Boerefijn*, Article 18, in: Freeman/Chinkin/Rudolf (eds.), The UN Convention on the Elimination of All Forms of Discrimination Against Women: A Commentary, 2012, p. 493, who refers to reviews in the absence of a report as an implied power, apparently also relying on considerations of effectiveness.

[443] Economic and Social Council, Final report on enhancing the long-term effectiveness of the United Nations human rights treaty system, UN Doc. E/CN.4/1997/74, 27.03.1997, para. 46.

[444] As far as the Convention against Torture is concerned, see *Bank*, Country-orientated procedures under the Convention against Torture: Towards a new dynamism, in: Alston/Crawford (eds.), The Future of UN Human Rights Treaty Monitoring, 2000, p. 148.

Hence, to secure the equal and fair treatment of all State parties taking part in the reporting procedure inevitably requires such action by treaty bodies. Reviews in the absence of a report thus emerge as indispensable in a twofold manner: they are the only means by which to secure any monitoring activity vis-à-vis non-compliant State parties, and they are the only means by which to uphold a comprehensive reporting calendar.

3. Alternative reading of article 36(2) CRPD

As regards article 36(2) CRPD, which entitles the Committee to review "significantly overdue" State parties in the absence of a report, "significantly overdue" cannot amount to any period of more than four years. Four years already constitute the regular reporting periodicity under CRPD. "Significantly overdue" must logically range between one to three years. Given that the Committees will strive for an overall eight-year periodicity, it is not too much to ask for to expect answers to LOIPRs one year after their request, let alone that the date of submission will be all the more predictable in the case of a comprehensive reporting calendar. In addition, "significantly overdue" must not necessarily be understood in a temporal dimension only. It can also be taken to mean what bearing the delay may have on the Committee's workload and the reviews of other contracting parties. If non-submission of reports clearly causes disorder and urges the Committee to spontaneously postpone or prepone reviews of other State parties, this may have *significant* repercussions on a variety of stakeholders and should be thus averted as much as possible. The term can therefore also be understood in the sense that the late submission has a significant impact on the entire reporting system under the Convention.

4. Remaining aspects of concern

a) Actual need to review State parties in the absence of a report

From a purely practical point of view, reviews in the absence of a report would not occur out of nowhere, even in the event of establishing a comprehensive reporting calendar. As analysed above, a master calendar would probably consist of an eight-year cycle.[445] According to the predictable review calendar, as proposed by the Human Rights Committee, a State party would receive its LOIPR in the first year, and would be expected to submit its answers the second year. The review would take place in the third year.[446] Since all Committees meet at least

---

[445] For developments among treaty bodies, see Report of the Chairs of the human rights treaty bodies on their thirty-second annual meeting, UN Doc. A/75/346, 14.09.2020, para. 46(g) with the establishment of an eight-year reporting cycle as far as the Covenant Committees are concerned.

[446] See for the most recent Rules of Procedure, Human Rights Committee, Rules of procedure of the Human Rights Committee, UN Doc. CCPR/C/3/Rev. 12, 04.01.2021, article 73(1) RoP, which stipulates that replies to LOIPRs shall in principle be examined within 12 months of the date of their submission.

biannually, each State party would be given at least one more session to submit its answers, and Committees could send at least a one-time reminder to the delinquent State party.

Furthermore, non-compliance by State parties must not be presumed as a deliberate attempt to avoid international scrutiny. It may well be the result of a lack of corresponding resources at the national level or of other reasons.[447] Hence, if the simplified reporting procedure and the introduction of a master calendar prove helpful in alleviating the reporting burden on State parties, a concomitant decrease of non-submitted reports is likely to be expected.

b) Sources of information for reviews in the absence of a report

Hidden behind the criticism that treaty bodies should focus on State reports is most likely the fear of State parties that in the absence of a report, too much focus could be placed on shadow reports by NGOs or other sources which are considered unreliable in the view of State parties, but which could bring systemic shortfalls and violations of rights more easily to light than the State report itself. The question arises which sources of information treaty bodies should draw on when they examine a State party in the absence of a report. A first point of reference is offered by article 36(2) CRPD, according to which information must be "reliable". Nevertheless, it is a term that certainly requires interpretation.[448] It is also striking that the Human Rights Committee, the CEDAW Committee and the Committee against Torture did not include any specification in their Rules of Procedure as to which sources they will rely on when they examine a State party in the absence of a report.[449]

The CESCR Committee and the CRC Committee have at least explained in their Working Methods that they will rely on all available information,[450] whereas the CMW Committee will only use "reliable information".[451] The CED Com-

---

[447] *Hennebel*, The Human Rights Committee, in: Mégret/Alston (eds.), The United Nations and Human Rights: A Critical Appraisal, Second Edition, 2020, p. 352.

[448] *Combrinck*, Article 36, Consideration of Reports, in: Bantekas/Stein/Anastasiou (eds.), The UN Convention on the Rights of Persons with Disabilities: A Commentary, 2018, p. 1080, arguing that the term "reliable information" can cover both the information submitted by independent monitoring institutions and civil society organizations.

[449] However, the Committee against Torture included provisions of a more general character in its Rules of Procedure with regard to possible sources of information, article 63 RoP CAT; see for the CEDAW Committee, articles 45–47 RoP CEDAW; in the Rules of Procedure adopted by the Human Rights Committee no comparable provisions are to be found. The latter, however, has explained in detail the relevance of NGOs for its work, Human Rights Committee, The relationship of the Human Rights Committee with non-governmental organizations, UN Doc. CCPR/C/104/3, 04.06.2012.

[450] CESCR Committee, Report on the thirty-sixth and thirty-seventh sessions, UN Doc. E/2007/22 (2007), para. 42; CRC Committee, Overview of the reporting procedures, UN Doc. CRC/C/33, 24.10.1994, para. 32.

[451] CMW Committee, Rules of Procedure, UN Doc. CMW/C/2, 08.02.2019, article 34(1) RoP.

mittee included in its Rules of Procedure article 52, which enumerates sources for "alternative reports",[452] but the provision is not expressly linked to the review process in the absence of a report. Still, said provision may suggest which kind of information the Committee will gather when it intends to review a State party without a report. The probably most accurate explanation of alternative sources has been adopted by the CERD Committee. The Committee will first seek to find information that has been submitted by the respective State party to organs of the United Nations. If these are non-existent, the Committee will adhere to information that has been adopted by organs of the United Nations regarding the respective State party.[453]

From the perspective of State parties, the approach of the CERD Committee will most likely be the preferred solution, as this information will be considered "reliable".[454] On the other hand, reports by civil society representatives, NGOs and other stakeholders are of utmost importance to treaty bodies, even when examining State parties under the standard reporting procedure or under the simplified reporting procedure.[455] Hence, treaty bodies will also rely on these sources for reviews in the absence of a report. Treaty bodies could be advised to establish guidelines in which they indicate what kind of information they rely on. Exemplary in that matter is, for instance, the enumeration of possible sources for the adoption of LOIPRs proposed by the Human Rights Committee.[456] Such a

---

[452] Explicit mention is made of "national human rights institutions, non-governmental organizations, associations of families of victims, other relevant civil society organizations, and individual experts", CED Committee, Rules of procedure, UN Doc. CED/C/1, 22.06.2012.

[453] Report of the Committee on the Elimination of Racial Discrimination (48th and 49th session), UN Doc. A/51/18 (1996), para. 608.

[454] Cf. *Mutzenberg*, NGOs, Essential Actors for Embedding Covenants in the National Context, in: Moeckli/Keller/Heri (eds.), The Human Rights Covenants at 50: Their Past, Present, and Future, 2018, p. 79, who describes that it is upon Committee members to monitor and assess the quality of NGO reports and that there have been "relatively few" instances in which NGO information was considered biased and non-independent.

[455] *McGaughey*, From gatekeepers to GONGOs: A taxonomy of Non-Governmental Organisations engaging with United Nations human rights mechanisms, Netherlands Quarterly of Human Rights 36 (2018), 111, 128, who observes that the key role of NGOs is to deliver critical information; generally on the contribution of NGOs to the work of UN human rights treaty bodies, see *Mutzenberg*, NGOs, Essential Actors for Embedding Covenants in the National Context, in: Moeckli/Keller/Heri (eds.), The Human Rights Covenants at 50: Their Past, Present, and Future, 2018, pp. 75–95, who examines the role of NGOs with a view to the reporting procedure, the adoption of General Comments and the individual complaints procedure; *Gaer*, Implementing international human rights norms: UN human rights treaty bodies and NGOs, Journal of Human Rights 2 (2003), 339; *Wiesberg*, The Role of Non-Governmental Organizations (NGOs) in the Protection and Enforcement of Human Rights, in: Symonides (ed.), Human Rights: International Protection, Monitoring, Enforcement, 2003, p. 356, who notes that treaty bodies are "heavily dependent on NGO information".

[456] Human Rights Committee, Focused reports based on replies to lists of issues prior to reporting (LOIPR): Implementation of the new optional reporting procedure (LOIPR procedure), UN Doc. CCPR/C/99/4, 29.09.2010, para. 12.

list could also precisely define which NGOs are entitled to provide shadow or alternative reports, or which NGOs have contributed under the reporting procedure. However, at the same time, such an approach also bears the risk of exposing these NGOs to intimidation and reprisals by State parties. As long as the Committees were to include rules on confidentiality, such an approach seems appropriate.[457]

IV. Conclusion on reviews in the absence of a report

Currently rather the exception than the rule, reviews in the absence of a State party are an important, if not the only, means to ensure regular monitoring activities vis-à-vis all parties to the treaty concerned. While such an approach certainly dispenses with the approach of maximum cooperation between treaty bodies and State parties and places more emphasis on international scrutiny than self-evaluation, it must be understood as an essential step in upholding a comprehensive reporting calendar. Practice by the Human Rights Committee or the CMW Committee indicate, at least to a certain extent, the willingness of these bodies to adhere more frequently to this specific review mode, if required. On that note, it is submitted here that reviews in the absence should ideally remain exceptional occurrences. Other proposals and ideas could also possibly render their conduction less indispensable. With a view to the mandate of treaty bodies, reviews in the absence of a report can be considered covered by a teleological treaty interpretation. The review procedure does not impose any new obligations on contracting parties. Although it might contradict the provisions governing the reporting procedure when read *stricto sensu*, reviews in the absence of a report emerge as indispensable in order to review State parties that are in constant breach with their reporting obligations. It must also not be overlooked that concluding observations in the absence of a report are of particular relevance for the State party under review anyways. It can benefit from them for further reporting cycles and reviews in the absence of a report hence do not only serve the objective of creating accountability.

In this vein, treaty bodies do possess the power to "regularly" review State parties in the absence of a report and such reviews do not necessarily have to present themselves as the *ultima ratio*. Such a legal possibility notwithstanding, it is of course desirable to seek the exchange of views by means of a constructive dialogue, and State parties should submit answers to LOIPRs.

To render reviews in the absence of a report more transparent, treaty bodies could be advised to establish common rules, which are to entail possible sources

---

[457] Such a possibility is also acknowledged by treaty bodies, Meeting of Chairpersons, Guidelines against Intimidation or Reprisals ("San José Guidelines"), UN Doc. HRI/MC/2015/6, 30.07.2015, para. 18, with the confidential transmission of information being mentioned as one of the possible preventive measures against intimidation and reprisals.

of information, common deadlines among the Committees, and approaches regarding the adoption of concluding observations in the absence of a report. Particularly the latter could also take into consideration whether State parties are given a last chance to comment on potential provisional concluding observations before they are made public, or whether they are immediately disseminated, which is the current approach of the Human Rights Committee.

E. Concluding observations and follow-up activities

After having considered State parties' reports or written replies to LOIPRs and after the constructive dialogue, each treaty body adopts country specific concluding observations. These are considered to be "at the heart of the review process",[458] as they form the basis for subsequent reports and can serve as "critical reference points for States Parties' record over time."[459] As with other steps under the reporting procedure, the approaches taken by the various treaty bodies differed.

I. Alignment of concluding observations

Similar to current developments in the alignment of the simplified reporting procedure, for instance, treaty bodies gradually developed a common approach for the adoption of concluding observations. At the beginning of the 2000s, all concluding observations roughly corresponded to the same structure: starting with a short introduction, followed by positive aspects and lastly the main part, consisting of areas of concern and corresponding recommendations which should be implemented in order to improve the human rights situation in the State party under review.[460] Nevertheless, as the devil is in the details, and despite the common general structure, treaty bodies still adhered to different formats and structures for the adoption of concluding observations.

1. Common format for concluding observations

The varying approaches in detail led the 23rd Meeting of Chairpersons to the adoption of points of agreement,[461] elaborated and presented to it by the Inter-

---

[458] *Oette*, The UN Human Rights Treaty Bodies: Impact and Future, in: Oberleitner (ed.), International Human Rights Institutions, Tribunals, and Courts, 2018, p. 101.

[459] *Oette*, The UN Human Rights Treaty Bodies: Impact and Future, in: Oberleitner (ed.), International Human Rights Institutions, Tribunals, and Courts, 2018, p. 101.

[460] *O'Flaherty*, The Concluding Observations of United Nations Human Rights Treaty Bodies, Human Rights Law Review 6 (2006), 27, 31.

[461] Report of the Chairs of the human rights treaty bodies on their twenty-third meeting, UN Doc. A/66/175, 22.07.2011, para. 18.

Committee.⁴⁶² These points of agreement were intended to serve as a basis for a common and clear format for concluding observations, applicable regardless of the treaty under review. In preparation for the 26th Meeting of Chairpersons in 2014, the Secretariat provided an overview of the related working methods of all treaty bodies, reiterated the points of agreement adopted in 2011, but developed the common format further. In doing so, it took into consideration both the recommendations made by the High Commissioner in her strengthening report and several other ideas developed during the multi-stakeholder consultation process.⁴⁶³

At the end of the 26th Meeting of Chairpersons, the Chairs endorsed a "Framework for the concluding observations".⁴⁶⁴ Still, it seems that the framework was understood more as a guideline than as something to be definitely implemented by each Committee. In this respect, the framework contained the additional remark that it was to be applied flexibly by each single treaty body in order to ensure that concluding observations would "respect and reflect the specificities of each convention and treaty body."⁴⁶⁵

Principally, the framework proposed to divide concluding observations into four main parts. First the introduction, mainly summarizing the single stages of the reporting procedure, which was to include the date of submission, the meetings of the Committee devoted to the consideration of reports or written answers, and the date of adoption of the concluding observations.⁴⁶⁶ The next section should highlight positive aspects, indicating inter alia whether a State party has made progress in the implementation of previous recommendations.⁴⁶⁷ The third part should focus on principal matters of concern and stipulate recommendations, which also forms the major part of concluding observations.⁴⁶⁸ Finally, the document should be concluded with a section on the implementation of recom-

---

⁴⁶² Report of the Inter-Committee Meeting working group on follow-up to concluding observations, decisions on individual complaints and inquiries, UN Doc. HRI/ICM/2011/3–HRI/MC/2011/2, 04.05.2011.

⁴⁶³ Concluding observations, Note by the secretariat, UN Doc. HRI/MC/2014/2, 14.04.2014, paras. 9–12.

⁴⁶⁴ Report of the Chairs of the human rights treaty bodies on their twenty-sixth meeting, UN Doc. A/69/285, 11.08.2014, Annex II.

⁴⁶⁵ Report of the Chairs of the human rights treaty bodies on their twenty-sixth meeting, UN Doc. A/69/285, 11.08.2014, para. 106.

⁴⁶⁶ Report of the Chairs of the human rights treaty bodies on their twenty-sixth meeting, UN Doc. A/69/285, 11.08.2014, Annex II, A.

⁴⁶⁷ Report of the Chairs of the human rights treaty bodies on their twenty-sixth meeting, UN Doc. A/69/285, 11.08.2014, Annex II, B.

⁴⁶⁸ Report of the Chairs of the human rights treaty bodies on their twenty-sixth meeting, UN Doc. A/69/285, 11.08.2014, Annex II, C, interesting to note is that recommendations are often rather cautiously worded, as it is mentioned that Committees "could" implement one of the proposals contained in the framework.

E. Concluding observations and follow-up activities   233

mendations, dissemination, and follow-up.[469] As apparent from current treaty body practice, each Committee adheres more or less to this framework.

2. References to other treaty bodies' concluding observations

Particularly interesting for the purpose of the thesis at hand is one of the framework's proposals that relates to the main part of concluding observations. In analogy to the adoption of LOIPRs, concluding observations should be accompanied by references to previous recommendations.[470] Presuming that a specific question in the LOIPRs was coupled with references to previous concluding observations, and also given that the respective Committee considers it necessary to adopt yet another recommendation in relation to the same topic, citations should be deemed appropriate. Without getting into a detailed analysis whether treaty bodies are inclined to include references, a perusal of concluding observations reveals an inconsistent pattern with dispersed references to preceding concluding observations.

The CRC Committee is supposedly the treaty body most prone to equip its current concluding observations with references to preceding findings. The Committee's readiness to proceed this way may be best illustrated by the concluding observations adopted vis-à-vis Australia[471] and Bosnia and Herzegovina,[472] both of which contained 20 relevant citations. However, concluding observations adopted vis-à-vis the Federated States of Micronesia[473] might perfectly serve as counterevidence. Here, only one reference can be detected in the whole document. Similar observations can be made with regard to all other treaty bodies. While certain documents could be considered indicative of a Committee's willingness to deliberately refer back to results from preceding reporting cycles, other documents leave the impression that the Committees are not aware at all of the fact that a State party had ever been under review before. Interestingly, the CESCR Committee and the Committee against Torture which were identified by *O'Flaherty* in 2006 as the treaty bodies "least inclined to even loosely refer to previous concluding observations",[474] are still ranging at the lower end of the scale, with the fewest citations of previous recommendations.

---

[469] Report of the Chairs of the human rights treaty bodies on their twenty-sixth meeting, UN Doc. A/69/285, 11.08.2014, Annex II, D.

[470] "The concern and/or the recommendation could reference previous recommendations of the Committee when appropriate (e.g., where the previous recommendation was implemented only partially or not at all)", Report of the Chairs of the human rights treaty bodies on their twenty-sixth meeting, UN Doc. A/69/285, 11.08.2014, Annex II, C.

[471] CRC Committee, Concluding observations on the combined fifth and sixth periodic reports of Australia, UN Doc. CRC/C/AUS/CO/5–6, 01.11.2019.

[472] CRC Committee, Concluding observations on the combined fifth and sixth periodic reports of Bosnia and Herzegovina, UN Doc. CRC/C/BIH/CO/5–6, 05.12.2019.

[473] CRC Committee, Concluding observations on the second periodic report of the Federated States of Micronesia, UN Doc. CRC/C/FSM/CO/2, 03.04.2020.

[474] *O'Flaherty*, The Concluding Observations of United Nations Human Rights Treaty Bodies, Human Rights Law Review 6 (2006), 27, 31.

II. Prioritization

Within the context of the current treaty body strengthening process, another feature of concluding observations is worth considering. Taking into consideration the current attempts to rationalize the reporting procedure and focus on fewer issues in a more thorough manner, prioritization of selected topics appears to be of utmost importance. The common framework recommended that treaty bodies should identify certain recommendations which require "priority attention" due to the gravity of the human rights concerns to which they relate.[475] Prioritization of specific issues has also been identified as a decisive factor that could possibly render concluding observations more beneficial and valuable to the State party concerned.[476] However, it has been also argued that any prioritization remains "a risky" activity, given its possible incentives to focus on fewer treaty provisions.[477]

Yet, these possible disadvantages were voiced at a time when both, the simplified reporting procedure and the current resource shortages, at least in their current severity, did not yet exist. While the former might be a reaction to the latter, both require treaty bodies to proceed in accordance with the motto "less is more".[478] A useful method to signal unequivocally to the State party under review that something needs more dedicated implementation efforts is to select certain recommendations for the formalized follow-up procedures. In contrast to the working methods and approaches in the context of adopting concluding observations, the procedures in place vary to a higher degree among the UN human rights treaty bodies. Thus, they merit closer examination and comparison in detail.[479]

---

[475] Report of the Chairs of the human rights treaty bodies on their twenty sixth meeting, UN Doc. A/69/285, 11.08.2014, Annex II.

[476] *O'Flaherty*, The Concluding Observations of United Nations Human Rights Treaty Bodies, Human Rights Law Review 6 (2006), 27, 45–46; see also *Ploton*, The Implementation of UN Treaty Body Recommendations, SUR International Journal on Human Rights 25 (2017), 219, 220, who argues to focus more on implementation and assessment and thereby on fewer issues.

[477] *O'Flaherty*, The Concluding Observations of United Nations Human Rights Treaty Bodies, Human Rights Law Review 6 (2006), 27, 46.

[478] *Krommendijk*, Less is more: Proposals for how UN human rights treaty bodies can be more selective, Netherlands Quarterly of Human Rights 38 (2020), 5.

[479] For a comparison of follow-up activities to views adopted under the individual complaints procedure, see *van Staden*, Monitoring Second-Order Compliance: The Follow-Up Procedures of the UN Human Rights Treaty Bodies, Czeck Yearbook of International Law 9 (2018), 329.

1. Follow-up to concluding observations

As described above, an important evolutionary step in enhancing the reporting procedure has been the development and implementation of a formal and written follow-up procedure to concluding observations.[480] As of 2020, eight out of nine treaty bodies had implemented formalized follow-up procedures to concluding observations, though differing in concrete design and details from Committee to Committee. Treaty bodies have developed different standards and criteria for the selection of recommendations to be included in a State party's follow-up report, different criteria concerning the assessment of State parties' replies, and have defined different time frames and deadlines for the submission of follow-up reports.[481] In order to harmonize and streamline their working methods in this matter as well, the Chairs to the human rights treaty bodies endorsed possible elements for a common aligned procedure for follow-up to concluding observations at their 30th Meeting in 2018.[482]

According to these elements, all treaty bodies should deploy a standard paragraph in their concluding observations for the identification of issues chosen for the follow-up procedure.[483] Ideally, treaty bodies should only choose between two to four recommendations for the follow-up process.[484] The selected recommendations should be "specific, measurable, achievable, realistic and time-bound" (the so-called "SMART-Formula") and moreover, in terms of criteria for the selection, recommendations should be "serious, urgent, protective and implementable within the relevant time frame".[485]

However, the Chairs gave the single treaty bodies leeway in determining which recommendations to choose for the follow-up procedure. In that regard, the framework indicated that the list of criteria was neither intended to be exhaustive nor cumulative.[486] Furthermore, the single Committees are vested with flexibility with regard to the time frame for the follow-up procedure. According to the common elements paper, it can last between one to two years, depending on the urgency of the topic addressed.

---

[480] See *supra*, Part III C.III.

[481] For the status by 2017, see Procedures of the human rights treaty bodies for following up on concluding observations, decisions and Views, UN Doc. HRI/MC/2017/4, 08.05.2017.

[482] Report of the Chairs of the human rights treaty bodies on their thirtieth meeting, UN Doc. A/73/140, 11.07.2018, Annex II, section A.

[483] Report of the Chairs of the human rights treaty bodies on their thirtieth meeting, UN Doc. A/73/140, 11.07.2018, Annex II, section A, para. (a).

[484] Report of the Chairs of the human rights treaty bodies on their thirtieth meeting, UN Doc. A/73/140, 11.07.2018, Annex II, section A, para. (d).

[485] Report of the Chairs of the human rights treaty bodies on their thirtieth meeting, UN Doc. A/73/140, 11.07.2018, Annex II, section A, para. (c).

[486] Report of the Chairs of the human rights treaty bodies on their thirtieth meeting, UN Doc. A/73/140, 11.07.2018, Annex II, section A, para. (c).

With a view to the assessment of the information provided for by State parties, all Committees may develop their own criteria. According to the common elements paper, they "remain within the purview of the follow-up rapporteur, coordinator or committee".[487] In the course of the assessment of follow-up information provided, the Committee may ask for additional information, and after having evaluated the State party's follow-up report, the results shall be made public.

a) Time frame for the follow-up report

Given the above-mentioned suggestion to establish an eight-year reporting cycle under each human rights treaty, and to cluster reviews by the Covenant Committees and the more specialized Committees in intervals of four years accordingly, treaty bodies should also strive for aligning the time frames for implementation and follow-up procedures. Most treaty bodies require State parties to submit their follow-up reports within one year. The CEDAW Committee does not adopt a general time frame and only requires the submission of information after one to two years, depending on the issue's urgency. The CMW Committee and the CESCR Committee require State parties to respond within two years.[488]

Treaty bodies should be advised to adopt a two-year deadline. This would result in a formalized dialogue between treaty bodies and State parties on a biennial basis. State parties would report to one of the clustered groups of treaty bodies every four years, and would interact with them every two years in between through the follow-up procedure.[489]

b) Criteria for the selection of concluding observations

On closer inspection, the common elements paper's paragraph on the criteria for the choice of which recommendations to include for the follow-up procedure does not prove to be particularly helpful. It is not straightforward, and seems to be an abstract summary of the criteria developed by the individual treaty bodies so far.

---

[487] Report of the Chairs of the human rights treaty bodies on their thirtieth meeting, UN Doc. A/73/140, 11.07.2018, Annex II, section A, para. (h).

[488] See for a general overview of the reporting deadlines under the follow-up procedure as determined by the various treaty bodies, Procedures of the human rights treaty bodies for following up on concluding observations, decisions and Views, UN Doc. HRI/MC/2017/4, 08.05.2017, para. 6; as far as the CESCR Committee is concerned, which did not deploy a written and formalized follow-up procedure at that time, see the most recent decision concerning its time frame, CESCR Committee, Report on the sixty-third and sixty-fourth sessions, UN Doc. E/2019/22 (2019), para. 36.

[489] *Shany/Cleveland*, Treaty Body Reform 2020: Has the time come for adopting a Global Review Calendar?, p. 4, who also opt for this solution, https://www.geneva-academy.ch/joomlatools-files/docman-files/Draft%20List%20of%20Submissions%20-%20Academic%20Platform%202020%20Review%20without%20Propositions%20.pdf (last access: 21.08.2023).

aa) Committee practice

The Human Rights Committee selects its recommendation on the basis of whether the recommendation is implementable within one year after its adoption, whether the recommendation requires immediate attention owing to the gravity of the referred situation or, alternatively, owing to the emergency of the situation. A situation is considered an emergency situation when non-action by the State party would constitute a major obstacle in the implementation of the Covenant, when remaining inactive in the recommendation's implementation would threaten the life or security of one or more persons, or if the selected issue has been on the agenda for a long time and has not yet been addressed by the State party.[490]

The Committee against Torture[491] seeks to select recommendations that may be realized within one year, and additionally deploys the rather vague "SMART-formula".[492] Furthermore, the Committee delimits its selection of issues to the effect that it choses recommendations which are likely to directly impact the situation of individuals, for instance with regard to legal safeguards for people deprived of their liberty.[493] The Committee thus identifies follow-up items by taking into consideration their possible impact on the ground.

The CEDAW Committee also refers to the SMART-formula in its revised guidelines on the follow-up procedure. It also takes into consideration which recommendations are suitable for "urgent short-term action", and will seek to select issues which pose "major [obstacles]" in the implementation of the Convention as such.[494] The Committee relies on an approach which focuses on gravity and urgency and is thereby comparable to the one chosen by the Human Rights Committee. The CERD Committee, in turn, bases its decision mainly on the

---

[490] Procedures of the human rights treaty bodies for following up on concluding observations, decisions and Views, Note by the Secretariat, UN Doc. HRI/MC/2017/4, 08.05.2017, para. 8; see also Human Rights Committee, Note by the Human Rights Committee on the procedure for follow-up to concluding observations, UN Doc. CCPR/C/108/2, 21.10.2013, para. 6.

[491] For the development of the follow-up procedure under CAT, see *Monina*, Article 19, State Reporting Procedure, in: Nowak/Birk/Monina (eds.), The United Nations Convention Against Torture and its Optional Protocol: A Commentary, Second Edition, 2019, paras. 75–86.

[492] Committee against Torture, Guidelines for follow-up to concluding observations, UN Doc. CAT/C/55/3, 17.09.2015, para. 9.

[493] Committee against Torture, Guidelines for follow-up to concluding observations, UN Doc. CAT/C/55/3, 17.09.2015, para. 7, further examples invoked by the Committee are the conduct of prompt and impartial investigations of alleged cases of torture or ill-treatment, the prosecution of suspects and the punishment of perpetrators of torture or ill-treatment or the possibility for victims to obtain redress.

[494] CEDAW Committee, Methodology of the follow-up procedure to concluding observations, 06.11.2019, para. 2, https://tbinternet.ohchr.org/_layouts/15/treatybodyexternal/Download.aspx?symbolno=INT%2FCEDAW%2FFGD%2F7102&Lang=en (last access: 21.08.2023).

criterion of whether the recommendations are detailed enough to enable the State party to provide for "substantive responses" within one year.[495] The CED Committee selects its issues for the follow-up procedure on the basis of whether these are "particularly serious, urgent, protective and/or can be achieved within a short period of time."[496]

The CRPD Committee deploys a comprehensive set of criteria, arguably resulting in the possibility to include nearly any recommendation adopted in its follow-up request. The Committee established the criteria whether the recommendation can be implemented in short, medium or long term, whether the issue identified would constitute a major obstacle in the implementation of the Convention as such, whether the implementation is feasible and measurable, whether the issues is serious and whether it is feasible to adopt implementation measures or short-term policies to implement the recommendations or to overcome the selected concerns.[497] The CESCR Committee selects its recommendations for the follow-up procedure based on their urgency and whether they are "attainable" within a time frame of 18 months.[498] The CMW Committee has not yet developed any specific guidelines concerning the selection of recommendations for the follow-up procedure.[499]

bb) Evaluation

A common criterion to be found among all human rights treaty bodies is the achievability of the specific recommendation within the set time frame for the follow-up procedure. Some treaty bodies single this requirement out as a specific and separate criterion, while others implicitly acknowledge such a choice by referring to the SMART-formula, which encompasses the factors "achievable" and "time-bound".

Surprising about the guidelines and criteria is, however, the lacuna of addressing the issue of useless repetition and duplication. While treaty bodies commenced to focus on the avoidance of negative duplication in the context of

---

[495] *Thornberry*, The International Convention on the Elimination of All Forms of Racial Discrimination: A Commentary, 2016, The Convention and the Committee, pp. 48–49; see also *Angst*, Artikel 9, in: Angst/Lantschner (eds.), ICERD: Internationales Übereinkommen zur Beseitigung jeder From von Rassendiskriminierung, Handkommentar, 2020, para. 42.

[496] Procedures of the human rights treaty bodies for following up on concluding observations, decisions and Views, Note by the Secretariat, UN Doc. HRI/MC/2017/4, 08.05.2017, para. 37.

[497] Report of the Committee on the Rights of Persons with Disabilities on its twelfth session, UN Doc. CRPD/C/12/2, 05.11.2014, Annex II, para. 2.

[498] CESCR Committee, Report on the sixtieth, sixty-first and sixty-second sessions, UN Doc. E/2018/22 (2018), Annex I, para. 4.

[499] Procedures of the human rights treaty bodies for following up on concluding observations, decisions and Views, Note by the Secretariat, UN Doc. HRI/MC/2017/4, 08.05.2017, para. 40; as far as apparent, this still holds true as of September 2021.

LOIPRs,[500] the possible elements for a common aligned methodology for follow-up procedure to concluding observations do not cover this topic at all. Provided that treaty bodies will only choose two to four recommendations, and additionally provided that similar issues may be raised before various treaty bodies, it might be even more essential to avoid duplication in the course of follow-up procedures than in LOIPRs.

Futile repetition is even more imaginable when taking into account that treaty bodies will possibly strive for limitations of topics in LOIPRs to a maximum number of 25 to 30. Even if coordination activities, comparable to the current *modus operandi* by the Committee against Torture in the selection for topics addressed by LOIPRs, become prevalent among all treaty bodies, this does not automatically foreclose any duplication. The Committees reserve the option to spontaneously raise topics during the constructive dialogue that might not have been included in LOIPRs. These topics might equally find their way into concluding observations and could be chosen for follow-up procedures.

The only treaty body which remotely addresses the need for avoiding repetition under the follow-up procedure is the CEDAW Committee. It determines in its methodology that issues chosen "should not include recommendations under other procedures."[501] It is ultimately starkly surprising that the potential risk of unnecessary overlap in the course of follow-up procedures has not yet come to the fore.[502]

c) Criteria for assessing State compliance

The possible elements for an aligned methodology expressly left it to the Committees to develop assessment criteria on their own. The only specification provided is the proposal to establish a grading scale, to help evaluate the information provided by State parties and assess the implementation of the recommendations adopted.[503] In practice, the approaches taken by the various treaty bodies, which comes as no surprise, differ. Neither the CERD Committee nor the CMW Committee make use of any grading system and are thus excluded from the following analysis.[504]

---

[500] See *supra* Part IV B.III.3.

[501] CEDAW Committee, Methodology of the follow-up procedure to concluding observations, 06.11.2019, para. 2, available under: https://tbinternet.ohchr.org/_layouts/15/treatybodyexternal/Download.aspx?symbolno=INT%2FCEDAW%2FFGD%2F7102&Lang=en (last access: 21.08.2023).

[502] Noting that duplication in the course of follow-up procedures should be avoided, Oberleitner, Agenda for Strengthening Human Rights Institutions, in: Oberleitner (ed.), International Human Rights Institutions, Tribunals, and Courts, 2018, p. 563.

[503] Report of the Chairs of the human rights treaty bodies on their thirtieth meeting, UN Doc. A/73/140, 11.07.2018, Annex II, section A, para. (h).

[504] Procedures of the human rights treaty bodies for following up on concluding observations, decisions and Views, Note by the Secretariat, UN Doc. HRI/MC/2017/4, 08.05.2017, para. 34.

aa) Committees with a single grading scheme

The Human Rights Committee, which was the first treaty body to introduce the practice of grading State parties in 2012,[505] and updated its criteria in 2016,[506] deploys grades that range from reply/action largely satisfactory (A), over partially satisfactory (B) to not satisfactory (C). If a State party has not responded to the follow-up request at all, the Human Rights Committee grades the respective State party with a "D", indicating "no cooperation". In the event of having taken measures which contravene recommendations adopted, or in the case of recommendations being deliberately rejected by a State party, the Committee will evaluate the implementation with an "E".

Striking about the Human Rights Committee's approach is the fact that its newly developed grading system is less complex than the one it had been using previously. The preceding grading scheme encompassed more nuanced grades, such as "B1" and "B2" for example, indicating substantive steps taken, but further action needed, and initial steps taken, but further action needed respectively.[507]

The CED Committee adopted an almost identical grading scheme that also ranges from A to E.[508] The division between satisfactory, partially satisfactory and unsatisfactory replies is also used by the CRPD Committee, but it neither uses a comparable grading scheme nor categories for the indication of non-cooperation or measures taken that contradict the recommendations made.[509]

The CESCR Committee, which has just recently adopted a more elaborate follow-up procedure, differentiates between sufficient and insufficient progress. The latter denotes that the State party has taken steps in response to the recommendations, but needs to take further action.[510] In addition, the Committee established two further categories which indicate either that a State party has provided insufficient information to enable the Committee to make an assessment, or that the State party has completely failed to reply to the follow-up request.[511]

---

[505] *Ploton*, The Implementation of UN Treaty Body Recommendations, SUR International Journal on Human Rights 25 (2017), 219, 221.

[506] Report of the Human Rights Committee (117th, 118th and 119th session), UN Doc. A/72/40 (2017), para. 53(b).

[507] Human Rights Committee, Note by the Human Rights Committee on the procedure for follow-up to concluding observations, UN Doc. CCPR/C/108/2, 21.10.2013, paras. 17–18.

[508] *Citroni*, Committee on Enforced Disappearances (CED), in: Ruiz Fabri/Wolfrum (eds.), Max Planck Encyclopedia of International Procedural Law, Online version, December 2018, para. 19; see also, by way of example, the latest follow-up report by the Committee, CED Committee, Report on follow-up to the concluding observations of the Committee on Enforced Disappearances, UN Doc. CED/C/19/4, 29.09.2020, para. 3.

[509] Report of the Committee on the Rights of Persons with Disabilities on its twelfth session, UN Doc. CRPD/C/12/2, 05.11.2014, Annex II, para. 4

[510] CESCR Committee, Report on the sixtieth, sixty-first and sixty-second sessions, UN Doc. E/2018/22 (2018), Annex I, para. 11.

[511] CESCR Committee, Report on the sixtieth, sixty-first and sixty-second sessions, UN Doc. E/2018/22 (2018), Annex I, para. 11.

bb) Committees with two grading schemes

The Committee against Torture and the CEDAW Committee have developed more sophisticated grading schemes.[512] While the scales applied by the Human Rights Committee, the CED, CRPD and CESCR Committee focus in parallel, and thus without differentiation, on both, actions taken and information provided, the Committee against Torture decided at its 55th session in 2015 to draw a distinction between the information received on the one hand and the assessment of the measures taken by the State party on the other hand.[513]

In relation to the *information received*, the Committee against Torture uses a scale that starts on its upper end with the assessment that the information submitted is "thorough and extensive" and directly relates to the respective recommendation (this information is considered satisfactory). On the next lower-level rank, information which is thorough and extensive, but which does not respond comprehensively to all the recommendations chosen by the Committee (this information is deemed partly satisfactory). At the bottom range information that is only "vague and incomplete", or which does not correspond to the selected recommendations (this information is evaluated as unsatisfactory).[514] Similar to other Committees, the Committee against Torture will make use of the category "no response" if the State party under review did not reply at all.[515]

The evaluation scheme concerning the *implementation* of the recommendation corresponds to the ones developed by the Human Rights Committee and the CED Committee. Grade "A" indicates that the recommendation has been fully or almost fully implemented. If a State party is graded "B", this signifies that the recommendation has been partially implemented. The grade may come in two different sub-grades. A State party is given a "B1" when it has taken substantive steps towards a recommendation's full implementation, but further action is still

---

[512] Until recently, the follow-up procedure developed by the Human Rights Committee was considered the most advanced, *Kosař/Petrov*, Determinants of Compliance Difficulties among 'Good Compliers': Implementation of International Human Rights Rulings in the Czech Republic, European Journal of International Law 29 (2018), 397, 419.

[513] For this distinction, see Committee against Torture, Guidelines for follow-up to concluding observations, UN Doc. CAT/C/55/3, 17.09.2015, paras. 18–20; see also for a short account of the procedure's development under CAT, *Monina*, Article 19, State Reporting Procedure, in: Nowak/Birk/Monina (eds.), The United Nations Convention Against Torture and its Optional Protocol: A Commentary, Second Edition, 2019, para. 75; *Ploton*, The Implementation of UN Treaty Body Recommendations, SUR International Journal on Human Rights 25 (2017), 219, 226–227, who considers the Committee against Torture's approach as "innovative".

[514] Committee against Torture, Guidelines for follow-up to concluding observations, UN Doc. CAT/C/55/3, 17.09.2015, paras. 18(a)–(c).

[515] Committee against Torture, Guidelines for follow-up to concluding observations, UN Doc. CAT/C/55/3, 17.09.2015, para. 19; Procedures of the human rights treaty bodies for following up on concluding observations, decisions and Views, UN Doc. HRI/MC/2017/4, 08.05.2017, para. 15.

needed. When further action is needed and the State party has only taken initial steps, it is graded with "B2". Further down the scale, grade "C" corresponds to unsatisfactory implementation, thus signifying that no measure has been taken, and "D" indicates that a State party has provided insufficient information to evaluate any implementation.[516] An "E" denotes that the State party has taken measures which contradict the recommendations chosen for the follow up procedure.[517] Last but not least, the Committee against Torture offers State parties to develop implementation plans focusing on issues that do not require immediate action.[518]

The CEDAW Committee used to adhere to a simple grading system as well,[519] but introduced in 2019 a system similar to the one deployed by the Committee against Torture.[520] It since then differentiates between the evaluation of the information received and the extent to which a State party has implemented recommendations. As far as the grading related to the information received is concerned, the CEDAW Committee seems to have fully copied the scheme developed by the Committee against Torture. Concerning the assessment of implementation activities, the CEDAW Committee seemed to copy the Committee against Torture's approach as well. However, it does not adhere to actual grades, but deploys categories such as "implemented", "substantially implemented", "partially implemented" and "not implemented".[521] Besides the fact that these categories essentially correspond to the grades "A", "B1", "B2", and "C" awarded by the Committee against Torture, the CEDAW Committee also takes recourse to the categories of insufficient information and measures taken which contravene the Committee's recommendations.[522]

---

[516] Committee against Torture, Guidelines for follow-up to concluding observations, UN Doc. CAT/C/55/3, 17.09.2015, para. 20.

[517] Committee against Torture, Guidelines for follow-up to concluding observations, UN Doc. CAT/C/55/3, 17.09.2015, para. 20.

[518] Committee against Torture, Guidelines for follow-up to concluding observations, UN Doc. CAT/C/55/3, 17.09.2015, para. 11.

[519] *Ploton*, The Implementation of UN Treaty Body Recommendations, SUR International Journal on Human Rights 25 (2017), 219, 226.

[520] Report of the Committee on the Elimination of Discrimination against Women (73rd, 74th and 75th session), UN Doc. A/75/38 (2020), Part two, decision 74/VIII, taken on 06.11.2019; see for the revised methodology of the CEDAW Committee, Methodology of the follow-up procedure to concluding observations, 06.11.2019, https://tbinternet.ohchr.org/_layouts/15/treatybodyexternal/Download.aspx?symbolno=INT%2FCEDAW%2FFGD%2F7102&Lang=en (last access: 21.08.2023).

[521] CEDAW Committee, Methodology of the follow-up procedure to concluding observations, 06.11.2019, para. 11, https://tbinternet.ohchr.org/_layouts/15/treatybodyexternal/Download.aspx?symbolno=INT%2FCEDAW%2FFGD%2F7102&Lang=en (last access: 21.08.2023).

[522] CEDAW Committee, Methodology of the follow-up procedure to concluding observations, 06.11.2019, para. 11, https://tbinternet.ohchr.org/_layouts/15/treatybodyexternal/Download.aspx?symbolno=INT%2FCEDAW%2FFGD%2F7102&Lang=en (last access: 21.08.2023).

cc) Evaluation

A common feature to be detected among all human rights treaty bodies that have introduced a grading scheme, except for the CESCR Committee, is the division between full implementation, partial implementation and recommendations yet to be implemented. What is more, the Committee against Torture and the CEDAW Committee developed a more sophisticated scale, with subgrades which indicate that certain recommendations have only partially been implemented. While the Human Rights Committee originally adhered to such a scheme as well, it changed its system in 2016 to a simpler scale that does not comprise subgrades.

With respect to the ongoing strengthening process and the related harmonization of working methods, treaty bodies should at least discuss adherence to a uniform grading system when evaluating the implementation of concluding observations.[523] In analogy to the methodology developed for LOIPRs, treaty bodies are advised to equally reflect on the problem of useless repetition in the context of follow-up procedures. Another decisive feature, so far only detectable in the Committee against Torture's approach, is the inclusion of any outstanding follow-up item under the next reporting cycle, and to reiterate the status of implementation in the next List of Issues Prior to Reporting.[524] As stated above, the approach enables the State party under review and the monitoring body to generate continuity in a long-term perspective.[525]

2. Prioritization by means of an integrated follow-up procedure

As evidenced by the example of the Committee against Torture's LOIPRs, there are many areas of substantive congruence, possibly addressed by various treaty bodies. At this point, and in contrast to the adoption of LOIPRs, the aspect of substantial coherence or diverging recommendations among different treaty bodies becomes more relevant. While references to other treaty bodies' documents in LOIPRs mainly serve the purpose of raising awareness among State parties about previous discussion in this matter and the topic's multidimensional character, references in concluding observations serve to attach more weight to a treaty body's own recommendation.

The first observation is, however, that references to other treaty bodies' recommendation are scarce, as well as references to the recommendations stemming from the UPR or to reports delivered by special procedure mandate holders. While it may well be convenient to subject cross-references to other treaty bodies' concluding observations to closer scrutiny with the aim of exploring

---

[523] *Ploton*, The Implementation of UN Treaty Body Recommendations, SUR International Journal on Human Rights 25 (2017), 219, 231.

[524] Committee against Torture, Guidelines for follow-up to concluding observations, UN Doc. CAT/C/55/3, 17.09.2015, para. 29; *Ploton*, The Implementation of UN Treaty Body Recommendations, SUR International Journal on Human Rights 25 (2017), 219, 227.

[525] See *supra* Part IV B.III.2.i).

(quasi-judicial) dialogue, the connectivity among human rights treaty bodies, or to analyse whether treaty bodies adopt (in-)coherent recommendations, the following section shall analyse a specific practice developed by the CRPD Committee. Said practice raises issues of competence and powers. At the same time, the practice may be considered as another option in signalizing priority to be given to certain recommendations by the State party under review by simultaneously drawing upon other treaty bodies' recommendations. Diverging concluding observations or those being at variance with each other will thus not be addressed in this chapter.[526]

a) Practice by the CRPD Committee

In line with the other Committees, the CRPD Committee only rarely refers to other treaty bodies' concluding observations. But in some of the few cases where references were included, the Committee went considerably beyond the practice of other treaty bodies. It explicitly recommended to implement concluding observations adopted by the cited Committees. For instance, in its concluding observations concerning Albania, the CRPD Committee recommended to "[implement] the recommendations made in 2016 by the Committee on the Elimination of Discrimination against Women"[527] and added the exact source of the latter. Almost identical recommendations can be found in concluding observations adopted with regard to Australia,[528] India,[529] and Saudi Arabia,[530] all of which comprised references to recommendations by the CEDAW Committee, and all of which were accompanied by the request to implement the specific findings by the CEDAW Committee.

Such a way of addressing concluding observations and recommendations adopted by other treaty bodies could potentially serve as a helpful means to rebut criticism that the establishment of a comprehensive reporting calendar, with two groups of treaty bodies monitoring a State party in intervals of four years each, would result in overly broad reporting gaps. Treaty bodies that belong to the second monitoring group could raise recommendations and their status of implementation which had been adopted four years ago by treaty bodies from the first group. In doing so, the Committees could establish a second and integrated kind of follow-up procedure, next to their own.

---

[526] See for such a study, *Tistounet*, The problem of overlapping among different treaty bodies, in: Alston/Crawford (eds.), The Future of UN Human Rights Treaty Monitoring, 2000, pp. 383–401.

[527] CRPD Committee, Concluding observations on the initial report of Albania, UN Doc. CRPD/C/ALB/CO/1, 14.10.2019, para. 14(c).

[528] CRPD Committee, Concluding observations on the combined second and third periodic reports of Australia, UN Doc. CRPD/C/AUS/CO/2–3, 15.10.2019, para. 54.

[529] CRPD Committee, Concluding observations on the initial report of India, UN Doc. CRPD/C/IND/CO/1, 29.10.2019, para. 33(a).

[530] CRPD Committee, Concluding observations on the initial report of Saudi Arabia, UN Doc. CRPD/C/SAU/CO/1, 13.05.2019, paras. 10(b) and 42(a).

As with all other proposals concerning the reform process, the question arises as to whether such an approach is covered by a treaty body's mandate. As a matter of fact, the Committees are only vested with the competence to monitor the implementation of their own treaty provisions, and to request corresponding follow-up information with a view to their own concluding observations.

b) Possible content of concluding observations

Treaty bodies can only legitimately address those issues in concluding observations which are covered by their respective treaties. These form the normative basis and justification for the Committees' pronouncements and recommendations as regards a State party's human rights record.[531] Any recommendation addressing "extraneous and non-treaty related issues" might be inappropriate and thus beyond a treaty body's mandate.[532] What is more, State parties may easily criticize supervisory bodies by claiming that their recommendations allegedly reach beyond the contours of the respective treaty.[533]

According to legal literature, the topics addressed in concluding observations can be divided into five categories, ranging from aspects related to the reporting procedure, substantive core issues, which are clearly covered by a treaty, over aspects covered by progressive treaty interpretation, "wider policy issues conducive to the full realization of the treaty concerned" and finally to issues reaching beyond the scope of the treaty concerned.[534] Nevertheless, any categorization and especially the question of what precisely constitutes a core issue covered by a human rights treaty already presumes a certain degree of interpretation. As aptly described, what Committees may or may not include in their concluding observations "has to be determined along a sliding scale".[535]

To stick to the classification proposed, the recommendation to implement other treaty bodies' recommendations rather approximates the lower end of said sliding scale. Any such concluding observation bears strong resemblance to recommendations to ratify other Conventions among the UN human rights core

---

[531] *Kälin*, Examination of state reports, in: Keller/Ulfstein (eds.), UN Human Rights Treaty Bodies: Law and Legitimacy, 2012, p. 50.

[532] *O'Flaherty*, The Concluding Observations of United Nations Human Rights Treaty Bodies, Human Rights Law Review 6 (2006), 27, 42, who ascertains that such practice raises at minimum issues of mandate and competency.

[533] Instructive in this sense is the Nigerian contribution to the 2020 co-facilitator process, next to criticism of too extensive interpretations undertaken by General Comments, for instance, the State party recommended to treaty bodies to "refrain from the practice of cross-referencing among treaty monitoring bodies, whose mandate and scope are not interrelated", submission available at: https://www.ohchr.org/en/calls-for-input/co-facilitation-process-treaty-body-review-2020 (last access: 21.08.2023).

[534] *Kälin*, Examination of state reports, in: Keller/Ulfstein (eds.), UN Human Rights Treaty Bodies: Law and Legitimacy, 2012, pp. 50–59.

[535] *Kälin*, Examination of state reports, in: Keller/Ulfstein (eds.), UN Human Rights Treaty Bodies: Law and Legitimacy, 2012, p. 50.

treaties, or are comparable to references to soft law documents adopted by the UN General Assembly or other international bodies, thus representing "extraneous" issues.[536]

With a view to the CRPD Committee's findings to implement recommendations adopted by the CEDAW Committee, a possible explanation might derive from the substantive provision forming the normative basis for the Committee's pronouncement in this subject matter. All of these specific recommendations were adopted under article 6 CRPD. Article 6 CRPD addresses the protection of women with disabilities, and is said to be the first provision among UN human rights core treaties to explicitly embrace the multi-facetted character of gender and disability-based discrimination.[537] What is more, article 6(2) CRPD stipulates that State parties shall take all appropriate measures to ensure the full development, advancement and empowerment of women, for the purpose of guaranteeing them the exercise and enjoyment of the human rights and fundamental freedoms set out in the CRPD. Described as a "new paradigm for international human rights treaties", the CRPD thus creates a nexus between gender and disability rights throughout its whole normative framework.[538] Arguably, the CRPD Committee is by virtue of its treaty already empowered to put a strong focus on women with disabilities. It could therefore be taken as entitled to recommend the implementation of similar recommendations made by the CEDAW Committee, as its own treaty explicitly addresses the intersectional and multi-layered discrimination of disabled women.[539]

The question arises whether all treaty bodies can recommend the implementation of concluding observations adopted by others. Of course, every Committee could formulate its own recommendation, being identical to those formulated by other treaty bodies. Yet, the concluding observation to implement other treaty bodies' recommendations signals the importance or urgency of the respective issue and arguably vests the recommendation with more persuasive force.

---

[536] *O'Flaherty*, The Concluding Observations of United Nations Human Rights Treaty Bodies, Human Rights Law Review 6 (2006), 27, 42.

[537] *Mykitiuk/Chadha*, Article 6, Women with Disabilities, in: Bantekas/Stein/Anastasiou (eds.), The UN Convention on the Rights of Persons with Disabilities: A Commentary, 2018, pp. 171–172.

[538] *Mykitiuk/Chadha*, Article 6, Women with Disabilities, in: Bantekas/Stein/Anastasiou (eds.), The UN Convention on the Rights of Persons with Disabilities: A Commentary, 2018, p. 188 with an enumeration of further provisions embodying the principle of gender equality under CRPD.

[539] See *Pyaneandee*, International Disability Law, A Practical Approach to the United Nations Convention on the Rights of Persons with Disabilities, 2019, p. 48, who observes that the CRPD Committee has focused on multiple and aggravated forms of discrimination against women and girls with disabilities, while other human rights treaty bodies, according to the author, must follow suit. But compare *Lord/Stein*, The Committee on the Rights of Persons with Disabilities, in: Mégret/Alston (eds.), The United Nations and Human Rights: A Critical Appraisal, Second Edition, 2020, p. 556, who wonder "whether the CRPD and the CRC and CEDAW treaty bodies will work cooperatively to develop cross-cutting jurisprudence."

E. Concluding observations and follow-up activities

Furthermore, from a purely legal point of view, it makes a difference whether the State party under review has continued to fail in its obligation to take due consideration of and implement the recommendation adopted by the other treaty body. The encouragement to implement another treaty body's recommendations, coupled with a second and distinct request, denotes implementation shortfalls with regard to two different treaties and thereby exceeds the mere repetition of recommendations. Put differently, a recommendation by another Committee remains unimplemented and is now followed-up by a different treaty body.

c) Legal arguments for an integrated follow-up procedure

On an abstract level, the UN human rights core treaties are considered part of a "family" of human rights treaties that share a common normative basis with the UDHR. Taking into consideration that the same argument has been advanced to establish a common point of reference between universal and regional human rights treaties,[540] the normative proximity between the UN human rights core treaties must be all the closer.

Based on this finding of a shared normative basis, *Payandeh* reaches the conclusion that "the nine human rights treaties do not contain different rights but protect different aspects of the same rights".[541] He illustrates the assumption made by pointing out several normative embodiments of the right to freedom of expression among UN human rights treaties, all of which are said to eventually relate to a "common concept of freedom of expression as a universal and inalienable right of every person."[542] The assertion that several normative embodiments of the same right ultimately pertain to the same abstract concept or normative standard is further bolstered by the conception of "multi-sourced equivalent norms" in general international law.[543] UN human rights treaties, overlapping to a certain extent with regard to substantive guarantees, precisely fit under the concept of multi-sourced equivalent norms, as a State party is bound by several UN human rights core treaties (different international sources) with partially almost identical rights (similar or identical normative content).

---

[540] *Ajevski*, Fragmentation in International Human Rights Law – Beyond Conflict of Laws, Nordic Journal of Human Rights 32 (2014), 87, 90.

[541] *Payandeh*, Fragmentation within international human rights law, in: Andenas/Bjorge (eds.), A Farewell to Fragmentation: Reassertion and Convergence in International Law, 2015, p. 306.

[542] *Payandeh*, Fragmentation within international human rights law, in: Andenas/Bjorge (eds.), A Farewell to Fragmentation: Reassertion and Convergence in International Law, 2015, p. 307.

[543] See for this conception *Broude/Shany*, The International Law and Policy of Multi-Sourced Equivalent Norms, in: Broude/Shany (eds.), Multi-Sourced Equivalent Norms in International Law, 2011, p. 5, who define multi-sourced equivalent norms as "two or more norms which are (1) binding upon the same international legal subject; (2) similar or identical in their normative content; and (3) have been established through different international instruments or 'legislative' procedures or are applicable in different substantive areas of the law."

Another argument can be drawn from one of the objectives of human rights reporting, as identified by the treaty bodies themselves in their harmonized Reporting Guidelines. According to these, the reporting procedure serves, inter alia, to enable State parties to comprehend the interrelatedness of human rights and to view their specific treaty commitment "within the wider context of the obligation of all States to promote respect for the rights and freedoms, set out in the Universal Declaration of Human Rights and international human rights instruments".[544] Presupposing that the reporting procedure indeed serves to allow State parties a better understanding of the superior normative framework of human rights, human rights treaty bodies must at least be able to offer guidance to State parties in achieving said understanding. In practice, this can be accomplished by the above observed practice developed by the CRPD Committee. Indications that another treaty body came across the same subject matter can signalize to the State party under review that implementation shortfalls possibly result from compound forms of discrimination, or that certain topics entail deeper structural problems that need to be overcome.

d) Practical arguments for an integrated follow-up procedure

Ultimately, treaty body practice demonstrates that the Committees are far from just focusing on the core of their own constituent treaty when reviewing State parties. For instance, since September 2015, some of the human rights treaty bodies systematically include references to the implementation of the United Nations Sustainable Development Goals in their recommendations and General Comments.[545] It has also been proposed that human rights treaty bodies could play a key role in implementing the standards contained in non-binding international documents, such as the relatively recently adopted "United Nations Declaration on the rights of peasants and other people working in rural areas" (UNDROP).[546] While these documents seem to constitute extraneous sources in the first place, it becomes obvious at second glance that most of the SDGs correspond to already existing human rights standards under the universal human rights treaties.[547] The UNDROP is also said to have taken inspiration from exist-

---

[544] Compilation of Guidelines on the Form and Content of Reports to be submitted by State Parties to the International Human Rights Treaties, Report of the Secretary-General, UN Doc. HRI/GEN/2/Rev. 6, 03.06.2009, para. 8.

[545] *Golay*, #ESCR and #SDGS, Practical Manual on the Role of United Nations Human Rights Mechanisms in Monitoring the Sustainable Development Goals that seek to realize economic, social and cultural rights, June 2020, pp. 41–49.

[546] *Golay*, The Role of Human Rights Mechanisms in Monitoring the United Nations Declaration on the Rights of Peasants, Research Brief, Geneva Academy, January 2020, p. 4; at least in its concluding observations on Guinea, the CESCR Committee included reference to the Declaration, CESCR Committee, Concluding observations on the initial report of Guinea, UN Doc. E./C.12/GIN/CO/1, 30.03.2020, para. 40.

[547] *Samarasinghe*, Human Rights and Sustainable Development: Together at Last?, in:

E. Concluding observations and follow-up activities   249

ing UN human rights treaties.[548] Thus, addressing these seemingly non-related (legal) sources can be justified by the fact that they may be covered by applying the respective human rights treaty through an even more group- or issue-specific lens. With a view to the SDGs, it appears that State parties also largely accept accompanying monitoring activities undertaken by treaty bodies, as they include answers to these specific questions in their reports.[549]

e) Identification of suitable topics for an integrated follow-up procedure

However, in the final analysis, even though various provisions might present themselves as closely related or belonging to a common concept, there might be differences with regard to their legal consequences, which depend on the "distinct political, normative and institutional environments in which they function."[550] It is therefore essential to determine comparable treaty provisions to article 6 CRPD, enabling Committees to monitor the implementation of similar provisions to be found in other human rights treaties, and to define criteria for the selection of provisions that present themselves as suitable for this kind of integrated follow-up procedure.[551]

In the course of the second reform initiative, the Secretariat developed a chart of congruence and included the latter in its draft guidelines on an expanded Core Document relevant to the work of all seven treaty bodies operating at that time.[552]

Browne/Weiss (eds.), Routledge Handbook on the UN and Development, 2020, p. 81; *Fredman*, Poverty and Human Rights: A Peril and a Promise, in: Akande et al. (eds.), Human Rights and 21st Century Challenges: Poverty, Conflict, and the Environment, 2020, p. 223, who notes that the SDGs are "strongly grounded" in human rights; for the own understanding of the Committees, see Report of the Chairs of the human rights treaty bodies on their twenty-seventh meeting, UN Doc. A/70/302, 07.08.2015, Annex I, with the Chairs underlining the "synergy between human rights, sustainable development and the environment."

[548] *Golay*, The Role of Human Rights Mechanisms in Monitoring the United Nations Declaration on the Rights of Peasants, Research Brief, Geneva Academy, January 2020, p. 4.

[549] See examples from recent State reports submitted to the CEDAW Committee, Ninth periodic report submitted by Honduras under article 18 of the Convention, due in 2020, UN Doc. CEDAW/C/HND/9, 01.04.2021, paras. 273–278 with a sub-section devoted to the implementation of the Sustainable Development Goals 2030; Seventh periodic report submitted by Armenia under article 18 of the Convention, due in 2020, UN Doc. CEDAW/C/ARM/7, 01.04.2021, paras. 251–254; Eighth periodic report submitted by Finland under article 18 of the Convention, due in 2018, UN Doc. CEDAW/C/FIN/8, 01.04.2021, paras. 265–268; see also *Samarasinghe*, Human Rights and Sustainable Development: Together at Last?, in: Browne/Weiss (eds.), Routledge Handbook on the UN and Development, 2020, p. 91 with similar observations.

[550] *Broude/Shany*, The International Law and Policy of Multi-Sourced Equivalent Norms, in: Broude/Shany (eds.), Multi-Sourced Equivalent Norms in International Law, 2011, p. 8.

[551] With a view to "substance uncertainty" and "incoherence" concerning indigenous peoples' rights, see *Charters*, Multi-Sourced Equivalent Norms and the Legitimacy of Indigenous Peoples' Rights under International Law, in: Broude/Shany (eds.), Multi-Sourced Equivalent Norms in International Law, 2011, pp. 300–304.

[552] Guidelines on an expanded core document and treaty-specific targeted reports and

The final guidelines adopted by the Meeting of Chairpersons, however, only addressed two substantive issues common to all treaties, which were non-discrimination and equality, and effective remedies.[553]

aa) Equality clauses

Each treaty contains a provision that enshrines the principle of equality.[554] Under the premise that the two Covenant Committees review State parties in a back-to-back fashion every eight years, and the more specialized Committees in between, the two equality provisions in the ICCPR and the ICESCR could serve as a normative basis to address topics raised by the issue- and group-specific treaty bodies. Whenever a certain vulnerable individual or group of individuals is discriminated against, this could possibly be covered by article 2(1) ICCPR or article 2(2) ICESCR as both provisions, being "substantially identical" to each other,[555] are open to any grounds of discrimination.[556] This is because next to the enumerated prohibited grounds of discrimination, both provisions include an umbrella clause[557] that covers discrimination based on *other status*.

The latter, according to both Covenant Committees, is understood as a flexible term which may evolve over time.[558] Thus, whenever an unjustified deprivation of Covenant rights by a State occurs, the Covenant Committees can presum-

---

harmonized guidelines on reporting under the international human rights treaties, Report of the secretariat, UN Doc. HRI/MC/2004/3, 09.06.2004, para. 20.

[553] Harmonized guidelines on reporting under the international human rights treaties, including guidelines on a common core document and treaty-specific documents, UN Doc. HRI/MC/2006/3, 03.05.2006, paras. 50–59; for a short overview of the concept of equality and its normative embodiments in universal and regional human rights treaties see *Clifford*, Equality, in: Shelton (ed.), The Oxford Handbook of International Human Rights Law, 2013, p. 420.

[554] The Convention against Torture is the only UN human rights core treaty that does not provide for a comparable equality clause, nevertheless, the principle of equality is referred to in the Convention's preamble.

[555] *Saul/Kinley/Mowbray*, The International Covenant on Economic, Social and Cultural Rights: Commentary, Cases, and Materials, 2014, Article 2(2), Non-discrimination, p. 174.

[556] *Henrard*, The Protection of Minorities through the Equality Provisions in the UN Human Rights Treaties: The UN Treaty Bodies, International Journal on Minority and Group Rights 14 (2007), 141, 153.

[557] *Nowak*, CCPR Commentary, Second revised Edition, 2005, Article 2, Domestic Implementation and Prohibition of Discrimination, para. 3.

[558] CESCR Committee, General Comment No. 20, Non-discrimination in economic, social and cultural rights (art. 2, para. 2, of the International Covenant on Economic, Social and Cultural Rights), UN Doc. E/C.12/GC/20, 02.07.2009, para. 27, cited at *Saul/Kinley/Mowbray*, The International Covenant on Economic, Social and Cultural Rights: Commentary, Cases, and Materials, Article 2(2), Non-discrimination, 2014, pp. 193–203, who list other grounds of discrimination addressed by the CESCR Committee, including disability, age, nationality, marital and family status, sexual orientation and gender identity, health status, place of residence and economic and social situation.

ably raise this issue under article 2(1) ICCPR and article 2(2) ICESCR respectively. Thereby they could be said to supervise the promotion of issue- or group-specific human rights in relation to the rights enshrined in their instruments.[559]

However, taking recourse to the rather unspecific and very broad equality provisions runs the risk of blurring the contours between the various human rights treaties, each in its own right focusing on a specific topic or vulnerable group. Besides, given the current trends regarding the rationalization and streamlining of the activities among treaty bodies, including targeted and focused reporting, while simultaneously seeking to minimize the work load of both State parties and treaty bodies, it is questionable whether addressing the recommendations made by more specialized treaty bodies via the broad equality provisions would prove helpful in the final analysis.[560]

State parties might also object to treaty bodies when these recommend the implementation of other treaty bodies' concluding observations, if such a monitoring activity is solely based on the rationale of treating all individuals equally by and under the law. Ultimately, even though each treaty contains an equality clause, its interpretation and application by the respective supervisory body does not necessarily lead to the same result.[561] There might be differences regarding possible justifications of unequal treatment, or with a view to positive measures aimed at achieving equality.[562]

bb) Congruent treaty provisions

There are, however, treaty provisions which are more congruent than others because of their specific scope of protection, sometimes coupled with (almost) identical wording.[563] For instance, article 15(1) CPRD prohibits torture and cruel, inhuman or degrading treatment or punishment and its wording is thus almost completely congruent with article 7 ICCPR. Article 15(2) CRPD, in turn, requires State parties to take all effective legislative, administrative, judicial or

---

[559] In this regard, see *Bourke Martignoni*, Sexual and Reproductive Rights at the Crossroads: Intersectionality and the UN Treaty Monitoring Bodies, in: Bribosia/Rorive (eds.), Human Rights Tectonics: Global Dynamics of Integration and Fragmentation, 2018, pp. 146–148, who observes that treaty bodies began to address multiple grounds of discrimination in the exercise of their mandates.

[560] *Krommendijk*, Less is more: Proposals for how UN human rights treaty bodies can be more selective, Netherlands Quarterly of Human Rights 38 (2020), 5, 8, arguing for "greater selectivity".

[561] For the interpretation of equality provisions, see *Clifford*, Equality, in: Shelton (ed.), The Oxford Handbook of International Human Rights Law, 2013, pp. 438–442.

[562] For a study on the equality and non-discrimination provisions among UN human rights treaties, see *Vandenhole*, Non-Discrimination and Equality in the View of the UN Human Rights Treaty Bodies, 2005.

[563] Guidelines on an expanded core document and treaty-specific targeted reports and harmonized guidelines on reporting under the international human rights treaties, UN Doc. HRI/MC/2004/3, 09.06.2004, para. 18.

other measures to prevent persons with disabilities from being subjected to the prohibited treatment under article 15(1) CRPD. The article is modelled after article 2 CAT,[564] the only difference being here that it is specifically devoted to the protection of disabled persons. Another example is *Payandeh's* observation relating to the right to freedom of expression, included through various similar, if not comparable, but nevertheless different normative embodiments in UN human rights treaties, all of which ultimately relate to the same universal and inalienable right pertaining to every individual, and finding a shared normative basis in the UDHR.[565] Textual resemblance or normative congruence with regard to the wording can thus serve as a first indicator in the search for suitable provisions.

Other provisions, with less textual resemblance, might possibly function as the normative basis to address cross-cutting issues found in other treaties as well. This, however, under the premise that the respective treaty body has interpreted the provisions further and has deepened or broadened the scope of protection to achieve normative consistency with relevant provisions under other UN human rights core treaties.

cc) Example of the right to water

One example shall be portrayed in more detail in the following. The chart of congruence developed by the Secretariat included, inter alia, the right to adequate food and clothing, to be found in article 11 ICESCR, article 6 ICCPR, article 5(e-iv) CERD, article 14(2-h) CEDAW and article 27(3) CRC. The list is completed with article 28 CRPD, which had not yet been adopted at the time of drafting the harmonized Reporting Guidelines.

In a more general context, the essence of these provisions is often summed up as the adequate standard of living, encompassing various components which are considered indispensable to living a dignified life. Conversely, focusing on other components comprised by the right to an adequate standard of living, the right to water finds mention in articles 14(2-h) CEDAW and 28(2-a) CRPD. Articles 11 ICESCR, 27 CRC and 5(e-iii) CERD lack any explicit reference to the right of water as such; article 24(2-c) CRC only mentions access to clean drinking water as a necessary prerequisite to the right to the enjoyment of the highest attainable standard of health. Nevertheless, the omission of water as an explicit component of an adequate standard of living under article 11 ICESCR and article 27 CRC did not prevent the CESCR and CRC Committee from construing these two provisions in a way that implies an implicit right to water.[566]

---

[564] *Fennell*, Article 15, Protection against Torture and Cruel or Inhuman or Degrading Treatment or Punishment, in: Bantekas/Stein/Anastasiou (eds.), The UN Convention on the Rights of Persons with Disabilities: A Commentary, 2018, p. 427.

[565] *Payandeh*, Fragmentation within international human rights law, in: Andenas/Bjorge (eds.), A Farewell to Fragmentation: Reassertion and Convergence in International Law, 2015, pp. 306–307.

[566] For the ICESCR, see *Saul/Kinley/Mowbray*, The International Covenant on Econom-

The CESCR Committee arrived at the conclusion that water should be included in the concept of adequate living standards. By reasoning that article 11 ICESCR contained a non-exhaustive list of elements pertaining to adequate living conditions because of the word "including" under article 11(1).[567] The CRC Committee, for its part, has explicitly linked the right to water to article 27 CRC, by raising the issue in its concluding observations adopted vis-à-vis several State parties.[568] This example demonstrates that the congruence of treaty provisions is not simply based on a congruent textual basis, but treaty interpretation can also lead to the incorporation of either new rights or further aspects which turn textually non-congruent treaty provisions into provisions with the same scope of protection.[569]

III. Conclusion on the follow-up procedure

Treaty bodies should be advised to explicitly recommend the implementation of other treaty bodies' recommendations when the normative basis under the two treaties in question is to a certain extent textually congruent or when similar provisions have been interpreted in a coherent manner. The latter, however, should be subject to the additional premise that both treaty bodies can build upon a certain body of "jurisprudence" or pronouncements which reflect their common interpretation (including General Comments and concluding observations repeatedly addressing the cross-cutting issue), thereby providing for legal certainty at least to some degree. While the substantive overlap has been often framed as a disadvantage that causes treaty bodies to work inefficiently, the preceding section has shown that there are also instances in which substantive overlap offers advantages. Presupposing an overall adherence to the simplified

---

ic, Social and Cultural Rights: Commentary, Cases, and Materials, 2014, Article 11, The Right to an Adequate Standard of Living, p. 899; for the CRC, see *Nolan*, Article 27, The Right to a Standard of Living Adequate for the Child's Development, in: Tobin (ed.), The UN Convention on the Rights of the Child: A Commentary, 2019, p. 1030.

[567] CESCR Committee, General Comment No. 15, The right to water (arts. 11 and 12 of the International Covenant on Economic, Social and Cultural Rights), UN Doc. E/C.12/2002/11, 20.01.2002, para. 3, cited at: *Saul/Kinley/Mowbray*, The International Covenant on Economic, Social and Cultural Rights: Commentary, Cases, and Materials, 2014, Article 11, The Right to an Adequate Standard of Living, p. 900; see also *de Albuquerque/Roaf*, The human rights to water and sanitation, in: Dugard et al. (eds.), Research Handbook on Economic, Social and Cultural Rights as Human Rights, 2020, p. 202 and pp. 204–208 with an overview of the CESCR Committee's clarification of the rights to water and sanitation.

[568] *Nolan*, Article 27, The Right to a Standard of Living Adequate for the Child's Development, in: Tobin (ed.), The UN Convention on the Rights of the Child: A Commentary, 2019, p. 1030.

[569] For a detailed analysis of how General Comment No. 15 was drafted and came into existence, see *Reiners*, Transnational Lawmaking Coalitions for Human Rights, 2021, pp. 78–89.

reporting procedure and the abidance by a comprehensive reporting calendar, the required coordination when addressing other treaty bodies' recommendations does not seem to pose insurmountable challenges. To this end, it might be also useful for treaty bodies to align their time frames for the follow-up procedure. It might then also be of added value to develop a common grading scale among all Committees.

Finally, concerns that focusing on recommendations made by other treaty bodies might have reverse effects on current strengthening efforts in rationalizing and rendering the reporting procedure more effective, could be refuted by greater efforts in coordination. For instance, treaty bodies could try not to include recommendations adopted by other Committees when the latter have chosen the specific recommendations for their own follow-up procedure. Given the restricted number of follow-up items under the current procedures, these should not be repeated unnecessarily. However, in situations where State parties have failed to deliver sufficient follow-up information or a recommendation has only been partially implemented, addressing this issue might serve as a good opportunity to not lose track of its implementation.

F. Conclusion on attempts at reform under the reporting procedure

The preceding part has analysed four attempts at reform which, implemented all together, could render the State reporting system before UN human rights treaty bodies more efficient and effective. The underlying premise is that the simplified reporting procedure becomes the default reporting procedure. As the procedure will focus on fewer issues, and given the overlap of treaty guarantees, it is even more essential that the various Committees coordinate their reporting activities so as to avoid futile repetition of the same topics.

As has become apparent, the need for cooperation to avoid negative duplication is given due consideration by the Committees and certain practices, such as the inclusion of cross-references or joint reviews, are already being explored by some. In this context, it is arguably the introduction of a comprehensive reporting calendar that could lead to greater gains with a view to coordination and thus the avoidance of negative and futile repetition.

Admittedly, the proposed periodicity of eight years might lead to long reporting intervals, which could nevertheless be shortened by the introduction of two clusters of treaty bodies and the additional introduction of an integrated follow-up procedure. In this context, it is also worth exploring how to achieve cooperation within the broader human rights protection architecture, which could possibly entail coordination of reporting under the UPR. Moreover, the practice of the CRPD Committee could be taken into consideration for further developments. Next to a treaty body's own follow-up procedure, other treaty bodies belonging to the second cluster could take up recommendations stemming from the first cluster, and raise the issue with specific reference another time. As the analysis has shown, suitable subject areas which allow several treaty bodies to raise the same issue under their own treaty do exist.

In order to guarantee regular review of all State parties, treaty bodies would need to develop a more rigid and stringent approach vis-à-vis non-reporting State parties. Reviews in the absence of a report could prove a suitable means in this matter. While such an approach should remain the *ultima ratio*, treaty bodies need to develop a less hesitant approach. As has been demonstrated, provided a comprehensive reporting calendar with predictable deadlines were to be consistently implemented, the need for reviews in the absence of a report would become less pressing. Treaty bodies should also be advised to take into consideration the problem of substantive overlap, not only as far as the application of the simplified reporting procedure is concerned, but also with a view to all other reform proposals, such as activities under the follow-up procedure or when reviewing State parties in the absence of a report.

With a view to the mandate of the Committees in implementing the reform proposals analysed above, many of them, indeed, can be implemented without the consent of State parties. The interpretation of the relevant treaty provisions governing the reporting procedure or establishing the Committees allow for many actions on the part of treaty bodies. Even though some proposals, such as the uniform and exclusive adherence to the simplified reporting procedure, are currently beyond their mandate, its mandatory implementation is not out of reach. Subsequent practice in accordance with article 31(3)(b) VCLT could prove helpful in that regard.

Ultimately, the COVID-19 pandemic has brought the treaty body system almost to a halt and has negatively affected the already stricken system. At the same time, the current situation offers the opportunity for a restart. Treaty bodies could also consider maintaining the practice of online dialogues and reviews,[570]

---

[570] See for instance CRC Committee, Concluding observations on the combined fifth and sixth periodic reports of Luxembourg, UN Doc. CRC/C/LUX/CO/5–6, 1.06.2021 paras. 1–2; CEDAW Committee, Concluding observations on the ninth periodic report of Denmark, UN Doc. CEDAW/C/DNK/CO/9, 09.03.2021, para. 3; Human Rights Committee, Concluding observations on the seventh periodic report of Finland, UN Doc. CCPR/C/FIN/CO/7, 03.05.2021, para. 1; CESCR Committee, Concluding observations on the second periodic report of Latvia, UN Doc. E/C.12/LVA/CO/2, 30.03.2021, para. 1; CRPD Committee, Concluding observations on the initial report of Estonia, UN Doc. CRPD/C/EST/CO/1, 05.05.2021, para. 3; Committee against Torture, Observations finales concernant le quatrième rapport périodique de la Belgique, UN Doc. CAT/C/BEL/CO/4, 25.08.2021, para. 2; CERD Committee, Concluding observations on the combined twentieth to twenty-second periodic reports of Belgium, UN Doc. CERD/C/BEL/CO/20–22, 21.05.2021, para. 2; CMW Committee, Concluding observations on the second periodic report of Chile, UN Doc. CMW/C/CHL/CO/2, 11.05.2021, para. 3; CED Committee, Concluding observations on the report submitted by Mongolia under article 29 (1) of the Convention, UN Doc. CED/C/MNG/CO/1, 11.05.2021, para. 1.

though it seems that these were only conducted in reaction to the extraordinary circumstances caused by the pandemic.[571] Nevertheless, these are worth considering, especially given that it is very burdensome for small States to appear before all the Committees. Such an approach should nevertheless be only applied if the technical arrangements are sufficient, both in Geneva and in the State party under review.

Finally, much depends on whether the Committees will seize the opportunity. Especially the discussions on the reporting calendar and still diverging working methods indicate that harmonization and alignment are difficult to achieve. Additionally, the velocity at which new reform proposals are spread among the treaty body systems could certainly be increased. Sometimes it also appears that some treaty bodies are or were not aware of changes within other Committees, although these changes could also turn out to be highly relevant for themselves. Therefore, the thesis' last part will focus on possible forms of cooperation among treaty bodies.

---

[571] See for instance, Report of the Committee on the Protection of the Rights of All Migrant Workers and Members of Their Families (32nd session), UN Doc. A/76/48 (2021), para. 9 with the Committee's decision to conduct online reviews if State parties would agree, see also para. 59 in the same document with the Committee considering working methods related to online reviews during the COVID-19 pandemic or similar crisis situations; similarly, the CED Committee considered online reviews as an option, but only under exceptional circumstances, Report of the Committee on Enforced Disappearances (17th and 18th session), UN Doc. A/75/56 (2020), para. 14; the CRPD Committee held an online dialogue with Estonia on an "exceptional, pilot basis", Report of the Committee on the Rights of Persons with Disabilities on its twenty-fourth session, UN Doc. CRPD/C/24/2, 30.04.2021, para. 19.

Part V

Institutionalized Cooperation among human rights treaty bodies

One of the positive features of Resolution 68/268 is that it considers all treaty bodies to belong to an interconnected system.[1] Nevertheless, one might question whether the various treaty bodies really do pertain to a system of connected bodies or whether they just have developed more and more harmonized and partially aligned working methods.[2] Considering that even the harmonization of minor changes in working methods has proven difficult, time-consuming, and challenging, it is questionable if the various treaty bodies have already achieved a level of integration at which they can really be considered a system of interconnected bodies.

The following section shall thus shed light on two fora of cooperation. These may be regarded as institutionalized linking elements in the midst of the several treaty bodies and could prove helpful in the strengthening process. These are the Meeting of Chairpersons and the Inter-Committee Meeting, the latter only existing between 2002 and 2011. Both serve, or more precisely served, in the case of the Inter-Committee Meeting, as fora for discussions among all Committees and allow treaty bodies to engage in a dialogue on specific issues relevant to the work of each Committee.[3]

Under the assumption that the fragmentation of human rights law has at least some kind of negative repercussions on the treaty body system, and that developing aligned and standardized working methods will prove beneficial to all stakeholders participating in the treaty body system, cooperation and coordination via inter-treaty body meetings might reduce incoherencies and are thus of added value.[4]

---

[1] *O'Flaherty*, The Strengthening Process of the Human Rights Treaty Bodies, American Society of International Law, Proceedings of the Annual Meeting 108 (2014), 285, 287.

[2] See, however, *Bernaz*, Continuing evolution of the United Nations treaty bodies system, in: Sheeran/Rodley (eds.), Routledge Handbook of International Human Rights Law, Abingdong 2013, p. 712, who reaches the conclusion that in light of the "sum of procedures used and common practice both adopted and encouraged by the treaty bodies" one can assume that the Committees form a system, even though the system "could certainly be more integrated".

[3] See *Kędzia*, United Nations Mechanisms to Promote and Protect Human Rights, in: Symonides (ed.), Human Rights: International Protection, Monitoring, Enforcement, 2003, p. 37, who describes the Meeting of Chairpersons as a "*sui generis* coordinating forum".

[4] *O'Flaherty/O'Brien*, Reform of UN Human Rights Treaty Monitoring Bodies: A Cri-

In the following, the development and evolution of the two "linkage Committees" will be traced first. Particularly with a view to the Meeting of Chairpersons, it is possible to detect four stages of its existence. The initial phase, a phase of improved organization, the period of parallel existence next to the Inter-Committee Meeting, and increasing trends towards consitutionalization after the abolishment of the Inter-Committee Meeting. In a second step, it will be analysed whether it is possible to vest the Chairs/the Meeting of Chairpersons with decision-making powers, which could provide necessary acceleration effects to the currently ongoing strengthening process.

A. Establishment and evolution of the "linkage Committees"

I. Initial phase

The origins of the Meeting of Chairpersons can be traced back to debates within the United Nations General Assembly Third Committee on the treaty bodies' annual reports. Because of the "proliferation" of reporting obligations under various international human rights instruments and the accompanying difficulties State parties were facing in submitting their reports, members of the Third Committee decided to propose a joint meeting of the organs charged with the reporting procedures.[5] Pursuant to General Assembly Resolution 38/117, adopted 16 December 1983, by which it requested the Secretary-General to consider the possibility of convening a meeting of "the Chairmen of the bodies entrusted with

---

tique of the Concept Paper on the High Commissioner's Proposal for a Unified Standing Treaty Body, Human Rights Law Review 7 (2007), 141, 159; see also *Kjærum*, The UN Reform Process in an Implementation Perspective, in: Lagoutte/Sano/Scharff Smith (eds.), Human Rights in Turmoil: Facing Threats, Consolidating Achievements, 2007, p. 17, who considers that solutions to the problem of duplication could be found "on the basis of greater coordination", realized via the Inter-Committee or the Meeting of Chairpersons; *Hampson*, An Overview of the Reform of the UN Human Rights Machinery, Human Rights Law Review 7 (2007), 7, 14 calling for more cooperation between treaty bodies themselves and other entities of the United Nations engaged in the protection of human rights.

Attempts at coordination are not unique to the human rights treaty bodies. Comparable to efforts among UN human rights treaty bodies, the Special Procedures have created a Coordination Committee, which shall help to generate increased synergies between mandate holders, to develop common working methods, or which shall enable mandate holders to speak with one voice, see in legal literature, *M'jid*, The UN Special Procedures System: The Role of the Coordination Committee of Special Procedures, in: Nolan/Freedman/Murphy (eds.), The United Nations Special Procedures System, 2017, p. 131.

[5] Report of the Human Rights Committee (17th, 18th and 19th session), UN Doc. A/38/40 (1983), para. 32.

the consideration of reports submitted under the relevant human rights instruments"[6], the first Meeting of Chairpersons took place in August 1984.[7]

The probably most important and relevant insight gained during the first four meetings was that each treaty body did, indeed, face similar challenges, such as non-compliance by State parties with a view to repeated non-submission of reports or reports of low quality, the burden of co-existing reporting procedures, and the need to enhance the implementation of recommendations adopted.[8] Additionally, all participants of the first Meeting of Chairpersons "were of the unanimous view" that it provided a very valuable opportunity to exchange views and discuss matters common to all treaty bodies. Consequently, such meetings should be organized on a regular basis in the future.[9]

Other than the identification of occasionally reoccurring topics in relation to the challenges faced under the reporting procedure by all Committees,[10] the first four Meetings of Chairpersons leave the impression of a rather uncoordinated approach by which the meetings were planned and ultimately convened. However, some of the participating treaty bodies had just taken up their activities, and it appears that the exchange of information and experiences made in the performance of their mandates played a pivotal role. In this context, the meetings also served as a useful means for treaty bodies to position themselves within the United Nations human rights protection architecture. The Meeting of Chairper-

---

[6] UN General Assembly, Resolution 38/117, Reporting obligations of the State parties to the International Covenants on Human Rights, UN Doc. A/RES/38/117, 16.12.1983, para. 5.

[7] For the first report of the newly established Meeting of Chairpersons, which was not yet called Meeting of Chairpersons, but "meeting of chairmen", see Reporting Obligations of State parties to the International Covenants on Human Rights and the International Convention on the Elimination of All Forms of Racial Discrimination, Note by the Secretary-General, UN Doc. A/39/484, 20.09.1984, Annex.

[8] Reporting Obligations of State parties to the International Covenants on Human Rights and the International Convention on the Elimination of All Forms of Racial Discrimination, Note by the Secretary-General, UN Doc. A/39/484, 20.09.1984, Annex, paras. 10 and 16 in particular.

[9] Reporting Obligations of State parties to the International Covenants on Human Rights and the International Convention on the Elimination of All Forms of Racial Discrimination, Note by the Secretary-General, UN Doc. A/39/484, 20.09.1984, Annex, para. 33.

[10] Compare the respective agendas, for the first meeting in 1984, Reporting Obligations of State parties to the International Covenants on Human Rights and the International Convention on the Elimination of All Forms of Racial Discrimination, Note by the Secretary-General, UN Doc. A/39/484, 20.09.1984, Annex; for the second meeting in 1988, Reporting Obligations of State parties to the United Nations Instruments on Human Rights, Note by the Secretary-General, UN Doc. A/44/98, 03.02.1989, Annex; for the third meeting in 1990, Effective Implementation of United Nations Instruments on Human Rights and Effective Functioning of Bodies Established Pursuant to such Instruments, Note by the Secretary-General, UN Doc. A/45/636, 30.10.1990, Annex; for the fourth meeting in 1992, Effective implementation of international instruments on human rights, including reporting obligations under international instruments on human rights, Note by the Secretary-General, UN Doc. A/47/628, 10.11.1992, Annex.

sons notably created a consciousness among treaty bodies that they "should not be viewed in isolation, but as a part of an overall system".[11]

Alongside the creation of awareness of the environment in which they were operating, treaty body Chairpersons additionally articulated the necessity for better external representation. At the the fourth Meeting of Chairpersons in 1992, the Chairs discussed the participation of treaty bodies in the preparatory process to the World Conference on Human Rights, set to take place in 1993. The representatives of the then existing Committees expressed that they had "been placed at disadvantage and thereby unable to make a full contribution to the preparatory process."[12] Due to their experiences, they decided to jointly articulate the need to be well-represented at such possible future meetings.[13]

Another argument militating for the treaty bodies being in a phase of orientation can be drawn from the report of the sixth Meeting of the Chairpersons. Although this meeting might not precisely fit into the "initial phase" anymore, it offers interesting insights into how the treaty bodies intended to organize linkages and relationships with other human rights mechanisms. Because of missing and inappropriate involvement of treaty body representatives in the preparations prior to the World Conference on Women in September 1995, the Chairpersons required the Secretary-General to provide the seventh Meeting of the Chairpersons with a report that should contain proposals on how to establish a "sui generis" status for human rights treaty bodies within the United Nations.[14]

II. Phase of increased and improved organization

The second phase of the Meeting of Chairpersons is best characterized by increased and improved organization. Even though the Meeting of Chairpersons and its internal structure did not evolve in a strict manner that would allow to precisely pin down a linear development in terms of coordination and profici-

---

[11] Reporting Obligations of State parties to the United Nations Instruments on Human Rights, Note by the Secretary-General, UN Doc. A/44/98, 03.02.1989, Annex, para. 63; see also the report of the third meeting in 1990, Effective Implementation of United Nations Instruments on Human Rights and Effective Functioning of Bodies Established Pursuant to such Instruments, Note by the Secretary-General, UN Doc. A/45/636, 30.10.1990, Annex, para. 57, with the Chairs highlighting the positive effects of increased and "greater interaction" between them.

[12] Effective implementation of international instruments on human rights, including reporting obligations under international instruments on human rights, Note by the Secretary-General, UN Doc. A/47/628, 10.11.1992, Annex, para. 32.

[13] Effective implementation of international instruments on human rights, including reporting obligations under international instruments on human rights, Note by the Secretary-General, UN Doc. A/47/628, 10.11.1992, Annex, para. 33 and paras. 77–82.

[14] Report of the sixth meeting of persons chairing the human rights treaty bodies, UN Doc. A/50/505, 04.10.1995, para. 22, with the CEDAW and CRC Committee being the two treaty bodies placed at disadvantage by their non-involvement.

ency, it is striking that between the fifth and the thirteenth Meeting of Chairpersons, meetings and the respective reports seemed to take on an increasingly coherent manner. One of the recommendations adopted at the fifth Meeting of Chairpersons in 1994 exemplifies this, since the Chairs "strongly [recommended]" that their meetings be "held annually instead of biennially",[15] which led to increased meeting time and thus allowed for intensified discussions and dialogues.

Not only were agenda items regularly revisited and reiterated at various consecutive meetings during the second phase, but these were discussed with simultaneous reference to conclusions and recommendations adopted on the same subject matter during previous meetings, thereby generating a higher degree of continuity.[16]

In addition, the Chairs began to consciously reflect on how to render the Meeting of Chairpersons more efficient as an institution. To that end, they proposed to provide "activities profiles" of all Committees prior to each meeting. These profiles should include "salient activities" and "relevant statistics".[17] To complement the "activities profiles", the Chairs requested the Secretariat to provide a kind of follow-up report that should focus on the steps taken by the single Committees in the implementation of the recommendations adopted at the Meeting of Chairpersons.[18]

Yet, it was not only the internal cooperation between treaty bodies that was fostered during this period, but also the cooperation between the treaty body system as a whole and other actors involved in the protection and promotion of human rights came to the fore, such as the Special Procedures Mandate Holders.[19] The eleventh Meeting of Chairpersons was thus used to organize a joint

---

[15] Report of the fifth meeting of persons chairing the human rights treaty bodies, UN Doc. A/49/537, 19.10.1994, para. 59.

[16] Compare in this matter the reports of the sixth, seventh and eight meeting with regard to the topic of gender perspectives within the work of treaty bodies: Report of the sixth meeting of persons chairing the human rights treaty bodies, UN Doc. A/50/505, 04.10.1995, paras. 34–35; Report of the seventh meeting of persons chairing the human rights treaty bodies, UN Doc. A/51/482, 11.10.1996, paras. 58–61; Report of the eighth meeting of persons chairing the human rights treaty bodies, UN Doc. A/52/507, 21.10.1997, paras. 62–64; or the report of the eighth, ninth and tenth meeting with regard to the possible introduction of focused reports on a limited range of issues: Report of the eighth meeting of persons chairing the human rights treaty bodies, UN Doc. A/52/507, 21.10.1997, para. 35; Report of the ninth meeting of persons chairing the human rights treaty bodies, UN Doc. A/53/125, 14.05.1998, paras. 30–31; Report of the persons chairing the human rights treaty bodies on their tenth meeting, UN Doc. A/53/432, 25.09.1998, paras. 29–31.

[17] Report of the eighth meeting of persons chairing the human rights treaty bodies, UN Doc. A/52/507, 21.10.1997, para. 73.

[18] Report of the eighth meeting of persons chairing the human rights treaty bodies, UN Doc. A/52/507, 21.10.1997, para. 74.

[19] The Special Procedures mandate holders meet annually since 1994, *M'jid*, The UN Special Procedures System: The Role of the Coordination Committee of Special Procedures, in: Nolan/Freedman/Murphy (eds.), The United Nations Special Procedures System, 2017, p. 132.

meeting with the sixth meeting of special rapporteurs and representatives, experts and chairpersons of working groups of the special procedures system of the Commission on Human Rights and of the advisory services programme.[20]

However, despite positive developments in terms of generating more continuity and thereby being able to conduct more thorough discussions, or the increased attempts to coordinate external relations, the Meeting of Chairpersons fell short in adoting feasible measures to overcome the challenges which were well-known by then. In order to foster and strengthen cooperation between the various Committees, the establishment of another linkage committee was thus eventually proposed, the so-called Inter-Committee Meeting. The idea of setting up a second body, with a specific focus on harmonizing practices under the reporting procedure, was first proposed at the twelfth Meeting of Chairpersons.[21]

III. Phase of parallel existence

1. Inter-Committee Meeting

At the thirteenth Meeting of Chairpersons in 2001, the Chairs resumed discussions on the idea of creating the Inter-Committee and discussed a background paper prepared by the Secretariat. The paper contained three possible topics to be dealt with by the newly created Inter-Committee meeting.[22] These three topics were to be the periodicity under the State reporting procedure, human trafficking, and reservations to UN human rights treaties.[23]

In the final analysis, the Meeting of Chairpersons reached the conclusion that the first Inter-Committee Meeting should be devoted to working methods only and not to substantive issues.[24] Pursuant to the recommendation by the Chairpersons, the first Inter-Committee Meeting was convened from 26 to 28 June 2002 and considered the methods of work and the issue of reservation to UN human rights core treaties.[25] As the meeting's outcome, it was agreed that a se-

---

[20] Report of the persons chairing the human rights treaty bodies on their eleventh meeting, UN Doc. A/54/805, 21.03.2000, Annex, paras. 33–36. In the following years, treaty body representatives and representatives of the special procedures system met regularly until June 2011, when the last joint meeting was held, Report of the Chairs of the human rights treaty bodies on their twenty-third meeting, UN Doc. A/66/175, 22.07.2011, Annex II, Report of the twelfth inter-committee meeting of the human rights treaty bodies, paras. 53–59.

[21] Report of the chairpersons of the human rights treaty bodies on their twelfth meeting, UN Doc. A/55/206, 19.07.2000, para. 70.

[22] Report of the chairpersons of the human rights treaty bodies on their thirteenth meeting, UN Doc. A/57/56, 05.02.2002, para. 63.

[23] Review of recent Development relating to the Work of the Treaty Bodies, Report by the Secretariat, UN Doc. HRI/MC/2001/2, 08.06.2001, paras. 27–52.

[24] Report of the chairpersons of the human rights treaty bodies on their thirteenth meeting, UN Doc. A/57/56, 05.02.2002, para. 63.

[25] Report of the first Inter-Committee Meeting of the Human Rights Treaty Bodies, UN Doc. HRI/ICM/2002/3, 24.09.2002.

cond Inter-Committee Meeting should be convened in two years in order to discuss the outstanding agenda items from the first Inter-Committee meeting,[26] which was affirmed by the fourteenth Meeting of Chairpersons, the latter immediately held afterwards.[27]

However, other than proposed, the second Inter-Committee was already convened one year later in 2003, as the Secretary-General requested the High Commissioner on Human Rights to consult with treaty bodies on new and streamlined reporting procedures.[28] Put in a larger context, the second Inter-Committee meeting was held one year earlier than originally envisaged due to the incentives set by the Secretary-General, which led to the second treaty body reform initiative.[29] The starting point of the latter is also reflected in the second Inter-Committee Meeting's agenda, which was mainly focusing on the Secretary-General's ideas on strengthening the human rights treaty body system.[30] At the same time, the Meeting of Chairpersons recommended that the Inter-Committee should henceforward be convened annually.[31] Its focus should rest on the coherent and consistent approach to substantive human rights issues, since it proved itself a "valuable forum for discussion."[32]

2. Meeting of Chairpersons

The Meeting of Chairpersons, in turn, assigned itself the role of facilitating discussions on technical and organizational issues, and maintaining responsibility for dialogue with State parties, the at the time still existing Commission on Human Rights, the Subcommission on the Promotion and Protection of Human Rights and other stakeholders, including United Nations entities and NGOs.[33] By assigning the task of developing a coherent and consistent approach to substantive human rights issues to the Inter-Committee Meeting, the Meeting of Chairpersons allocated much of its original workload to the newly founded body.

---

[26] Report of the first Inter-Committee Meeting of the Human Rights Treaty Bodies, UN Doc. HRI/ICM/2002/3, 24.09.2002, para. 81.
[27] Report of the chairpersons of the human rights treaty bodies on their fourteenth meeting, UN Doc. A/57/399, 11.09.2002, para. 61.
[28] Report of the Chairpersons of the human rights treaty bodies on their fifteenth meeting, UN Doc. A/58/350, 05.09.2003, Annex I, Report of the second inter-committee meeting of human rights treaty bodies, para. 1.
[29] See *supra* Part II B.
[30] Report of the Chairpersons of the human rights treaty bodies on their fifteenth meeting, UN Doc. A/58/350, 05.09.2003, Annex I, Report of the second inter-committee meeting of human rights treaty bodies, paras. 11–22.
[31] Report of the Chairpersons of the human rights treaty bodies on their fifteenth meeting, UN Doc. A/58/350, 05.09.2003, para. 50.
[32] Report of the Chairpersons of the human rights treaty bodies on their fifteenth meeting, UN Doc. A/58/350, 05.09.2003, para. 50.
[33] Report of the Chairpersons of the human rights treaty bodies on their fifteenth meeting, UN Doc. A/58/350, 05.09.2003, para. 51.

Even though it was the Meeting of Chairpersons which officially decided to retain the main responsibility for keeping in dialogue with State parties, the Inter-Committee gradually took over more and more tasks of the Meeting of Chairpersons. For instance, it appears that the Inter-Committee began to fulfil the role of a spokesperson between treaty bodies and other stakeholders, as discussions with NGOs or informal consultations with State parties were included in its agenda, though originally pertaining to the Meeting of Chairpersons.[34]

In 2007, at the sixth Inter-Committee Meeting, it was decided that meetings would henceforth be held twice a year, so as to ensure increasing harmonization across the treaty body system,[35] which was endorsed by the nineteenth Meeting of Chairpersons.[36] Nonetheless, only four years later in 2011, the last Inter-Committee Meeting took place.[37] With the twelfth Inter-Committee Meeting, the phase of coexistence between the Meeting of Chairpersons and the Inter-Committee as a second forum of exchange came to an end, since the twenty-third Meeting of Chairpersons decided to abolish the Inter-Committee.[38] Reasons for the abolishment, according to the Chairpersons, were the low compliance and implementation rate of recommendations adopted by the Inter-Committee Meeting and limited financial resources.[39] The Inter-Committee Meeting was supposed to be substituted by thematic working groups, established by the Chairs when considered necessary. These working groups should dedicate their attention to "issues of common interest, including the harmonization of treaty body jurisprudence."[40] Additionally, the Chairs justified the Inter-Committee's abolishment with an "increasing overlap between their meetings and the Inter-Committee".[41] This finding is somewhat ironic since the Inter-Committee was

---

[34] Report of the chairpersons of the human rights treaty bodies on their twenty-first meeting, UN Doc. A/64/276, 10.08.2009, Annex I, Report of the eighth inter-committee meeting of human rights treaty bodies, paras. 34–48; Report of the chairs of the human rights treaty bodies on their twenty-second meeting, UN Doc. A/65/190, 06.08.2010, Annex II, Report of the eleventh inter-committee meeting of the human rights treaty bodies, paras. 32–39.

[35] Report of the chairpersons of the human rights treaty bodies on their nineteenth meeting, UN Doc. A/62/224, 13.08.2007, Annex, Report of the sixth inter-committee meeting of human rights treaty bodies, para. 48(ii).

[36] Report of the chairpersons of the human rights treaty bodies on their nineteenth meeting, UN Doc. A/62/224, 13.08.2007, para. 23.

[37] Report of the Chairs of the human rights treaty bodies on their twenty-third meeting, UN Doc. A/66/175, 22.07.2011, Annex II, Report of the twelfth inter-committee meeting of the human rights treaty bodies.

[38] Report of the Chairs of the human rights treaty bodies on their twenty-third meeting, UN Doc. A/66/175, 22.07.2011, para. 25.

[39] Report of the Chairs of the human rights treaty bodies on their twenty-third meeting, UN Doc. A/66/175, 22.07.2011, para. 24.

[40] Report of the Chairs of the human rights treaty bodies on their twenty-third meeting, UN Doc. A/66/175, 22.07.2011, para. 25.

[41] Report of the Chairs of the human rights treaty bodies on their twenty-third meeting, UN Doc. A/66/175, 22.07.2011, para. 24.

originally intended to lead to decreased overlap and better coordination between the treaty bodies, but itself ended up duplicating the Meeting of Chairperson's mandate.

IV. Phase of "constitutionalization" of the Meeting of Chairpersons

After the abolishment of the Inter-Committee Meeting, the Meeting of Chairpersons held its next meeting in 2012.[42] Whereas the Meeting of Chairpersons fell dormant during the phase of parallel existence, it now regained momentum. A perusal of the 2012 meeting's agenda reveals that it came back to address more issues than it did during previous meetings. Particular attention was devoted to *Pillay's* report on the treaty body strengthening process and the reform proposals contained therein.[43] Further indicative of a reinvigorated Meeting of Chairpersons is the fact that, in comparison to previous meetings, the Chairs also resumed the practice of convening consultations with State parties or other entities on a regular basis, starting at the twenty-fifth meeting in 2013.[44]

Most noteworthy, the Chairs began to regularly chose agenda items for the upcoming Meeting of Chairpersons,[45] with the provisional agenda becoming ever more detailed.[46] Additionally, a run-through of all annual reports adopted between 2014 and 2020 demonstrates that each Meeting of Chairpersons took up one major aspect contained in Resolution 68/268. All reports considered together, the Meeting of Chairpersons covered almost comprehensively all aspects comprised in Resolution 68/268. Noteworthy in this respect is also the meeting conducted in 2022, as the Chairs reached many conclusions regarding the reform

---

[42] Report of the Chairs of the human rights treaty bodies on their twenty-fourth meeting, UN Doc. A/67/222, 02.08.2012.

[43] Report of the Chairs of the human rights treaty bodies on their twenty-fourth meeting, UN Doc. A/67/222, 02.08.2012, paras. 7–15 and paras. 32–34.

[44] Report of the Chairs of the human rights treaty bodies on their twenty-fifth meeting, UN Doc. A/68/334, 19.08.2013, paras. 26–34, with the Chairs holding informal consultations with States and with civil society organizations and the International Coordinating Committee of national human rights institutions.

[45] See in that regard, Report of the Chairs of the human rights treaty bodies on their twenty-fourth meeting, UN Doc. A/67/222, 02.08.2012, para. 39; Report of the Chairs of the human rights treaty bodies on their twenty-fifth meeting, UN Doc. A/68/334, 19.08.2013, para. 50.

[46] See in comparison to previous meetings the decisions adopted at the twenty-sixth Meeting of Chairpersons for the twenty-seventh meeting's agenda, Report of the Chairs of the human rights treaty bodies on their twenty-sixth meeting, UN Doc. A/69/285, 11.08.2014, para. 115; see for the provisional agenda of the thirty-first Meeting of Chairpersons in 2019 (the last one prior to the COVID-19 pandemic, which had a serious impact on the annual Meeting of Chairpersons), Provisional agenda and annotations, UN Doc. HRI/MC/2019/1, 12.04.2019.

process and possible future developments.⁴⁷ Also, especially activities in recent years, such as the endorsement of elements concerning a common aligned procedure, and the conscious selection of issues to be addressed in more detail during upcoming meetings, prove that the Meeting of Chairpersons is working continuously with the aim of achieving progress with regard to the harmonization of working methods and procedures.⁴⁸

V. Evaluation of the two "linkage committees"

Any evaluation of the Inter-Committee and the Meeting of Chairpersons and their contribution so far to the strengthening process appears ambiguous. The work of the Inter-Committee Meeting in particular allowed treaty bodies to discuss and harmonize jurisprudence, general comments and working methods,⁴⁹ and "many contributors recommended reviving and institutionalizing joint meetings" in the form of Inter-Committee Meetings.⁵⁰

---

⁴⁷ Report of the Chairs of the human rights treaty bodies on their thirty-fourth annual meeting, UN Doc. A/77/228, 26.07.2022.

⁴⁸ Proposals relating to the reporting procedure, the constructive dialogue and concluding observations were discussed at the twenty-sixth meeting in 2014, Report of the Chairs of the human rights treaty bodies on their twenty-sixth meeting, UN Doc. A/69/285, 11.08.2014, paras. 15–54; the elaboration of General Comments and the issue of reporting compliance were taken up at the twenty-seventh meeting in 2015, Report of the Chairs of the human rights treaty bodies on their twenty-seventh meeting, 07.08.2015, UN Doc. A/70/302, paras. 21–29; discussions on the common core document were conducted at the twenty-eighth meeting in 2016, Report of the Chairs of the human rights treaty bodies on their twenty-eighth meeting, UN Doc. A/71/270, 02.08.2016, paras. 23–25; an "interim" conclusion was reached at the twenty-ninth meeting in 2017, Report of the Chairs of the human rights treaty bodies on their twenty-ninth meeting, UN Doc. A/72/177, 20.07.2017, para. 26; follow-up activities came into focus in 2018 during the thirtieth meeting, Report of the Chairs of the human rights treaty bodies on their thirtieth meeting, UN Doc. A/73/140, 11.07.2018, paras. 18–21 and para. 68 with reference to Annex II for the respective decision/endorsement; the 31ˢᵗ meeting in 2019 endorsed a common framework for the simplified reporting procedure, Report of the Chairs of the human rights treaty bodies on their thirty-first annual meeting, UN Doc. A/74/256, 30.07.2019, Annex II.

⁴⁹ *Gaer*, The Institutional Future of the Covenants, A World Court for Human Rights?, in: Moeckli/Keller/Heri (eds.) The Human Rights Covenants at 50: Their Past, Present, and Future, 2018, p. 341, who points to the Inter-Committee Meeting's goal of "breaking the stranglehold that committee chairs had on the harmonization and reform efforts"; *Bernaz*, Continuing evolution of the United Nations treaty bodies system, in: Sheeran/Rodley (eds.), Routledge Handbook of International Human Rights Law, 2013, p. 714, who highlights the Inter-Committee Meeting's contribution to the adoption of harmonized reporting guidelines.

⁵⁰ *Callejon et al.*, Optimizing the UN Treaty Body System, p. 28, even though it is submitted here that the clear focus of the Inter-Committee laid on the harmonization of working methods and that the issues of general comments and jurisprudence were only touched upon; see also *Egan*, The United Nations Human Rights Treaty System: Law and Procedure, 2011, p. 472, who emphasizes that the Inter-Committee demonstrates the treaty bodies' willingness to observe and learn from each other.

Meanwhile, the input of the Meeting of Chairpersons was considered less valuable on the grounds that "these meetings face legitimacy and governance challenges" and that "decisions adopted by the Chairpersons in joint meetings have never been implemented because other members have not endorsed them."[51] It is true that the Meeting of Chairpersons fell short with regard to useful and feasible recommendations in the phase of parallel existence. However, it must be borne in mind that both linkage Committees ended up duplicating their mandates and that it was the Inter-Committee Meeting which undertook most of the substantial work during the phase of parallel existence.

Furthermore, the Meeting of Chairperson's value should not be solely assessed on the basis of its current or more recent contributions to the strengthening process.[52] Quite to the contrary end, with particular hindsight to its initial phase, the Meeting of Chairpersons served and continues to serve as the only forum among all individual treaty bodies that enables them to speak with one voice and to remain constantly in a formalized and institutionalized dialogue. It also serves to spread newly emerging ideas among the system, though admittedly sometimes in an inchmeal fashion. Proceeding only incrementally, however, must not obscure the fact that recommendations as formulated by the Meeting of Chairpersons can subtly influence the various Committees.[53] They might even exert pressure on those Committees which might initially be reluctant to accept certain reform proposals.[54]

To lend more weight to its importance, reference shall be made to its overall development and the concomitant improvements in terms of continuity and internal structures. It is also crucial to note that prevailing and chronic scarcity of financial and human resources affects the Meeting of Chairpersons no less than it affects each single treaty body in the proper performance of its mandate.[55]

---

[51] *Callejon et al.*, Optimizing the UN Treaty Body System, p. 29.

[52] See *Cleveland*, Enhancing Human Rights Connectivity for the Treaty Body System, Document submitted for the Treaty Body Review Conference, Geneva, 8 – 9 December 2016, p. 3 who considers the Meeting of Chairpersons as "vital" but at the same "insufficient" for generating "meaningful communication" between the various treaty bodies, https://www.geneva-academy.ch/joomlatools-files/docman-files/Draft%20List%20of%20Submissions%20-%20Academic%20Platform%202020%20Review%20without%20Propositions%20.pdf (last access: 21.08.2023).

[53] As an example, reference can be made to the CEDAW Committee's decision to reinstate the simplified reporting procedure and its application to a growing number of State parties, see *supra* Part III B.II.6.

[54] *Alston*, The Committee on Economic, Social and Cultural Rights, in: Mégret/Alston (eds.), The United Nations and Human Rights: A Critical Appraisal, Second Edition, 2020, p. 448; *Evatt*, The Future of the Human Rights Treaty System: Forging Recommendations, in: Bayefsky (ed.), The UN Human Rights Treaty System in the 21st Century, 2000, p. 294, noting that individual treaty bodies did not always give due consideration to the Meeting of Chairpersons.

[55] The lack of financial resources was ultimately also one of the major reasons for the abolishment of the Inter-Committee Meeting, Report of the Chairs of the human rights treaty bodies on their twenty-third meeting, UN Doc. A/66/175, 22.07.2011, para. 24.

Moreover, other practical obstacles clearly hamper its functioning, such as the very limited meeting time only once a year,[56] the steady fluctuation in the membership of any kind of "linkage Committee" due to the varying and non-synchronized terms of office as prescribed by the various treaties,[57] and the obvious need for the single Committees/Chairs to be given enough time beforehand to discuss and prepare their respective contributions to the annual meetings.[58] These obstacles clearly cause the Meeting of Chairperson's mills to mostly grind slowly. This conclusion leads to the next section, which will deal with a proposal to possibly enhance the Meeting of Chairperson's mandate and its efficiency.

B. Decision-making powers of "linkage Committees"

To accelerate the process of harmonizing working methods among the various human rights treaty bodies, it has been suggested to enhance the role of the Chairs, or to vest the "linkage committees" with decision-making powers regarding procedural aspects respectively.

I. Vesting Chairs with decision-making powers

Early forms of such a proposal can be found in the report of the ninth Inter-Committee Meeting, where it was discussed whether the individual Committee members present had the power to act on behalf of their Committees and to take decisions on behalf of them.[59] While generally divided on this issue, the majority

---

[56] *Egan*, Reform of the UN Human Rights Treaty Body System, in: Mégret/Alston (eds.), The United Nations and Human Rights: A Critical Appraisal, Second Edition, 2020, p. 661.

[57] For this observation, see Report of the chairpersons of the human rights treaty bodies on their twenty-first meeting, UN Doc. A/64/276, 10.08.2009, Annex II, Report of the ninth inter-committee meeting of human rights treaty bodies, para. 21.

[58] *Abashidze/Koneva*, The Process of Strengthening the Human Rights Treaty Body System: The Road towards Effectiveness or Inefficiency?, Netherlands International Law Review 66 (2019), 357, 374; *Schöpp-Schilling*, Treaty Body Reform: The Case of the Committee on the Elimination of Discrimination Against Women, Human Rights Law Review 7 (2007), 201, 204, who observes a "cumbersome and time-consuming process" with regard to subsequent discussions within individual Committees on the implementation of proposals stemming from the Meeting of Chairpersons.

[59] Report of the chairpersons of the human rights treaty bodies on their twenty-first meeting, UN Doc. A/64/276, 10.08.2009, Annex II, Report of the ninth inter-committee meeting of human rights treaty bodies, para. 21 and para. 9, with the term "binding" being used; another indirect proposal of that kind can be found in statements of the CMW and CRC Committee during discussions on the unified standing treaty body, the CMW Committee proposed to "upgrade" the Inter-Committee Meeting and to provide it with a broader mandate to develop concrete proposals, Report of the Working Group on the Harmonization of Working Methods of Treaty Bodies, UN Doc. HRI/MC/2007/2, 09.01.2007, para. 9. The CRC Committee proposed the establishment of a "coordination committee" or a "management bureau",

of Inter-Committee members could at least agree on a common denominator. Treaty body representatives could take decisions on behalf of their Committees as far as "organizational matters" were concerned, but decisions on "substantive issues" should still be subject to further endorsement by the individual Committees.[60]

The next essential consideration of vesting representatives of Committees (in particular the Chairs) with decision-making power was made at one of the expert seminars on the occasion of *Pillay's* multi-stakeholder initiative in Poznan in September 2010. The discussants refined the idea to vest Chairs with decision-making powers and developed the so-called "Poznan formula".[61] In order to shift "from a 'light' to an 'advanced' coordination and harmonization mode",[62] "Chairpersons should be empowered to adopt measures on those working methods and procedural matters, which are common across the Treaty Body system and which have previously been discussed within each of the Committees. Such a measure would be implemented by all Treaty Bodies, unless a Committee subsequently dissociates itself from it."[63]

In essence, the Poznan formula, if applied, would partially render the Meeting of Chairpersons into a decision-making body, with the restriction that each Committee needs to discuss the subject matter first, and that they later retain the possibility to reverse the decision imposed on them.[64]

II. Hesitant implementation of the "Poznan formula"

However, despite its possible acceleration effect in harmonizing procedural matters,[65] the Chairs seemed to proceed rather cautiously with a view to the subse-

---

para. 6. There were also discussions on possible decision-making powers of such a body, paras. 12–13; see also in legal literature, *Schöpp-Schilling*, Treaty Body Reform: The Case of the Committee on the Elimination of Discrimination Against Women, Human Rights Law Review 7 (2007), 201, 204, who remarked that Chairs were lacking decision-making power.

[60] Report of the chairpersons of the human rights treaty bodies on their twenty-first meeting, UN Doc. A/64/276, 10.08.2009, Annex II, Report of the ninth inter-committee meeting of human rights treaty bodies, para. 21.

[61] *Egan*, The United Nations Human Rights Treaty System: Law and Procedure, 2011, p. 472.

[62] The Poznan Statement on the Reforms of the UN Human Rights Treaty Body System, para. 16, https://www2.ohchr.org/english/bodies/HRTD/docs/PoznanStatement.pdf (last access: 21.08.2023).

[63] The Poznan Statement on the Reforms of the UN Human Rights Treaty Body System, para. 17, available at: https://www2.ohchr.org/english/bodies/HRTD/docs/PoznanStatement.pdf (last access: 21.08.2023).

[64] See, however, *Egan*, Transforming the UN Human Rights Treaty System: A Realistic Appraisal, Human Rights Quarterly 42 (2020), 762, 784, who argues that the Poznan could even jeopardize any attempts to assign Chairs a leading role in the strengthening process because, in her opinion, the formula appears to be too weak.

[65] See *Egan*, The United Nations Human Rights Treaty System: Law and Procedure, 2011,

quent implementation of the "Poznan formula". Though formally endorsing the formula during their next gathering in 2011, they wished to have the matter discussed further in the individual Committees so as to "seek approval for a stronger statement."[66]

The reticent attitude towards fully implementing the Poznan formula is further mirrored by following Meetings of Chairpersons, which merely reiterated the recommendation to adopt measures on working methods and procedural issues of common concern across the treaty body system, but without any further clarification as to whether they were actually inclined to apply the formula with respect to a concrete reform proposal.[67] From 2014 onwards, an even less determinate rhetoric is to be found in the annual reports. Now, frequent mention was made of the Chairpersons' mandate to formulate "conclusions" in ensuring coherence across the treaty bodies and standardizing working methods.[68] Still, the Chairs also repeated the recommendation to implement the Poznan formula with the exact same language as used in previous reports.[69]

The partial shift from vesting Chairs with the power to *adopt measures* to the mere competence of *formulating conclusions* is supposedly owed to General Assembly Resolution 68/268. Said resolution had only taken up the possibility of formulating conclusions, which is clearly less than adopting measures, the latter implying a certain kind of decision-like act at least.[70] Noteworthy is also the complete omission of any reference to the Poznan formula's language in the Chairpersons' reports from 2016 until 2018. Indeed, reference was only made to the encouragement of formulating conclusions as stipulated by Resolution 68/268.[71]

---

p. 476, who considers the Poznan formula as "a critical" recommendation in the process of harmonization. Thereby she seems to contradict herself, considering her statement cited one footnote above.

[66] Report of the Chairs of the human rights treaty bodies on their twenty-third meeting, UN Doc. A/66/175, 22.07.2011, para. 9.

[67] Report of the Chairs of the human rights treaty bodies on their twenty-fourth meeting, UN Doc. A/67/222, 02.08.2012, para. 34; and Report of the Chairs of the human rights treaty bodies on their twenty-fifth meeting, UN Doc. A/68/334, 19.08.2013, para. 48.

[68] Report of the Chairs of the human rights treaty bodies on their twenty-sixth meeting, UN Doc. A/69/285, 11.08.2014, para. 76.

[69] Report of the Chairs of the human rights treaty bodies on their twenty-sixth meeting, UN Doc. A/69/285, 11.08.2014, para. 77.

[70] UN General Assembly, Resolution 68/268, Strengthening and enhancing the effective functioning of the human rights treaty body system, UN Doc. A/RES/68/268, 09.04.2014, para. 38.

[71] Report of the Chairs of the human rights treaty bodies on their twenty-eighth meeting, UN Doc. A/71/270, 02.08.2016, para. 74; Report of the Chairs of the human rights treaty bodies on their 29th meeting, UN Doc. A/72/177, 20.07.2017, para. 28; Report of the Chairs of the human rights treaty bodies on their thirtieth meeting, UN Doc. A/73/140, 11.07.2018, para. 64.

III. Recent discussion on decision-making powers

Yet, in 2019, the Chairs came back to explicitly mentioning the Poznan formula. They recalled their "decision, taken at their previous meetings" to adopt measures which "should be implemented by all treaty bodies unless a treaty body subsequently dissociated itself from the system."[72] The most firmly formulated statement in relation to the Poznan formula was, however, included in the 2020 Chairpersons' report. Among the common concerns and proposals conveyed to the co-facilitators of the 2020 treaty body review process, the Chairs clearly sought to empower and strengthen their own role. They proposed that "treaty bodies should ensure that Committee Chairs are mandated to take decisions in respect of working methods and procedures, which are common across the treaty body system and have previously been discussed and agreed to within each of the Committees, with particular reference to reporting and individual communications procedures."[73]

Striking about this statement is not only the clear-cut use of the term "decision", which exceeds the terms "to adopt measures" and "to formulate conclusions", as previously used in the Poznan formula, Resolution 68/268 and the Chairs' annual reports, but also the exact point of reference for the application of such powers. While previously rather nebulous references had been made to "organizational matters", "procedural matters common across the treaty body system", "working methods", or "methodologies", the Chairs now seem to demonstrate their willingness to vest the Chairs with decision-making powers in relation to working methods that directly concern the reporting and individual complaints procedures. In this way, the Chairs now defined a more precise field of the formula's application than they had ever done before.[74]

IV. Legal mandate of treaty bodies in implementing the "Poznan formula"

The above-mentioned discrepancy between the General Assembly's envisaged enhanced role of treaty body Chairpersons and the one contained in the Poznan Statement is possibly an expression of what is referred to as the "legitimacy challenge"[75] the Meeting of Chairpersons allegedly faces, or of what has been

---

[72] Report of the Chairs of the human rights treaty bodies on their thirty-first annual meeting, UN Doc. A/74/256, 30.07.2019, para. 57.

[73] Report of the Chairs of the human rights treaty bodies on their thirty-second annual meeting, UN Doc. A/75/346, 14.09.2020, para. 46(c).

[74] See also the 2023 Conclusions of the Chairs of the human rights treaty bodies on the OHCHR Working Paper – Options and guiding questions for the development of an implementation plan for the conclusions of the human rights treaty body Chairs at their 34th meeting in June 2022 (A/77/228, paras. 55–56), paras. 8–11, as one of the most unequivocal reaffirmation to implement the formula.

[75] *Callejon et al.*, Optimizing the UN Treaty Body System, p. 29.

labelled as the "problematic format"[76] of the annual meetings. Indeed, the enhancement of the role of Chairpersons is not left uncontested, particularly by parties to the human rights treaties.

In the ongoing 2020 treaty body review process, several State parties opposed the possibility of vesting the Chairs with further reaching competencies. Some State parties argued, for instance, that "[suggestions] by the chairs have to be approved by each treaty-body, in accordance with its respective rules of procedure".[77] Other State parties seemed to be more supportive of a strengthened Meeting of Chairperson's mandate,[78] while others, in turn, seem inclined to an invigorated Meeting of Chairpersons, simultaneously leaving it uncertain how this is to be accomplished in concrete terms.[79] Common to both proponents and opponents of an enhanced mandate of the Meeting of Chairpersons, however, is that neither of them addresses the issue from a legal perspective as such. The same applies to legal commentators,[80] which justifies a closer look at the legal questions and possible solutions which arise in connection with the application of the "Poznan formula".

---

[76] Cf. *Abashidze/Koneva*, The Process of Strengthening the Human Rights Treaty Body System: The Road towards Effectiveness or Inefficiency?, Netherlands International Law Review 66 (2019), 357, 371–375.

[77] The Consideration of the State of the Human Rights Treaty Body System, Submission by the "African Group" and Bahrain, para. 27, these State parties argued further that "[other] initiatives by chairpersons of the human rights treaty body non-related to the methods of work and organizational matters often lead to an increase in the workload and the expenditures of the treaty body and shall, therefore, be avoided."; Position of the Russian Federation regarding the review of the implementation of provisions of UN GA Resolutions 68/268 on Strengthening and Enhancing the Effective Functioning of the Human Rights Treaty Body System, para. 13, both available at https://www.ohchr.org/en/calls-for-input/co-facilitation-process-treaty-body-review-2020 (last access: 21.08.2023).

[78] See for instance HRTBs Questionnaire- Bangladesh position, which states: "We believe the treaty bodies should enjoy the liberty of determining the scope of the chairperson's coordinating role.", https://www.ohchr.org/en/calls-for-input/co-facilitation-process-treaty-body-review-2020 (last access: 21.08.2023).

[79] Contributions submitted by Costa Rica on behalf of 43 other State Parties to the 31st meeting of Chairs – Towards the 2020 treaty body review, 20.07.2019, p. 3, https://tbinternet.ohchr.org/_layouts/15/treatybodyexternal/Download.aspx?symbolno=INT/CHAIRPERSONS/CHR/31/28571&Lang=en (last access: 21.08.2023); see also *Abashidze/Koneva*, The Process of Strengthening the Human Rights Treaty Body System: The Road towards Effectiveness or Inefficiency?, Netherlands International Law Review 66 (2019), 357, 374.

[80] *Rodley*, The Role and Impact of Treaty Bodies, in: Shelton (ed.), The Oxford Handbook of International Human Rights Law, 2013, p. 647, who only mentions in passing "legal and even political obstacles" as regards Chairs' decision-making powers; *Callejon et al.*, Optimizing the UN Treaty Body System, p. 29, with the sole mention of a legitimacy challenge that the Meeting of Chairpersons is facing.

1. Legal problems in the application of the "Poznan formula"

As mentioned in the Poznan statement, vesting the Chairpersons with decision-making powers should not interfere with the "autonomy and specificities of treaty bodies".[81] Nevertheless, applying the Poznan formula inevitably entails, to a certain degree, subjecting treaty bodies to external influence, which automatically and logically signifies a concomitant loss of autonomy.

The Poznan formula can only live up to its full potential in accelerating harmonization across the treaty body system if the Chairs are given leeway to discuss ideas and to modify proposals as part of the decision-making process. One may think of a scenario in which several ideas regarding a reform proposal are presented to the Meeting of Chairpersons by different treaty bodies. If the Chairs were then to discuss these proposals and would eventually agree on one of the various ideas developed, all Committees opting for another possibility would have to accept a different idea other than the one submitted. Working methods were thus influenced by decisions partially emanating from distinct treaty regimes. This poses two, closely related, legal questions that can only be answered conclusively together.

First, are Chairpersons mandated to act, and even more importantly, to take decisions on behalf of their respective treaty bodies? Second, is it permissible to apply any such decision-making power as envisaged by the Poznan formula, namely with the immediate implementation of measures that originate outside the treaty body's constituent treaty, and thus result from different treaty regimes?

2. Internal rules governing the Chairpersons' mandates

It is worth noting that none of the nine human rights core treaties contains any provision which explicitly mentions the Chairperson's mandate, which therefore justifies a closer look at the Rules of Procedure adopted by the various Committees.

a) Ordinary powers during treaty body sessions

First and foremost, it is a Chair's task to preside over their respective Committee's sessions, which finds expression in the commonly established rule among all treaty bodies that the Chairperson shall "control the proceedings of the Committee"[82] so as to ensure maintenance of order during the meetings. For this purpose, a Chairperson is vested with various powers, such as to direct the dis-

---

[81] The Poznan Statement on the Reforms of the UN Human Rights Treaty Body System, para. 16, available at: https://www2.ohchr.org/english/bodies/HRTD/docs/PoznanStatement.pdf (last access: 21.08.2023).

[82] Article 33 RoP CESCR; Article 37 RoP CERD; Article 26(1) RoP CMW; Article 46(2) RoP CRC; Article 29(2) RoP CED; Article 37 RoP Committee against Torture; Article 30(2) RoP CEDAW; Article 33(2) RoP CRPD; Article 40 RoP Human Rights Committee.

cussions, to accord the right to speak to individual Committee members, to call a speaker to order if remarks prove not relevant to the subject under discussion, and more generally, the power to rule on points of order.[83] However, these powers only concern the conduct of business during a Committee's session. They relate to internal and organizational matters. These rules therefore do not indicate how the Committees perceive the powers of their Chairpersons in external relations and decision-making processes.

b) Rules governing a Committee's control over its Chairperson

More instructive are, however, those provisions which stipulate that the respective Chairperson "shall remain under the authority of the Committee" when exercising the functions conferred upon them by the respective treaty and the respective Rules of Procedure. This rule can be found in each Committee's Rules of Procedure,[84] albeit with minor variations.

Such a provision might very likely imply that the Chairs, in the view of the various Committees, shall not have any further reaching powers than the Committee itself in plenary. Yet, the rule could alternatively be taken to mean that a Chair is barred from unilaterally imposing decisions upon their Committee without the latter having the ability to eventually reverse these decisions. Put differently, the Poznan formula does not necessarily contradict this specific rule. Any decision taken by the Chairs on behalf of their Committees is amenable to change. According to the Poznan formula, the Committees hence retain the possibility of subsequently dissociating themselves from the measures/decisions adopted.[85]

Further illustrative of the Chairs being possibly able to act on behalf of their Committees are rules on their representative function, though only to be found in the Rules of Procedure of three Committees. Article 19(2) RoP of the Human Rights Committee, article 17(4) RoP CED and article 18(3) RoP CEDAW accordingly all provide that their "Chair shall represent the Committee at United Nations meetings in which the Committee is officially invited to participate." Thereby, these three Committees recognize at least a representative function of their Chairs in relation to official meetings convened under the auspices of the United Nations. Nevertheless, the fact that these Committees consider their Chairs as representatives at United Nations meetings does not automatically reveal anything about further powers.

---

[83] See for example the powers of the Chair to the CRPD Committee, Article 33 RoP CRPD, UN Doc. CRPD/C/1/Rev. 1, 10.10.2016.

[84] Article 16(2) RoP CMW; Article 19(1) RoP Human Rights Committee; Article 18(2) RoP CRPD; Article 25(2) RoP CRC; Article 17(2) RoP CED; Article 16 RoP CESCR; Article 18(1) RoP Committee against Torture; Article 18(2) RoP CEDAW; Article 17 RoP CERD.

[85] This possibility is also included in the latest proposal made by the Chairs on this matter, Report of the Chairs of the human rights treaty bodies on their thirty-second annual meeting, UN Doc. A/75/346, 14.09.2020, para. 46(c).

c) Exceptional intersessional powers

Finally, two treaty bodies expressly vest their Chairs with the power to act on behalf of their Committees. The Rules of Procedure of both, the Committee against Torture and the CED Committee provide that "between sessions, at times when it is not possible or practical to convene a special session of the Committee [...], the Chairperson is authorized to take action to promote compliance with the Convention on the Committee's behalf if he/she receives information which leads him/her to believe that it is necessary to do so."[86]

While the wording still suggests that action taken by the Chairs on behalf of their Committees remains exceptional, given that any such action is only permissible between sessions and under the premise that it is not possible or practical to convene a special session, the two Chairs nevertheless enjoy a certain range of discretion. The measures taken are dependent on the belief whether they are necessary. Beyond the discretion granted to the Chairs, resulting from the rather vague and non-defined term "necessary", actions in accordance with article 18(2) RoP CAT and article 17(3) RoP CED relate to a considerable field of application. Such measures can be taken to promote compliance with the Convention, which clearly correlates with activities under the State reporting and individual complaints procedure. Consequently, decisions taken in accordance with these rules could encompass activities that directly affect the Committee-State party relationship.

d) Methods of voting

Closely connected to the question of whether Chairs may act on behalf of their Committees are the decision-taking modi and voting methods. Most of the Committees expressly refer to decisions adopted by consensus as the default voting method, by either stipulating it as the first rule,[87] or by clarifying that prior to the adoption of a decision by a majority of votes, the respective Committee "shall endeavour" to reach its decisions by consensus.[88]

The Human Rights Committee and the CRC Committee are the only treaty bodies that established the rule that any decision shall be made by a majority of the members present.[89] Nevertheless, these two Committees acknowledge the principle of consensus as well. Both complemented their respective rule therefore with a footnote, indicating that the "method of work should normally allow for attempts to reach decisions by consensus before voting".

---

[86] Article 18(2) RoP Committee against Torture and article 17(3) RoP CED with identical language.
[87] Article 34(1) RoP CRPD; article 31(1) RoP CED; article 27(1) RoP CMW; article 31(1) RoP CEDAW.
[88] Article 46 RoP CESCR; article 50(2) RoP Committee against Torture.
[89] Article 52 RoP Human Rights Committee and article 59 RoP CRC.

The lack of express rules in this matter is explained, at least as far as the Human Rights Committee is concerned, by disagreement among Committee members on whether to formally include the consensus principle in the Committee's Rules of Procedure.[90] The CERD Committee is therefore the only treaty body that has not incorporated the principle of consensus in its Rules of Procedure.[91] Yet, in practice, the Committee also strives for the adoption of decisions by consensus, at least with regard to recommendations adopted under the reporting procedure.[92]

3. Relevant treaty provisions

Based on the Rules of Procedure analysed above, it becomes apparent that the Committees generally seek to reach decisions by consensus. Beyond that, it is a general rule among all treaty bodies that Chairs should principally remain under the authority and control of the Committees acting in plenary. At the same time, this general rule does not come without some exceptions, such as the power to act on behalf of a Committee in exceptional inter-sessional situations, or the representative function as recognized by some treaty bodies. Taking into consideration the specific language of the Chairs' proposals conveyed to the co-facilitators of the 2020 treaty body review process, in which it is stated that the Chairs "should ensure that Committee Chairs are mandated to take decisions in respect of working methods and procedures",[93] it is imaginable that the Committees will vest their Chairs with further powers through amendments to their respective Rules of Procedures.

While treaty bodies can certainly adopt their own Rules of Procedure and thereby enjoy "relatively far-reaching autonomy",[94] the power to adopt internal rules is subject to the restriction that they must not contradict the respective Committee's constituent treaty.[95] Hence, any amendment of Rules of Procedure in order to enable Chairs to act on behalf of their Committees must be taken in accordance with provisions and principles established under the treaties. This

---

[90] *McGoldrick*, The Human Rights Committee: Its Role in the Development of the International Covenant on Civil and Political Rights, 1991, p. 48.

[91] See article 50 RoP CERD, which requires the Committee to take decisions by a two-thirds majority of its members present and voting.

[92] *Thornberry*, The International Convention on the Elimination of All Forms of Racial Discrimination: A Commentary, The Convention and the Committee, 2016, pp. 47–48, who adds that consensus might be "thin", though.

[93] Report of the Chairs of the human rights treaty bodies on their thirty-second annual meeting, UN Doc. A/75/346, 14.09.2020, para. 46(c).

[94] *Nowak*, CCPR Commentary, Second revised Edition, 2005, Article 39, Officers and Rules of Procedure, para 3; with specific view to the First Optional Protocol and the related Rules of Procedure, *Møse/Opsahl*, The Optional Protocol to the International Covenant on Civil and Political Rights, Santa Clara Law Review 21 (1981), 271, 278.

[95] *Boerefijn*, The Reporting Procedure under the Covenant on Civil and Political Rights: Practice and Procedures of the Human Rights Committee, 1999, p. 36.

raises the question as to whether decisions taken by a single Committee member, the Chairperson, contradict the treaties themselves. Besides, in a second step, it must be analysed whether there are provisions that would allow the treaty bodies to submit themselves to external influence by the Meeting of Chairpersons, which implies, as aforementioned, a loss of independence and autonomy to a certain extent.

a) Requirement of acting as "the Committee"

In correspondence to the aforementioned "relatively far-reaching autonomy" in adopting Rules of Procedure, only a few treaties contain precise prescriptions as to their mandatory content. Only article 39(2) ICCPR and article 18(2) CAT respectively prescribe the quorums and voting methods of the two Committees, while in all other treaties there is only the general provision that each treaty body shall establish its own Rules of Procedure.

Article 39(2) ICCPR stipulates that twelve members shall constitute a quorum and decisions of the Committee shall be made by a majority vote of the members present. Similarly, article 18(2) CAT provides that six members shall constitute a quorum and that decisions shall also be adopted by a majority vote of the members present. In relation to all other treaties, which equally applies to the ICCPR and CAT, it can be ascertained that it is "the Committee" which considers State parties' reports, examines individual communications and carries out every other action. In principle, given a strict reading of all these provisions referring to "the Committee", this could imply the necessity to act in plenary and hence as a single organ.[96]

In keeping with such a reading, treaty bodies could only reach decisions regardless of the subject matter, by respecting the quorum stipulated in their treaty, provided that such a provision is included in the treaty, and only when acting as a plenary organ. The requirement to take decisions by a majority vote and the usage of the term "the Committee" seem to, at first glance, prevent the Committees from vesting their Chairs with further reaching powers.

On the other hand, both the requirement that the Committees act as a single organ and the autonomy of treaty bodies in determining their own Rules of Procedure enjoy an equal normative level. Therefore, the question arises as to whether these two principles could eventually be reconciled with each other, so as to allow ample usage of the latter without violating the former. In other words,

---

[96] For this possible interpretation of the term "the Committee" in relation to the question whether treaty bodies could split up in parallel chambers to examine State reports, see *Callejon et al.*, Optimizing the UN Treaty Body System, p. 42; with a view to the individual complaints procedure, *Kretzmer*, Commentary on Complaint Processes by Human Rights Committee and Torture Committee Members: The Human Rights Committee, in: Bayefsky (ed.), The UN Human Rights Treaty System in the 21st Century, 2000, p. 163, who argues that there is a "legal constraint" on establishing chambers with decision-making powers and that any decision must be approved by the Committee in plenary.

Committees could act in plenary and take a decision by consensus to confer certain powers upon individual Committee members. If such actions were taken by "the Committee", or if the quorum requirements in the cases of CAT and ICCPR were respected, these decisions would not contravene treaty provisions. The Committees would have acted as "the Committee".

The practice of treaty bodies also reveals a perforation of the consensus principle and demonstrates that the Committees are far from always acting in plenary. Under the reporting procedure, Committees appoint, for instance, country rapporteurs who are tasked with the drafting of LOIPRs/List of Issues and with the adoption of draft concluding observations after the constructive dialogue.[97] In addition, committees sometimes also work in parallel chambers.[98] Besides, so-called follow-up rapporteurs have been appointed,[99] who are tasked with receiving information from the State party under review concerning the implementation of recommendations adopted, as well as with assessing and evaluating this information, and communicating with the State party during the follow-up procedure.[100]

All these delegations of powers and work demonstrate an increasing division of labour, even in external relation to State parties. Ultimately, despite the delegation of certain tasks and the concomitant transferral of certain powers to individual Committee members, the treaty bodies as plenary bodies, and hence as "the Committee", retain the overall control over the various rapporteurs, chambers and working groups. Nothing else would ultimately apply in the event of the Poznan formula's application. The Committees would retain the overall authority, as they could subsequently dissociate themselves from any decision taken. Vesting Chairpersons with the power to act on behalf of their respective Committees and to take decisions does not contradict treaty provisions and could thus be incorporated in the various Committees' Rules of Procedure. The only mandatory requirement, however, is that the Committees maintain the ability to eventually later overturn and reverse such a decision.

---

[97] *Combrinck*, Article 36, Consideration of Reports, in: Bantekas/Stein/Anastasiou (eds.), The UN Convention on the Rights of Persons with Disabilities: A Commentary, 2018, p. 1069; *Boerefijn*, Article 18, in: Freeman/Chinkin/Rudolf (eds.), The UN Convention on the Elimination of All Forms of Discrimination Against Women: A Commentary, 2012, p. 498.

[98] Speaking positively of the review of State parties in dual chambers and suggesting to institutionalize this practice, *Seibert-Fohr*, The UN Human Rights Committee, in: Oberleitner (ed.), International Human Rights Institutions, Tribunals, and Courts, 2018, p. 134.

[99] *Monina*, Article 19, State Reporting Procedure, in: Nowak/Birk/Monina (eds.), The United Nations Convention Against Torture and its Optional Protocol: A Commentary, Second Edition, 2019, paras. 79–80; *Combrinck*, Article 36, Consideration of Reports, in: Bantekas/Stein/Anastasiou (eds.), The UN Convention on the Rights of Persons with Disabilities: A Commentary, 2018, p. 1075.

[100] *Tomuschat*, Human Rights: Between Idealism and Realism, Third Edition, 2014, p. 233.

b) External influence via the Meeting of Chairpersons

Yet, applying the Poznan formula does not only require vesting the Chairs with decision-making powers, but also subjects treaty bodies to external influence. Treaty bodies are only tasked with the oversight of their constituent instruments. Decisions and activities concerning their implementation may principally only be taken by the respective treaty body. Each decision taken jointly by all Chairs present at the annual Meeting of Chairpersons, and then subsequently implemented by each Committee, would however arise from, or would at least be partially influenced by, other treaty regimes.

A more institutionalized Meeting of Chairpersons could wield decisive influence. This could for example mean that provided a proposal made by the CED or CMW Committee gained acceptance at the Meeting of Chairpersons and were later adopted by the Chairs, all other Committees would have to, as a matter of principle, comply with the decision taken. In such a case, the proposal of a treaty body in whose constituent treaty only about 50 to 60 States are parties would influence the performance of all other Committees' mandates and would therefore indirectly affect the legal relations between these Committees and their State parties, which need not necessarily be parties to the treaty whose Committee made the prevailing proposal. At first sight, this might appear less problematic, as the Meeting of Chairpersons seeks to take decisions by consensus, but as previous chapters have shown, subsequent discussions within the individual Committees and the slow implementation of decisions adopted reveal that there is still disagreement, even when a decision has been officially taken at the Meeting of Chairpersons. Decisions adopted by consensus therefore can also be a strategic choice of the Meeting of Chairpersons to demonstrate cohesiveness, while internally there may well still be disagreement about individual modalities. With a view to the influence of a strengthened Meeting of Chairpersons, at least two treaty provisions among the UN human rights core treaties merit closer attention, which could argue for Committees to immediately defer to decisions taken by the Meeting of Chairpersons.

aa) Article 28 CED

Article 28(1) CED establishes the duty for the CED Committee to cooperate with other relevant organs tasked with the protection of all persons against enforced disappearances and mentions inter alia "treaty bodies instituted by international instruments".[101]

---

[101] Article 28(1) CED reads as follows: "In the framework of the competencies granted by this Convention, the Committee shall cooperate with all relevant organs, offices and specialized agencies and funds of the United Nations, with the treaty bodies instituted by international instruments, with the special procedures of the United Nations and with the relevant regional intergovernmental organizations or bodies, as well as with all relevant State institutions, agencies or offices working towards the protection of all persons against enforced disappearances."

Given that article 28(1) CED imposes the specific duty to cooperate with other treaty bodies, it could be argued that at least the CED Committee could submit itself to external influence by other treaty bodies in the form of decisions taken at the Meeting of Chairpersons. However, any kind of cooperation the CED Committee seeks to achieve is subject to the "framework of the competencies granted by this Convention", according to said provision.

The restriction to the framework of the competencies granted by the Convention proves to be of limited help in the determination as to how far the cooperation of the CED Committee can reach, as the formulation neither clarifies, nor delineates the boundaries of the Committee's mandate. The further requirement that the cooperation shall be advantageous to the protection of all persons against enforced disappearances rather suggests that any kind of cooperation in accordance with article 28(1) CED shall aim at providing better substantive protection for the victims of enforced disappearance. The provision seeks to consolidate efforts by international actors who dedicate their activities to the protection of all persons against enforced disappearances. At first glance, this thus seems to indicate that article 28(1) CED addresses cooperation to ensure adequate protection of individuals rather than providing for than inter-Committee cooperation as far as procedural harmonization is concerned.

However, pursuant to article 28(2) CED, the Committee shall consult other treaty bodies, in particular the Human Rights Committee, "with a view to ensuring the consistency of their respective observations and recommendations." Hence, article 28(2) CED seems to indicate to what extent cooperation between treaty bodies governed by article 28(1) CED shall take place, since the former refers to a wide range of other actors, whereas article 28(2) CED only mentions other treaty bodies, and in particular the Human Rights Committee. The provision could thus be considered *lex specialis* to the more general provision of article 28(1) CED as it is specifically limited to other treaty bodies instituted by relevant international human rights instruments.

Nevertheless, it must be noted that article 28(2) CED imposes the duty to *consult* other treaty bodies. This wording implies that the CED Committee is obliged to pro-actively seek guidance by other Committees. Seeking guidance, however, does not necessarily equate with cooperation on equal footing between the various treaty bodies, as would be the case of a strengthened Meeting of Chairpersons. Moreover, the provision explicitly refers to the "consistency" of observations and recommendations only. It therefore addresses the potential substantive overlap and possible deviating interpretations undertaken between the CED Committee and other treaty bodies, and in particular the Human Rights Committee. The provision thus aims at securing a consistent body of jurisprudence among those actors involved in the protection against enforced disappearances. Such an assumption is further bolstered by the fact that article 28 CED, read together with article 27 CED, was included to soothe those voices in the drafting process that advocated against the establishment of yet another treaty body.[102] Opponents of the creation of another treaty with another supervisory body preferred the adoption of an optional protocol either to the Convention against Torture or to the ICCPR on the grounds that the Human Rights Committee or the Committee against Torture had already acquired a "substantial case-law" on enforced disappearance,[103] and those States were thus concerned with normative consistency.

bb) Article 38(b) CRPD

Whereas article 28 CED specifically addresses the problem of substantive overlap, cooperation in form of a more institutionalized Meeting of Chairpersons might be covered by article 38(b) CRPD. The provision obliges the CRPD Committee to consult other relevant treaty bodies to ensure consistency inter alia as regards reporting guidelines.[104] Analogous to article 28 CED, the CRPD Committee has the duty to consult other "relevant bodies instituted by international human rights treaties, a term which most likely covers other treaty bodies at the UN level.[105] In respect of the express reference to reporting guidelines by article 38(b) CRPD, subjecting the CRPD Committee to the influence of an invigorated Meeting of Chairperson could be reconciled with article 38(b) CRPD as far as procedural harmonization is concerned. Contrary to article 28(1) CED and analogous to article 28(2) CED, however, the Committee shall *consult* other treaty bodies and the consultation is subject to the further restriction that any such activities are deemed appropriate. Last but not least, the provision not only addresses the harmonization of reporting guidelines, but also requires the CPRD Committee to consult other treaty bodies with a view to ensure the consistency of recommendations and suggestions. This wording is reminiscent of article 28 CED and suggests that article 38(b) CRPD refers rather to harmonization in terms of substance. Said interpretative result is also bolstered by the last half-sentence of article 38(b) CRPD, which provides that any consultation activity shall help to

---

[102] *de Frouville*, The Committee on Enforced Disappearances, in: Mégret/Alston (eds.), The United Nations and Human Rights: A Critical Appraisal, Second Edition, 2020, pp. 588–589.

[103] *de Frouville*, The Committee on Enforced Disappearances, in: Mégret/Alston (eds.), The United Nations and Human Rights: A Critical Appraisal, Second Edition, 2020, pp. 583–584.

[104] Article 38(b) CRPD reads as follows: "The Committee, as it discharges its mandate, shall consult, as appropriate, other relevant bodies instituted by international human rights treaties, with a view to ensuring the consistency of their respective reporting guidelines, suggestions and general recommendations, and avoiding duplication and overlap in the performance of their functions."

[105] See *Bantekas*, Article 38, Relationship of the Committee with Other Bodies, in: Bantekas/Stein/Anastasiou (eds.), The UN Convention on the Rights of Persons with Disabilities: A Commentary, 2018, p. 1117, who rightly emphasizes that reference to overlapping mandates and duplication "is only meaningful if an action or activity is undertaken by two or more entities making use of the same resources and attending to the same subject matter".

avoid duplication and overlap in the performance of treaty bodies and what implies the avoidance of substantive overlap.

Given the meaning of the term "to consult" and the focus on avoiding substantive incoherence, also article 38(b) CRPD does not cover the mandate of an invigorated Meeting of Chairpersons with decision-making powers regarding procedural harmonization. Even if one were to assume, by construing the provisions very broadly, that article 28 CED and article 38(b) CPRD would allow for enhanced cooperation in the form of the Meeting of Chairpersons being vested with decision-making powers, eventually only two out of nine treaties do exhibit such a "cooperation-provision" anyway.

4. Reconciliation between autonomy and external influence

The search for express provisions which could enable the treaty bodies to subject themselves to external influence by a Meeting of Chairpersons with increased decision-making powers put aside, the power to establish their own Rules of Procedure shall be revisited one last time.

Within their own treaty regime, treaty bodies acting in plenary can delegate certain functions and concomitant powers to individual treaty body members unless the plenary organ is not exempt from retaining overall authority and control. It is already common practice for the various Committees to perform their mandates based on a certain division of labour. As long as the decision to vest individual members with further reaching powers is taken in accordance with the required quorums and by the Committees as plenary organs, any such decision seems possible.

At this juncture, the criteria, and factors for the classification of treaty bodies powers shall be given due consideration. A distinction may be made between decisions pertaining exclusively to internal matters and those affecting external relations between State parties and treaty bodies.[106] The scenario that the Committees would apply certain working methods prescribed by the Meeting of the Chairpersons could hence simply be understood as an expression of the power to determine their own Rules of Procedure. Their autonomy in establishing Rules of Procedure and working methods could be understood as encompassing decisions on how decisions themselves are arrived at and taken. Besides, the external influence of the Meeting of Chairpersons notwithstanding, the Committees would retain the overall control in the last resort, and could thus reverse any measure taken by the Chairs.

Furthermore, in following the Poznan formula, the treaty bodies would not task a non-related international institution with the decision-making process. Rather to the opposite, it has to be recalled that each Committee is represented in

---

[106] See *Ulfstein*, Treaty Bodies and Regimes, in: Hollis (ed.), The Oxford Guide to Treaties, Second Edition, 2020, p. 419, who distinguishes between powers relating only to internal matters and those which would "impose new substantive obligations" on contracting parties.

the Meeting of Chairpersons by its own Chair, with this person pressing the respective Committee's view developed during preceding discussions within the individual Committee. Since measures taken by the Meeting of Chairpersons shall relate to features and functions common to all Committees, which are established by human rights treaties that are considered belonging to the same "family", incompatible decisions that are contradictory to already existing working methods, are almost utterly out of question. It could also be argued that decisions are taken by consensus, and should an individual chairperson have genuine doubts about the decision, he or she would also be left with a veto against the decision.

Ultimately, a decisive distinction must be drawn according to whether a given decision is internal or external in nature. Admittedly, a clear-cut differentiation is hard to undertake since any decision related to working methods will, sooner or later, directly or indirectly, affect the legal relationship between treaty bodies and State parties. Approaching the question from the extremes, the decision to apply the simplified reporting procedure as the default procedure, or to introduce another kind of follow-up procedure, both directly affecting or adding legal obligations imposed on State parties, are beyond an enhanced mandate of the Meeting of Chairpersons. On the other hand, features contained in the common elements paper on the simplified reporting procedure, such as contributions by single Committees to the establishment of a database concerning the use of the simplified reporting procedure,[107] the inclusion of standard paragraphs in LOIPRs to remind State parties that other questions than those enumerated in LOIPRs could possibly be raised during the constructive dialogue,[108] or the development of internal guidelines for the drafting of LOIPRs,[109] do not, at least predominantly, affect the Committee-State party relationship. These are thus all examples for a possible application of the Poznan formula. As far as less unequivocal features are concerned, an assessment on a case-by-case basis might be necessary. Such assessment could take into consideration the criteria identified in the context of delineating a treaty body's powers as developed above.

---

[107] Report of the Chairs of the human rights treaty bodies on their thirty-first annual meeting, UN Doc. A/74/256, 30.07.2019, Annex II, para. (e).

[108] Report of the Chairs of the human rights treaty bodies on their thirty-first annual meeting, UN Doc. A/74/256, 30.07.2019, Annex II, para. (g).

[109] Report of the Chairs of the human rights treaty bodies on their thirty-first annual meeting, UN Doc. A/74/256, 30.07.2019, Annex II, para. (k).

C. Conclusion and outlook

In summary, both the Inter-Committee Meeting and especially the Meeting of Chairpersons, notwithstanding criticism levelled at the latter, have contributed to the ongoing strengthening process. In reaction to the time-consuming and incremental decision-making process within the individual Committees, and subsequently within the Meeting of Chairpersons and then yet again within the various treaty bodies, possibly resulting in another referral back to the Meeting of Chairpersons the next year, the idea to enhance the role of Chairpersons by vesting them with decision-making powers relating to harmonization of working methods has emerged.

As has become apparent, vesting the Chairs with the power to take decisions on behalf of their Committees with regard to procedural matters is covered by treaty law. Key legal safeguards, which must be respected in any event, are that the single Committees retain overall control and that decisions taken by the Chairs do not directly affect legal obligations incumbent on State parties. Yet, cooperation via the Meeting of Chairpersons is by no means the ultimate and completely watertight solution. It has to be borne in mind that much depends, first and foremost, on the willingness and capacity of the individual Chairs, and second, decisions reached by the Meeting of Chairpersons do not necessarily present themselves as the most suitable solution to a problem. Furthermore, as with the work of the individual treaty bodies, the Meeting of Chairpersons and its proper functioning are largely dependent on the service provided by the Secretariat.

On that note, it is crucial to mention that vesting the Chairpersons with further reaching powers is not the only means by which treaty bodies can seek to increase coordination and cooperation. During more recent meetings, the idea surfaced to mandate single Committee members to form inter-Committee working groups, which would then meet between the sessions of the Meeting of Chairpersons.[110] In practice, all treaty bodies, except for the CESCR Committee, have already designated one of their individual members as focal point or rapporteur with respect to reprisals against persons and groups engaging with United Nations human rights treaty bodies and who shall exchange information intersessionally, resulting in a better flow of information between the various treaty bodies.[111] What is more, decisive preparatory work on the 2019 treaty body po-

---

[110] Report of the Chairs of the human rights treaty bodies on their thirtieth meeting, UN Doc. A/73/140, 11.07.2018, Annex III; however, the establishment of working groups had been already proposed after the abolishment of the Inter-Committee Meeting, cf. Report of the Chairs of the human rights treaty bodies on their twenty-third meeting, UN Doc. A/66/175, 22.07.2011, para. 25, see also *supra* Part V A.3.b).

[111] Role of treaty body focal points and rapporteurs with respect to reprisals against persons and groups engaging with United Nations human rights treaty bodies, UN Doc. HRI/MC/2019/2, 15.04.2019; in case of the CESCR Committee, its own Bureau acts as a focal

sition paper was accomplished by a meeting in February 2019, composed of Chairpersons and focal points of each Committee.[112] In 2019, the Human Rights Committee started to appoint focal points to strengthen the relation and cooperation with some of the other treaty bodies and regional human rights mechanisms,[113] and completed its list of focal points with further appointments in 2020, now covering relationships with all of the UN human rights treaty bodies.[114]

Noteworthy in that matter is also the establishment of an informal working group, composed of either Chairs or focal points, charged with finding suggestions in relation to the impact of COVID-19 on the modalities of work, and on the substantive contributions of treaty bodies related to the human rights implications of COVID-19.[115] Curiously, the working group, which was composed of 19 members from ten treaty bodies, gathered on a monthly basis via online-meetings and seems to provide valuable input to the Meeting of Chairpersons.[116] In its report, it requested the Meeting of Chairpersons, inter alia, to clarify the mandate of the working group, to strengthen synergies, and proposed to plan future sessions of the Meeting of Chairpersons well in advance.[117] The latter corresponds to the observation made above that the Meeting of Chairpersons is undergoing a process of professionalization and constitutionalization as an institution in its own right. It appears that this informal working group serves comparable purposes as the Inter-Committee Meeting, but with a considerably more dynamic and flexible approach. Said dynamic is probably owed to the fact that the working group meets monthly and quite flexibly online. Such an approach, however, requires the constant dedication of the participating Committee members and only adds to their existing workload.[118]

Thus, besides efforts in institutionalizing the Meetings of Chairpersons, more informal, intersessional and even bilateral cooperative approaches are evident and it will be interesting to see which of these two models will prevail, or even both, as the case may be.

---

point, Practices of the human rights treaty bodies on intimidation and reprisals and issues for further action by the Chairs, UN Doc. HRI/MC/2022/2, 21.03.2022, Annex I.

[112] Report of the Chairs of the human rights treaty bodies on their thirty-first annual meeting, UN Doc. A/74/256, 30.07.2019, para. 12.

[113] Report of the Human Rights Committee (123rd, 124th and 125th session), UN Doc. A/74/40 (2019), para. 56.

[114] Report of the Human Rights Committee (126th, 127th and 128th session), UN Doc. A/75/40 (2020), para. 50.

[115] Report of the Chairs of the human rights treaty bodies on their thirty-second annual meeting, UN Doc. A/75/346, 14.09.2020, paras. 30–39.

[116] Report of the Chairs of the human rights treaty bodies on their thirty-third annual meeting, UN Doc. A/76/254, 30.07.2021, Annex II.

[117] Report of the Chairs of the human rights treaty bodies on their thirty-third annual meeting, UN Doc. A/76/254, 30.07.2021, Annex II, para. 12.

[118] Taking into consideration the 2022 report, this approach seems to prevail, Report of the Chairs of the human rights treaty bodies on their thirty-fourth annual meeting, UN Doc. A/77/228, 26.07.2022, para. 55 No. 5.

Conclusions

That the UN human rights treaty bodies have been and are in a precarious situation is nothing new. Against the background of past attempts at reform, the discussions that these reform proposals triggered and their eventual outcome, it is hardly surprising that the 2020 treaty body review process came to nothing rather than maintaining the momentum which was present during the initial phase of *Pillay's* multistakeholder consultation process. State parties seemed to have missed the opportunity to direct the strengthening process to the next level.

However, the human rights treaty bodies themselves should not lean on possible actions by State parties; instead, it is their autonomy and their own legal mandate by which changes in the system can be brought about.

Conclusion No. 1: Past attempts at reform and the drafting of the UN human rights treaties strongly indicate that the most promising stakeholder to bring about sustainable and lasting change to the treaty body system are the United Nations human rights treaty bodies themselves.

Since the inception of each Committee, there has been a gradual development of their respective working methods and approaches under the various functions they exercise. It is also safe to assume that their evolution will continue. In order to determine which legal possibilities are intrinsic to human rights treaty bodies in the context of the treaty body strengthening process, it is necessary to interpret their constituent instruments, from which they derive their mandate and their very existence.

The interpretation of human rights treaties is subject to allegedly specialized methods of interpretation, which arguably focus more on teleological aspects of interpretation and seek to render rights and guarantees effective. With regard to an invigorated treaty body system with more efficient monitoring, effectiveness-orientated interpretation seems compelling. Such an interpretation can lead to the broadening of treaty provisions.

However, any interpretation of UN human rights treaties, and any interpretation of those provisions that establish the treaty bodies and vest them with their powers, must take due account of the fact that treaty bodies ultimately exhibit a weaker mandate when compared to regional human rights courts. In addition, State parties might more easily oppose the extension of their powers, which is owed exactly to the assumption of treaty bodies being somewhat weaker or inferior to regional human rights courts. The question which accordingly arises is not so much about whether procedural provisions may be interpreted in a progressive fashion, but more about where to draw the boundaries, e.g., to which possible limitations any progressive interpretation of procedural provisions is subject.

Conclusion No. 2: Effectiveness-orientated interpretation applies to both substantive and procedural provisions of UN human rights treaties, which is nevertheless subject to limitations.

Conclusion No. 3: To determine limitations for any extension of powers enjoyed by UN human rights treaty bodies by means of interpretation, the following parameters shall guide any such interpretation: is there a sufficient, and possibly strong, textual and thus normative basis provided for in the treaties? In the case of a weak or even inexistent normative basis, is the contentious power in question indispensable in a sense that without its introduction the treaty body could no longer perform one of its functions? Does the introduction of new powers significantly affect existing legal obligations of contracting parties, or even introduce new obligations for State parties? Is the legal relationship between the treaty body and the State parties directly concerned, or does the extension of powers predominantly affect internal matters?

Taken together, these parameters can guide any interpretation of procedural provisions under the treaties. A lack of one of these parameters might be outweighed by the presence of others, or *vice versa*.

The measures on which the focus of this thesis has been placed are only a snapshot of the last few years, and part of an arguably open-ended evolutionary process. Instructive in this sense is the introduction of possible focused reviews at the two latest annual Meetings of Chairpersons. Interesting to note in this context is also that the simplified reporting procedure, which could be considered the predecessor of the focused reviews, has not even been implemented by all treaty bodies as the default procedure so far, while discussions on yet another review mode unfold. Whereas progress and innovative ideas are certainly vital for the effective functioning of the treaty bodies, their introduction and implementation should not come too hastily. Reforming the system step by step and at a reasonable speed seems appropriate.

With a view to the concrete reform proposals under the reporting procedure analysed in more detail, all of them should be implemented together. To this end, possible disadvantages caused by the implementation of one proposal alone could be outweighed. The uniform application of the simplified reporting procedure thereby serves as the basic premise. The procedure's application entails more focused reports, and can help to alleviate both the workload on the Committees and the reporting burden imposed on State parties. Presupposed that the financial situation of treaty bodies will not significantly improve in the next years, and given the very limited meeting time, dispensing with comprehensive reviews of every single treaty guarantee seems indispensable. In a next step, treaty bodies should be advised to harmonize the various reporting periodicities. However, it seems that their alignment constitutes a rather delicate topic, as Chairs, so far, could not agree on a common denominator with regard to the future calendar's final design. Nevertheless, the decision to adopt an eight-year calendar must be recognised as a significant one.

Provided that the introduction of a reporting master calendar with two groups of treaty bodies that review State parties in intervals of eight years, which is the solution opted for in this thesis, might lead to broad reporting gaps, integrated follow-up procedures could refute certain criticism. Reviews in the absence of a report emerge as another means by which non-compliant State parties are still put under scrutiny. Otherwise, they could evade monitoring by treaty bodies for a considerable period of time. There are more examples, but the point is that it is only the holistic consideration of the reporting procedure as such that will provide lasting and sustainable change. For example, reference shall be made to the avoidance of substantive overlap. While the effects of negative overlap and useful repetition occupy a prominent place in the discussions on the implementation of the simplified reporting procedure, these topics are hardly addressed in the context of the follow-up procedure, nor have treaty bodies considered how to handle overlap in possible reviews in the absence of a report vis-à-vis the same State party. Therefore, any future reflection and creative thinking on how to render the treaty body system more efficient must bear in mind that adjustments on one side of the system will inevitably necessitate further adjustments on the other side.

Conclusion No. 4: In relation to current strengthening activities, treaty bodies should consider the implementation of the various reform proposals portrayed above as being contingent on each other. The simplified reporting procedure should become and stay the default *modus operandi*. Adhering to one reporting procedure exclusively allows the establishment of a comprehensive reporting calendar, with dates for both, the submission and review of reports. To uphold any such calendar, reviews in the absence of a report emerge as a necessary means to do so.

Conclusion No. 5: The omnipresent risk of substantive overlap and futile repetition must be borne in mind by treaty bodies when implementing reform proposals. At the same time, substantive overlap also holds advantages, such as the possibility to shorten broad reporting intervals by addressing other treaty bodies' concluding observations and raising questions about their implementation. It becomes evident that the overlap is neither a deficit nor any advantage as such; what matters is a conscious approach to this issue.

Next to considerations on the impact of certain reform proposals on the reporting procedure, the legal powers of treaty bodies with regard to current reform efforts have been put into focus. Any proposal advanced, no matter how compelling, cannot provide an improvement if its implementation lies outside the Committees' mandates and may therefore be prevented by a reluctant or even hostile attitude on the part of States. Applying the parameters summarized under Conclusion No. 3, the thesis has analysed whether treaty bodies can ultimately implement the various reform proposals on their own, thus without State consent. In most of the cases, this appears possible, with the mandatory introduction of the simplified reporting procedure being a decisive exception. The latter is the only example where treaty bodies are exempt from taking unilateral action.

Conclusion No. 6: The implementation of most of the suggestions being currently discussed are covered by the mandates of treaty bodies. The extension of reporting intervals, regular reviews in the absence of a report, and following-up on other treaty bodies' recommendations are all covered by the Committees' mandates. To this end, effectiveness-orientated interpretation, within the limits as proposed in this thesis, is possible.

Therefore, one can safely assume that effectiveness-orientated interpretation is indeed suited to procedural provisions under a human rights treaty that set up a monitoring body. As long as such an interpretation is not guided by unreflective considerations of effectiveness, the extension of powers in concrete terms is absolutely possible.

Conclusion No. 7: In cases where a treaty body cannot initially implement certain reform proposals on its own, treaty interpretation in accordance with article 31(3)(b) VCLT might be a promising and alternative avenue. Presupposing a consistent State practice in the application of a treaty, the Committees could try to gather and provide evidence as to the existence of an agreement on the part of State parties. The Committee practice could thus trigger ensuing subsequent practice in accordance with article 31(3)(b) VCLT.

The analysis of the discussions among treaty bodies has also revealed that coordination and cooperation are necessary for any feasible and lasting strengthening effort. Even though the various Committees are considered to belong to a system, as it was, for instance, stated in Resolution 68/268, it has been demonstrated in the foregoing analysis that cooperation and coordination are not easy to achieve. Sometimes, despite the agreement to implement certain measures adopted at the inter-Committee level, individual Committees might eventually be reluctant to implement the measures anyway.

Therefore, improved and increased cooperation and coordination among the Committees is required. For this purpose, the Meeting of Chairpersons plays an important role. It is currently the only institutionalized forum in the midst of all treaty bodies to discuss issues of common concern. In analogy to the constant refinement and development of the reporting procedure, the Meeting of Chairpersons underwent an evolutionary process in its own right and, notwithstanding critique of its mandate and output, contributed to the strengthening process. With a view to increasing joint efforts in aligning and harmonizing working methods, the idea of vesting the Meeting of Chairpersons with decision-making powers has been analysed more closely. The idea seems possible, though subject to two restrictions. First, the individual treaty bodies must be able to reverse any decision taken by the Chairs. Second, far-reaching decisions that would interfere to a great extent with the autonomy of the individual treaty bodies are not covered by an invigorated Meeting of Chairpersons' mandate. Furthermore, even though a strengthened Meeting of Chairpersons could prove helpful in the current strengthening process, it must not be overlooked that it has limited capacities. Two of its greatest weaknesses continue to be its limited meeting time and steady fluctuation of members. Regarding the latter, a strengthened Meeting of Chairpersons also presupposes the willingness of all participating Chairs to seize the forum's opportunities.

Conclusion No. 8: The Meeting of Chairpersons can play a pivotal role in the strengthening process, notwithstanding factual obstacles, such as limited meeting time or non-existent financial resources.

Conclusion No. 9: Vesting Chairs with decision-making powers is legally possible, subject to the restriction that the individual Committees retain the possibility of reversing such a decision.

Actions taken by the Meeting of Chairpersons in reaction to the COVID-19 pandemic, such as the establishment of an informal working group to address the impact of the pandemic on the work of the UN human rights treaty bodies, could shed light on ways and means how to render the Meeting of Chairpersons more efficient. Comparable to the Inter-Committee Meeting, decisive preparatory work could be outsourced to informal working groups that prepare and draft proposals which are then discussed at the annual Meeting of Chairpersons. While such an approach would allow for more in- and output generated by the Meeting of Chairpersons, it is simultaneously dependent on the personal capacity of Committee members, and would render the decision-making process and the preceding preparatory process less transparent. And while the inter-Committee cooperation has mainly focused on procedural matters, it might now be time to also focus on achieving coherence in terms of substantive standards. Human rights treaty bodies could be advised to jointly incorporate "trending" issues in their work, with a possible focus on the avoidance of substantial overlap under the reporting procedure. Topics, such as business and human rights or climate change and human rights can be addressed through the lens of several treaties, depending on whether one might focus on a certain discriminatory dimension, or alternatively on State parties' positive obligations to protect individuals under their jurisdiction from climate change-induced harm, just to mention a few examples of a theoretically non-exhaustive list. The Meeting of Chairpersons might present itself as an appropriate forum for launching first initiatives and activities in these matters.

Furthermore, when time has passed and more treaty bodies than the Human Rights Committee and the Committee against Torture have developed a more "judicial" profile, it might be of major importance to analyse their *modus operandi* under the individual complaints procedure. With a view to the system's capacity and taking into consideration the ever-growing number of individual communications filed with treaty bodies, ways to handle possible floods of communications are of utmost importance. First steps have been taken by the CESCR Committee in this matter. It recently introduced a pilot views procedure,[1] comparable to the pilot-judgment procedure developed by the ECtHR.

---

[1] See Article 20 Draft RoP CESCR, Draft Rules of procedure under the Optional Protocol

On that note, it might be crucial to reiterate another time, though therefore possibly even banal to state, that the current treaty body system is operating at its breaking point, specifically in terms of financing and support by the Secretariat. However, other human rights treaties are in sight and with the treaty on business and human rights, another treaty is already in the making. While this thesis has demonstrated that treaty bodies themselves have considerable potential in rendering the exercise of their mandates more efficient, there are ultimately limits to what they can accomplish. It is thus crucial that sufficient funding and resources are provided to the Committees. However, this also raises the question of whether it will continue to be appropriate in the future to leave the observation and monitoring of the core human rights treaties to bodies which, by virtue of their constituent instruments, are designated to operate part-time. Without prejudice to the benefits of a possible World Court of Human Rights, such an endeavour should only be explored when there is sufficient and forthright support by the majority of State parties. As long as this support is lacking, it would be highly risky to dispense with the current system despite its flaws.

With regard to all further reform projects, analyses focusing on the Committees, and strengthening efforts undertaken by the treaty bodies themselves, one definite conclusion can be drawn. Since the UN human rights treaty bodies are considered weak, are attributed a status *sui generis* and only partially exhibit (quasi-)judicial elements, it is all the more important that they operate in a purely legal context. This signifies that their activities must be governed by and in conformity with the law. It is the valid interpretation of their own constituent instruments in accordance with the general rules of interpretation that decisively contributes to their resilience.

---

to the International Covenant on Economic, Social and Cultural Rights, UN Doc. E/C.12/69/R.1, 26.03.2021.

Bibliography

Abashidze, Aslan, The Complementary Role of General Comments, in: Bassiouni, M. Cherif/Schabas, William A. (eds.), New Challenges for the UN Human Rights Machinery: What Future for the UN Treaty Body System and the Human Rights Council Procedures?, Intersentia, Cambridge 2011, pp. 137–148.

Abashidze, Aslan/Koneva, Aleksandra, The Process of Strengthening the Human Rights Treaty Body System: The Road towards Effectiveness or Inefficiency?, Netherlands International Law Review 66 (2019), 357–389.

Ajevski, Marjan, Fragmentation in International Human Rights Law – Beyond Conflict of Laws, Nordic Journal of Human Rights 32 (2014), 87–98.

Akthar, Rajnaara C./Nyamutata, Conrad, International Child Law, Fourth Edition, Routledge, London 2020.

Alston, Philip, Out of the Abyss: The Challenges Confronting the New U. N. Committee on Economic, Social and Cultural Rights, Human Rights Quarterly 9 (1987), 332–381.

–, The Committee on Economic, Social and Cultural Rights, in: Alston, Philip (ed.), The United Nations and Human Rights: A Critical Appraisal, First Edition, Clarendon Press, Oxford 1992, pp. 473–508.

–, The Purposes of Reporting, in: Manual on Human Rights Reporting, HR/PUB/91/1 (Rev. 1), 1997.

–, Against a World Court for Human Rights, Ethics & International Affairs 28 (2014), 197–212.

–, The Committee on Economic, Social and Cultural Rights, in: Mégret, Frédéric/Alston, Philip (eds.), The United Nations and Human Rights: A Critical Appraisal, Second Edition, Oxford University Press, Oxford 2020, pp. 439–476.

Alston, Philip/Quinn, Gerard, The Nature and Scope of States Parties' Obligations under the International Covenant on Economic, Social and Cultural Rights, Human Rights Quarterly 9 (1987), 156–229.

Alvarez, Jose E., Constitutional Interpretation, in: Coicaud, Jean-Marc/Heiskanen, Veijo (eds.), The legitimacy of international organizations, United Nations University Press, Tokyo 2001, pp. 104–154.

Andenas, Mads/Bjorge, Eirik (eds.), A Farewell to Fragmentation: Reassertion and Convergence in International Law, Cambridge University Press, Cambridge 2015.

Angst/Lantschner (eds.), ICERD: Internationales Übereinkommen zur Beseitigung jeder From von Rassendiskriminierung, Handkommentar, Nomos, Baden-Baden 2020.

Arato, Julian, Subsequent Practice and Evolutive Interpretation: Techniques of Treaty Interpretation over Time and Their Diverse Consequences, The Law and Practice of International Courts and Tribunals 9 (2010), 443–494.

Aust, Anthony, Modern Treaty Law and Practice, Third Edition, Cambridge University Press, Cambridge 2013.

Azaria, Danae, The Legal Significance of Expert Treaty Bodies Pronouncements for the Purpose of the Interpretation of Treaties, International Community Law Review 22 (2020), 33–60.

Bank, Roland, Country-orientated procedures under the Convention against Torture: Towards a new dynamism, in: Alston, Philip/Crawford, James (eds.), The Future of UN Human Rights Treaty Monitoring, Cambridge University Press, Cambridge 2000, pp. 145–174.

Bantekas, Ilias/Stein, Michael Ashley/Anastasiou, Dimitris (eds.), The UN Convention on the Rights of Persons with Disabilities: A Commentary, Oxford University Press, Oxford 2018.

Banton, Michael, International Action Against Racial Discrimination, Clarendon Press, Oxford 1996.

Baratta, Roberto, Should Invalid Reservations to Human Rights Treaties be Disregarded?, European Journal of International Law 11 (2000), 413–425.

Bayefsky, Anne F., Introduction, in: Bayefsky, Anne F. (ed.), The UN Human Rights Treaty System in the 21st Century, Kluwer Law International, The Hague 2000, pp. xvii–xx.

Baylis, Elena A., General Comment 24: Confronting the Problem of Reservations to Human Rights Treaties, Berkeley Journal of International Law 17 (1999), 277–329.

Beiter, Klaus Dieter, The Protection of the Right to Education by International Law: Including a Systematic Analysis of Article 13 of the International Covenant on Economic, Social and Cultural Rights, Martinus Nijhoff Publishers, Leiden 2006.

Bernaz, Nadia, Continuing evolution of the United Nations treaty bodies system, in: Sheeran, Scott/Rodley, Nigel S. (eds.), Routledge Handbook of International Human Rights Law, Routledge, Abingdon 2013, pp. 707–723.

–, Conceptualizing Corporate Accountability in International Law: Models for a Business and Human Rights Treaty, Human Rights Review 22 (2021), 45–64.

Bjorge, Eirik, The Evolutionary Interpretation of Treaties, Oxford University Press, Oxford 2014.

–, The Convention as a Living Instrument: Rooted in the Past, Looking to the Future, Human Rights Law Journal 36 (2016), 243–255.

Blokker, Niels M., International Organizations or Institutions, Implied Powers, in: Peters, Anne (ed.), Max Planck Encyclopedia of Public International Law, Online version, April 2009.

Boerefijn, Ineke, The Reporting Procedure under the Covenant on Civil and Political Rights: Practice and Procedures of the Human Rights Committee, Intersentia, Antwerp 1999.

–, Impact on the Law on Treaty Reservations, in: Kamminga, Menno T./Scheinin, Martin (eds.), The Impact of Human Rights Law on General International Law, Oxford University Press, Oxford 2009, pp. 63–98.

Bohning, Roger, The ILO and the New UN Convention on Migrant Workers: The Past and Future, International Migration Review 25 (1991), 698–709.

Boisson de Chazournes, Laurence, Plurality in the Fabric of International Courts and Tribunals: The Threads of a Managerial Approach, European Journal of International Law 28 (2017), 13–72.

Bossuyt, Marc J., Guide to the "travaux préparatoires" of the International Covenant on Civil and Political Rights, Martinus Nijhoff Publishers, Dordrecht 1987.

Bourke Martignoni, Joanna, Sexual and Reproductive Rights at the Crossroads: Intersectionality and the UN Treaty Monitoring Bodies, in: Bribosia, Emmanuelle/Rorive, Isabelle (eds.), Human Rights Tectonics: Global Dynamics of Integration and Fragmentation, Intersentia, Cambridge 2018, pp. 141–162.

Bowman, Michael, Towards a Unified Treaty Body for Monitoring Compliance with UN Human Rights Conventions? Legal Mechanisms for Treaty Reform, Human Rights Law Review 07 (2007), 225–249.

Bradley, Curtis A./Goldsmith, Jack L., Treaties, Human Rights, and Conditional Consent, University of Pennsylvania Law Review 149 (2000), 399–468.

Brems, Eva, Smart human rights integration, in: Brems, Eva/Ouald-Chaib, Saïla (eds.), Fragmentation and Integration in Human Rights Law: Users' Perspectives, Edward Elgar Publishing, Cheltenham 2018, pp. 165–194.

Broecker, Christen/O'Flaherty, Michael, The Outcome of the General Assembly's Treaty Body Strengthening Process, Universal Rights Group, Policy Brief, Geneva 2014.

Brölmann, Catherine, Specialized Rules of Treaty Interpretation: International Organizations, in: Hollis, Duncan B. (ed.), The Oxford Guide to Treaties, Second Edition, Oxford University Press, Oxford 2020, pp. 524–542.

Broude, Tomer, Keep Calm and Carry on: Martti Koskenniemi and the Fragmentation of International Law, Temple International & Comparative Law Journal 27 (2013), 279–292.

Broude, Tomer/Shany, Yuval, The International Law and Policy of Multi-Sourced Equivalent Norms, in: Broude, Tomer/Shany, Yuval (eds.), Multi-Sourced Equivalent Norms in International Law, Hart Publishing, Oxford 2011, pp. 1–15.

Brown, Chester, A Common Law of International Adjudication, Oxford University Press, Oxford 2007.

–, Inherent Powers in International Adjudication, in: Romano, Cesare P.R./Alter, Karen J./Shany, Yuval (eds.), The Oxford Handbook of International Adjudication, Oxford University Press, Oxford 2013, pp. 828–847.

Brunnée, Jutta, Treaty Amendments, in: Hollis, Duncan B. (ed.), The Oxford Guide to Treaties, Second Edition, Oxford University Press, Oxford 2020, pp. 336–354.

Buckley, Carla M./Donald, Alice/Leach, Philip (eds.), Towards Convergence in International Human Rights Law: Approaches of Regional and International Systems, Brill Nijhoff, Leiden 2016.

Buga, Irina, Modification of Treaties by Subsequent Practice, Oxford University Press, Oxford 2018.

Burgers, J. Herman/Danelius, Hans, The United Nations Convention against Torture: A Handbook on the Convention against Torture and Other Cruel, Inhuman or Degrading Treatment or Punishment, Martinus Nijhoff Publishers, Dordrecht 1988.

Burrows, Noreen, The 1979 Convention on the Elimination of All Forms of Discrimination Against Women, Netherlands International Law Review 32 (1985), 419–460.

Bustelo, Mara R., The Committee on the Elimination of Discrimination Against Women at the Crossroads, in: Alston, Philip/Crawford, James (eds.), The Future of UN Human Rights Treaty Monitoring, Cambridge University Press, Cambridge 2000, pp. 79–112.

Byrnes, Andrew, The Other Human Rights Treaty Body: The Work of the Committee on the Elimination of Discrimination against Women, Yale Journal of International Law 14 (1989), 1–67.

–, The Committee against Torture, in: Alston, Philip (ed.), The United Nations and Human Rights: A Critical Appraisal, First Edition, Oxford University Press, Oxford 1992, pp. 509–546.

–, The Committee on the Elimination of Discrimination against Women, in: Hellum, Anne/Aasen, Henriette Sinding (eds.), Women's Human Rights: CEDAW in International, Regional and National Law, Cambridge University Press, Cambridge 2013, pp. 27–61.

–, The Committee against Torture and the Subcommittee for the Prevention of Torture, in: Mégret, Frédéric/Alston, Philip (eds.), The United Nations and Human Rights: A Critical Appraisal, Second Edition, Oxford University Press, Oxford 2020, pp. 477–518.

–, The Committee on the Elimination of Discrimination Against Women, in: Mégret, Frédéric/Alston, Philip (eds.), The United Nations and Human Rights: A Critical Appraisal, Second Edition, Oxford University Press, Oxford 2020, pp. 393–438.

Cabrera-Ormaza, Maria Victoria, International Labour Organization, in: Oberleitner, Gerd (ed.), International Human Rights Institutions, Tribunals, and Courts, Springer, Singapore 2018, pp. 227–249.

Çalı, Başak, Specialized Rules of Treaty Interpretation: Human Rights, in: Hollis, Duncan B. (ed.), The Oxford Guide to Treaties, Second Edition, Oxford University Press, Oxford 2020, pp. 504–523.

Callejon, Claire/Kemileva, Kamelia/Kirchmeier, Felix/Zipoli, Domenico, Optimizing the UN Treaty Body System, Academic Platform Report on the 2020 Review, The Geneva Academy.

Campbell, A. I. L., The Limits of the Powers of International Organisations, International Comparative Law Quarterly 32 (1983), 523–533.

Carraro, Valentina, The United Nations Treaty Bodies and Universal Periodic Review: Advancing Human Rights by Preventing Politicization?, Human Rights Quarterly, 39 (2017), 943–970.

–, Electing the experts: Expertise and independence in the UN human rights treaty bodies, European Journal of International Relations 25 (2019), 826–851.

, Promoting Compliance with Human Rights: The Performance of the United Nations' Universal Periodic Review and Treaty Bodies, International Studies Quarterly 63 (2019), 1079–1093.

Charters, Claire, Multi-Sourced Equivalent Norms and the Legitimacy of Indigenous Peoples' Rights under International Law, in: Broude, Tomer/Shany, Yuval (eds.), Multi-Sourced Equivalent Norms in International Law, Hart Publishing, Oxford 2011, pp. 289–319.

Chauville, Roland, The Universal Periodic Review's first cycle: successes and failures, in: Charlesworth, Hilary/Larking, Emma (eds.), Human Rights and the Universal Periodic Review, Cambridge University Press, Cambridge 2014, pp. 87–108.

Cheeseman, Chloe, Harmonising the Jurisprudence of Regional and International Human Rights Bodies: A Literature Review, in: Buckley, Carla M./Donald, Alice/Leach, Philip (eds.), Towards Convergence in International Human Rights Law: Approaches of Regional and International Systems, Brill Nijhoff, Leiden 2016, pp. 595–627.

Chetail, Vincent, Committee on the Protection of the Rights of All Migrant Workers and Members of their Families (CMW), in: Ruiz Fabri, Hélène/Wolfrum, Rüdiger (ed.), Max Planck Encyclopedia of International Procedural Law, Online version, August 2018.

–, The Committee on the Protection of the Rights of All Migrant Workers and Members of Their Families, in: Mégret, Frédéric/Alston, Philip (eds.), The United Nations and Human Rights: A Critical Appraisal, Second Edition, Oxford University Press, Oxford 2020, pp. 601–644.

Chinkin, Christine, Reservations and Objections to the Convention on the Elimination of All Forms of Discrimination against Women, in: Gardner, J. P./Higgins, Rosalyn (eds.), Human Rights as general Norms and a State's Right to opt out: Reservations and Objections to Human Rights Conventions, The British Institute of International and Comparative Law, London 1997, pp. 64–84.

–, Human Rights, in: Bowman, Michael J./Kritsiotis, Dino (eds.), Conceptual and Contextual Perspectives on the Modern Law of Treaties, Cambridge University Press, Cambridge 2018, pp. 509–537.

Christoffersen, Jonas, Impact on General Principles of Treaty Interpretation, in: Kamminga, Menno T./Scheinin, Martin (eds.), The Impact of Human Rights Law on General International Law, Oxford University Press, Oxford 2009, pp. 37–62.

Citroni, Gabriella, Committee on Enforced Disappearances (CED), in: Ruiz Fabri, Hélène/Wolfrum, Rüdiger (eds.), Max Planck Encyclopedia of International Procedural Law, Online version, December 2018.

Cleveland, Sarah H., Enhancing Human Rights Connectivity for the Treaty Body System, Document submitted for the Treaty Body Review Conference, Geneva, 8–9 December 2016, https://www.geneva-academy.ch/joomlatools-files/docman-files/Draft%20List%20of%20Submissions%20-%20Academic%20Platform%202020%20Review%20without%20Propositions%20.pdf (last access: 21.08.2023).

Clifford, Jarlath, Equality, in: Shelton, Dinah (ed.), The Oxford Handbook of International Human Rights Law, Oxford University Press, Oxford 2013, pp. 420–445.

Collister, Heather, Rituals and implementation in the Universal Periodic Review and the human rights treaty bodies, in: Charlesworth, Hilary/Larking, Emma (eds.), Human Rights and the Universal Periodic Review, Cambridge University Press, Cambridge 2014, pp. 109–125.

Connors, Jane, The Human Rights Treaty Body System, in: Chesterman, Simon/Malone, David M./Villalpando, Santiago (eds.), The Oxford Handbook of United Nations Treaties, Oxford University Press, Oxford 2019, pp. 377–396.

Coomans, Fons, The Role of the UN Committee on Economic, Social and Cultural Rights in Strengthening Implementation and Supervision of the International Covenant on Economic, Social and Cultural Rights, Verfassung und Recht in Übersee 35 (2002), 182–201.

–, The UN Committee on Economic, Social, and Cultural Rights, in: Oberleitner, Gerd (ed.), International Human Rights Institutions, Tribunals, and Courts, Springer, Singapore 2018, pp. 143–168.

Corkery, Allison/Saiz, Ignacio, Progressive realization using maximum available resources: the accountability challenge, in: Dugard, Jackie/Porter, Bruce/Ikawa, Daniela/Chenwi, Lilian (eds.), Research Handbook on Economic, Social and Cultural Rights as Human Rights, Edward Elgar Publishing, Cheltenham 2020, pp. 275–300.

Corten, Olivier/Klein, Pierre (eds.), The Vienna Conventions on the Law of Treaties: A Commentary, Volume I, Oxford University Press, Oxford 2011.

Craven, Matthew, The International Covenant on Economic, Social, and Cultural Rights: A Perspective on its Development, Oxford University Press, Oxford 1995.

–, Legal differentiation and the concept of the human rights treaty in international law, European Journal of International Law 11 (2000), 489–519.

Crawford, James, The UN human rights treaty system: A system in crisis?, in: Alston, Philip/Crawford, James (eds.), The Future of UN Human Rights Treaty Monitoring, Cambridge University Press, Cambridge 2000, pp. 1–12.

–, Brownlie's Principles of Public International Law, Ninth Edition, Oxford University Press, Oxford 2019.

Crawford, James/Keene, Amelia, Interpretation of the human rights treaties by the International Court of Justice, The International Journal of Human Rights 24 (2020), 935–956.

Creamer, Cosette D./Simmons, Beth A., The Proof Is in the Process: Self-Reporting Under International Human Rights Treaties, American Journal of International Law 114 (2020), 1–50.

de Albuquerque, Catarina/Roaf, Virginia, The human rights to water and sanitation, in: Dugard, Jackie/Porter, Bruce/Ikawa, Daniela/Chenwi, Lilian (eds.), Research Handbook on Economic, Social and Cultural Rights as Human Rights, Edward Elgar Publishing, Cheltenham 2020, pp. 202–226.

de Frouville, Olivier, The Committee on Enforced Disappearances, in: Mégret, Frédéric/Alston, Philip (eds.), The United Nations and Human Rights: A Critical Appraisal, Second Edition, Oxford University Press, Oxford 2020, pp. 579–600.

de Schutter, Olivier, Towards a New Treaty on Business and Human Rights, Business and Human Rights Journal 1 (2015), 41–67.

–, The Formation of a Common Law of Human Rights, in: Bribosia, Emmanuelle/Rorive, Isabelle (eds.), Human Rights Tectonics: Global Dynamics of Integration and Fragmentation, Intersentia, Cambridge 2018, pp. 3–40.

de Schutter, Olivier/Sant'Ana, Matthias, The European Committee of Social Rights (the ECSR), in: de Beco, Gauthier (ed.), Human Rights Monitoring Mechanisms of the Council of Europe, Routledge, Abingdon 2012, pp. 71–99.

de Zayas, Alfred, Petitions before the United Nations Treaty Bodies: Focus on the Human Rights Committee's Optional Protocol Procedure, in: Alfredsson, Gudmundur/Grimheden, Jonas/Ramcharan, Bertrand G./de Zayas, Alfred (eds.), International Human Rights Monitoring Mechanisms: Essays in Honour of Jakob Th. Möller, Second Revised Edition, Martinus Nijhoff Publishers, Leiden 2009, pp. 35–76.

Della Fina, Valentina/Cera, Rachele/Palmisano, Guiseppe (eds.), The United Convention on the Rights of Persons with Disabilities: A Commentary, Springer, Cham 2017.

Devereux, Annemarie/Anderson, Catherine, Reporting under International Human Rights Treaties: Perspectives from Timor Leste's Experience of the Reformed Process, Human Rights Law Review 8 (2008), 69–104.

Dimitrijevic, Vojin, State Reports, in: Alfredsson, Gudmundur/Grimheden, Jonas/Ramcharan, Bertrand G./de Zayas, Alfred (eds.), International Human Rights Monitoring Mechanism, Essays in Honour of Jakob Th. Möller, First Edition, Kluwer Law International, The Hague 2001, pp. 185–200.

Djeffal, Christian, Static and Evolutive Treaty Interpretation: A Functional Reconstruction, Cambridge University Press, Cambridge 2016.

Doek, Jaap E., The CRC: Dynamics and Direction of Monitoring its Implementation, in: Invernizzi, Antonella/Williams, Jane (eds.), The Human Rights of Children, From Vision to Implementation, Ashgate Publishing, Farnham 2011, pp. 99–116.

Dominguez-Redondo, Elvira, The Universal Periodic Review – Is There Life beyond Naming and Shaming in Human Rights Implementation?, New Zealand Law Review 4 (2012), 673–706.

Dörr, Oliver, The Strasbourg Approach to Evolutionary Interpretation, in: Abi-Saab, Georges/Keith, Kenneth/Marceau, Gabrielle/Marquet, Clément (eds.), Evolutionary Interpretation and International Law, Hart Publishing, Oxford 2019, pp. 115–122.

Dörr, Oliver/Schmalenbach, Kirsten (eds.), Vienna Convention on the Law of Treaties: A Commentary, Second Edition, Springer, Berlin 2018.

Dzehtsiarou, Kanstantsin, European Consensus and the Evolutive Interpretation of the European Convention on Human Rights, German Law Journal 12 (2010), 1730–1745.

Egan, Suzanne, The United Nations Human Rights Treaty System: Law and Procedure, Bloomsbury Professional, Haywards Heath 2011.

–, Strengthening the United Nations Human Rights Treaty Body System, Human Rights Law Review 13 (2013), 209–243.
–, Transforming the UN Human Rights Treaty System: A Realistic Appraisal, Human Rights Quarterly 42 (2020), 762–789.
–, Reform of the UN Human Rights Treaty Body System, in: Mégret, Frédéric/Alston, Philip (eds.), The United Nations and Human Rights: A Critical Appraisal, Second Edition, Oxford University Press, Oxford 2020, pp. 645–664.
Engström, Viljam, Understanding Powers of International Organizations: A Study of the Doctrines of Attributed Powers, Implied Powers and Constitutionalism – with a Special Focus on the Human Rights Committee, Åbo Akademi University Press, Åbo 2009.
–, Constructing the Powers of International Institutions, Martinus Nijhoff Publishers, Leiden 2012.
Evans, Christine, The Committee on the Rights of the Child, in: Mégret, Frédéric/Alston, Philip (eds.), The United Nations and Human Rights: A Critical Appraisal, Second Edition, Oxford University Press, Oxford 2020, pp. 519–546.
Evatt, Elizabeth, The Future of the Human Rights Treaty System: Forging Recommendations, in: Bayefsky, Anne F. (ed.), The UN Human Rights Treaty System in the 21st Century, Kluwer Law International, The Hague 2000, pp. 287–297.
Fischer, Dana D., Reporting under the Covenant on Civil and Political Rights: The First Five Years of the Human Rights Committee, American Journal of International Law 76 (1982), 142–153.
Fitzmaurice, Malgosia, Interpretation of Human Rights Treaties, in: Shelton, Dinah (ed.), The Oxford Handbook of International Human Rights Law, Oxford University Press, Oxford 2013, pp. 739–771.
Flinterman, Cees, The United Nations Human Rights Committee, Some Reflections of a Former Member, Netherlands Quarterly of Human Rights 33 (2015), 4–8.
Flinterman, Cees/Liu, Ginney, CEDAW and the Optional Protocol: First Experiences, in: Alfredsson, Gudmundur/Grimheden, Jonas/Ramcharan, Bertrand G./de Zayas, Alfred (eds.), International Human Rights Monitoring Mechanisms: Essays in Honour of Jakob Th. Möller, Second Revised Edition, Martinus Nijhoff Publishers, Leiden 2009, pp. 91–97.
Fredman, Sandra, Poverty and Human Rights: A Peril and a Promise, in: Akande, Dapo/Kuosmanen, Jaakko/McDermott, Helen/Roser, Dominic (eds.), Human Rights and 21st Century Challenges: Poverty, Conflict, and the Environment, Oxford University Press, Oxford 2020, pp. 222–246.
Freeman, Marscha A./Chinkin, Christine/Rudolf, Beate (eds.), The UN Convention on the Elimination of All Forms of Discrimination Against Women: A Commentary, Oxford University Press, Oxford 2012.
Gaer, Felice D., Implementing international human rights norms: UN human rights treaty bodies and NGOs, Journal of Human Rights 2 (2003), 339–357.
–, A Voice Not an Echo: Universal Periodic Review and the UN Treaty Body System, Human Rights Law Review 7 (2007), 109–139.
–, Implementing Treaty Body Recommendations: Establishing Better Follow-Up Procedures, in: Bassiouni, M. Cherif/Schabas, William A. (eds.), New Challenges for the UN Human Rights Machinery: What Future for the UN Treaty Body System and the Human Rights Council Procedures?, Intersentia, Cambridge 2011, pp. 107–121.
–, The Institutional Future of the Covenants, A World Court for Human Rights?, in: Moeckli, Daniel/Keller, Helen/Heri, Corina (eds.), The Human Rights Covenants at 50: Their Past, Present, and Future, Oxford University Press, Oxford 2018, pp. 334–356.

Gaggioli, Gloria, The Strength of Evolutionary Interpretation in International Human Rights Law, in: Abi-Saab, Georges/Keith, Kenneth/Marceau, Gabrielle/Marquet, Clément (eds.), Evolutionary Interpretation and International Law, Hart Publishing, Oxford 2019, pp. 103–114.

Gardiner, Richard, Treaty Interpretation, Second Edition, Oxford University Press, Oxford 2015.

–, The Vienna Convention Rules on Treaty Interpretation, in: Hollis, Duncan B. (ed.), The Oxford Guide to Treaties, Second Edition, Oxford 2020, pp. 459–488.

Gautier, Philippe, The Reparation for Injuries Case Revisited: The Personality of the European Union, Max Planck Yearbook of United Nations Law 4 (2000), 331–361.

Ghandhi, Sandy, The Human Rights Committee and Interim Measures of Relief, Canterbury Law Review 13 (2007), 203–226.

Giegerich, Thomas, Vorbehalte zu Menschenrechtsabkommen: Zulässigkeit, Gültigkeit und Prüfungskompetenzen von Vertragsgremien: Ein konstitutioneller Ansatz, ZaöRV 55 (1995), 713–782.

–, Treaties, Multilateral, Reservations to, in: Peters, Anne (ed.), Max Planck Encyclopedia of Public International Law, Online version, September 2020.

Giegling, Jule, Challenges and Chances of a Written State Report: Analysis and Improvement of a Monitoring Instrument on the Implementation of Human Rights, Berliner Wissenschafts-Verlag, Berlin 2021.

Golay, Christophe, The Role of Human Rights Mechanisms in Monitoring the United Nations Declaration on the Rights of Peasants, Research Brief, Geneva Academy, January 2020.

–, #ESCR and #SDGS, Practical Manual on the Role of United Nations Human Rights Mechanisms in Monitoring the Sustainable Development Goals that seek to realize economic, social and cultural rights, Academy Briefing No. 16, Geneva Academy, June 2020.

Goodman, Ryan, Human Rights Treaties, Invalid Reservations, and State Consent, American Journal of International Law 96 (2002), 531–560.

Hafner, Gerhard, Subsequent Agreements and Practice: Between Interpretation, Informal Modification, and Formal Amendment, in: Nolte, Georg (ed.), Treaties and Subsequent Practice, Oxford University Press, Oxford 2013, pp. 105–122.

Hall, Christopher Keith, The Duty of States Parties to the Convention against Torture to Provide Procedures Permitting Victims to Recover Reparations for Torture Committed Abroad, European Journal of International Law 18 (2007), 921–937.

Hampson, Françoise J., An Overview of the Reform of the UN Human Rights Machinery, Human Rights Law Review 7 (2007), 7–27.

Hartman, Joan F., Derogation from Human Rights Treaties in Public Emergencies – A Critique of Implementation by the European Commission and Court of Human Rights and the Human Rights Committee of the United Nations, Harvard International Law Journal 22 (1981), 1–52.

Harvey, Philip, Monitoring Mechanisms for International Agreements Respecting Economic and Social Human Rights, Yale Journal of International Law 12 (1987), 396–420.

Helfer, Laurence R., Forum Shopping for Human Rights, University of Pennsylvania Law Review 148 (1999), 285–400.

–, Not Fully Committed? Reservations, Risk, and Treaty Design, Yale Journal of International Law 31 (2002), 367–382.

–, Pushback Against Supervisory Systems: Lessons for the ILO from International Human Rights Institutions, in: Politakis, George P./Kohiyama, Tomi/Lieby, Thomas (eds.),

ILO100 – LAW FOR SOCIAL JUSTICE, International Labour Office, Geneva 2019, pp. 257–278.

Helfer, Laurence R./Slaughter, Anne-Marie, Toward a Theory of Effective Supranational Adjudication, Yale Law Journal 107 (1997), 273–391.

Hellum, Anne/Ikdahl, Ingunn, Committee on the Elimination of Discrimination Against Women (CEDAW), in: Ruiz Fabri, Hélène/Wolfrum, Rüdiger (eds.), Max Planck Encyclopedia of International Procedural Law, Online version, January 2019.

Hennebel, Ludovic, The Human Rights Committee, in: Mégret, Frédéric/Alston, Philip (eds.), The United Nations and Human Rights: A Critical Appraisal, Second Edition, Oxford University Press, Oxford 2020, pp. 339–392.

Henrard, Kristin, The Protection of Minorities through the Equality Provisions in the UN Human Rights Treaties: The UN Treaty Bodies, International Journal on Minority and Group Rights 14 (2007), 141–180.

Hertig Randall, Maya, The History of the Covenants: Looking Back Half a Century and Beyond, in: Moeckli, Daniel/Keller, Helen/Heri, Corina (eds.), The Human Rights Covenants at 50: Their Past, Present, and Future, Oxford University Press, Oxford 2018, pp. 7–30.

Heyns, Christof/Killander, Magnus, Universality and the Growth of Regional Systems, in: Shelton, Dinah (ed.), The Oxford Handbook of International Human Rights Law, Oxford University Press, Oxford 2013, pp. 670–697.

Heyns, Christof/Viljoen, Frans (eds.), The Impact of the United Nations Human Rights Treaties on the Domestic Level, Kluwer Law International, The Hague 2002.

Ingelse, Chris, The UN Committee against Torture: An Assessment, Kluwer Law International, The Hague 2001.

Jardón, Luis, The Interpretation of Jurisdictional Clauses in Human Rights Treaties, Anuario Mexicano de Derecho Internacional 8 (2013), 99–143.

Jhabvala, Farrokh, The Practice of the Covenant's Human Rights Committee, 1976–82: Review of State Party Reports, Human Rights Quarterly 6 (1984), 81–106.

Johnstone, Rachael Lorna, Cynical Savings or Reasonable Reform? Reflections on a Single Unified UN Human Rights Treaty Body, Human Rights Law Review 7 (2007), 173–200.

–, Streamlining the Constructive Dialogue: Efficiency from States' Perspectives, Bassiouni, M. Cherif/Schabas, William A. (eds.), New Challenges for the UN Human Rights Machinery: What Future for the UN Treaty Body System and the Human Rights Council Procedures?, Intersentia, Cambridge 2011, pp. 59–93.

Kälin, Walter, Examination of state reports, in: Keller, Helen/Ulfstein, Geir (eds.), UN Human Rights Treaty Bodies: Law and Legitimacy, Cambridge University Press, Cambridge 2012, pp. 16–72.

Kälin, Walter/Künzli Jörg, The Law of International Human Rights Protection, Second Edition, Oxford University Press, Oxford 2019.

Kanetake, Machiko, UN human rights treaty monitoring bodies before domestic courts, International and Comparative Law Quarterly 67 (2018), 201–232.

Keane, David, Mapping the International Convention on the Elimination of All Forms of Racial Discrimination as a Living Instrument, Human Rights Law Review 20 (2020), 236–268.

Kędzia, Zdzisław, United Nations Mechanisms to Promote and Protect Human Rights, in: Symonides, Janusz (ed.), Human Rights: International Protection, Monitoring, Enforcement, Ashgate Publishing, Aldershot 2003, pp. 3–90.

Keller, Helen/Grover, Lena, General Comments of the Human Rights Committee and their legitimacy, Keller, Helen/Ulfstein, Geir (eds.), UN Human Rights Treaty Bodies: Law and Legitimacy, Cambridge University Press, Cambridge 2012, pp. 116–198.

Keller, Helen/Marti, Cedric, Interim Relief Compared: Use of Interim Measures by the UN Human Rights Committee and the European Court of Human Rights, Zeitschrift für ausländisches öffentliches Recht und Völkerrecht 73 (2013), 325–372.

Keller, Helen/Ulfstein Geir, Introduction, in: Keller, Helen/Ulfstein, Geir (eds.), UN Human Rights Treaty Bodies: Law and Legitimacy, Cambridge University Press, Cambridge 2012, pp. 1–15.

Kessing, Peter Vedel, New Optional Protocol to the UN Torture Convention, Nordic Journal of International Law 72 (2003), 571–592.

Kilkelly, Ursula, The CRC at 21: Assessing the Legal Impact, Northern Ireland Legal Quarterly 62 (2011), 143–152.

Killander, Magnus, Interpreting Regional Human Rights Treaties, Sur-International Journal on Human Rights 13 (2010), 145–169.

Kirkpatrick, Jesse, A Modest Proposal: A Global Court of Human Rights, Journal of Human Rights 13 (2014), 230–248.

Kjærum, Morten, Approaches to Reservations by the Committee on the Elimination of Racial Discrimination, in: Ziemele, Ineta (ed.), Reservations to Human Rights Treaties and the Vienna Convention Regime: Conflict, Harmony or Reconciliation, Martinus Nijhoff, Leiden 2004, pp. 67–77.

–, The UN Reform Process in an Implementation Perspective, in: Lagoutte, Stéphanie/Sano, Hans-Otto/Scharff Smith, Peter (eds.), Human Rights in Turmoil: Facing Threats, Consolidating Achievements, Martinus Nijhoff Publishers, Leiden 2007, pp. 7–23.

–, State Reports, in: Alfredsson, Gudmundur/Grimheden, Jonas/Ramcharan, Bertrand G./de Zayas, Alfred (eds.), International Human Rights Monitoring Mechanisms; Essays in Honour of Jakob Th. Möller, Second Revised Edition, Martinus Nijhoff Publishers, Leiden 2009, pp. 17–24.

Klabbers, Jan, An Introduction to International Institutional Law, Second Edition, Cambridge University Press, Cambridge 2009.

–, Formal Intergovernmental Organizations, in: Katz Cogan, Jacob/Hurd, Ian/Johnstone, Ian (eds.), The Oxford Handbook of International Organizations, Oxford University Press, Oxford 2016, pp. 133–151.

Klein, Eckart, Impact of Treaty Bodies on the International Legal Order, in: Wolfrum, Rüdiger/Röben, Volker (eds.), Developments of International Law in Treaty Making, Springer, Berlin 2005, pp. 571–580.

Klein, Eckart/Kretzmer, David, The UN Human Rights Committee: The General Comments – The Evolution of an Autonomous Monitoring Instrument, German Yearbook of International Law 58 (2015), 189–230.

Kohen, Marcelo G., Keeping Subsequent Agreements and Practice in Their Right Limits, in: Nolte, Georg (ed.), Treaties and Subsequent Practice, Oxford University Press, Oxford 2013, pp. 34–45.

Korkelia, Konstantin, New Challenges to the Regime of Reservations under the International Covenant on Civil and Political Rights, European Journal of International Law 13 (2002), 437–477.

Kosař, David/Petrov, Jan, Determinants of Compliance Difficulties among 'Good Compliers': Implementation of International Human Rights Rulings in the Czech Republic, European Journal of International Law 29 (2018), 397–425.

Kretzmer, David, Commentary on Complaint Processes by Human Rights Committee and Torture Committee Members: The Human Rights Committee, in: Bayefsky (ed.), The UN Human Rights Treaty System in the 21st Century, The Hague 2000, pp. 163–167.

–, Human Rights, State Reports, in: Peters, Anne (ed.), Max Planck Encyclopedia of Public International Law, Online version, October 2008.

–, The UN Human Rights Committee and International Human Rights Monitoring, Straus Institute Working Paper No. 12, 2010.

Kretzmer, David/Klein, Eckart, The Human Rights Committee: Monitoring State Parties' Reports, Israel Yearbook on Human Rights 45 (2015), 133–167.

Krommendijk, Jasper, The Domestic Impact and Effectiveness of the Process of State Reporting under UN Human Rights Treaties in the Netherlands, New Zealand and Finland: Paper-pushing or policy prompting?, Intersentia, Cambridge 2014.

–, Less is more: Proposals for how UN human rights treaty bodies can be more selective, Netherlands Quarterly of Human Rights 38 (2020), 5–11.

Łącki, Paweł, Consensus as a Basis for Dynamic Interpretation of the ECHR – A Critical Assessment, Human Rights Law Review 21 (2021), 186–202.

Langford, Malcolm/Porter, Bruce/Brown, Rebecca/Rossi, Julieta (eds.), The Optional Protocol to the International Covenant on Economic, Social and Cultural Rights: A Commentary, Pretoria University Law Press, Pretoria 2016.

Lansdown, Gerison, The reporting process under the Convention on the Rights of the Child, in: Alston, Philip/Crawford, James (eds.), The Future of UN Human Rights Treaty Monitoring, Cambridge University Press, Cambridge 2000, pp. 113–128.

Leary, Virginia A., The International Labour Organisation, in: Alston, Philip (ed.), The United Nations and Human Rights: A Critical Appraisal, First Edition, Clarendon Press, Oxford 1992, pp. 580–619.

Leckie, Scott, The Committee on Economic, Social and Cultural Rights: Catalyst for change in a system needing reform, in: Alston, Philip/Crawford, James (eds.), The Future of UN Human Rights Treaty Monitoring, Cambridge University Press, Cambridge 2000, pp. 129–144.

Letsas, George, Strasbourg's Interpretive Ethic: Lessons for the International Lawyer, European Journal of International Law 21 (2010), 509–541.

–, The ECHR as a living instrument: its meaning and legitimacy, in: Føllesdal, Andreas/Peters, Birgit/Ulfstein, Geir (eds.), Constituting Europe: The European Court of Human Rights in a National, European and Global Context, Cambridge University Press, Cambridge 2013, pp. 106–141.

Lijnzaad, Liesbeth, Reservations to UN-Human Rights Treaties: Ratify and Ruin?, Martinus Nijhoff Publishers, Dordrecht 1995.

Limon, Marc/Montoya, Mariana, The Universal Periodic Review, Treaty Bodies and Special Procedures: A connectivity study, June 2019.

Lixinski, Lucas, Treaty Interpretation by the Inter-American Court of Human Rights: Expansionism at the Service of the Unity of International Law, European Journal of International Law 21 (2010), 585–604.

Lord, Janet E./Stein, Michael Ashley, The Committee on the Rights of Persons with Disabilities, in: Mégret, Frédéric/Alston, Philip (eds.), The United Nations and Human Rights: A Critical Appraisal, Second Edition, Oxford University Press, Oxford 2020, pp. 547–578.

M'jid, Najat Maalla, The UN Special Procedures System: The Role of the Coordination Committee of Special Procedures, in: Nolan, Aoife/Freedman, Rosa/Murphy, Thérèse (eds.), The United Nations Special Procedures System, Brill Nijhoff, Leiden 2017, pp. 131–140.

Mac-Gregor, Eduardo Ferrer, What Do We Mean When We Talk about Judicial Dialogue: Reflections of a Judge of the Inter-American Court of Human Rights, Harvard Human Rights Journal 30 (2017), 89–128.

McCall-Smith, Kasey L., Reservations and the Determinative Function of the Human Rights Treaty Bodies, German Yearbook of International Law 54 (2011), 521–563.

–, Mind the Gaps: The ILC Guide to Practice on Reservations to Human Rights Treaties, International Community Law Review 16 (2014), 263–305.

McConnell, Lee, Assessing the Feasibility of a Business and Human Rights Treaty, International and Comparative Law Quarterly 66 (2017), 143–180.

McGaughey, Fiona, From gatekeepers to GONGOs: A taxonomy of Non-Governmental Organisations engaging with United Nations human rights mechanisms, Netherlands Quarterly of Human Rights 36 (2018), 111–132.

McGoldrick, Dominic, The Human Rights Committee: Its Role in the Development of the International Covenant on Civil and Political Rights, Clarendon Press, Oxford 1991.

–, The United Nations Convention on the Rights of the Child, International Journal of Law and the Family 5 (1991), 132–169.

McGrogan, David, On the Interpretation of Human Rights Treaties and Subsequent Practice, Netherlands Quarterly of Human Rights 32 (2014), 347–378.

McGrory, Glenn, Reservations of Virtue? Lessons from Trinidad and Tobago's Reservation to the First Optional Protocol, Human Rights Quarterly 23 (2001), 769–826.

McQuigg, Ronagh J.A., Is it time for a UN treaty on violence against women?, The International Journal of Human Rights 22 (2018), 305–324.

Mechlem, Kerstin, Treaty Bodies and the Interpretation of Human Rights, Vanderbilt Journal of Transnational Law 42 (2009), 905–947.

Medina Quiroga, Cecilia, The Role of International Tribunals: Law-Making or Creative Interpretation?, in: Shelton, Dinah (ed.), The Oxford Handbook of International Human Rights Law, Oxford University Press, Oxford 2013, pp. 649–669.

Meier, Benjamin Mason/Kim, Yuna, Human Rights Accountability through Treaty Bodies: Examining Human Rights Treaty Monitoring for Water and Sanitation, Duke Journal of Comparative and International Law 26 (2015), 139–228.

Meron, Theodor, Human Rights Law-Making in the United Nations: A Critique of Instruments and Process, Clarendon Press, Oxford 1986.

Moeckli, Daniel, Interpretation of the ICESCR: Between Morality and State Consent, in: Moeckli, Daniel/Keller, Helen/Heri, Corina (eds.), The Human Rights Covenants at 50: Their Past, Present, and Future, Oxford University Press, Oxford 2018, pp. 48–74.

Moeckli, Daniel/White, Nigel D., Treaties as 'Living Instruments', in: Bowman, Michael J./Kritsiotis, Dino (eds.), Conceptual and Contextual Perspectives on the Modern Law of Treaties, Cambridge University Press, Cambridge 2018, pp. 136–171.

Morijn, John, Reforming United Nations Human Rights Treaty Monitoring Reform, Netherlands International Law Review 58 (2011), 295–333.

Møse, Erik/Opsahl, Torkel, The Optional Protocol to the International Covenant on Civil and Political Rights, Santa Clara Law Review 21 (1981), 271–332.

Mowbray, Alastair, A New Strasbourg Approach to the Legal Consequences of Interim Measures, Human Rights Law Review 5 (2005), 377–386.

–, Between the will of the Contracting Parties and the needs of today, in: Brems, Eva/Gerards, Janneke (eds.), Shaping Rights in the ECHR: The Role of the European Court of Human Rights in Determining the Scope of Human Rights, Cambridge University Press, Cambridge 2013, pp. 17–37.

Murray, Rachel, The African Charter on Human and Peoples' Rights: A Commentary, Oxford University Press, Oxford 2019.

Mutzenberg, Patrick, NGOs, Essential Actors for Embedding Covenants in the National Context, in: Moeckli, Daniel/Keller, Helen/Heri, Corina (eds.), The Human Rights Covenants at 50: Their Past, Present, and Future, Oxford University Press, Oxford 2018, pp. 75–96.

Naldi, Gino, Interim Measures in the UN Human Rights Committee, International and Comparative Law Quarterly 53 (2004), 445–454.

Neuman, Gerald L., Giving Meaning and Effect to Human Rights, The Contribution of Human Rights Committee Members, in: Moeckli, Daniel/Keller, Helen/Heri, Corina (eds.), The Human Rights Covenants at 50: Their Past, Present, and Future, Oxford University Press, Oxford 2018, pp. 31–47.

Nowak, Manfred, CCPR Commentary, Second revised Edition, N.P. Engel Verlag, Kehl 2005.

–, Comments on the UN High Commissioner's Proposals Aimed at Strengthening the UN Human Rights Treaty Body System, Netherlands Quarterly of Human Rights 31 (2013), 3–8.

–, A World Court of Human Rights, in: Oberleitner, Gerd (ed.), International Human Rights Institutions, Tribunals, and Courts, Singapore 2018, pp. 271–290.

Nowak, Manfred/Birk, Moritz/Monina, Giuliana (eds.), The United Nations Convention Against Torture and its Optional Protocol: A Commentary, Second Edition, Oxford University Press, Oxford 2019.

Nowak, Manfred/McArthur, Elizabeth, The United Nations Convention Against Torture: A Commentary, First Edition, Oxford University Press, Oxford 2008.

O'Flaherty, Michael, The Concluding Observations of United Nations Human Rights Treaty Bodies, Human Rights Law Review 6 (2006), 27–52.

–, Reform of the UN Human Rights Treaty Body System: Locating the Dublin Statement, Human Rights Law Review 10 (2010), 319–335.

–, The United Nations Human Rights Treaty Bodies as Diplomatic Actors, in: O'Flaherty, Michael/Kędzia, Zdzisław/Müller, Amrei/Ulrich George (eds.), Human Rights Diplomacy: Contemporary Perspectives, Martinus Nijhoff Publishers, Leiden 2011, pp. 155–171.

–, The High Commissioner and the Treaty Bodies, in: Gaer, Felice D./Broecker, Christen (eds.), The United Nations High Commissioner for Human Rights: Conscience for the World, Martinus Nijhoff Publishers, Leiden 2014, pp. 99–119.

–, The Strengthening Process of the Human Rights Treaty Bodies, American Society of International Law, Proceedings of the Annual Meeting 108 (2014), 285–288.

O'Flaherty, Michael/O'Brien, Claire, Reform of UN Human Rights Treaty Monitoring Bodies: A Critique of the Concept Paper on the High Commissioner's Proposal for a Unified Standing Treaty Body, Human Rights Law Review 7 (2007), 141–172.

O'Flaherty, Michael/Tsai, Pei-Lun, Periodic Reporting: The Backbone of the UN Treaty Body Review Procedure, in: Bassiouni, M. Cherif/Schabas, William A. (eds.), New Challenges for the UN Human Rights Machinery: What Future for the UN Treaty Body System and the Human Rights Council Procedures?, Intersentia, Cambridge 2011, pp. 37–56.

Oberleitner, Gerd, Menschenrechtsschutz durch Staatenberichte, Peter Lang, Frankfurt am Main 1998.

–, Agenda for Strengthening Human Rights Institutions, in: Oberleitner, Gerd (ed.), International Human Rights Institutions, Tribunals, and Courts, Springer, Singapore 2018, pp. 551–569.

Odello, Marco/Seatzu, Francesco, The UN Committee on Economic, Social and Cultural Rights: The Law, Process and Practice, Routledge, Abingdon 2013.

Oette, Lutz, The UN Human Rights Treaty Bodies: Impact and Future, in: Oberleitner, Gerd (ed.), International Human Rights Institutions, Tribunals, and Courts, Springer, Singapore 2018, p. 95–115.

Opsahl, Torkel, The General Comments of the Human Rights Committee, in: Jekewitz, Jürgen/Klein, Karl Heinz/Kühne, Jörg Detlef/Petersmann, Hans/Wolfrum, Rüdiger (eds.), Des Menschen Rechts zwischen Freiheit und Verantwortung: Festschrift für Karl Joseph Partsch zum 75. Geburtstag, Duncker & Humblot, Berlin 1989, pp. 273–288.

–, The Human Rights Committee, in: Alston, Philip (ed.), The United Nations and Human Rights: A Critical Appraisal, Clarendon Press, First Edition, Oxford 1992, pp. 369–443.

Orakhelashvili, Alexander, Restrictive Interpretation of the Human Rights Treaties in the Recent Jurisprudence of the European Court of Human Rights, European Journal of International Law 14 (2003), 529–568.

–, The Interpretation of Acts and Rules in Public International Law, Oxford University Press, Oxford 2008.

Pace, John P., The United Nations Commission on Human Rights: 'A Very Great Enterprise', Oxford University Press, Oxford 2020.

Pappa Christoph, Das Individualbeschwerdeverfahren des Fakultativprotokolls zum Internationalen Pakt über bürgerliche und politische Rechte, Stämpfli+Cie AG, Bern 1996.

Partsch, Karl Joseph, The Racial Discrimination Committee, in: Alston, Philip (ed.), The United Nations and Human Rights: A Critical Appraisal, First Edition, Clarendon Press, Oxford 1992, pp. 339–368.

Pasqualucci, Jo M., Interim Measures in International Human Rights: Evolution and Harmonization, Vanderbilt Journal of Transnational Law 38 (2005), 1–49.

Payandeh, Mehrdad, Fragmentation within international human rights law, in: Andenas, Mads/Bjorge, Eirik (eds.), A Farewell to Fragmentation: Reassertion and Convergence in International Law, Cambridge 2015, pp. 297–319.

Pazartzis, Photini/Merkouris, Panos, Final Report on The UN Human Rights Committee and other Human Rights Treaty Bodies, TRICI-Law Paper No. 007/2020.

Pedone, Joanne/Kloster, Andrew R., New Proposals for Human Rights Treaty Body Reform, Journal of Transnational Law & Policy 22 (2012–2013), 29–84.

Peters, Anne, The refinement of international law: From fragmentation to regime interaction and politicization, International Journal of Constitutional Law 15 (2017), 671–704.

Pillay, Navanethem, Strengthening the United Nations human rights treaty body system, A report by the United Hight Commissioner for Human Rights, June 2012.

Ploton, Vincent, The Implementation of UN Treaty Body Recommendations, SUR International Journal on Human Rights 25 (2017), 219–235.

Pyaneandee, Coomara, International Disability Law, A Practical Approach to the United Nations Convention on the Rights of Persons with Disabilities, Routledge, Abingdon 2019.

Ramcharan, Bertrand G., Modernizing the UN Human Rights System, Brill Nijhoff, Leiden 2019.

Rehof, Lars Adam, Guide to the *Travaux Préparatoires* of the United Nations Convention on the Elimination of All Forms of Discrimination Against Women, Martinus Nijhoff Publishers, Dordrecht 1993.

Reiners, Nina, Transnational Lawmaking Coalitions for Human Rights, Cambridge University Press, Cambridge 2021.

Riedel, Eibe, Committee on Economic, Social and Cultural Rights (CESCR), in: Peters, Anne (ed.), Max Planck Encyclopedia of Public International Law, Online version, November 2010.
–, International Covenant on Economic, Social and Cultural Rights (1966), in: Peters, Anne (ed.), Max Planck Encyclopedia of Public International Law, Online version, April 2011.
–, Global Human Rights Protection at the Crossroads: Strengthening or Reforming the System, in: Breuer, Marten/Epiney, Astrid/Haratsch, Andreas/Schmahl, Stefanie/Weiß, Norman (eds.), Der Staat im Recht, Festschrift für Eckart Klein zum 70. Geburtstag, Duncker & Humblot, Berlin 2013, pp. 1289–1306.
Rietiker, Daniel, The Principle of "Effectiveness" in the Recent Jurisprudence of the European Court of Human Rights: Its Different Dimensions and Its Consistency with Public International Law – No Need for the Concept of Treaty Sui Generis, Nordic Journal of International Law 79 (2010), 245–277.
Rivera, Humberto Cantú, The UN Human Rights Council: Achievements and Challenges in Its First Decade, in: Oberleitner, Gerd (ed.), International Human Rights Institutions, Tribunals, and Courts, Springer, Singapore 2018, pp. 49–68.
Roberts, Anthea, Subsequent Agreements and Practice: The Battle over Interpretive Power, in: Nolte, Georg (ed.), Treaties and Subsequent Practice, Oxford University Press, Oxford 2013, pp. 95–102.
Rodley, Nigel S., The United Nations Human Rights Council, Its Special Procedures, and Its Relationship with the Treaty Bodies: Complementarity or Competition?, in: Boyle, Kevin (ed.), New Institutions for Human Rights Protection, Oxford University Press, Oxford 2009, pp. 49–74.
–, Duplication and Divergence in the Work of the United Nations Human Rights Treaty Bodies: A Perspective from a Treaty Body Member, American Society of International Law Proceedings 105 (2011), 512–515.
–, UN treaty bodies and the Human Rights Council, in: Keller, Helen/Ulfstein, Geir (eds.), UN Human Rights Treaty Bodies: Law and Legitimacy, Cambridge University Press, Cambridge 2012, pp. 320–355.
–, The Role and Impact of Treaty Bodies, in: Shelton, Dinah (ed.), The Oxford Handbook of International Human Rights Law, Oxford University Press, Oxford 2013, pp. 621–648.
Rosenne, Shabtai, Provisional Measures in International Law: The International Court of Justice and the International Tribunal for the Law of the Sea, Oxford University Press, Oxford 2004.
Salem, Nora, Sharia Reservations to Human Rights Treaties, in: Peters, Anne (ed.), Max Planck Encyclopaedia of International Public Law, Online version, March 2020.
Samarasinghe, Natalie, Human Rights and Sustainable Development: Together at Last?, in: Browne, Stephen/Weiss, Thomas G. (eds.), Routledge Handbook on the UN and Development, Routledge, London 2020, pp. 80–95.
Sarkin, Jeremy, The 2020 United Nations human rights treaty body review process: prioritising resources, independence and the domestic state reporting process over rationalising and streamlining treaty bodies, The International Journal of Human Rights 25 (2021), 1301–1327.
Saul, Ben/Kinley, David/Mowbray, Jacqueline, The International Covenant on Economic, Social and Cultural Rights: Commentary, Cases, and Materials, Oxford University Press, Oxford 2014.

Schabas, William A., Reservations to the Convention on the Rights of the Child, Human Rights Quarterly 18 (1996), 472–491.

–, U.N. International Covenant on Civil and Political Rights, Nowak's CCPR Commentary, Third revised Edition, N. P. Engel, Kehl 2019.

Scheinin, Martin, How to Untie a Tie in the Human Rights Committee, in: Alfredsson et al. (eds.), International Human Rights Monitoring Mechanism: Essays in Honour of Jakob Th. Möller, First Edition, Kluwer Law International, The Hague 2001, pp. 129–145.

–, Reservations by States under the International Covenant on Civil and Political Rights and its Optional Protocols, and the Practice of the Human Rights Committee, in: Ziemele, Ineta (ed.), Reservations to Human Rights Treaties and the Vienna Convention Regime: Conflict, Harmony or Reconciliation, Martinus Nijhoff, Leiden 2004, pp. 41–57.

–, The Proposed Optional Protocol to the Covenant on Economic, Social and Cultural Rights: A Blueprint for UN Human Rights Treaty Body Reform Without Amending the Existing Treaties, Human Rights Law Review 6 (2006), 131–142.

Schermers, Henry G./Blokker, Niels M., International Institutional Law: Unity within Diversity, Sixth Revised Edition, Brill Nijhoff, Leiden 2018.

Schlütter, Birgit, Aspects of human rights interpretation by the UN treaty bodies, in: Keller, Helen/Ulfstein, Geir (eds.), UN Human Rights Treaty Bodies: Law and Legitimacy, Cambridge University Press, Cambridge 2012, pp. 261–319.

Schmahl, Stefanie, Kinderrechtskonventionen mit Zusatzprotokollen, Handkommentar, Zweite Auflage, Nomos, Baden-Baden 2017.

Schmidt, Markus G., Follow-up Mechanisms Before UN Human Rights Treaty Bodies and the UN Mechanisms Beyond, in: Bayefsky, Anne F. (ed.), The UN Human Rights Treaty System in the 21st Century, Kluwer Law International, The Hague 2000, pp. 233–249.

–, Follow-Up Activities by UN Human Rights Treaty Bodies and Special Procedures Mechanisms of the Human Rights Council – Recent Developments, in: Alfredsson, Gudmundur/Grimheden, Jonas/Ramcharan, Bertrand G./de Zayas, Alfred (eds.), International Human Rights Monitoring Mechanisms: Essays in Honour of Jakob Th. Möller, Second Revised Edition, Martinus Nijhoff Publishers, Leiden 2009, pp. 25–34.

Schöpp-Schilling, Hanna Beate, Reservations to the Convention on the Elimination of All Forms of Discrimination against Women: An Unresolved Issue or (No) New Developments?, in: Ziemele, Ineta (ed.), Reservations to Human Rights Treaties and the Vienna Convention Regime: Conflict, Harmony or Reconciliation, Martinus Nijhoff, Leiden 2004, pp. 3–39.

–, Treaty Body Reform: The Case of the Committee on the Elimination of Discrimination Against Women, Human Rights Law Review 7 (2007), 201–224.

Schwelb, Egon, Civil and Political Rights: The International Measures of Implementation, American Journal of International Law 62 (1968), 827–868.

Seibert-Fohr, Anja, The Effect of Subsequent Practice on the European Convention on Human Rights, Considerations from a General International Law Perspective, in: van Aaken, Anne/Mutoc, Iulia (eds.), The European Convention on Human Rights and General International Law, Oxford University Press, Oxford 2018, pp. 61–82.

–, The UN Human Rights Committee, in: Oberleitner, Gerd (ed.), International Human Rights Institutions, Tribunals, and Courts, Springer, Singapore 2018, pp. 117–141.

Shah, Sangeeta/Sivakumaran, Sandesh, The Use of International Human Rights Law in the Universal Periodic Review, Human Rights Law Review 21 (2021), 265–301.

Shany, Yuval, The Effectiveness of the Human Rights Committee, in: Breuer, Marten/Epiney, Astrid/Haratsch, Andreas/Schmahl, Stefanie/Weiß, Norman (eds.), Der Staat im Recht, Festschrift für Eckart Klein zum 70. Geburtstag, Berlin 2013, pp. 1307–1324.

Shany, Yuval/Cleveland, Sarah H., Treaty Body Reform 2020: Has the time come for adopting a Global Review Calendar? https://www.geneva-academy.ch/joomlatools-files/docman-files/Draft%20List%20of%20Submissions%20-%20Academic%20Platform%202020%20Review%20without%20Propositions%20.pdf (last access: 21.08.2023).

Shelton, Dinah, The Legal Status of Normative Pronouncements of Human Rights Treaty Bodies, in: Hestermeyer, Holger P./König, Doris/Matz-Lück, Nele/Röben, Volker/Seibert-Fohr, Anja/Stoll, Peter-Tobias/Vönkey, Silja (eds.), Coexistence, Cooperation and Solidarity, Liber Amicorum Rüdiger Wolfrum Volume I, Martinus Nijhoff Publishers, Leiden 2012, pp. 553–576.

–, Inherent and Implied Powers of Regional Human Rights Tribunals, in: Buckley, Carla M./Donald, Alice/Leach, Philip (eds.), Towards Convergence in International Human Rights Law: Approaches of Regional and International Systems, Brill Nijhoff, Leiden 2016, pp. 454–489.

Simma, Bruno/Hernandez, Gleider I., Legal Consequences of an Impermissible Reservation to a Human Rights Treaty: Where Do We Stand?, in: Cannizzaro, Enzo (ed.), The Law of Treaties Beyond the Vienna Convention, Oxford University Press, Oxford 2011, pp. 60–85.

Skubiszewski, Krzysztof, Implied Powers of International Organizations, in: Dinstein, Yoram (ed.), International Law at a Time of Perplexity: Essays in Honour of Shabtai Rosenne, Martinus Nijhoff Publishers, Dordrecht 1989, pp. 855–868.

Slaughter, Anne-Marie, A Typology of Transjudicial Communication, University of Richmond Law Review 29 (1994), 99–137.

Smith, Lucy, Monitoring the CRC, in: Alfredsson, Gudmundur/Grimheden, Jonas/Ramcharan, Bertrand G./de Zayas, Alfred (eds.), International Human Rights Monitoring Mechanisms: Essays in Honour of Jakob Th. Möller, Second Revised Edition, Martinus Nijhoff Publishers, Leiden 2009, pp. 109–116.

Stein, Michael Ashley/Lord, Janet E., Monitoring the Convention on the Rights of Persons with Disabilities: Innovations, Lost Opportunities, and Future Potential, Human Rights Quarterly 32 (2010), 689–728.

Subedi, Surya P., The Effectiveness of the UN Human Rights System, Reform and the Judicialisation of Human Rights, Routledge, Abingdon 2017.

Swaine, Edward T., Treaty Reservations, in: Hollis, Duncan B. (ed.), The Oxford Guide to Treaties, Second Edition, Oxford University Press, Oxford 2020, pp. 285–306.

Thornberry, Patrick, Confronting Racial Discrimination: A CERD Perspective, Human Rights Law Review 5 (2005), 239–269.

–, The International Convention on the Elimination of All Forms of Racial Discrimination: A Commentary, Oxford University Press, Oxford 2016.

Tistounet, Eric, The problem of overlapping among different treaty bodies, in: Alston, Philip/Crawford, James (eds.), The Future of UN Human Rights Treaty Monitoring, Cambridge University Press, Cambridge 2000, pp. 383–402.

Tobin, John, Seeking to Persuade: A Constructive Approach to Human Rights Treaty Interpretation, Harvard Human Rights Journal 23 (2010), 1–50.

–, The UN Convention on the Rights of the Child: A Commentary, Oxford University Press, Oxford 2019.

Tolley, Howard Jr., The U.N. Commission on Human Rights, Westview Press, Boulder 1987.
Tomuschat Christian, Human Rights: Between Idealism and Realism, Third Edition, Oxford University Press, Oxford 2014.
–, International Covenant on Civil and Political Rights (1966), in: Peters, Anne (ed.), Max Planck Encyclopedia of Public International Law, April 2019.
–, The Human Rights Committee, in: Peters, Anne (ed.), Max Planck Encyclopedia of Public International Law, Online version, April 2019.
Tyagi, Yogesh, The UN Human Rights Committee, Practice and Procedure, Cambridge University Press, Cambridge 2011.
Ulfstein, Geir, The international Judiciary, in: Klabbers, Jan/Peters, Anne/Ulfstein, Geir (eds.), The Constitutionalization of International Law, Oxford University Press, Oxford 2009, pp. 126–152.
–, Individual Complaints, in: Keller, Helen/Ulfstein, Geir (eds.), UN Human Rights Treaty Bodies: Law and Legitimacy, Cambridge University Press, Cambridge 2012, pp. 73–115.
–, Law-making by human rights treaty bodies, in: Liivoja, Rain/Petman, Jarna (eds.), International Law-making: Essays in Honour of Jan Klabbers, Routledge, London 2014, pp. 249–257.
–, The Human Rights Treaty Bodies and Legitimacy Challenges, in: Grossman, Nienke/Cohen, Harlan Grant/Follesdal, Andreas/Ulfstein, Geir (eds.), Legitimacy and International Courts, Cambridge University Press, Cambridge 2018, pp. 284–304.
–, Interpretation of the ECHR in light of the Vienna Convention on the Law of Treaties, The International Journal of Human Rights 24 (2020), 917–934.
–, Treaty Bodies and Regimes, in: Hollis, Duncan B. (ed.), The Oxford Guide to Treaties, Second Edition, Oxford University Press, Oxford 2020, pp. 414–431.
van Alebeek, Rosanne/Nollkaemper, André, The legal status of decisions by human rights treaty bodies in national law, in: Keller, Helen/Ulfstein, Geir (eds.), UN Human Rights Treaty Bodies: Law and Legitimacy, Cambridge University Press, Cambridge 2012, pp. 356–413.
van Alphen Fyfe, Monique/Fiti Sinclair, Guy, Supervisory and Review Procedures: International Labour Organization (ILO), in: Peters, Anne (ed.), Max Planck Encyclopedia of Public International Law, Online version, April 2020.
van Staden, Andreas, Monitoring Second-Order Compliance: The Follow-Up Procedures of the UN Human Rights Treaty Bodies, Czeck Yearbook of International Law 9 (2018), 329–356.
Vandenhole, Wouter, The Procedures before the UN Human Rights Treaty Bodies: Divergence or Convergence?, Intersentia, Antwerp 2004.
–, Non-Discrimination and Equality in the View of the UN Human Rights Treaty Bodies, Intersentia, Antwerp 2005.
Verheyde, Mieke/Goedertier, Geert, A Commentary on the United Nations Convention on the Rights of the Child, Articles 43–45: The UN Committee on the Rights of the Child, Martinus Nijhoff Publishers, 2006.
Voeten, Erik, Borrowing and Nonborrowing among International Courts, The Journal of Legal Studies 39 (2010), 547–576.
Volger, Helmut, Die Stärkung der Vertragsorgane im UN-Menschenrechtssystem, MenschenRechtsMagazin 20 (2015), 107–116.
Wagner, Niklas Dominik, Internationaler Schutz sozialer Rechte, Die Kontrolltätigkeit des Sachverständigenausschusses der IAO, Nomos, Baden-Baden 2001.

Walker, Simon, International Human Rights Law: Towards Pluralism or Harmony? The Opportunities and Challenges of Coexistence: The View from the UN Treaty Bodies, in: Buckley/Donald/Leach (eds.), Towards Convergence in International Human Rights Law: Approaches of Regional and International Systems, Leiden 2016, pp. 491–515.

Webb, Philippa, International Judicial Integration and Fragmentation, Oxford University Press, Oxford 2013.

White, Nigel D., The law of international organisations, Third Edition, Manchester University Press, Manchester 2017.

Wiesberg, Laurie S., The Role of Non-Governmental Organizations (NGOs) in the Protection and Enforcement of Human Rights, in: Symonides, Janusz (ed.), Human Rights: International Protection, Monitoring, Enforcement, Ashgate Publishing, Aldershot 2003, pp. 347–372.

Wyatt, Julian, Intertemporal Linguistics in International Law: Beyond Contemporaneous and Evolutionary Treaty Interpretation, Hart Publishing, Oxford 2020.

Ziemele, Ineta/Liede Lāsma, Reservations to Human Rights Treaties: From Draft Guideline 3.1.12 to Guideline 3.1.5.6, European Journal of International Law 24 (2013), 1135–1152.

Zimmermann, Andreas/Tams, Christian J. (eds.), The Statute of the International Court of Justice: A Commentary, Third Edition, Oxford University Press, Oxford 2019.

Index

Alston proposals 31 ff.
– Final report 33
– Initial report 31
– Interim report 32
Annual meeting time 124, 127 ff., 261

Budgetary constraints 7, 46, 128

CED Committee
– Additional information procedure 146 ff.
– Congruence between ICCPR and CED 25
– Establishment 24 ff.
CEDAW Committee
– Reporting frequencies 199 f.
– Reviews in the absence of a report 217 f.
CERD Committee
– Reporting frequencies 198
– Reviews in the absence of a report 213 f.
CESCR Committee
– Establishment 18 f.
– Mandate 19, 92
– Reviews in the absence of a report 214
Chairpersons 273
– Intersessional powers 275 f.
– Representational authority 277 ff.
Chart of congruence 37, 249
CMW Committee
– Establishment 23 f.
– Reporting frequencies 202 f.
– Reviews in the absence of a report 218
Co-facilitators' review process 49 ff., 271, 276
Cold War 15, 80, 137
Combination of periodic reports 203
Committee against Torture
– Establishment 21 f.
– Reporting frequencies 200 f.
– Reviews in the absence of a report 215 f.

Common Core Document 37, 145
Compliance 212, 228, 239 ff., 259
Concluding observations
– CEDAW Committee 82 f.
– Common structure 231 ff.
– Cross-references 233
– Human Rights Committee 80 ff.
– Legal background 79 ff.
Conference of State parties 129 ff.
Congruence 37, 252
– between ICCPR and CED 25
Content of State reports 174 ff.
Cooperation among treaty bodies 257 ff.
CRC Committee
– Establishment 22
– Reporting frequencies 201
– Reviews in the absence of a report 215
Cross-references 165 ff., 233, 243
Cross-regional group, *see also* Like-minded group
CRPD Committee
– Establishment 27
– Reporting frequencies 202
– Reviews in the absence of a report 219

Decision-making powers 268 ff.
Digital uplift 50, 285
Drafting process 29

Eastern Bloc 16, 80, 137
Economic and Social Council 18, 176
Equality clauses 250
European Court of Human Rights 59, 71
Extension of legal powers 113 ff.

Focal points 284 f.
Follow-up procedure
– Concluding observations 89 ff.
– Grading schemes 240 ff.

- Individual complaints 93
- Normative basis 90 ff., 93 ff.

Forum shopping 10

Fragmentation
- decisional 10
- Human rights law 9, 164, 247, 252
- International law 9

General Assembly 31, 44 f., 51, 127 ff., 258 f.

General Comment No. 24, *see also* Severance approach to reservations

General Comments
- Functions 85 f.
- Normative basis 86 ff.

Harmonized reporting guidelines 36, 137

High Commissioner for Human Rights 38, 41

Human Rights Committee
- Reporting guidelines 136
- Reservations to the ICCPR 104 ff.
- Reviews in the absence of a report 216 f.

ILC Guidelines on Reservations 111

Implied powers 73 ff., 93, 114, 129
- Application to treaty bodies 77 ff.
- Narrow and broad approach 76
- Origin 74

Individual complaints procedure 93 f., 102, 110, 114, 134, 291

Initial reports 152 ff.

Inquiry procedure 3

Integrated follow-up procedure 247 ff.

Inter-American Court of Human Rights 59, 71

Inter-Committee Meeting 36, 112, 262 ff.

Inter-state complaints mechanism 3, 72

Intergovernmental process 44 ff., 124

Interim measures 71, 96 ff.
- Binding force 99 ff.
- Legal mandate 96 ff.
- Normative basis 99 ff.

International Labour Organization 23, 203

International Law Commission 106, 109, 117

Interpretation 55 ff.
- effectiveness-orientated 61, 65, 70, 72 f., 94, 113 f., 206 f., 225 ff.
- teleological 61, 91, 134, 205

Intersectionality 251

Judicial Dialogue 166 ff.

Legal mandate of treaty bodies 78 ff., 178, 204 ff., 212, 230 f., 271 ff.

Like-minded group 44 ff., 90, 222

List of Issues Prior to Reporting 154, *see also* Simplified reporting procedure
- Cross-references 167
- inter-Committee coordination 170
- Substantive overlap 164

Living-instrument approach 59, 71

Loizidou v. Turkey (Preliminary Objections) 70 f.

Loss of autonomy 273

Malbun I meeting 35

Malbun II meeting 40

Meeting of Chairpersons
- Establishment 258 ff.
- Influence on the strengthening process 149 ff., 194 f., 220 f., 265 ff.

Methods of voting 275 f.

Multi-sourced equivalent norms 247

Multistakeholder approach 41

Navanethem Pillay 41

Negative repetition 149, 170, 239

Non-compliance 6, 212 f., 228

Object and purpose of human rights reporting 134 ff.

Poznan formula 269 ff.

Prioritization 234, 243 f.

Procedural provisions 70

Proliferation of treaty bodies 17, 29

Quasi-judicial bodies 67 f.

Reparation for Injuries Advisory Opinion 74, 76

Reporting calendar
- Cluster 187 ff., 212, 236
- comprehensive 183
- Proposal 42

Reporting fatigue 11, 164
Reporting guidelines 36 f., 137 f., 248, 281
– harmonized 37 f.
Reporting intervals 184, 196
– Decrease 197
Reservations 103 ff.
– ILC Guide to Practice on Reservations 109, 111
– Impermissibility 104 ff.
– Legal mandate 106 ff.
– Presumption of severability 112
Resolution 68/268 46 ff., 131, 181, 257, 265
Review
– back-to-back 170, 188
– Clustered 187
– Pairing of treaty bodies 186
– Single consolidated 188
Reviews in the absence of a report 212 ff.
– Legal mandate 221 ff.
– Sources of information 228 ff.
Right to water 252
Rules of interpretation 55
– specialized 56, 70
Rules of procedure 97, 172, 212

Severance approach to reservations 104 ff., 110 ff.
Shadow reports 228
Simplified reporting procedure 139 ff.
– Alignment among treaty bodies 152 ff.
– Cross-references 165 ff.
– Initial reports 152 f.

– Origins 140 ff.
– Substantive overlap 164
Single State report 35, 188, 190
SMART-formula 235, 237 f.
Sources of information 228 ff.
Specialization of international law 9
Standard reporting procedure 140, 173
State report, consolidated 34, 36, 51, 188
Subsequent practice 115 ff., 180 ff., 207
– Constituent elements 120 ff.
– Introduction of LOIPRs 180 ff.
Substantive overlap 11, 149, 164 ff., 253, 280
Sustainable Development Goals 248

Teleological approach, *see also* Interpretation
Time frame for follow-up 236
Treaty amendments 123 ff.
Treaty on business and human rights 29

UN Commission on Human Rights 15
UN Declaration on the rights of peasants and other people working in rural areas 248
UN Secretary-General 35, 37, 48
Unified standing treaty body 38 ff.
Universal Declaration of Human Rights 15, 137, 248
Universal Periodic Review 208 ff.

World Court of Human Rights 53, 292

Jus Internationale et Europaeum

edited by

Thilo Marauhn and Christian Walter

The impact of international and European law on national legal systems is increasing constantly. This development presents an immense challenge, since what is involved is no longer the mere enforcement of international and European legal standards, but also the incorporation of the necessary adjustments into the national legal systems. Apart from the practical difficulties often involved, theories have yet to be developed for this procedure, something still very much at the beginning in public law, which continues to have an ambivalent attitude to international and European law. The goal pursued by the *Jus Internationale et Europaeum* series is to make a contribution to the theoretical and dogmatic penetration of public law by internationalization and Europeanization and to offer solutions for the practical problems resulting from this. This series accepts habilitations, outstanding dissertations and comparable monographs which deal with legal issues at the interface between national public law and international law or with subjects pertaining to genuine international or European law. A special focus is on works which bridge the gap between fundamental questions and the practical application of the law.

ISSN: 1861-1893
Suggested citation: JusIntEu

All available volumes can be found at *www.mohrsiebeck.com/jusinteu*

Mohr Siebeck
www.mohrsiebeck.com